Byron and the Websters

Byron and the Websters

*The Letters and Entangled Lives
of the Poet, Sir James Webster
and Lady Frances Webster*

JOHN STEWART

McFarland & Company, Inc., Publishers
Jefferson, North Carolina, and London

The unpublished letters of Lord Byron. Edited with a critical essay on the poet's philosophy and character, by H.S. Schultess-Young. London: R. Bentley, 1872, pp. 159–166. PR4381.A3 S38 1872. Used by kind permission of the Department of Special Collections, Charles E. Young Research Library, UCLA.
Letters of Lord Byron, Sir James Webster-Wedderburn, and Lady Frances Webster-Wedderburn courtesy The Trustees of the National Library of Scotland.
Forged letter from Lord Byron to Sir James Webster-Wedderburn, dated 23 August 1813, courtesy the Harry Ransom Humanities Research Center, The University of Texas at Austin.
Forged letter from Lord Byron to Sir James Webster-Wedderburn, dated 17 June 1817, reproduced by kind permission of the President and Council of the Royal College of Surgeons of England.

John Stewart is also the author of the following books, all from McFarland: *Confederate Spies at Large: The Lives of Lincoln Assassination Conspirator Tom Harbin and Charlie Russell* (2007). *African States and Rulers,* 3d ed. (2006). *Broadway Musicals, 1943–2004* (2006). *The British Empire: An Encyclopedia of the Crown's Holdings, 1493 through 1995* (1996). *Italian Film: A Who's Who* (1994). *Moons of the Solar System: An Illustrated Encyclopedia* (1991). *Antarctica: An Encyclopedia* (2 volumes; 1990).

LIBRARY OF CONGRESS CATALOGUING-IN-PUBLICATION DATA

Stewart, John, 1952–
Byron and the Websters : the letters and entangled lives of the poet, Sir James Webster and Lady Frances Webster / John Stewart.
p. cm.
Includes bibliographical references and index.

ISBN-13: 978-0-7864-3240-0
softcover : 50# alkaline paper ∞

1. Byron, George Gordon Byron, Baron, 1788–1824 — Relations with women. 2. Byron, George Gordon Byron, Baron, 1788–1824 — Friends and associates. 3. Byron, George Gordon Byron, Baron, 1788–1824 — Correspondence. 4. Webster-Wedderburn, Frances, 1793–1837 — Correspondence. 5. Webster-Wedderburn, James, 1788–1840 — Correspondence. 6. Aristocracy (Social class) — Great Britain — Biography. 7. Great Britain — Social life and customs — 19th century. I. Title.
PR4382.S67   2008   821.'7 — dc22 [B]   2008005158

British Library cataloguing data are available

©2008 John Stewart. All rights reserved

No part of this book may be reproduced or transmitted in any form or by any means, electronic or mechanical, including photocopying or recording, or by any information storage and retrieval system, without permission in writing from the publisher.

Cover image: On the cover: (left to right) James W. Wedderburn, Lord Byron, Lady Frances Wedderburn; background Shutterstock ©2007
Manufactured in the United States of America

*McFarland & Company, Inc., Publishers
Box 611, Jefferson, North Carolina 28640
www.mcfarlandpub.com*

For Gayle Winston
and to Bold Webster and Lady Frances,
without whom this book would, literally,
not have been possible

Acknowledgments

Professor Charles E. Robinson, University of Delaware
Jean Ferguson, Reference Desk, Perkins Library, Duke University
Dr. Carl Thompson, University of Nottingham at Trent
Ellen Daugman, of Wake Forest University Library
Bevis Hillier
Jane Singer
Martin Davies
Barclay's Bank
Jamie Andrews of the Manuscript Department of the British Library
Professor Peter W. Graham, Virginia Tech
Ann Fleming, of Cuckfield, Sussex
Peter Cochran
Mike Herring
Gayle Winston
Richard Workman, University of Texas
Tim Burnett
Ruth Boreham and David McClay
Genie Guerard, UCLA

Table of Contents

Acknowledgments   vii
Introduction   1

1. The '45   5
2. Childe Webster   7
3. Hussar   12
4. Lady Frances   18
5. Arms   21
6. Dandy   23
7. Vis à Vis   26
8. The Groom of Abydos   29
9. Aston Hall   33
10. Byron's Song   36
11. Vive l'Empereur   38
12. Master Shallow   90
13. Waterloo: Ball, Battle and Poem   94
14. Monument to a Dead Son   119
15. The Sucking Salamander   123
16. Nantes   131
17. The Duel   139
18. Sir James   152
19. Kiss Me, Hardy   153
20. Reconciliation   156
21. The Kidnapping   168
22. When We Two Parted   173
23. The Death of Byron   175

24. Baronet	176
25. Wedderburn vs. Wedderburn	180
26. The Robbing of Lady Frances	183
27. The Molesting of Lady Frances	186
28. The Death of Lady Frances	191
29. James's Death at Cooney's Tavern	194
30. Post Mortem	197
Bibliography	201
Index	203

Introduction

From 1806 until 1824 Sir James Webster-Wedderburn was an intimate of Lord Byron, and for that he earned his place as a footnote in literary and social history. Arguably the most offensive, despised and ridiculed dandy of the Regency period, Webster was, by so being, admirably qualified for membership of the Prince Regent's inner circle. Indeed, that princely ring almost demanded such virtues of its members. James was more than just a stunning example of what has been called "the upper class twit"; he was a nasty individual, a vicious wastrel, and egotistical to the point of aggressive and dangerous narcissism. Yet he came from a good background, was admirably educated, and could be amusing at times. In his youth he had been an accomplished and determined athlete, a natural sportsman, who performed unprecedented feats in endurance races, both on foot and on horse, and it was his sporting achievements and ruddy vigor that led to his nickname, Bold Webster. However, he frittered away his physical gifts as he did his plural family fortunes, and instead of achieving something positive, which he quite clearly could have done, he chose to be a profligate fool, and that is how he is remembered.

He did do a few things right, although probably inadvertently and with mixed motives, and certainly always with "tragick consequences" to himself and others. One springs to mind: He married the daughter of the Earl of Mountnorris. Lady Frances Caroline Annesley, celebrated as one of the most beautiful women of her day, was very young when the happy event took place with her bold Hussar. If she had been but a few years older — and her personality had had time to develop the considerableness it attained in later years — she would never have countenanced the possibility of such a union, but desperation to escape her family led to the decision that deprived her of what one genuinely senses could have been her true place in history.

Nevertheless, Lady Frances is much better remembered than her husband, mainly because of the notorious affairs she indulged in with Byron and Wellington, and because, at a few choice points in her life, she was the most discussed woman in Europe.

James would openly talk about his extramarital conquests to anyone who would listen, but Lady Frances kept her private life quiet — her *real* private life, that is. From early in their marriage James's boorish behavior forced her to look elsewhere for the one thing she really wished for: love, something James was incapable of giving, except to himself.

One of the two great Websterian puzzles that has tormented Byron scholars for decades is why Byron should have tolerated James Webster as a friend for all those years. The answer is finally revealed in this book.

Lady Frances thought she had found true happiness with Byron, but he proved to be, in many respects, as much a dud as Bold Webster. That the great poet was not the all-round great man is glaringly evident from the forty-odd extant letters Lady Frances wrote to him. The letters a person writes reveal only what the writer wishes to be revealed. It is the letters written to that person that help round out the picture — and the letters written to Byron by Lady Frances force us to revise, to some extent, our picture of the man.

Byron kept Lady Frances's letters, despite her persistent pleadings that he burn them. He knew as well as she did that discovery would put her in great danger, but when he died in 1824 they were still among his possessions. After all is said and done, he had let her down in the most pernicious manner. Byron's executors likewise refused to destroy them, and the letters, along with another forty or so from Bold Webster, became part of the Murray Archives, that priceless museum of memorabilia stored over the decades by Byron's publisher, John Murray, of Albemarle Street, London. Finally, in the early 21st century, John Murray closed its doors and sold the archives to Scotland. The Webster letters now reside in the National Library of Scotland, available for anyone to peruse. Those quoted in this book are all part of the Murray Archives, unless otherwise stated. The same is true for the Byron letters quoted. All letters that belong in the Murray Archives were reproduced with kind permission from those archives.

Having now broached the issue of Lady Frances's affair with Byron, we forge ahead to the second great Websterian question that has been plaguing Byron scholars: Did Byron spare her, as he claimed?

The puzzle has seemed impossible to solve. Debate has raged. And all the while, the answer has been present in the Lady Frances letters, quite available to any researcher.

Yet no more than a handful of authors have ever looked at these Lady Frances letters, and then for other reasons. In 1939 George Paston (a woman) published *To Lord Byron*, a compilation of letters written by a select sampling of Byron's lady friends, and it is evident from her penciled notes on Lady Frances's letters that she was the first ever to look at them. But her sense of scholarship did not match her Victorian enthusiasm, and besides, she was dying. Whether Peter Quennell, the preeminent Byron scholar of his age, never even laid eyes on the late Miss Paston's work or he did, indeed, finish it as purported (hence Paston and Quennell's being listed as the authors), the result is awful, a travesty of research and integrity, and a tragedy of hopelessly missed opportunities.

If Paston had only turned one page more, or had but struggled that little bit harder to decipher certain passages, then she would have been the one to answer the great question: Did Byron spare Lady Frances at Aston Hall, or did he physically consummate the relationship with this lady who was, without doubt, one of his principal and most famous conquests?

Finally, now, the answer to the question is revealed in the letters, in black and white, unequivocally, with no room left to argue the point.

Après Byron Lady Frances had her notorious "affair" with Wellington. Again, this interlude has called forth a thousand questioning voices, but they all ask essentially the same question: Did the duke physically consummate what was clearly a romantic and passionate relationship? In this case it is not so much Lady Frances's letters, but rather merely a cursory study of her genealogy that would have revealed the truth, if any scholar had ever seriously attempted to get to the bottom of this.

After the scandal of the Iron Duke, she set her sights on lesser metals. Because she had to, Lady Frances metamorphosed from a hopeless romantic platonic into a very hot carnal adventurer, although this new condition was not really new at all, just dormant. She became notorious within the closed circles of the noble and the dandy for her "peculiar mode of manifesting preference" toward the objects of her desire. This "mode" is startlingly revealed in her letters to another of her paramours, Regency dandy Scrope Davies. One note in particular is so graphic that it all but revolutionizes our concept of upper-class Regency sexual practices.

It took Scrope Davies to unleash the volcano, but once he had, he was not man enough to handle it. Perhaps we might ask: Who would be?

The 21 letters from Lady Frances to Scrope, at the height of their wild affair in 1818–19, reveal not only Lady Frances's development as a human being, but also her profundity, her daring (something she had always had, as we can see from her letters to Byron, but which now, half a decade later, had become the stuff of legend), and above all, her sexual abilities.

These letters to Scrope Davies were discovered only 30 years ago when the famous dandy's trunk was opened in London, amid much fanfare. One and a half of these letters were published by T.A.J. Burnett in his 1981 biography of Scrope Davies (*The Rise and Fall of a Regency Dandy*), but aside from that, nothing. Here, for the first time, the letters have been transcribed in their entirety, including the one which will likely become notorious—the letter of the "sucking salamander."

Bold Webster managed to stay married to Fanny, but despite the production of several children, the marriage was a fiction, held together by the restraints of the times and also by the convenience that, for a while anyway, they were useful to one another.

As the Websters were on such close terms with big players of the day, it is inevitable that much of the biographical information about them comes from works on, and letters by, the great poet and the great general, and from other books on the Regency period and its personalities. However, the heart of the story, in many ways, is Lady Frances's letters to Byron and Scrope Davies, unpublished until now. In addition, as the great-great-great-grandson of Bold Webster and Fanny, and also twice the third cousin of Byron (albeit four times removed), the author is privy to a certain amount of inside information, now revealed for the reader's pleasure.

1
The '45

Bonnie Prince Charlie landed on Scottish soil in July 1745. Although Charles Edward Stewart (in French form Stuart, there being no "w" in that language) is popularly imagined as a rosy-cheeked little lad in frilly clothes, he was, in fact, 24 years of age, and his hour had finally come. The intention of the Stewarts was to kick German George out of Britain and restore the throne to the rightful heir, Charlie. He was that season's bright ray of hope for the Highlanders, just as his father had been thirty years before. Like the Old Pretender in '15, Charles Edward would fail, but not before his name went down in song.

The chieftains flocked to the cause, each one putting a regiment in the field. Each regiment consisted of companies organized by lesser dignitaries, one of whom was Robert Wedderburn of Pearsie, sheriff clerk of Forfarshire since April 7, 1738, who raised and headed the Glen Prosen Company of Clova men for Lord Ogilvy's second battalion.

As is well known, after a promising start the campaign ended tragically when the rag-tag army came up against Butcher Cumberland at Culloden, in the north of Scotland, on April 6, 1746, and in the aftermath George II made sure there would be no more Jacobite risings. In the wake of the final battle the Highlanders who were not captured fled into the mountains.

Wedderburn of Pearsie had helped Ogilvy escape, thereby becoming a fugitive himself, with a price on his head. For several weeks Pearsie hid out in a cave at Cat Law, a hill over 2000 feet high between Glen Prosen and Glen Isla in the Forfarshire highlands northwest of Kirriemuir. He came down only after he had secured a protection warrant from the lord chief justice clerk. Later, he was able to resume his business in Dundee.

Pearsie's elder brother, Sir John Wedderburn, 5th Baronet of Blackness, who had also served with Ogilvy, was not so fortunate. He was captured at Culloden and hanged, drawn and quartered in London on November 28, 1746, his baronetcy being forfeited.

John and Robert were only two of the children of Alexander Wedderburn, the old 4th Baronet of Blackness, who had died as late as 1744. John inherited the title but little else, as the estate of Blackness had been sold some years previous in order to satisfy the old baronet's monumental debts. As a consequence, the younger generation of Wedderburns, the ones who fought in the '45, were all (relatively) broke.

Following the execution of the 5th Baronet, his sons and several other Wedderburns, afraid for their lives because they too had fought with Ogilvy, fled to Jamaica. The decades after the '45 were not a safe period of time for a Jacobite to be in Scotland. These Jamaican exiles, in an effort to retrieve their family's lost fortunes, started a company called Wedderburn & Co., and they prospered.

Robert Wedderburn of Pearsie's mother-in-law had married again after her first husband died. She and her second husband, a Dundee merchant named Webster, had produced, among others, James and David Webster. These two started their business life as Messrs Webster, druggists, and were now expanded into Webster & Co. of Clapham, with their head office at East &

West India House, 35 Leadenhall Street. They also happened to be the home correspondent for Messrs Wedderburn & Co. of Jamaica.

Pearsie's fourth and youngest son, David Wedderburn, was only 15 when he left Dundee in 1772 and ventured down to London to work for his half-uncles at Webster & Co. He settled into the firm and into society as a West India merchant, duly becoming junior partner.

Sir James Webster-Wedderburn (Bold Webster), in a note to his manuscript history of the family, says, "For fifty years, 1780–1830, the several firms in Leadenhall Street, though not equally distinguished for prudence, were all alike remarkable for liberal and honourable character, and during more than one period of mercantile distress, when the Bank of England hesitated to discount bills for many reputable houses, no bill of the Wedderburns was ever delayed for an instant."

Old Robert Wedderburn died, six days after his 82nd birthday, on February 19, 1786, seven years after he had sold the estate of Pearsie to his second son, Charles. His widow did not long survive him. The *Times* of January 8, 1788, listed as deceased "on the 6th instant, in Dundee, Mrs Wedderburn, relict of Robert Wedderburn, Esq., of Pearsie."

2

Childe Webster

Bold Webster was born James Webster Wedderburn at Clapham, Surry (as they spelled Surrey then), on May 31, 1788, the eldest son of David Wedderburn and Elizabeth Read. A memorandum later written by his mother gives his birthday as May 30 (with doubt!), and later still, James himself gave 1789 as the year; nevertheless, his birth date was definitely May 31, 1788. His mother had probably tried to forget the event, while James himself, ever the egomaniac, simply lied to make himself younger. The name Webster was from his father's mother's half-brother, James Webster.

Elizabeth Read's memorandum is worth more than a mention. Written as a letter to her late husband's cousin John Wedderburn on July 30, 1819, from Brigton, in the county of Forfarshire (also known as Angus), this letter is in the John Wedderburn collection. It reads:

> To the best of my knowledge and memory the following is correct. David Wedderburn [Elizabeth Read's husband] was born at Dundee [he was actually born at Pearsie] 15 Aug. 1756 [it was actually 1757], married there the 28th December, 1785, to Elizabeth Read [the writer of this memorandum], who was born at Logie, Co. Angus, the 13th of Oct., 1770 (daughter of Alexander Read of Logie and Ann Fletcher). He [David Wedderburn] died at Bath 21 March 1801.
>
> My son James was born 30th May [this is the aforementioned error], I think the year 1788 [this time she is right], but he is just two days older than your brother James [she was right here too; the James and John were the sons of John Wedderburn of Clapham — also known as John Wedderburn of Spring Garden, for his estate in Jamaica — himself the son of Thomas of Cantra, younger brother of Robert Wedderburn of Pearsie] ... his marriage I am rather in doubt about, but I think it took place in Jan. 1811 [she was wrong again, but she had admitted that probability], to Lady Frances Caroline Annesley; they have had issue, a daughter Lucy and son Charles Byron, the latter died at Nantz [Nantes] in 1817. My eldest daughter Anne [Bold Webster's sister] was born at Clapham, 2nd March, 1791, and married Aug. 1814, to Captain Archibald Douglas, of the 52nd Foot, has issue Elizabeth, William and Mary. My 2nd daughter Mary was born at Clapham, 15 Sept., 1793, and married 22 March 1814 [this should be 25 March 1815] to George Hawkins, of Harnish House, Wilts. They have no issue. My son Charles Wedderburn [he was born Charles Wedderburn Webster, last name Webster, middle name Wedderburn, in accordance with old man Webster's will — and he, similarly to his brother, would eventually change to Charles Webster Wedderburn] was born in London 10th Sept. 1799. My son David was born in London 10 August 1801, and died at Brigton 14 May [she means 14 July] 1816, and was buried there.

John Wedderburn of Spring Garden, son of Cantra, arrived in London in 1789, after 25 years in the West Indies, and became a new partner in the firm. This move would have far-reaching consequences.

On December 28 of that 1789, old man Webster died. The *Times* reported:

> Yesterday morning, at his seat at Clapham, James Webster, Esq., Merchant of London, who is reported to have left behind him upwards of ONE HUNDRED THOUSAND POUNDS! [the *Times*'s capitals and exclamation point], which was accumulated from a very trivial outset in life. Born at Dundee in Scotland, his first appearance in London was as a clerk at only 15 [pounds] a

year from which, by an impartial and strict attention to business, added to the honour of his dealings, he arose to this pre-eminence. His brother, Mr David Webster, died exactly almost to a day, two years past, and was buried in the Parish of St Andrew Undershafts [sic], Leadenhall-street — and at the particular request of the deceased, the top of the vault was left for his interment with his brother.

In his will, proved in the Prerogative Court of Canterbury on January 13, 1790, old James Webster left money and property to his wife Catherine, his brothers John, George and Thomas, and to George Webster's five daughters. Also to "James Webster Wedderburn (son of the said David Wedderburn) on his attaining 21." Other legatees were Charles Wedderburn of Pearsie (David's brother), and his wife Ann Read; Elizabeth Wedderburn (David's sister), wife of James Graham of Balmuir; Catherine Wedderburn (David's sister), wife of Robert Stewart, of Dundee; Isabella Wedderburn (David's sister), wife of the Rev. James Stormonth, of Airly; John Wedderburn (i.e. John, of Spring Garden, one of the partners in the company); Louisa Dorothea Wedderburn (the daughter of Sir John, the 6th Baronet, and granddaughter of the executed 5th baronet); James Wedderburn of Inveresk (younger son of the executed baronet, and later a Colvile-Wedderburn); and James Wedderburn, of Trelawny, Jamaica (brother of John Wedderburn of Spring Garden).

Webster left to his half-nephew David Wedderburn "various sums of money, the leasehold houses in Leadenhall Street and at Clapham, and other property, on condition that he and his heirs male shall immediately, on the death of the said James Webster take the surname of Webster only, in lieu and stead of Wedderburn, and shall forthwith obtain a legal license so to do."

A sum of £6,000 was also left, after all the legacies were paid, for founding an academy for 30 boys 12 to 16 years of age and 35 girls in Dundee. The executors of the will were David Wedderburn, John Webster (the testator's brother), and John Wedderburn.

So, on January 13, 1790, David obtained a royal license to change his name from Wedderburn to Webster, and thus became David Wedderburn Webster — no hyphens. The firm changed its name to Wedderburn, Webster & Co.

The *Times* of January 20, 1790, reported: "Jan. 19. The King has been pleased to grant to David Wedderburn of London, merchant, son of Robert Wedderburn, late of Pearsie, in North Britain, deceased, and his issue, his Royal Licence and authority to assume and take the surname of Webster only, and also to bear the arms of Webster pursuant to the last will and testament of James Webster, late of Clapham Common, in the County of Surry, Esq., deceased."

Young James Webster (né Wedderburn), then, grew up as the son of a well-connected West India merchant. His uncle was Fletcher Read (or Reid), one of the wealthiest men in Britain, a great sporting blood (he is mentioned as such in Conan Doyle's wonderful novel *Rodney Stone*) who would later introduce his nephew into those circles. James himself would, in no time at all, become a major blood himself, as well as a sportsman of great note, who would take on any race if the stakes were high enough.

Sir James Webster-Wedderburn, from a miniature. From the author's collection, also by kind permission of Tatton Hewetson.

In 1796 David Webster (formerly Wedderburn) and his cousin John Wedderburn of Spring Garden took into partnership another of their cousins, young David (later Sir David Wedderburn of Ballindean, 1st Baronet), the eldest son of Sir John Wedderburn, the so-called 6th Baronet (himself the son of the executed 5th Baronet). Young David had just turned 21, and the company was now called Wedderburn Webster & Co. (no comma). This partnership was scheduled to last for seven years, David and John to get five-twelfths each and young David to get two-twelfths. If John or the older David were to die then young David would get one-third, and the other two-thirds would be split between the survivor and the heirs of the deceased. The older David did die, in 1801, and left his share in his will to his family. The company was re-formed after David's death, with John Wedderburn of Spring Garden becoming the chief partner until his death in 1820.

James Webster was educated at home, in Clapham, his tutor being John Campbell, who in 1798 had just come down from Scotland to London. This tutoring position was Mr. Campbell's first employment. A minister's son from Cupar, Fife, he was eighteen years old at the time, and this new milieu did little to satisfy a young man from his austere background.

Campbell was a truly remarkable character whose astonishing gifts seem to have been equally balanced by a plethora of punishing defects, as if the gods had created him for the sheer sport of watching him fight his way through life. A university student at the age of ten, the kindest of men, a paragon of industry and application, and, although no natural wit, a storehouse of good stories, Plain John Campbell was just that: plain. Indeed, he was notoriously ugly and awkward, with a severe Fife accent. This trio of natural disfavors thwarted him at every turn. In a very definite sense he failed at least once: The woman he loved could never be his. She was one of the most beautiful women in Europe, married, far above him in station, and by the time Campbell achieved the confidence to succeed she had passed beyond not only his reach but his desire, and he settled for someone else.

Reminiscing about those first days in London, he says in his autobiography, *Life of John, Lord Campbell, Lord High Chancellor of Great Britain*:

> My companions had to present themselves at the India House, and I was to find out the residence of Mr Webster, on Clapham Common. Thither was I carried by the Clapham stage, and I was installed in my new office. Mr Webster was very good-natured but not a very wise man, and I soon discovered that he had not much authority in his own house. Madame was mistress in everything. She was young, beautiful, gay, and fond of admiration. My pupil was a boy of about nine or ten years of age who had been taught to read English pretty well, but whom I was to initiate in the first rudiments of Latin....
>
> I had no particular grievance to complain of, and I believe I was treated with all the consideration that could have been reasonably expected, but I found my situation from the beginning very irksome, and it became more and more unbearable. The company frequenting the house consisted chiefly of West India merchants and East India captains, and the conversation turned on the price of sugars, the rate of freights, and the trifling gossip of the day....

Another — regular, nay continual — guest is not mentioned by the future lord chancellor, probably because he was too inexperienced in the ways of the flesh and the devil to see what was going on. That visitor was Robert Douglas. Born in Dundee on April 12, 1773, eldest son of William Douglas, an overspending Scotch laird of Brigton in Forfarshire, Robert had been educated in a multitude of disciplines in a variety of countries and was thus a man of the world. By the time he was appointed clerk in the Home Office in London and was renting rooms in Pall Mall, he was a man on the make, his due having been squandered before he could even get his hands on it. Not to mention (but we will) three gossipy but salient points: Firstly, he was of an amorous nature; secondly, so was Mrs. Webster, not quite three years Douglas's senior and still very attractive; and thirdly, Mrs. Webster's husband, David, was a sick man, though able to procreate with some regularity until his premature death — or was he? A genealogically stimulating question.

Campbell goes on:

> I exerted myself to the utmost for the improvement of my pupil, and I continued with him for nearly two years, at the end of which time, if he was rather deficient in longs and shorts, he was well acquainted with the principles of grammar, he had a good notion of composing in Latin prose, and he could read and be amused with Ovid's 'Metamorphoses.'
>
> Mr Webster purchased a fine country house at Shenley Hill in Hertfordshire, where we spent the following summer [1798]. Mrs Webster, wishing to take a lead in fashionable life, induced her husband to rent a splendid mansion at the west end of the town [London], first in Bruton Street and then in Upper Grosvenor Street. She did not think it genteel that her son's tutor should sleep or eat in the house, and to my great satisfaction lodgings were taken for me in Conduit Street, my appointments were increased that I might provide for my own board, and unless during the hours of study I was entirely my own master.

The 169-acre property on the pleasing eminence known as Shenley Hill, formerly belonging to Samuel Gambier, had been bought by David Webster at Mr. Christie's auction, which he held at his Great Room on Pall Mall at 1 o'clock on June 7, 1798. (This is James Christie and the same Christie's that would become so famous as an auction house.) The property consisted of a singularly elegant and compact freehold villa, or mansion, and small part copyhold of inheritance. Features included roomy stabling for eight horses, two coach houses, numerous attached and detached offices of every description suited for the elegant villa and farm, and excellent kitchen gardens with hothouse and fully cropped melon-ground. The garden was surrounded by lofty walls clothed with choice fruit trees, and a beautiful pleasure ground included a capacious lawn fringed with rich plantations, valuable plants and shrubs seated in an elegant paddock of 54 acres, and several rich enclosures all around—all told, 87 acres and 8 poles, with a beautiful command of rich and extensive prospects. It was plentifully supplied with excellent water, and was situated about a mile from the Great North Road, that stretched between Barnet and St Alban's, and 16 miles from London, a healthy and sporting part of the county of Herts.

In a letter to his father, Campbell wrote from Shenley Hill on August 9, 1798, "The family left Clapham on July 10, but I was left behind in Surry for a fortnight."

On April 22, 1799, Campbell wrote to his brother from No. 18 Warwick St., Golden Square, Westminster, "I am about to leave London in a fortnight. Whither I shall then go I am perfectly uncertain! Mr and Mrs Webster and the family return to the country, but it appears extremely improbable that I shall accompany them."

But Campbell did accompany the Websters, for on May 23, 1799, he wrote his father from Shenley Hill, "You will be happy to learn that I am here in high health and spirits."

On June 8, 1799, Campbell wrote to his brother from Shenley Hill, and on December 11, 1799 to his father from 10 Upper Grosvenor Street, London. On January 16, 1800, he again wrote his father, "I now write to you for the last time from Upper Grosvenor Street."

This time Campbell had had enough. He left the Websters in order to be entered as a student at Lincoln's Inn, and so began a great legal career. However, he does not disappear from the story of Bold Webster.

In his autobiography Campbell writes:

> I left the Websters on very friendly terms, and I continued to visit them and to be treated by them with kindness. Mr Webster, within a year afterwards, died, and his widow contracted a second marriage with a gentleman of the name of Douglas. They afterwards consulted me about their affairs when I was rising to eminence at the Bar, and I had the satisfaction of being of considerable use to them. The son went to a public school, entered the Army, married a daughter of the Earl of Mountnorris, and became Sir James Webster Wedderburn.

According to the Harrow records, in September 1800 a Mr. Webster did enter the school, aged 12. This is James. He left the same term, however, unplaced. He was probably intolerable.

There is a false tradition that it was at Harrow that James met Byron for the first time; the truth is they did not meet until 1806. Byron was born on January 22, 1788, son of Mad Jack Byron and Caroline Gordon of Gight; at the age of 10 he became 6th Baron Byron of Rochdale. He was at Harrow from the summer term of 1801 to 1805. Webster had left Harrow by the time Byron arrived. The headmaster of Harrow during this period was the Reverend Joseph Drury, at least until March 1805, when he was succeeded by Dr. Butler.

On March 21, 1801, James's father died, and the executors of David's estate placed Shenley Hill with James Christie. After extensive advertising in the *Times* and elsewhere, Christie again auctioned it off in his Great Room on August 25.

James's mother, having now passed from very rich to very *very* rich, went away with her younger children and rented Langham House in Suffolk. In June 1802, at the village church of Langham, she married again, to Robert Douglas of Brigton. In November of that year Douglas resigned his clerkship at the Home Office and busied himself with producing a son, William Douglas, who was born on August 4, 1803, in London, while Robert and his wife were there visiting from Langham House. It would not be long before the family moved again, from Langham to the nearby and picturesque village of Aldeburgh.

Sir John Wedderburn of Ballindean, the soi-disant 6th Baronet Blackness, James's late father's first cousin, died on June 13, 1803, aged 74.

3

Hussar

In 1804 James Webster entered the 10th Light Dragoons (Prince of Wales's Own), as a cornet, aged 16, and therefore did not go up to Cambridge, as some authorities have suggested (he is not listed in the *Alumni Cantabrigienses*, the complete list of all men admitted to Cambridge). In 1806 James's regiment became the 10th Hussars (later the 10th Royal Hussars), the first Hussar regiment in the British Army. The regiment's officers, including James, were sometimes nicknamed "The Elegant Extracts."

In a (much later) letter from Byron to Lady Hardy the poet mentions that James was a Hussar, and Elizabeth Longford says in her book *Years of the Sword* that Lady Frances had married a Hussar officer in 1810. The regimental records of the 10th Royal Hussars tell us that J.W. Webster joined that regiment as a cornet in 1809, became a lieutenant in 1810, and served with them until 1811. However, evidence that the dates on these regimental records are in error is preponderant. Fred Henning's classic book on bare-knuckle boxing, *Fights for the Championship*, tells us that James was a lieutenant by 1807, although with the 11th Hussars (and this is wrong, too, as that regiment was the 11th Dragoons then, and did not convert to Hussars until 1840). This enigma will sort itself out as the story of James unfolds.

Around 1806 James changed his name subtly to James Wedderburne Webster, adding an "e" to his middle name simply to make it ten percent more weighty (he would joke about this at his own expense).

This was the period during which he first met Byron. In the aforementioned letter to Lady Hardy, written by Byron from Genoa on February 17, 1823, the great poet indicates (but does not specifically say) that he met Bold Webster at a period later than Harrow, when Byron was a Collegian (i.e. at Cambridge, which he was between 1805 and 1808), and Bold Webster was a Hussar.

Again, in a letter to James, Byron wrote on September 2, 1813, "My Dear Webster, you are just the same generous and I fear—careless gentleman of the years of indifferent memory 1806–7." This letter will be reproduced more fully in its correct chronological place in this book.

James was well known as a champion pedestrian, walking and running great distances for money. He was also a noted horse rider. Ready cash was no object to this Regency roué. For a wager of 500 guineas he walked from Ipswich to Whitechapel, 70 miles, easily. Accompanied by his friend Gentleman John Jackson, the former boxing champion, he covered 65 miles in 19 hours, and thus had five hours to do the remainder. A week or two later he rode his favorite mare, Buzzard, over the same distance. The *Times* of September 8, 1807, tells of this latter adventure in the form of an anecdote (they edited; their omissions are included here in brackets):

> A match was made against time, some time since, by ——[Lieutenant] Webster, nephew of the late [celebrated] Fletcher Read, Esq., which excited a good deal of speculation [and the result of which has struck the *cognoscenti* with astonishment]. Mr Webster undertook, for a wager of 600 guineas, to ride a favorite horse, his property, from Ipswich to London, a distance of 70 miles, in [the short space of] five hours. Sunday morning [this should read, 'On Monday morning, Sept.

7, at an early hour'] Mr Webster commenced his journey from Ipswich, [and the sporting circles line the road from the Metropolis; anxiety never has been more strongly excited] and the horse [this should read, 'The animal'] ran the first 20 miles in an hour and ten minutes, when the rider halted for a few minutes and gave the horse a portion of wine and water. [The animal had to perform fourteen miles an hour at starting, and it kept on at a running rate the whole of the distance.] Whitechapel Church was the extent of the journey, at which place the horse and its rider arrived in four hours and 50 minutes, [having performed the journey] ten minutes less than the given time. [Mr W rides about nine stone. The wonderful equestrian performance of Mr Webster has excited a good deal of rivalship in the sporting world].

The *Weekly Messenger* of September 13, 1807, printed the article in full.

Fletcher Read had died only that year, on January 24, at Shepperton, near London, aged 34.

James's riding feat, to which there is also a reference in the *Farrington Diary* published in 1920, sounds like the one described in the book *Brighton*, by Osbert Sitwell and Margaret Barton. Discussing the Prince Regent's famous ride to London and back in 10 hours — 108 miles in all — it adds a footnote, "Some years later his record was to be broken by a Mr Webster, who rode from Westminster Bridge to Brighthelmstone [the old name for Brighton], on one of his own phaeton horses in 3 hours 20 mins, an average of over 16 miles an hour. He stopped only once on the way — to swallow a glass of wine, and to pour the rest of the contents of the bottle down the panting animal's throat."

George Gordon, Lord Byron

For these feats James became known as Bold Webster, although Malcolm Elwin, in his book *Lord Byron's Wife*, says that this was an ironic name created by Byron because Webster had quarreled with Charles Skinner Matthews at the Newstead party. This is wrong; James was known as Bold Webster long before that party.

Fred Henning tells us that on the evening of July 12, 1807, a new heavyweight, Bob Gregson, was presented at the Fives Court, St. Martin's Street, Leicester Square, in an exhibition bout against Isaac Bitton, in which Bob acquitted himself very well. The fancy that night included Major Morgan, Captain Mellish (Henry Francis Mellish, of the 10th Hussars, who would die in 1817), and Lt. Wedderburne Webster of the 11th Dragoons, nephew of (the late) Fletcher Read. Webster became one of Gregson's backers in the championship fight near Newmarket on October 14 against John Gully. Gregson lost.

After a short spell on the 65-ton man o' war *Lion*, James Webster was admitted a student at Lincoln's Inn (presumably on the suggestion of John Campbell, his erstwhile tutor) on May 25, 1808. His admission record says, "James Wedderburn Webster, aged 20, eldest son of David Webster late of Shanly Hill [should be Shenley Hill], co. Herts." He did not stay there long, not being cut out for the rigors of study or for a career which demanded liberal application of a sane and balanced judgment.

In a letter to Gentleman John Jackson, the grand'homme of boxing at that time, dated October 4, 1808, N.A. [Newstead Abbey], Notts., Lord Byron says, "If you see Bold Webster, remember me to him, and tell him I have to regret Sydney, who has perished, I fear, in my rabbit warren, for we have seen nothing of him for the last fortnight." It is not absolutely clear who Sydney was. It may have been a mutual friend, but, in that case, one feels that such a fate would have been not only well-reported in the newspapers but lampooned too. Sydney is more likely to have been Webster's dog.

Byron had taken up residence at Newstead, his ancestral home, in September 1808, having (says Tom Moore) "received the place in a most ruinous condition from the hands of its late occupant Lord Grey de Ruthyn."

Thomas Moore, a significant character in this story, was a hugely successful Irish poet, nine years older than Byron and Bold Webster, who had come to London. Through his singing talent and the good offices of Lord Moira, he had become a friend of the Prince of Wales, with whom he was eventually to split over the issue of Catholic emancipation, Moore being a Catholic and fervent Irish nationalist. In 1811 he began his long and famous friendship with Byron.

John Jackson, who had been the British bare-knuckle champion from 1795 to 1800, had, even before winning the title from Daniel Mendoza, become the gentleman-tutor to the fancy in the manly art of self-defense. Toward the end of the first decade of the 19th century, he was still teaching the likes of Byron and Webster at his rooms. Indeed, as Henning says, in *Fights for the Championship*, "Not to have taken lessons from Mr Jackson was a positive neglect of a gentleman's ordinary education. Byron was a staunch admirer, friend and pupil." We know, from later letters, that Bold Webster was too.

In 1808 James was living at Brighton, as was Byron with his friends Scrope Davies and John Cam Hobhouse. It was here that Byron brought a girl dressed as a boy (as described in Gronow's *Reminiscences*), a somewhat strange episode that Webster and others would often talk about later. This was Caroline Cameron, Byron's sixteen-year-old prostitute friend, whom he would introduce as his brother Gordon.

Of the Brighton period, Benita Eisler, in her 1999 book *Byron*, quotes Gronow's *Reminiscences* I, 152–3, in T. Moore (I), I, 147: "A Cambridge friend, Wedderburn Webster, was struck by the [and then quoting Webster] 'dexterous manner in which Byron used to get into his boat; for while standing on the beach I once saw him vault into it with the agility of a harlequin, in spite of his lame foot.'" Fiona MacCarthy quotes this too, at least the latter part of the quote, in her *Byron: Life and Legend*. However, this is not a quote from Webster, but from Gronow himself.

Whenever Lord Byron was in London he would go to Manton's shooting gallery in Davies Street to get in some practice, being constantly fearful for his life in a duel. On one occasion in 1808 Wedderburn Webster accompanied him. Byron boasted to Joe Manton (the most well known gunsmith of his day) that he (the poet) was the best shot in London. "No, my Lord," replied Manton, "not the best; but your shooting today was respectable." Byron (in the company of Webster) left the shop in a rage. (This from Gronow.)

In 1809, when James reached his majority, he came into a large amount of money from old man Webster's will. He spent it faster than seems humanly possible, and by 1813 was broke. It was the gambling, more than anything — the reckless wagering of huge sums at the fights and the races. Henning tells us that Wedderburn Webster was at the February 1, 1809, championship fight at Epsom Downs between Jem Belcher and Tom Cribb. Being thus a noted member of the fancy, James could be relied upon to lose more on one boxing match than the average English working man made in a lifetime.

James's great sporting days — as a participant, that is — were over by 1809. He now confined himself to the pleasures of spectating and, above all, wagering. James would bet on all the pedestrian events he could get to. Pedestrianism was what we would call track and field today, except that it was all track and no field. Pole-vaulting and high jumping, triple jumping and throwing the hammer had yet to be established as events, but running and, especially, long distance walking were immensely popular, and threw up notables such as Captain Hewetson, Mr. Howe, Mr. Downes, Captain Aiken, Mr. Athol, Wedderburn Webster (of course), and without doubt the greatest of them all, and the only pedestrian to come down in legend, Captain Robert Barclay.

The *Times* of March 21, 1809, gives us the first of many blow-by-blow accounts of Captain Barclay's famous walk: "It was related some time since that this pedestrian had offered to back himself for 1000 guineas to go a thousand miles in the same number of hours." It goes on to say that "the match had been made with Mr Webster," and that "Capt. B. will undertake the prodigious task on the 1st of June at Newmarket on a piece of turf."

What this means was not that James was doing any walking, but that he was laying out a lot of cash over the outcome. Barclay duly set out on his staggering mission, sustained for six weeks on cold beef steaks and mutton chops and two bottles per day of port wine, fighting off vandals who would occasionally smash the lanterns that lit his way at night, sleeping every couple of hours only to be awakened by an alarm clock. Up he would spring, fit as a fiddle, guzzling more port and sinking his choppers into a slab of dead sheep, until he finally crossed the finish line, and James lost another cool thousand.

In April 1809 Byron, who was about to leave for the Continent (it was his first trip out of Britain), threw a party for his best friends at the newly-renovated and now comfortable Newstead Abbey, where they all got drunk. Although there was horseplay, it was not the degenerate orgy that has been sometimes later depicted. As Byron recalled in a letter to John Murray (the publisher) of November 19, 1820, "We went down to Newstead together — where I had got a famous cellar — and Monk's dresses from a masquerade warehouse.— We were a company of some seven or eight, with an occasional neighbor or so for visitors — and used to sit up late in our friars' dresses, drinking burgundy, claret, champagne, and what not — out of the skull-cup, and all sorts of glasses, and buffooning all round the house, in our conventual garments."

A few days after their arrival, one of the friends, Charles Skinner Matthews, who was of ill-health and irritable, threatened to throw Bold Webster out of a window "in consequence of I know not what commerce of jokes" (Byron's quote). Webster went to Byron and said that his respect and regard for him as a host would not permit him to call out any of his guests, and that therefore he would go to town the next morning. "He did," Byron wrote. "It was in vain that I represented to him that the window was not high, and the turf under it was particularly soft. Away he went."

Webster apologized for his behavior in a letter written to "The Honble. The Lord Byron, Newstead Abbey, near Nottingham": "My Dear Byron, I cannot express the regret I really feel at having left the social throng in the abrupt way my own evil genius impel'd me to do — I sent you a seal yesterday. I assure you the motto is what I sh'd really feel on losing the 'Bart.' If you think I am not worthy of that trifling memento pray throw the seal into the fire. If otherwise & you keep it — my wish is fully gratified —."

This reference to "losing the 'Bart'" is a private one, presumably something to do with a failed shot at a baronetcy, and at this remove, it remains, unfortunately, inscrutable.

Webster continued:

> Davies & I think of paying you a visit next week — if my conversation has not sicken'd you that is — & as you never <u>write</u> you may inform me by <u>proxy</u> whether my presence is acceptable to yr Lordship?—
> Davies has just told me to my astonishment that the papers have teem'd with nothing else but the well known hospitality of Newsteads [sic] convivial board & 'of Mr Wedderburn Webster having join'd the noble Irony'— who the author is I know not & I dare say you <u>care</u> not —

> I sincerely feel anxious for the restablishment [sic] of my friend Matthews' health! I hope to hear of his recovery — with kind remembrance to him, my friend Hobhouse & Mr Claridge, believe me in grt [great] sincerity, truly y'rs Dear Byron, WedderburnWebster [that's how he was signing his name then]. 11 April [1809], Blade's Hotel [London].

John J. Claridge — "dull Claridge" — was an old friend from Harrow. The "immortal Davies" was their mutual friend Scrope Berdmore Davies, first name pronounced "scroop," as in the first syllable of "scruples" — or lack of. Davies had been baptized on New Year's Day, 1783, in Horsley, Glos, the son of the Reverend Richard Davies, Vicar of Horsley, by his wife Margaretta Berdmore. Schooled at Eton, then Cambridge, he was famous as an athlete, a Regency wit and dandy, a womanizer, and Byron's friend.

John Cam Hobhouse, the writer, was a couple of years older than Byron and Webster. He had been born on June 27, 1786, at Redlands, near Bristol, the eldest son of Ben Hobhouse, of Cottles House, Wilts, later a baronet, by his wife Charlotte Cam. While at Trinity College, Cambridge (Cambridge being on the River Cam), with Byron, John Cam founded the Whig Club and the Amicable Society. A lawyer, he became a prominent politician and succeeded his father as Second Baronet Hobhouse in 1831. For his contributions to the country, he was raised to the peerage as Baron Broughton of Broughton-de-Gyfford in 1851. He died on June 3, 1869, in London. Although he was a far more noble character than Bold Webster, he does share one thing with that unworthy, and that is that he is chiefly remembered for his long friendship with Byron (he was the best man at Byron's wedding in 1815, and would be one of the two executors of his will). The same is true for both Tom Moore and Scrope Davies.

These gentlemen, then — notwithstanding Hobhouse's foray into politics and his elevation to the peerage — would never have existed to posterity without Byron. However, Scrope Davies may, in his own little way, have proved to be immortal after all. But that's a tale for 1818.

From Newstead Byron sent this letter, on April 12, 1809: "Dear Webster, I shall be very happy to see you again with or without the immortal Davies, pray come down soon as I am obliged to be in town on the 23rd. — Your seal will be very acceptable and no doubt the motto will be classical. I hope your watch is in the custody of [Stracey?] for here it is not. Believe me Dr. W. yours very sincerely, Byron."

By 1809 James was back in the 10th Hussars, as a lieutenant. Regimental records tell us that the 10th spent the summer of 1809 at Brighton, Sussex, then moved to Romford, Essex, until April 1810, when they went on to Islington.

Byron, together with Hobhouse, left on his European tour on July 2. Among his Lordship's retinue were his staid and melancholy valet, William Fletcher; Robert Rushton, his young general servant, son of one of Byron's Rochdale tenants; and old Joe Murray, his faithful butler. After a month and a half in the Iberian Peninsula, Byron sent Rushton (who was sick) and old Murray back home, keeping Fletcher. After a few weeks in Malta, they finally got to Greece in late September 1809. On Christmas Day, 1809, the party arrived in Athens where they spent a few months. Some sources say that sometime during their Athens stay, in 1810, they were joined for a while by James Webster; this has to be doubted, however, owing to lack of hard evidence. If James did go East, then he was on a short furlough from his army duties.

It wasn't all play for Byron — although there was a lot of play — as he began work on *Childe Harold's Pilgrimage* during this trip. Although he seems to have had no sense of the fact, this was the poem that was going to make him a star.

On May 2, 1810, the 10th Hussars were back in Romford (this was one day before Byron swam the Hellespont), and on May 16 the Hussars returned to Brighton and Lewes, where they stayed until May 16, 1812. On March 6, 1811, the 10th Hussars became the 10th Royal Hussars (being the Prince of Wales's Regiment). At this time they invented hurdle racing over the downs at Brighton, and the 10th were prominently to the fore in fashionable sporting and racing events.

Hobhouse returned to England in July 1810, but Byron continued on in Greece, having fallen in love with the country and some of its denizens. Despite repeated warnings from his lawyer, John Hanson, that he was bankrupting himself by his wild spending, he refused to sell Newstead.

Hanson was more than just the lawyer. He had been Byron's financial adviser since the young nobleman inherited the title, and was also, in many ways though none of them official, the future poet's guardian.

There is a miniature of Bold Webster done in 1813 by French artist Louis-Marie Autissier (1772–1830). It says on the back, "Lieut. Wedderburne Webster, 10th P.W.O. Dragoons, Sept. 1810." The regimental name is not necessarily here an anachronistic ascription, because the two terms, Dragoons and Hussars, were still being used interchangeably at that stage. This miniature was given to Bold Webster's son Major George (who had a tendency to carry on the Wedderburne spelling) by a fellow officer who had had it for many years, originally having bought it from a dealer who claimed it had been picked up on the field of Waterloo. Who had dropped it on that battlefield remains a mystery, and why anyone should have been carrying a miniature of Bold Webster in such a dangerous place is an even bigger puzzle. Webster himself was not anywhere near the discomfiting sound of cannon fire, so perhaps he had a secret admirer, or his wife may have had one. It is absolutely unconscionable even to conceive that Wellington might have been toting a miniature of Bold Webster on the field of the most famous battle in history.

At any rate, Major George's wife, Caroline, came into possession of this miniature, and then gave it to her daughter Annie, who gave it to her niece Betty Valentia Stewart, and from there it went to Betty Valentia's son, William Stewart (this author's father).

4

Lady Frances

On December 8, 1810, at the fashionable church of St. Marylebone, Westminster (Byron was baptized here), James Wedderburn Webster married the seventeen-year-old Lady Frances Caroline Annesley, eldest of the three surviving daughters of Arthur, 8th Viscount Valentia and 1st Earl of Mountnorris, by his second wife, Sarah, daughter of Sir Henry Cavendish, Baronet, of Doveridge Hall, Derbyshire, and Sarah, Baroness Waterpark (created 1792). "Highly pedigreed," as Fiona MacCarthy describes Lady Frances in her 2002 biography of Byron.

The Earl of Mountnorris's first marriage, to Lucy Lyttelton, had produced his heir, George, as well as a couple of daughters, Juliana and Hester. Hester had married a Macleod, but Juliana Lucy, the second daughter, is definitely worth dwelling upon a little longer. She was baptized on October 28, 1772, at Upper Arley, Worcestershire, and on July 4, 1789, she married John Barry-Maxwell, who would become Lord Farnham, a great Irish landlord. She would die in 1833, and Lord Farnham in 1838. This would all be fairly straightforward if it weren't for the fact that Juliana Lucy would have, many years later, a youngest (half) sister named Juliana Lucy.

Mountnorris's first wife died, and he married Sarah Cavendish. Henry Arthur was the first child from that marriage who survived. They would call him Arthur. Then came Lady Frances Caroline Annesley, on May 28, 1793; Lady Catherine, on July 16, 1795; and finally, Juliana Lucy, on November 21, 1797, in Camolin, in Wexford, Ireland.

By the time the second Juliana Lucy was born, the first one had long been married to Lord Farnham, so perhaps Mountnorris felt that there should be a new Juliana Lucy Annesley. Something like that. It is a very odd case, not unique, but definitely unusual.

James's mother's memorandum is wrong in giving the date of his marriage to Lady Frances as January 1811, and the *Wedderburn Book* (a huge, two-volume, vastly impressive 1898 work by one of the Wedderburns) is wrong in giving it as October 8, 1810. The *Annual Register*, volume 52, page 414, and the *Gentleman's Magazine*, as well as the Marylebone parish records themselves, give the date as December 8, 1810. The *Gentleman's Magazine* says, "By special

The Countess Mountnorris, mother of Lady Frances Webster-Wedderburn. From the author's collection.

4. *Lady Frances*

The Countess Mountnorris and family. Standing: Lady John Somerset, Honorable Henry Annesly, Lady Frances Webster-Wedderburn; sitting: Lady Mountnorris; kneeling: Lady Juliana Bayly. From the author's collection.

licence, James-Wedderburn Webster, Esq., of Clapham, to the Right-Hon. the Lady Frances Caroline Annesley, second [sic] daughter of the Earl of Mountnorris, and sister to Viscount Valentia."

James did well by this marriage, even though, according to the *Life and Letters of Lady Melbourne*, James's brother told Byron this was a marriage of convenience. Aside from other considerations, he had married a lady described by Austin K. Gray, in his book *Teresa*, as "that wistful beauty, Lady Frances Webster." Peter Quennell, in his book *Byron: The Years of Fame*, describes Lady Frances as "slender, fair, with long, dark eyelashes. She moved through life fragile, acquiescent and subdued." André Maurois says of her, "Lady Frances was very pretty, but had an air of fragility."

Much emphasis is placed upon her "fragility" and like qualities. However, Lady Frances was a lot tougher than a mere surface inspection would reveal. The fragile quality was, to some extent, cultivated, for that was the way many played the game in those days. One must never lose sight of the fact that Lady Frances came from a hardy breed—i.e., the British aristocracy.

Quennell calls Webster "that scribbler and bore," and claims these qualities grew "all the worse" with his marriage. But Quennell is jumping the gun on two counts here. First, as hard as it is to imagine from what came later, Bold Webster was not yet a bore; and second, he had not yet begun to write. Quennell also tells us, in a misquote, that Lady Frances married to escape a bad-tempered family. This is true, and Byron mentions this (the poet actually uses the phrase "ill-tempered") in his October 1, 1813, letter to Lady Melbourne.

Lady Melbourne, Byron's arch-confidante, was the wife of Peniston Lamb, 1st Viscount Melbourne, and mother of William Lamb, 2nd Viscount Melbourne and future prime minister, who was married to one of Byron's memorable amours, the notorious Lady Caroline Lamb, nicknamed within her circle as "The Lamb." Lady Melbourne was born Elizabeth Milbanke, daughter of Ralph Milbanke, 5th Bart., and sister of Ralph Milbanke, 6th Bart., and therefore aunt of Annabella Milbanke, who would become Byron's wife. Byron described Lady Melbourne as "the best, and kindest, and ablest female I have ever known, old or young."

After his marriage James quit the army again, temporarily, and he and Lady Frances moved to James's house, 48 Albemarle Street, Clapham. Henning tells us that Wedderburn Webster was at Bob Gregson's pub, *The Castle*, in Holborn, on January 30, 1811, when Bob presented his new protégé, Heskin Rimmer, to a group of bloods which included Wedderburn Webster and the 8th Marquess of Tweeddale (who in 1828 would become the brother-in-law of John Cam Hobhouse).

Lady Frances Webster-Wedderburn. By kind permission of Martin Davies.

5

Arms

On February 4, 1811, James was granted Arms by the Lord Lyon of Scotland. The curious thing is that he is listed as Sir James Webster Wedderburn, K.B., when in fact he was not knighted until 1822. K.B. could have meant one of only three things in 1811: Knight Banneret, but as this title went out just after 1611 it seems unlikely, if not impossible; Knight of the Bath (after 1814 called KCB), too prestigious an order for James to lie about it (and certainly to have received); or Knight Bachelor, the lowest knight, one who did not belong to any order. There was no roll of knights bachelor before 1902, so it was possible in 1811 to lie about it and get away with it. But surely with the Lord Lyon he would have had to have furnished some sort of proof. This is mysterious.

Notwithstanding, the grant [*Lyon Register*, ii. 61] reads undeniably thus:

> To all and sundry whom these presents do or may concern. We, Thomas Robert, Earl of Kinnoull, etc., Lord Lyon King at Arms, do hereby certify and declare that the Ensigns Armorial belonging and pertaining to Sir James Webster Wedderburn, K.B., of Clapham in the county of Surry, eldest son of David Wedderburn, alias Webster, of Shenley Hill, in the county of Herts, Esquire, who, in obedience to the will of James Webster, Esq., of Clapham aforesaid, his uncle, obtained his Majesty's Licence to assume the name of Webster, which David Wedderburn was third son of Robert second son of Sir Alexander Wedderburn of Blackness, Baronet, and which Sir James Webster Wedderburn, K.B. has also assumed the surname Webster, in virtue of the foresaid Royal Licence to David Wedderburn his father, and is married to the Right Honourable Lady Frances Caroline Annesley, second [sic] daughter of Arthur, Earl of Mount-Norris [sic]:— Are matriculated in the public registers of the Lyon Office and are blazoned [described, with pomp] as on the margin thus viz: Quarterly [an escutcheon, or shield, divided into quarters], first and fourth Argent [heraldic term for silver] a fess [horizontal division within the middle of the flag] between three weavers' shuttles, gules [red], tipped and furnished with quils [sic] of yarn, Or [gold], for the surname of Webster; second and third Argent, a cheveron [sic] between three roses gules, for Wedderburn. Above the shield is placed an helmet, befitting his degree, with a mantling gules [red drapery tied to the helmet above the shield], the doubling Argent [silver mantlings borne about the achievement of arms], and on a wreath of his liveries is set for crest an Eagle's head erased proper ["erased" means with the head ripped off, leaving a jagged edge], this motto, 'In Deo Spero,' on a compartment below the shield, on which is the motto, 'Non Degener,' are placed for supporters (he being the Chief of the surname Webster in Scotland, a surname at one time very numerous in the county of Forfar) [a curious statement of chieftainship, as he had no Webster blood] on this dexter [right] side a lion rampant [i.e. with forepaws in the air, as if attacking; unless otherwise stated the lion always faces dexter], and on the sinister [left] a stag proper; both of them ["proper" means that the animal is represented in its natural color], and in an escroll above the crest collared gules [i.e., with a red collar, or crown, around their necks], and thereto affixed a chain passing between their forelegs and reflexed over their backs of the same ["reflexed," more often seen as "reflected," meaning when the chain is turned around and thrown over the animal's back], each of them holding in its mouth a thistle proper. Which Armorial Ensigns above blazoned We do hereby ratify, confirm and assign to the said Sir James Webster Wedderburn and the heirs male of his body as their proper arms and bearing in all times coming. In testimony whereof these presents are subscribed by James Home of Linhouse,

Esquire, Our deputy, and the seal of Our office is appended hereunto at Edinburgh this fourth day of February in the year of Our Lord one thousand eight hundred and eleven — Lyon Office, Edinburgh, 4th Feb. 1811. This patent is duly entered in the records of the Lyon Office by me John Kerr, herald, painter, and keeper of records. James Home, Lyon Depute.

It is worth noting that in this 1811 grant his name is Webster Wedderburn, no hyphen, as given at birth. This seems to be indicating that he was changing his name back from Wedderburne Webster (or Wedderburn Webster). This was not the only time he changed his name, and other people could not keep up with him in this regard. They continued to call him by whatever they had known him as, and this accounts for the variants of his name as seen in print over the years.

Although obvious, it is also worth noting, in light of the confusion over the title of "K.B.," that James's father, David, is not Sir David; therefore James's putative title, in this granting of arms, was not hereditary but acquired during his lifetime, more precisely before February 4, 1811. As he was only 22 at the time and had done nothing to deserve a knighthood, one must certainly be led toward the suspicion that there was some graft and corruption going on in the Lord Lyon's office — unless possibly James's friend the Prince of Wales had been kind enough to award him such an honor or at least to have had it arranged. If this royal benediction was indeed, bestowed, there is no record of it. However, the same Prince of Wales's granting of James's later (1822) knighthood, which was much more celebrated by his contemporaries — perhaps because the prince was now king — even though it should have been a somewhat superfluous title (as James already had a knighthood in 1811), is just as absent in the record-books.

But truly, the most bizarre thing is this: Given that before he was knighted in 1822 James would have given his left hand for the title "Sir," if he had it as early as 1811, why didn't he flaunt it? Something is irreconcilable here.

6

Dandy

Precisely one day after Bold Webster took out arms, almost as if he had known the shape of things to come, the government passed the Regency Act. George III had been subject to fits of madness before, but by now his condition was more or less permanent. He would remain king until he died, of course, but he could not reign. So his eldest son, the Prince of Wales, was appointed regent. Hence the term "Regency period," the space of time between 1811 and 1820 when Prinnie, as he was known to his intimates, ruled the land for his father.

The prince regent set the trend in many ways, being the leading man in a nation full of leading men. He spoke several languages, was at ease in any company, and reputedly had 7,000 romantic affairs. But in other ways, he was the victim of fashion dictated by others, notably that of Beau Brummell, the king of the dandies.

The term "dandy," as it came to be applied in those days, describes a different creature from the one of a century later, when "dandies" such as Oscar Wilde and Algernon Swinburne roamed the earth. No, the Regency dandy was a quite different animal.

Fashion, like every other facet of a subculture with more available money than sense, either evolves naturally or takes a quick turn as the result of an idea which catches on. Gentlemen of a certain type have always, throughout history, desired to be set apart, to be the cynosure of other men's—not women's—eyes.

In the 18th century, for example, at least for a time, there not only existed, but reigned, the macaroni. Based on a word used throughout Europe meaning a homosexual of extraordinarily effeminate appearance and manner, this term seemed snug for the gent who effected his debut as such in mid–Georgian London. Bizarre even in his own day, the macaroni lisped and gasped, fainted, blushed, uttered and stuttered in staccato, and trained himself to achieve upper vocal registers that would, in the end, amid a welter of other psychological and physiological factors, lead to the "macaroni walk." An awesome creature, loathsome, indeed, to those of lesser aspirations, what finally did him in was his own absurdity and lack of education in the natural sciences. Under the force of competition his wig had been growing, in altitude and complexity, topped off with a little hat that could only be doffed using the point of a rapier. So tall and so elaborate was this hairpiece that the macaroni began to experience difficulty in safe locomotion. Of course, this could not last, as the poor man could not move for fear of disturbing his peruke; and so he died out.

But the impulse that drove the macaroni continued to find expression in the fop. Again, alarmingly effeminate, over-dressed, over-powdered, over-perfumed, aspiring to aristocracy, the fop lisped and offended his way along St. James's Street at the drop of a hat, at all times the object of ridicule. The Scarlet Pimpernel (in his alter role, of course) is the archetypical fop.

Then came the dandy. It was Beau Brummell who invented dandyism. Well-spoken was the dandy, witty, educated, very bright, unpowdered and unscented, bathed to the minute, dressed well—very well—albeit conservatively, in an immaculate frock coat, waistcoat, an elaborate cravat, neatly-pressed trousers, and, at times, a top hat, although he was ambitious to show off his hair style, which was, almost unbelievably and for that very reason, as plain as Napoleon's. His boots, which he polished with champagne following Brummell's lead, were tasteful (nay, almost potable) and of a cut and shine to bring warmth to the heart of a slightly sozzled recruiting officer. Above all other considerations, the dandy's clothes were impossibly expensive. Brummell was asked once how much it took a dandy per year for clothing. His reply was £800.

A dandy took five hours to dress before he even dared venture out into the street. The mirror was his friend, his advisor, his critic, his servant, his amour, but ultimately his master. Without the mirror the dandy would have been like a Wild West gunfighter without a revolver. He would have been unable to function. He took fashion that seriously. It was the look in the eyes of acquaintances that told the story, that revealed the efficacy of his looking-glass. That look he lived for, did the dandy, for it was all he really had to live for — except for the brilliant conversation (another hallmark of this well-spoken creature), the fine food and the gambling.

Spending so much time getting ready naturally precluded work or industry of any kind. Dandyism was a full-time occupation for rich layabouts — or at least for layabouts who ran up tailors' bills with such lack of mercy that they deserved the fate that befell most of them — insanity, suicide, syphilis, poverty, despair, solitary confinement in a dingy boarding house on the Continent. Fate caught up with most of them, which is more than can be said for most of their outraged creditors.

There was George Brummell, of course, the doyen of the Regency bucks, and his chief deputy Lord Alvanley. Also there were the Count d'Orsay; Golden Ball Hughes (named, unfortunately, not for any anatomical prodigy, but rather because he was born Ball); Charles Howard, the Drunken Duke of Norfolk; me Lords Hertford, Yarmouth, Rutland, Worcester (father and son, or rather perhaps one and the same, given the bizarre state of things dandy), Argyll and Barrymore (the 6th Duke and 8th Earl respectively); Sir John Lade, the one with the foul-mouthed wife; Poodle Byng, named after his dog rather than his father; Beau Petersham, fashion setter with a notorious duel upon his far horizon; Sir Henry Mildmay and Sir Skiffy Skeffington; the Americans — or at least American by virtue of having been over there — Colonel Hanger and Banastre Tarleton; and finally Henry Pierrepoint, Tom Foley, Scrope Davies, and Wedderburn Webster.

> My dear Scrope, lend me two hundred pounds; the banks are shut, and all my money is in the three percents. It shall be repaid tomorrow morning. Yours, George Brummell.
> My dear George, 'tis unfortunate, but all my money is in the three percents. Yours, S. Davies.

A craze at the time was coaching. Clubs were formed — the Four-in-Hand Club, the Four Horse Club, the Whip Club — the more virile members of which would take the reins of a barouche landau and, setting out from London, test the patience of their less-propelled contemporaries and the safety of perambulating peasants and their charges as they thundered down the rutted roads to the Pack Horse in Turnham Green or the Castle Inn at Salt Hill to partake of luncheon.

At any given moment, to be seen flying through the countryside yelling, "Bang up for Salt Hill" would be, among others, Bold Webster with his four chestnuts, Captain Morgan with his four bays, Lord Hawke with his bright ones and Captain (later Sir) Felix Agar with his iron bays, Sir John Rogers with his blacks, and the veteran coachman Sir Jack Lade, all dressed in their uniform of dark green frock coat, brass or gilt buttons, leather breeches, top boots, and broad-brimmed beavers.

A curious footnote of synchronicity: the landlady of the Pack Horse a few generations prior — Mrs. Henrietta Partridge — was the most famous publican of her day. In the mid–1760s she upped and took over the Castle Inn, near Slough. On the night of March 29, 1773, seventeen men died there as the result of bad turtle soup. It was quite a scandal. For a year Mrs. Partridge couldn't pull them in with a hook, but she survived, eventually quitting the inn business and opening a school for girls in Hammersmith. Her great granddaughter would marry Bold Webster's son in 1853 in Corfu.

The Regency period was no different from any other arbitrarily categorized period in English history in that new things happened in every walk of life, and, to the same extent that every other era was and is unique, the Regency period was too. It gave us the Romantic Poets—Byron, Shelley, Keats, Wordsworth, Southey and Coleridge too, and Jane Austen, and Walter Scott of North Britain, and Constable, Gainsborough, Reynolds, and Beau Nash.

7

Vis à Vis

One good thing about getting arms was that one was invited to functions. On February 26, 1811, the prince regent held his first public levee of the year. Lt. Wedderburne Webster, mentioned in the list of distinguished characters, was one of those presented to His Highness. Not Sir but Lieutenant, one notices.

On April 30, 1811, Byron set out on the long journey home from exotic parts, contracting malaria as he did so. On June 19, in a long letter to his friend John Cam Hobhouse, written on board the frigate *Volage*, he says, "Bold Webster (by way of keeping up that epithet, I suppose) has married, and, bolder still, a sister of Lord Viscount Valentia, and, boldest of all, has published letters to the Commander-in-Chief! Corpo di Caio Mario! what will the world come to? I take this to be one of the newest events 'under the sun.' Had he no friend, no relation, no pitying monitor to snatch the manuscript from one devil to save it from the other? Pray are the letters in prose or verse?"

Incidentally, the captain of the *Volage* was named Hornby. Byron describes him as "a gentlemanly and pleasant man." Although there are no further references to Hornby's having hobnobbed with Byron, it is tempting to speculate that perhaps it was through this seaman that Byron met the Reverend George Hornby, the priest who married Captain William Dixon and Cecilia Pierina Gironci in Corfu in 1823. The daughter of the Dixons would marry the son of the Websters at Corfu in 1853.

Soon after Byron's return from Greece (July 14, 1811), he submitted *Childe Harold* for publication, threw several parties for his old friends, and ordered a vis à vis built by the famous London carriage-maker Philip Godsall, of 103 Long Acre. However, Benita Eisler says, in her book *Byron*, "Realizing the impracticality of a two-seater for his social life, involving, as it often did, parties of friends, he later agreed to exchange his occasional vehicle, plus 200 guineas, for Webster's coach"—Webster, of course, being Bold Webster, "the unstable character who had been the butt of practical jokes at Newstead" (*Byron: a Biography*, by Leslie A. Marchand).

Byron wrote to Webster on July 29, 1811, from Reddish's Hotel in St. James's Street, where Byron had taken lodgings on January 9, 1809, before he set out for Europe on his two-year trip. Bold Webster was then living at Dean's Court, Wimborne, in Dorset. The poet says:

> My Dear Webster. As this eternal vis a vis seems to sit heavy on your soul, I beg leave to apprise you that I have arranged with Goodsall [he means Godsall]; you are to give me the promised wheels, & the lining, with the box at Brighton, & I am to pay him the stipulated sum.—I am obliged to you for your favorable opinion & trust that the happiness you talk so much of will be stationary, and not take those freaks to which the Felicity of common mortals is subject.—I do very sincerely wish you well, & am so convinced of the Justice of your matrimonial arguments, that I shall follow your example as soon as I can get a sufficient price for my Coronet.—In the mean I should be happy to drill for my new situation, under your auspices, but Business,

inexorable Business, keeps me here — your letters are forwarded. — If I can serve you in any way, command me, I will endeavour to fulfill your requests as awkwardly as another. I shall pay you a visit perhaps in the Autumn. Believe Dr W, yrs unintelligibly, B.

Two days after the deal had been struck with Webster, the carriage arrived, but with a faded and worn interior instead of the new one Byron had stipulated. The poet was not amused, and wrote to Bold Webster from Reddish's Hotel, on July 31, 1811:

My Dear W.W. I always understood the Lining was to accompany the Carriage, if not the Carriage may accompany the Lining; for I will have neither one or the other. In short, to prevent squabbling, this is my determination, so decide: — if you leave it to my feelings (as you say) they are very strongly in favour of the said lining. — 200 Gs. [guineas] for a carriage with ancient lining!!! Rags & Rubbish! You must write another pamphlet my dear W. before — but pray do not waste your time & eloquence in expostulation, because it will do neither of us good, but decide — content or not content — The best thing you can do for the Tutor you speak of, will be to send him in your vis (with the Lining) to the University of Gottingen, how can you suppose (now that my own Bear is dead) that I have any situation for a German Genius of his kind till I get another, or some children. [We do not know who this tutor is] — I am infinitely obliged to you for your invitations, but I cant [sic] pay so high for a second hand chaise to make my friends a visit. — The Coronet will not grace the 'pretty vis' till your tattered lining ceases to disgrace it. — Pray favour me with an answer, as we must finish the affair one way or another immediately before next week. — Believe me, yrs very truly, Byron.

James wrote a note in his manuscript of the letter saying, "Byron was more than strict about trifles," but that is understating what he really felt. There is certainly the threat of a duel in the last part of this letter.

Perhaps in consequence of this veiled threat, in August 1811 Webster was very upset over the confusion of the carriage. Byron wrote a hugely conciliatory letter to him, from Newstead Abbey, on August 24, 1811, a letter which contained the first of many blandishments to take up a career in politics:

My dear W. — Conceiving your wrath to be somewhat evaporated & your Dignity recovered from the Hysterics into which my innocent note from London had thrown it, I should feel happy to be informed how you have determined on the disposal of this accursed Coach, which has driven us out of our Good humour & Good manners to a complete Standstill, from which I begin to apprehend that I am to lose altogether your valuable correspondence. — Your angry letter arrived at a moment, to which I shall not allude further, as my happiness is best consulted in forgetting it. — You have perhaps heard also of the death of poor Matthews, whom you recollect to have met at Newstead. — He was one whom his friends will find it difficult to replace, nor will Cambridge ever see his equal — .

Charles Skinner Matthews had been a little ahead of Byron at Trinity. He drowned in the Cam on August 3, 1811. His screams as he struggled to free himself from the weeds were remembered many years afterwards by some of his contemporaries.

"I trust you are on the point of adding to your relatives instead of losing them," continues the poet,

and of friends a man of fortune will always have a plentiful stock — at his Table. — I dare say now you are gay — & connubial & popular so that in the next parliament we shall be having you a County Member. — But beware your Tutor, for I am sure he Germanized that sanguinary letter, you must not write such another to your constituents; for myself (as the mildest of men) I shall say no more about it. — Seriously, mio Caro W. if you can spare a moment from Matrimony, I shall be glad to hear that you have recovered from the pucker into which this Vis (one would think it had been a Sulky) has thrown you. — You know I wish you well — & if I have not inflicted my society upon you according to your own Invitation, it is only because I am not a social animal, & should feel sadly at a loss amongst Countesses and Maids of Honour, particularly being just come from a far Country, where ladies are neither carved for [sic], or fought for, or danced after, or mixed at all (publicly) with the Men-folks, so that you must make allowances for my natural diffidence & two years travel.— But (God and yourself willing) I shall certes pay my promised visit, as I shall be in town, if Parliament meets in October.— In the mean time let me hear from you (without a privy Council) and believe me, in sober sadness, yours very sincerely, Byron.

James replied quickly, in a letter undated but almost certainly August 25 or 26, 1811:

Deans Court, Wimborne. My Dear B, Our correspondence w'd have certainly for ever stood still had I not been favor'd with y'r epistle as those very very feelings which impel my nature to value you as a <u>friend now</u> <u>w'd before</u> as certainly have made me respect you as an Ennemy [sic]— But a truce to such <u>unbecoming</u> thoughts as <u>ode sparring</u> of every description from the magnanimous <u>Jackson</u>! [i.e. the pugilist] down to my own poor scribbling—

You lest [sic] know what is become of the 'accursed coach' you allude to. As Godsall of course informed me he had credited me with 200 guineas from your acct. & paying for new wheels & the <u>memorable</u> lining—

'So pray be happy with your new bought vis' 'or cease Dear B either to spar or quit.'

Now when you are tired of it let me know & I will try & find as ready a purchaser for you as I once myself proved— Do you know Wm Bankes well— He & his famille dined here yesterday. He boasts much of his extreme intimacy with '<u>your Lordship</u>'— I was very near him at Dinner <u>me misere</u>! for I think he talks the most <u>sublime</u> stuff I ever heard—.

William Bankes was, indeed, a good friend of Byron's; they had met at Cambridge. Bankes was an Egyptologist, son of the member for Corfe Castle, and notorious homosexual. He was caught with a guardsman in Green Park and effectively banished from England. About the same age as Byron and Bold Webster, he outlived them both, dying in 1855.

Webster continued his letter, "Apropos to sublimity I enclose you a Hares critique on Lady J Grey, &c, as a good thing— as hares are still too young to be devour'd treat the cantling [he might mean canting] gently pray—."

Byron's friend Francis Hodgson had written *Lady Jane Grey, a Tale; and other Poems*, which had been published in 1809. Naylor Hare (1753–1815, a friend of the gambling Duchess of Devonshire) criticized this piece, and it was this critique Webster was sending Byron.

Webster's letter continues:

Now my Dear B., I really feel for you & altho' I know y'r mind capable of great energy— still without you have some particular favor'd friend with you— time must be sad & sober— I was much shocked at Poor Mathews' [sic] death. I hope that wretched fatality won't visit all y'r friends & light upon your poor humble servant—!

Who the maids of Honor are here I know not at any rate— I think a regular maid of honor & a fille de joie [a lady of the evening, so to speak]— ignominious— vide my Lord Lyttelton's definition of that sacred courtly character, but you must fear nothing here as our Countess is a very <u>tame</u> one for these savage times & our young ladies are far from <u>pregnant</u>— Only beware of your <u>lordly heart</u>— I need not repeat how delighted we sh'd be to see you & if you are <u>melancholick</u>— as folk say— I am sure you w'd find pleasure in my cara sposa's conversation [now, what does this mean!]— how does Newstead look. I ever thought it a sweet place—

I take my leave of you, with a sincere profession of friendship & a most ardent wish to see you soon here— & interim to hear from you—

Tout à vous, Wedderburn Webster.

This was the last time the vis was mentioned. Byron, from now on, studiously ignored any reference to it.

8

The Groom of Abydos

A few days later, from Newstead Abbey, on August 31, 1811, Byron responded somewhat scathingly:

> My dear W.—I send you back your friend's letter & though I don't agree with his Canons of Criticism, they are not the worse for that.—My friend Hodgson is not much honoured by the Comparison to the 'Pursuits of L' [*The Pursuits of Literature*, a satirical poem written by T.J. Mathias in 1797] which is notoriously as far as the poetry goes the worst written of it's [sic] kind, the world has long been but of the opinion viz. that it's sole merit lies in the Notes, which are indisputably excellent.— had Hodgson's 'Alternative' been placed with the 'Baviad' [written by William Gifford in 1794], the compliment had been higher to both, for surely the Baviad is as much superior to H's poem, as I do firmly believe H's poem to be to the 'Pursuits of Literature.'—Your correspondent talks for talking's sake when he says Lady J. Gray [sic] is neither 'Epic, dramatic, or legendary.' Who ever said it was 'epic' or 'dramatic'? he might as well say his letter was neither 'epic or dramatic,' the poem makes no pretensions to either character 'Legendary' it certainly is, but what has that to do with it's merits? all stories of that kind founded on facts are in a certain degree legendary, but they may be well or ill written without the smallest alteration in that respect.—When Mr Hare prattles about the 'Economy' &c. he sinks sadly; all such expressions are the mere cant of a schoolboy hovering around the Skirts of Criticism.—Hodgson's tale is one of the best efforts of his Muse, & Mr H's approbation must be one of more consequence, before any body will reduce it to a 'Scale,' or be much affected by 'the place' he 'assigns' to the productions of a man like Hodgson.—But I have said more than I intended & only beg you never to allow yourself to be imposed upon by such 'commonplace' as the 5th form letter you sent me.—Judge for yourself.—I know the Mr Bankes you mention though not to that 'extreme' you seem to think, but I am flattered by his 'boasting' on such a subject (as you say) for I never thought him likely to 'boast' of anything which was not his own—I am not 'melancholick' pray what 'folk' dare to say any such thing? I must contradict them by being merry at their expence [sic].—I shall invade you in the course of the Winter, out of envy, as Lucifer looked at Adam & Eve.—Pray be as happy as you can, & write to me that I may catch the infection. Yrs ever, Byron.

In August 1811 Capt. Rees Howell Gronow wrote in a letter, "I know very little of Lord Byron personally, but lived with two of his intimate friends, Scrope Davies and Wedderburn Webster, from whom I frequently heard many anecdotes of him." Gronow (1794–1865), a Glamorganshire-born veteran of the playing fields of both Eton and Waterloo (two very similar experiences in many ways), a Grenadier Guardsman turned politician who later lived at Chesterfield Street in Mayfair (as did the Webster-Wedderburns and as had Beau Brummell), is best remembered as a dandy and the quintessential gossip columnist of his day.

On September 2, 1811, from Newstead Abbey, Byron wrote to Scrope Davies, who had invited him to come and visit, "I am also invited by Bold Webster, who is reconciled with as little reason as he was angry." Here, Byron is referring to James Webster's rather sudden departure from Newstead in 1809, after Matthews had threatened to defenestrate him.

In writing to Webster from Newstead Abbey on October 10, 1811, Byron says:

Dear Webster.—I can hardly invite a gentleman to my house a second time who walked out of it the first in so singular a mood, but if you had thought proper to pay me a visit, you would have had a 'Highland Welcome'—I am only just returned to it out of Lancashire where I have been on business to a Coal manor of mine near Rochdale, & shall leave it very shortly for Cambridge & London. My companions, or rather companion (for Claridge alone has been with me) have not been very amusing, & as to their 'sincerity,' they are doubtless sincere enough for a man who will never put them to the trial.—Besides, you talked so much of your conjugal happiness, that an invitation from home would have seemed like Sacrilege, & my rough Bachelor's Hall would have appeared to little advantage after the Bower of 'Armida' [from Tasso] where you have been reposing—I cannot boast of my social powers at any time, & just at present they are more stagnant than ever—Your brother in law [George Annesley, Viscount Valentia] means to stand for Wexford, but I have reasons for thinking the Portsmouth interest will be against him, however I wish him success.—Do you mean to stand for any place next elections? What are your politics? I hope Valentia's Lord is for the Catholics.—You will find Hobhouse at Enniscorthy, in the contested county. Pray what has seized you? Your last letter is the only one in which you do not rave upon matrimony, are there no symptoms of a young W.W. & I shall never be a Godfather?—I believe I must be married myself soon, but it shall be a secret & a surprise.—However, knowing your exceeding discretion I shall probably entrust the secret to your silence at a proper period. You have it is true invited me repeatedly to Dean's Court, & now when it is probably I might adventure there, you wish to be off.—Be it so.—If you address your letters to this place they will be forwarded wherever I sojourn.—I am about to meet some friends at Cambridge and on to town in November—the papers are full of Dalrymple's Bigamy, (I know the man) What the Devil will he do with his Spare-rib?—He is no beauty, but as lame as myself.—He has more ladies than legs, what comfort to a cripple! Sto sempre umilisssimo servitore [always your most humble servant], Byron.

Captain Dalrymple had, indeed, done the dirty deed, and it was, as Byron said, in all the papers.

James Webster is mentioned in passing in a letter by Byron to John Cam Hobhouse from Newstead Abbey on October 13, 1811.

It was at this time that a choirboy type named John Edleston, a friend of Byron's, died. Several recent biographers of Byron have made probes into the possible homosexual life of Byron; in other words, was he or wasn't he? Fiona MacCarthy, in her 2002 biography of the poet, says, "Early in November he [Byron] shows signs of paranoia in a letter to Hobhouse, reporting James Wedderburn Webster's indiscreet reference to a boy, a 'Hyacinth.'" MacCarthy writes that there was an implication that this boy was rentable at the rate of £200 a year. She also says, "'Bold' Webster threw in reckless comments on his brother-in-law Lord Valentia, a known homosexual [this is the brother of Lady Frances]."

The letter to Hobhouse to which Fiona MacCarthy refers was written on November 2, 1811, from 8 St. James's St., London, where the poet had taken up residence only four days before:

Bold Webster dropped in after dinner & managed to annoy Hodgson with his absurdity, he talked of H's satire & particularly his address to the 'Electric!!!' [Eclectic] Critics, and Porson's edition of Phocion!!! and finished by asking H if he had ever redde his (W's) pamphlet!!! He made one cursed speech which put me into a fever, about ena paidi [Greek for 'a boy'] & made Hodgson nearly sink into the earth, who unluckily recollected our telling him the 'two hundred a year' proffer pro iakinthos [for the Hyacinth]. He then to mend matters entered into a long defence of his brother in law, without any occasion as nobody had mentioned his name, persisted in spite of all endeavours to make him change ye. subject, & concluded by saying that Ld. Courtney was 'called Cousin by the King of Prussia!!!' Now all this is a verbatim conversation of Bold W—You will think me Banksizing but it is fact Per Dio!

Hobhouse's reply included "the beastly talk of that fool of fools Bold Webster—Why you do not cut him dead I do not understand." (See Fiona MacCarthy's *Byron: Life and Legend*).

Whatever anyone may make of Byron's homosexuality (or lack of it), James never seems to have been tarred with the same brush. Some have inferred, to their discredit as researchers, that this may be why Byron put up with someone like Bold Webster. The reasons for Byron's putting up with Webster are discussed at the end of this book, but Webster was not a homosexual. Byron maybe, but not Webster.

On November 3, 1811, the poet had some more news of Webster, in another letter to Hobhouse from St. James's Street. Byron said:

> Bold Webster is in a scrape with the Morning Post, Morning Chronicle, & all the Posts Morning & Evening, about some letters on politics with which he has lately been tying Cannisters to his tail, they charged him ten pounds for inserting one of these precious billets & if they had asked a hundred the disgrace to the paper was honestly worth it.—It is in vain that wife, relations, friends, & enemies have risen up in fierce opposition to his malady, nothing but a thumbscrew or a whitloe on the itching finger can quell his scribbling.—He has exposed himself, nay hurt himself, for he was soliciting a Scotch place, & wrote a defence of Ld. Fingal [the senior Irish Catholic peer, embroiled in Irish politics] by way of ingratiating himself with Ministers!!! & the worst of it is that everybody knew this devil of a defence to be his, though sans signature, & for fear they should not be told it unto all men.—His wife is very pretty, and I am much mistaken if five years hence she don't give him reason to think so [Byron as minor but successful prophet]. Knowing the man one is apt to fancy these things, but I really thought she treated him, even already, with a due portion of conjugal contempt, but I dare say this was only the megrim of a misogynist.
> At present he is the happiest of men, and has asked me to go with them to a tragedy to see his wife cry!

This incident that Byron mentions, and others like it, are important in understanding Bold Webster's sexual drive, and indeed his life's ego-bound motive in general. Benita Eisler has this to say of this incident, for readers who might not be able to grasp its meaning from the original Byron letter:

> His Cambridge crony, 'Bold' Webster, oafish mascot of their group, had taken to himself a beautiful, rich and well-born young bride, Lady Frances Annesley.... Eager to display his prize Webster importuned Byron with invitations to visit them in the country, but, failing to lure his friend from town, arranged an evening at the theater so his guest could admire Lady Frances's superior sensibilities as she wept through the tragic proceedings onstage. Writing to Hobhouse, Byron made sport of this fresh instance of Webster's idiocy. With the eye of a predator he had noticed that the young bride already treated her husband with a certain contempt.

James was a "Cambridge crony" only if one stretches the term Cambridge—he was a friend of Byron's from the poet's days at the university, but he himself was not a student there, and a "mascot" he certainly was not. Oafish as he may have been, he was part of the group, and oafish is not really the adjective for James, no matter what other pejorative descriptors apply. However, pretty much everyone was agreed that the Websters' marriage was already on the rocks.

Another letter from Byron to Hobhouse, from the same address, on November 8, 1811, says, "All Webster's connections are at their Wits' end to cure him of his malady, they have applied to me to talk to him seriously on ye. subject, & I have talked, but to no purpose, for he lost his temper, & invited me to a Controversy in the Newspapers!!! Valentia is vastly annoyed, & so is W's spouse, but nothing will do, he persists in his laudable design of becoming ridiculous."

Also to Hobhouse, from St. James's St., on November 17, 1811, "Webster is vanished with his wife." Byron said, in the same letter, "Wr will be a noble subject for cuckoldom in three years, though he has managed to impregnate her Ladyship, which consequently can be no very difficult task. She is certainly very pretty, & if not a dunce, must despise her 'Bud' heartily. She is not exactly to my taste, but I daresay Dragoons would like her."

A sidelight here is that Bernard Grebanier, in his book *The Uninhibited Byron*, tells us that the poet stayed twice at Aston Hall, and that the first time was followed two weeks later by this November 17 letter. This is inaccurate, as Webster was living in Dorset at this time, not at Aston Hall; further, Byron does not seem to have stayed with the Websters, even at Dorset, at this time, certainly not in the early part of November. Webster did not even begin to rent Aston Hall until 1813. Byron did visit the Websters on occasion at that address, but the first time was not until September 1813, and the times after that were all in October of that year—just one long, interrupted, visit.

On December 7, 1811, Byron wrote the first of several (extant) letters to James from 8 St. James's Street:

> My dear W.—I was out of town during the arrival of your letters, but forwarded all on my return.—I hope you are going on to your satisfaction & that her Ladyship is about to produce an heir with all his mother's Graces & all his Sire's good qualities. You know I am to be a Godfather, Byron Webster! a most heroic name, say what you please.—Dont be alarmed, my 'caprice' won't lead me into Dorset, no, Bachelors for me, I consider you as dead to us, & all my future devoirs are but tributes of respect to your Memory—Poor fellow, he was a facetious companion & well respected by all who knew him, but he is gone, sooner or later we must all come to it.—I see nothing of you in the papers, the only place where I don't wish to see you, but you will be in town in the winter. What doest thou do? Shoot, hunt, & 'wind up ye. clock' as Caleb Quotem [a character in the 1808 play *The Review, or The Wags of Windsor*, by George Colman the Younger] says, thou art vastly happy I doubt not—I see your brother in law at times, & like him much, but we miss you much; I shall leave town in a fortnight to pass my Xmas in Notts—Good afternoon Dear W. believe me, Yrs ever Most truly B.

In a letter to John Cam Hobhouse, written from St. James's St. on December 15, 1811, Byron says, "Bold Webster is preparing Caudle for his spouse, & I am to be a Godfather!"

On March 2, 1812, James's first child, Lucy Sarah Anne Wedderburn-Webster, was born in Piccadilly, London. Unfortunately for Bold Webster, Lucy was a girl, and so could not be named after Byron. Rumor later had it that Lucy was born in Paris and baptized in Brussels, but, according to Lucy herself, she was born in Piccadilly. And besides, Bold Webster never even visited France until 1814.

However, as a gift for the occasion Byron gave Webster a copy of *Childe Harold's Pilgrimage*, which was published that very week amid much fanfare. This particular copy was on record as still in existence at least as late as 1946, bound in green straight-grained morocco by Messrs Thompson & Wrightson. According to the 1946 record their ticket was still inside the front cover, where there was also the armorial bookplate of James Wedderburn Webster. A presentation inscription in the author's hand appears on leaf "B," and says "To J.W. Webster Esqre. from his sincere friend & well-wisher the Author. Mh 12th, 1812." Below this are two lines, a direct quote from Horace's *Epistles*, in Byron's hand:

> Albi nostrorum sermonum candide judex
> Quid nunc te dicam facere?

Lady Frances was a guest at the first drawing-room held by the queen in two years, in fact since the king's birthday in 1810. The ladies of the realm had been deprived of court all that time, but the event at St. James's Palace, on April 30, 1812, was splendid enough to make up for the lapse.

This was also a period of change for James's mother, Mrs. Elizabeth Douglas. Her father-in-law, William Douglas, was forced to sell, in 1811, the estate of Brigton in order to satisfy his creditors. By this time Elizabeth wanted a home of her own, instead of the series of rented houses she had been taking. That year provided all the money with which to purchase Brigton from the legal machinery that held it, and thus it became the property of Robert Douglas of Brigton, who then, over the course of the ensuing three years, proceeded to fix it up, refurnish it (all with his wife's money, of course) and get it ready for their occupation. In 1814 the Douglases left Suffolk and headed north, staying for a while in Newby Wiske, in Yorkshire, and then finally arriving at their new home, Brigton, where they were to spend the rest of their lives.

9

Aston Hall

We now come to a period, 1813, where the lives of both James and Lady Frances are chronicled in some detail, thanks to the fact that Byron was staying with them at Aston Hall for a short time, and while there fell in love with Lady Frances. His letters and diary entries are not only revealing, they are extensive. The multi-volume book *Byron's Letters and Journals*, edited by Leslie A. Marchand, is really a one-stop shop for this material, at least for the letters written by Byron to other people.

In addition to this Byron material are the 40 or so highly secret (and, for the most part, never before published) letters from Lady Frances to Byron, which comprise the extant correspondence that started during this period and was to go on until the poet's death in 1824. Although Byron's letters to her, both replies and ones he sent off his own bat, no longer exist (he either destroyed them, or sent them on to Lady Melbourne, or they were destroyed on his behalf), we can, by juxtaposing his comments with those of others (mainly Lady Melbourne) about the contents of certain of Lady Frances's letters, build up quite a fascinating picture of their relationship.

Aston Hall is the second-most famous house of its name in England, not to be confused with the much larger stately home near Birmingham, the one owned by the Holte family. The one James rented ready-furnished was an elegant mansion surrounded by 75 acres of parkland in Yorkshire, on the turnpike-road between the towns of Worksop and Sheffield, and five miles from Rotherham. Even though it was very close to the Nottinghamshire border, it was still in Yorkshire. Notwithstanding, James Webster usually addressed his letters from "Aston Hall, Worksop, Notts." Notts was a better address, and besides, Newstead was in that county. It was the second incarnation of this particular Aston Hall, built 1762–72 by John Carr for the 4th Earl of Holderness and bought in 1773 by Sir Harry Verelst, former governor of Bengal, in whose family it would remain until 1928 (it was subsequently a hospital, and is now a luxury hotel). The pile commanded a beautiful and extensive view of the surrounding countryside, and consisted of three stories. The ground floor (or basement, as they called it then) boasted a large entrance hall, a library, and two smaller rooms, as well as most convenient offices of every description. On the first floor were to be found a billiard hall; breakfast; dining and drawing rooms; four bedrooms; and one dressing room. The attics contained six excellent bedrooms and one dressing room. There were also two good servants' rooms, and, if that wasn't enough, granaries over the stables. The property had most commodious outbuildings—a brew house, wash house, laundry, stabling for 17 horses, a very productive kitchen garden, a vine house, orchards, and so forth. The whole place was peculiarly adapted for the residence of any sportsman, being within eight miles of the Earl of Scarborough's kennels.

Parenthetically only, the referred-to 7th Earl of Scarborough's son John Lumley, the future 8th Earl, had no legal issue, but he made up for it on the other side of the blanket with a Frenchwoman who had been kicked out of her house by her husband. Their illegitimate children took the name Savile-Lumley, and son John, 1st Baron Savile of Rufford, was the father of the 2nd Baron who would marry the widowed Gertrude Violet Helyar, granddaughter of Bold Webster and Fanny.

On July 25, 1813, Byron wrote to James Webster from 4 Bennet St., St. James's, London. This letter, in manuscript form at the Academy of Sciences, Moscow, begins, "My dear Webster, I have just heard of your present residence"

Indeed, Aston Hall was the very house in which, as Byron later told Tom Moore, Captain Jack Byron, the poet's father, had adulterated with Lady Carmarthen after they eloped, and produced Augusta, the poet's half-sister.

Byron continues:

> Rushton tells me that you offered him a situation last Spring on your Agricultural establishment for which he is well adapted having been educated for that purpose. If you still wish to have him — though it is eventually my intention to provide for him — it would be a very good thing for him for a few years— as I am now going abroad almost immediately — & having parted with Newstead — & not quite arranged my Rochdale concerns, I am rather at a loss for his present employment. On this of course you will act as you think proper — his own statement led me to write to you on this subject.— He is honest — good tempered & has had a very fair education — as far as a country school could give. Will you favour me with an answer when convenient.— I have been very little in town this year & quite ignorant of all your movements.— I hope however that LF [Lady Frances] has increased your happiness & family & have little doubt of your welfare which I wish you sincerely. If I prolonged this letter I should only talk to you of myself a topic not very interesting & of which you have had too much already — my Egotism therefore shall briefly end in my begging you to believe that I ever am yours very truly & affectly, Byron.

Bold Webster replied from "Aston Hall, Rotheram [sic]," on the last day of the month, "My Dear Byron, I have some reason to be surprised on seeing a letter from you — after so <u>determined</u> an interval of silence on y'r part & particularly when I have a right to presume you received 3 very kind letters from me w'ch you never answer'd —."

This is not a particularly good way to win friends and influence people. It is Webster the ego-ridden little boy, "me, me, me." No one else counts in this world. Although Byron had his own motives for writing the letter he did to Webster — i.e., the poet had to unload Rushton quickly, and there was the ever-growing desire to meet Lady Frances — he was still doing Webster a favor even by talking to him. A more reasonable man than Webster might have understood this, but not Bold W. He was his own sun-king, and his only subject.

But he hasn't yet finished his castigation: "I am unfortunate under these events in not being able to forget some hours in our early Days ye recollection of w'ch can <u>now</u> only tend to <u>aggravate</u> ye Distance at w'ch you have thought fit to place our Intercourse —."

There are people who would read too much into this last paragraph. He carries on, "No conduct however on ye past can ever give me offence — It can neither provoke my Enmity — however unimportant it might be nor can it destroy that regard w'ch you can only blame our former Intimacy for having given birth to —."

He could talk humble, could Webster, self-effacement being something he had learned along the way, but only as an academic exercise. He didn't mean it. As in so many other aspects of his life, he knew the routine but he didn't feel. This made him, ultimately, a spectator of life, not a participant.

He continues:

> It was singular that I had been to take a long farewell of Newstead ye day on w'ch y'r letter arrived — I spent an hour there (not ye most lively in my life) with Old Murray [Byron's butler, Joe Murray] — in ye recollection of former times there — He is extremely attached to you & deplores Newstead [i.e. the losing of it] m'ch [much]. Is it really effectually sold? —
> Pray excuse me — I am much interested in y'r welfare — ye <u>estate</u> appears sadly neglected —

> Don't leave ye antique Boards on ye Dining Room Chimney Piece a Prey to sacrilegious hands—or ay [any] other memento of y'r familial antiquity—I heard much of Mrs C who we dined with & more of a certain picture now moved from ye abbey—.

One can guess at the identity of Mrs. C, but a guess will not do. As for the picture/abbey reference, that is simply too obscure to interpret.

Bold Webster continues, "Chaworth has been grinding a Miller's wife for such ye Miller means to prosecute him—."

He must here be referring to the Chaworths of Annesley Hall, in Nottinghamshire. Mary Chaworth, Byron's first romantic affair (1803) and a distant cousin, was the grandniece of Lord Chaworth, who had been run through by Byron's great-uncle. Mary would marry Jack Musters. As to the grinding of the miller's wife, this promising scandal did not make the papers.

Says Webster:

> I was to have been in Sicily this month & lose a large bet malgré on ye occasion—When do you go abroad—May I beg to know y'r plans, who goes with you? You cannot fill a letter with any subject more interesting to me—
>
> I can pay you no compliment in proportion to ye strong receicts [receipts, which means "reviews"] of ye 'Giaour'—it contains indeed some admirable passages—ye vision of Leila is extremely chaste & sublime ye reflections & simile to ye Butterfly are beautifully traced—& tho' a fragment it contains some prodigiously fine strokes of fancy—
>
> Ye character of ye whore is of no common complexion & we must all admit it certainly bears ye features of a master in ye first school—

John Murray had published Byron's latest epic, *The Giaour*, on June 5, 1813. This legendary publishing house, founded in 1768, was not only Byron's publisher, but also that of Walter Scott, Jane Austen, and (in time) Darwin, George Borrow, and Livingstone. There were several successive heads of the firm, all called John Murray. John the Second was the friend of Byron, and, after the poet's death in 1824, along with Byron's executors, he was responsible for burning Byron's manuscript journals—to protect the great poet's reputation.

The letter goes on:

> I first saw Rushton by accident at Mansfield—I wish much to have him in my service from ye opinion I know you entertain of his Honesty—
>
> He w'd have a most eligible situation with me & during y'r absence I think he may be better off with me than with at least may [many] others—Let me know if he comes & when I may expect him—
>
> I should always be his friend in y'r absence—as far as my ability goes [an interesting codicil]—
>
> May I beg to hear from you soon. I have prolonged this scrawl for I have really had no time to shorten it & conclude with Lady Fanny's best remembrance & y'r truly affect'ly, J Wedderburne Webster. July 31, 1813.

There is of course a P.S. "Send me a copy of ye 'Giaour' as you did ye Childe—Don't forget to write in ye Title Page as that makes it alone valuable to me.—"

Byron's reply says:

> My Dear Webster, I am, you know, a detestable correspondent, and write to no one person whatever. You therefore cannot attribute my silence to anything but want of good breeding or good taste, and not to any more atrocious cause; and as I confess the fault to be entirely mine—why—you will pardon it.
>
> I have ordered a copy of the *Giaour* (which is nearly doubled in quantity in this edition) to be sent, and I will first scribble my name in the title page. Many and sincere thanks for your good opinion of book, and (I hope to add) author.
>
> Rushton shall attend you whenever you please, though I should like him to stay a few weeks, and help my other people in forwarding my chattels. Your taking him is no less a favour to me than him, and I trust he will behave well. If not, your remedy is very simple; only don't let him

be idle; honest I am sure he is, and I believe good-hearted and quiet. No pains has [sic] been spared, and a good deal of expense incurred in his education; accounts and mensuration, etc., he ought to know, and I believe he does.

I write this near London, but your answer will reach me better in Bennet Street, etc. (as before). I am going very soon, and if you would do the same thing — as far as Sicily — I am sure you would not be sorry. My sister, Mrs L, goes with me — her spouse is obliged to retrench for a few years (but he stays at home), so that his link boy prophecy (if ever he made it) recoils upon himself.

"Mrs L" is Augusta Leigh, the poet's married half-sister, with whom Byron had a summer affair that year. That relationship resulted in the production of issue, Elizabeth Medora, in 1814 — at least, it is as certain as can be that the girl was Byron's, and not that of Col. George Leigh (Augusta's first cousin and husband, formerly of the 10th Dragoons). As for this "link boy prophecy," I have been unable to run it down.

"I am truly glad to hear of Lady Frances's good health," Byron continues. "Have you added to your family? Pray make my best respects acceptable to her Ladyship.

"Nothing will give me more pleasure than to hear from you as soon and as full as you please. Ever most truly yours, Byron."

This last letter from Byron, dated August 12, 1813, was in reply to Webster's letter of July 31, but in the meantime Webster had written another to "Rt Hon Lord Byron, 4 Bennet St, St James, London," from "Aston Hall, Rotheam [sic]," which the poet seems not to have yet received, even though it was franked on August 2.

My Dear Byron,
By ye last letter I received from you, <u>mine</u> had evidently not been received — Yours w'd have superceded [sic] ye necessity of it —

I am glad I am to have Rushton, as I think it would be a comfortable place for himself & as you observe ye remedy in those cases is always open & easy to both parties— He & I had no settlement as to wages but I wish m'ch you w'd fix this for me. I know you could neither name extravantly [sic] large on my acc't or too low on his— I leave ye time of his coming to y'r own Discretion, with this remark, that ye sooner he comes in next month, as my House will probably be then full ye more acceptable & convenient to me. I fear you will think I want to <u>monopolise y'r Establishment</u>, but a regard for them as belonging to you & some view I confess of utility to myself actuates me — This leads to ye question of what do you propose for old Murray? If you have nothing better he w'd be extremely usefull to me —& you c'd not oblige me more than by agreeing to ye arrang't I propose — you I suppose will always hold him a <u>pensioner</u> & whatever you may choose to continue in that shape, I <u>w'd make up</u> to handsome wages— If you liked it, I am sure he w'd find a comfortable asylum — he is too old for an active place, & mine w'd be ye vey [very] thing. He will make a good <u>shadow</u> of a <u>Butler</u> & I c'd confidently trust him with rec'ing money &c in my absence from home w'ch is frequent & protracted —

As this plan will alter ye fate of my present Intendant, pray send me y'r wishes on ye suject [sic] as soon as possible —

We went on an immense party to Newstead yesterday — I mentioned this to him [i.e., to Joe Murray] & said I w'd consult you — Of course he is completely Devoted to you in ey [every] sense as he ought to be —

Y'r '<u>Giaour</u>' is ye <u>Testament</u> of every one here — it is justly & extremely admired; you are indeed ye Idol Poet of ye Day —'Carpe Diem' when ye time & ye world is yours— ye '<u>aurorae filii</u>' are few indeed now of Days—!

Sir Francis Bacon had not coined the term "aurorae filii," but he had reminded readers of it. It means "sons of the morning," yet to the poets it could imply one of two things: the bright young boys of their day, the scholars, the ones who would change the world; and also duelists, who always arranged their fatal encounters at the break of day, presuming that the constabulary would not yet be awake to stop them. Webster himself would, a few years hence, become a filius aurorae himself, but only in the latter sense.

James was sent a copy of the *Giaour*, but it must have been from someone else because on the same day (August 12) that Byron wrote to Webster, Webster wrote a letter to "the Rt. Hon. Lord Byron, Bennet St, St James, London. It was dated "Aston Hall, Aug. 12, 1813," and was franked two days later in Rotherham. It was quite a nasty and remonstrating letter in places, and undeservedly so. It reads:

> My Dear Byron, I have been in anxious expectation to learn ye fate of Rushton, for some days past as it Disarranges my Establishment in ye mean time — Pray inform me by return of Post if he is coming or <u>not</u>. If he <u>is</u> I wish him to come immed'ly as I am going to Lord Scarsdales this month — I have received a late edition of ye Giaour, but y'r having omitted what I beged [he had written begged, but deleted the second g] you to do leaves me only to <u>conjecture</u> it came from <u>you</u> — I am how'r much obliged to you for it — .

Nathaniel Curzon, 2nd Baron Scarsdale, lived in — well, anywhere he wanted, really, but his seat, as it were, was the amazing Kedleston Hall, just north of Derby, and a couple of hour's hard ride from Aston Hall. Scarsdale's wife, Sophia, was the sister of Judith Noel, who became the wife of Admiral Sir Ralph Milbanke, 6th Bart. The admiral and Judith were the parents of Anne Isabella (known as Annabella) Milbanke, who would become Byron's wife on January 2, 1815. The Noel girls, Judith and Sophia, were the daughters of Edward Noel, 1st Viscount Wentworth.

Webster continues to Byron, "Untill I hear from you in answer to my last letter, I have no right & little inclination to prolong this in w'ch perhaps I oblige you mch [i.e. much] —

"With ey [every] kind wish, believe me ever y'r sincere friend, W."

There is a P.S.: "I beg to know immed'ly abt Rushton, as it really inconveniences me at present."

A note from James Webster, to Byron, undated but from this very time, reads, "The sooner Rushton appears ye more convenient to me. But study yr own wishes first, 'Room for my Lord! O — Stand by and bow.' Diaboliad."

Webster is quoting, fairly faithfully, from Charles Churchill's 1761 poem, "An Epistle to Robert Lloyd," which in turn had quoted from Pope's *Dunciad*. Webster, as we have already seen, despite all his faults, was not under-educated.

There are a couple of forged Byron letters to James from 1813. One, undated, is now in Myers, Catalogue 4, Summer 1962. I have been quite unable to find this letter. None of the major Byron scholars or librarians can help either. The reference "Myers" has been traced, in a vague and insubstantial way, to an art dealer in London, but there the trail ends.

This letter and the other do not seem to have been created by Major Byron. In Theodore G. Ehrsam's book *Major Byron* there is a list of forgeries perpetrated by the major. These two 1813 letters are not on the list. Whoever did them remains unknown.

Major Byron was a shadowy figure (even in his own time), claiming to be George Gordon de Luna Byron, the biological result of a legal marriage between the great poet and one Countess de Luna, of Cadiz, Spain. The most any thinking person would give the forger is that his conception may have been Byronic, the poet having been in Cadiz in July and August of 1809 during his European tour. Curiously, the great 20th century opera singer Amelita Galli-Curci claimed to be a niece of the Countess de Luna, of Cadiz, but dates prevent it from being the same lady.

The second forgery, dated August 23, 1813, is in manuscript form at the Harry Ransom Humanities Research Center, The University of Texas at Austin by whose permission it is reproduced here. The purported envelope says: "Geo. Byron. To Webster Wedderburn, Esq., Holland House, London." This is an odd address to attribute to James, as he was living then at Aston Hall, in Yorkshire. The letter itself reads:

> Bennet Street — Aug. 23d, 1813. My dear Webster — Alas! I know too well that my case is out of reach of advice — out of the reach of consolation. But it is some relief to the wounded heart to impart its tale of misery — What would I not give to exchange this rabid fury which vexes me, for

> your quiet, sanctified stomach — Well, no one stage of suffering lasts for ever — We should grow reconciled to it at length, I suppose, if it did — I am stupid, and lose myself in what I write — I write rather what answers to my feelings than express my present ones — When you have the inclination I shall be very glad to see you — This morning I received a few lines from A [Annabella Milbanke] — She would share life and death — heaven and hell — with me. She lives but for me — and I know I have been tearing her life with my cursed ways of going on. — What you say of Harry is really distressing — I fear for his christianity [sic] — They will certainly circumcise him — I supped last night with Davis [Scrope Davies] — My habits are changing, I think, i.e. from drunk to sober — whether I shall be happier or not, remains to be proved — Apropos — the whole alphabet of Boyle's register are in a state little short of purgatory — according to report a lady of haut ton was found hanging at the bedpost in her lord's garter — he being a Knight of that 'august order' — but has been restored to her family and a select party of 500 of her friends — Believe me ever and truly, yrs, Byron.

The bit about Harry, whoever he was, evidently falling into the hands of the Turks, and the subsequent part of this letter defy explanation.

On August 27, 1813, Webster dashed off a note to Byron, with no preamble:

> Pray say what ship do you go out in? Who are y'r company? Have you any room?
> I am sorry for Leigh & had forgot his liberal prophecy — I am going to Lord Scarsdales for ye Derby races where I must endeavr [i.e. endeavor] to be as gay & giddy as my cotemparies [sic] w'ch is no easy task either —
> Pray write to me immed'ly & oblige Dear Byron yours ever — W —
> Aug. 27, 1813.

Webster wasn't lying. That very day he made the trip to Lord Scarsdale's, and returned to Aston Hall on the morrow. On August 29 he wrote another letter to the poet:

> My Dear Byron, I returned from L'd Scarsdale's yesterday & finding no reply to a letter I wrote you ab't ye fate of Old Murray, I am obliged to trouble you at present. If the letter has never reached you, it was merely to say that if you have no <u>better</u> view for him you c'd not <u>favor me</u> more than by letting him come to me, & if (as I presume) you will continue his annuity being no object to you, I will make up his salary 45 francs, w'ch with a place where no activity or work is required w'd render ye <u>Evening</u> of <u>his Long Day</u> comfortable — in your absence his life I am sure has few enjoyments.
> I wish well to ey [every] thing that belongs to you & if you don't object may make so arrangement. He is extremely attached to you, as he ought to be —
> Have you ay [any] room in ye ship you go out in? Pray tell me, & what is ye expence?
> I met his Grace of Devon — Petersham, Aylesford &c &c at ye Scarsdales else I sh'd have found it vey [very] triste, Races have few charms for me —.

Heneage Finch, 5th Earl of Aylesford, was two years older than Webster and Byron, but appears only en passant in this story. Petersham, on the other hand, needs some introduction, as he is a major character in the Webster saga. Eight years older than Bold W, nevertheless he was a good friend of long standing, until he blotted his copybook, as we shall see. One of the roaring dandies of the Regency period, Charles Stanhope was the son of the 3rd Earl Harrington. It was customary for the eldest son of the Earls Harrington to sport the inferior title Viscount Petersham until such time as they succeeded their father as Earl Harrington, which our Petersham would do as 4th Earl in 1829.

Webster continues:

> In my last I beged [sic] <u>you</u> to settle what I am to give <u>Rushton</u>. When you can spare him, let him come, but desire him to hold no parlies with my Domestics untill he sees <u>me</u>, else it might derange ye <u>oeconomy</u> of a but <u>badly regulated</u> house — our old friend Francis Stanhope [one of Lord Petersham's brothers] & his cara moitié comes here next week. She is very pretty & more interesting than generally follows where beauty only leads.
> I wish most solemnly I c'd <u>serve you</u> in <u>any way</u>, either <u>now</u> or when you are <u>gone</u>. We have <u>few years</u> & <u>fewer friends</u> in this life — but you may ever command y'r sincere f'd [friend] —

P.S. Will you be Godfather to my next Garçon — as it was to have been ye last time — write ab't Murray immediately —
Aston Hall. Aug. 29. 13.

About this time, but impossible to fix more minutely in time, is a note Bold Webster sent up to Byron in London, while the former was in town:

The Bearer will wait, or call again for an answer but—
P.S. You may be assured of this— that I must have <u>very weighty reasons</u> that prevent my calling upon you — adio! [sic] —

On September 2, 1813, Byron replied to James's frantic Rushton-related letters of August:

My dear Webster — You are just the same generous and I fear — careless gentleman of the years of <u>indifferent</u> memory 1806-7 — but I must not burthen you with my entire household. — Joe [Murray] is I believe necessary for the present as a fixture to keep possession till every thing is arranged — & were it otherwise — you dont know what a perplexity he would prove — honest and faithful but fearfully superannuated — now <u>this</u> I ought & do bear — but as he has not been 50 years in your family — it would be rather hard to convert your mansion into a hospital for decayed domestics — Rushton is or may be made useful & I am less <u>compunctious</u> on his account — 'Will I be godfather?' Yea — verily — I believe it is the only species of parentage I shall ever encounter — for all my acquaintance — Powerscourt — Jocelyn — yourself — Delawarr — Stanhope — with a long list of happy &c. are married — most of them my Juniors too — and I as single & likely to remain so as — nay — more than if I were seventy —.

Most of Byron's friends were indeed married. Richard Wingfield, 5th Viscount Powerscourt, who was a couple of years younger than Byron, had just that very year married the daughter of the Earl of Roden. Roden's son, Robert Jocelyn, the future 3rd Earl and an old friend of Byron's from Harrow, had also married in 1813. Jocelyn's son would (much later) marry Hobhouse's daughter. George West, three years younger than Byron and also an old Harrovian, had been 4th Earl De La Warr since infancy, and 1813 saw him too fall victim to matrimony (with the daughter of the Earl of Dorset). Francis Stanhope, nine months Byron's junior, had also married, as, of course, had Bold Webster.

The poet continued:

If it is a Girl why not also?— Georgina — or even Byron will make a classical name for a spinster — if Mr Richardson's Sir Charles Grandison is any authority in your estimation [Harriet Byron was the heroine in that novel]. — My ship is not settled — my passage in the Boyne was only for one servant — & would not do of course — you ask after the expence [sic] — a question no less interesting to the married than to the single — unless things are much altered no establishment in the Mediterranean countries could amount to a quarter of the expenditure requisite in England for the same or an inferior household. — I am interrupted — & have only time to offer my best thanks for all your good wishes and intentions — and to beg you will believe me equally yours ever, B. P.S. Rushton shall be sent on Saturday next.

Webster replied to Byron's September 2 letter, addressing it to "The Hon. Lord Byron, 4 Bennet St, St James, London." Dated "Sept. 4, 1813, Aston" and franked two days later, the reply read:

My Dear Byron, I am sorry you lay an embargo on Joe [Murray]. He w'd have been invaluable to me —
If Rushton has not left town when you receive this let him go to Lord M'tNorris, 23 Piccadilly, by 7 o'clock next Wednesday morning & my sister Lady C [Lady Catherine Annesley, actually his sister-in-law] will bring him on my carriage down. If he has, n'importe —
I fancy you will be some time before you go. C'd you do a charitable act & run down here for a few days? —
If you may be seen I'll invade you for 5 minutes at 7 o'clock on Wednesday morning, ergo give an order for ye admittance —
I shall only arrive in Town that morning to mail & shall leave it again by 8 for this [i.e., Aston Hall] — Untill then <u>ever</u> yours J. Wedderburne Webster."

P.S. I hear you have been ill — if you have need ay [any] <u>physicians</u> who are <u>poets</u>— pray let me know —
Aston Hall — Sept. 4. 13
Pray settle what I am to give Rushton?

Byron's reply (now in manuscript form in the Robert H. Taylor College, Princeton University Library) followed to James, on September 6, 1813: "My dear Webster — This will be delivered to you by Rushton who sets off tomorrow, & I have directed him to make the best of his way to your mansion. As I wrote to you recently at some length [September 2] I will not now further encroach upon your time than to say I shall always be glad to hear from or of you & ever am, very faithfully yrs. Biron [sic]. P.S. Have you ever [heard of] a mansion untenanted in a decent situation within ten miles of your neighborhood?"

James replied to Byron's September 6 letter from "Aston Hall, Sept. 13. 13":

> My Dear <u>Biron</u>, I feel some reluctance to acknowledge ye changing ye <u>y</u> in ye old name — as I think ye 'Crete Byron' so m'ch more correct — how'r I obey —
> I did anticipate much pleasure in seeing you on Wednesday, but I only arrived at Hatfield in time to meet Lady Cath [erine Annesley] & having comp. [one assumes he means 'completed'] here on Thursday I had no time to lose —
> Rushton I saw in ye carriage & he is regularly instated in his new office. I think he will be useful to me — I shall certainly be not wanting in befriending him when he desires it —
> I have a place near this [place] w'd just suit you & that a Priory too — Let me know if <u>you want</u> a place? Will you <u>oblige</u> me & come down <u>here</u> — I will promise you shall be as m'ch isolé as if you were on ye Brow of Zitna! [this is very clearly what it says, but the reference remains elusive] — & you shall have a sett of rooms entirely to yourself — only let me know what y'r <u>antipathies</u> are — as tho' with ye <u>best intentions</u> they vary in men so m'ch their [sic] is no guarding ag'st them — D'Epernon used to faint at the sight of a leveret — Bacon was apt to swoon at ye Eclipse of ye moon & Poor Bayle fell into convulsions at ye sound of water coming thro' a cock! [i.e., a faucet] — These & may [i.e. many] other such <u>horrors</u> I will guard y'r nerves from, only pray come down here if only for a week — Doncaster Races are on ye 27th & y'r presence will be a novelty of m'ch attraction —.

Apparently James was correct in his anecdotal references to great men's bizarre weaknesses. The Duc d'Epernon would, indeed, faint at the sight of a leveret, although he was fine when a hare leaped past. However, that same hare would cause the great astronomer Tycho Brahe to keel over. According to legend, Francis Bacon would be as moonstruck as Bold Webster indicates. As for Pierre Bayle, the French philosopher, one's mind boggles.

> I was invaded by ye <u>Ghost</u> of Lord Grantley to Day & have hardly recover'd my nerves w'ch must account for <u>some</u> of ye nonsense & ye perfect unintelligibility of this letter — write & say if you are obstinate & I uncharitable — if you are <u>not</u> you will pay a visit to y'r ever, Dear B, W —.

A day later Byron received Webster's letter, and on September 15, 1813, he responded to the invitation — or, as Paston and Quennell put it, "Though Byron professed a peculiar terror of *ennui*, he felt a curious attraction towards bores themselves; and since at the moment he had little to occupy him, he accepted the invitation in a friendly letter":

> My dear Webster — I shall not resist your second invitation & shortly after the receipt of this you may expect me. — You will excuse me from ye. races — as a guest I have no 'antipathies' & few preferences — you wont mind however my <u>not</u> dining with you — every day at least. — When we meet we can talk over our respective plans — mine is very short & simple — viz — to sail when I can get a passage — if I remained in England — I should live in ye. country — & of course in the vicinity of those whom I know would be most agreeable. — I did not know that Jack's graven image was at Newstead — if it be — pray transfer it to Aston — It is my hope to see you so shortly — tomorrow or the next day — that I will not now trouble you with my speculations — ever yrs very faithfully, Byron. P.S. I don't know how I came to sign myself with ye. 'i' it is the old spelling — & I sometimes slip into it — when I say I can't dine with you — I mean that sometimes I dont dine at all — of course when I do — I conform to all hours & domestic arrangements —.

Byron set out to conquer Lady Frances—that much seems clear—in order to forget Augusta Leigh. Peter Gunn, in his book *My Dearest Augusta*, tells us that the poet had heard that Lady F was a "pretty, pleasant woman" [this is a misquote from Byron's letter below] and went to Aston Hall to transfer his "regards to another" [Gunn is in concurrence here with most biographers]. But it did not work out the way Byron planned.

The September 21, 1813, letter to Lady Melbourne from Aston Hall reads in part, "My stay at Cambridge was very short, but feeling feverish and restless in town I flew off, and here I am on a visit to my friend Webster, now married and (according to ye Duke of Buckingham's curse) 'settled in ye country.' His bride, Lady Frances, is a pretty, pleasing woman, but in delicate health, and, I fear, going—if not gone—into a decline."

André Maurois, in his book *Byron*, completely misinterprets this passage. He writes that the poet, "observing the pallor of her skin and the hectic gleam of her eyes," wondered if she would live. This is an astonishingly free French interpretation—not at all accurate—and it then suffers further from being translated into English by Hamish Miles.

Byron continues in the same letter, "Stanhope [Lord Petersham's brother] and his wife—pretty and pleasant too, but not at all consumptive—left us today, leaving only ye family, another single gentleman, and your slave. The sister, Ly Catherine, is here too, and looks very pale from a <u>cross</u> in her love for Lord Bury (Lord Albemarle's son); in short, we are a society of happy wives and unfortunate maidens."

Maurois has this to deduce from the above Byronic passage: "Her sister, Lady Catherine Annesley, was no less frail, both of them blondes, with long upturning eyelashes and mournful deeply-ringed eyes. Webster, a plump, jovial fellow, seemed out of place amid all these anaemic Graces."

Encore, M. Maurois has seen only what he wanted to see. Lady Catherine was no more or less frail than her sister, and generally speaking, these ladies were not anemic at all—only at certain moments of their lives, as is true with everyone. They would hardly have been the great beauties of their age if they had been as sickly as the Frenchman makes them out to be.

As for James being plump and jovial, he was never jovial, and he was certainly not plump at this point in his life; his figure, at 25, still held from the time he had been a great athlete. He did not start to gain weight until much later.

Picking up Byron in the same letter:

> The place is very well, and quiet, and the children only scream in a low voice, so that I am not much disturbed, and shall stay a few days in tolerable repose. W don't want sense, nor good nature, but both are occasionally obscured by his suspicions, and absurdities of all descriptions; he is passionately fond of having his wife admired, and at the same time jealous to jaundice of everything and everybody. I have hit upon the medium of praising her to him perpetually behind her back, and never looking at her before his face; as for her, I believe she is disposed to be very faithful, and I don't think anyone now here is inclined to put her to the test. W himself is, with all his jealousy and admiration, a little tired; he has been lately at Newstead, and wants to go again. I suspected this sudden penchant, and soon discovered that a foolish nymph of the Abbey about whom fortunately I care not, was the attraction ["apparently one of the servant girls," hazards Fiona MacCarthy in *Byron: Life and Legend*]. Now if I wanted to make mischief I could extract much good perplexity from a proper management of such events; but I am grown so good, or so indolent, that I shall not avail myself of so pleasant an opportunity of tormenting mine host, though he deserves it for poaching. I believe he has hitherto been unsuccessful, or rather it is too astonishing to be believed. He proposed to me, with great gravity, to carry him over there, and I replied, with equal candour, that he might set out when he pleased, but that I should remain here to take care of his household in the interim—a proposition which I thought very much to the purpose, but which did not seem at all to his satisfaction. By way of opiate he preached me a sermon on his wife's good qualities, concluding by an assertion that in all moral and mortal qualities, she was very like 'Christ!!!' I think the Virgin Mary would have been a more appropriate typification; but it was the first comparison of the kind I ever heard, and made

me laugh till he was angry, and then I got out of humour too, which pacified him, and shortened the panegyric. Lord Petersham is coming here in a day or two, who will certainly flirt furiously with Lady F, and I shall have some comic Iagoism with our little Othello. I should have no chance with his Desdemona myself, but a more lively and better dressed and formed personage might, in an innocent way, for I really believe the girl is a very good, well-disposed wife, and will do very well if she lives, and he himself don't tease her into some dislike of her lawful owner.

Again, this Byron "if she lives" quote is over-statement, under-statement, exaggeration, hyperbole, and just something to say. One must not infer from it, as Maurois and others have done, that Lady Frances was at death's door. She wasn't.

He ends with, "I am asked to stay for the Doncaster races, but I am not in plight, and am a miserable beau at the best of times; so I shall even return to town, or elsewhere."

Peter Quennell, in his book *Byron: The Years of Fame*, paraphrases part of this letter when he says, "Webster, who had a passion for seeing his wife admired, was also preposterously jealous." He also describes Webster as "a verbose and self-important personage" and "an unfaithful and ridiculous busybody."

On September 25, 1813, Byron was at Stilton, and wrote James a letter from there. (This letter is here reproduced by kind permission of the president and council of the Royal College of Surgeons of England, who are in possession of the original, in manuscript form.) "My dear Wr — Thus far can I 'report progress' & as a solid token of my remembrance I send you a cheese of 13 lbs to enable your digestion to go through ye. race week."

Cheese binds, and in those privy-less days of yesteryear the well-to-do would, in lieu of desperation, carry with them a stone of Stilton. This Byronic gift to Bold Webster was also the poet's little contribution to the retention of that matter of which Bold W was so full, the excretion of which would thus deprive the poet and his associates of a good deal of fun.

"It will go tonight —," he continues, "pray let your retainers enquire after it — the date of this letter will account for so homely a present.— On my arrival in town I will write more at length on our different concerns — in ye. meantime I wish you & yours all the gratification at Doncaster you can wish for yourselves.— My love to ye. faithless Nettle (who I dare say is wronging me during my absence) & my best compts. to all in your house who will receive them — ever dear W, yrs truly B. P.S. I fully intend to rejoin you on Saturday if nothing very particular occurs to prevent me."

Nettle was a poodle that Byron admired enormously, and which Webster gave to the poet as a gift while at Aston Hall.

On September 27, 1813, Byron wrote to Thomas Moore, "I have been in the country, and ran away from the Doncaster races. It is odd,—I was a visitor in the same house which came to my sire as a residence [Aston Hall] with Lady Carmarthen ... and they thrust me into an old room, with a nauseous picture over the chimney, which I should suppose my papa regarded with due respect, and which, inheriting the family taste, I looked upon with great satisfaction. I staid a week with the family, and behaved very well — though the lady of the house is young, and religious, and pretty, and the master is my particular friend. I felt no wish for anything but a poodle dog, which they kindly gave me."

Bold Webster received Byron's Stilton and letter on September 27, and dashed off a letter (dated simply Sept. 1813) to "The Lord Byron, Bennet St, St James, London":

My Dear Byron, I received y'r letter with infinite pleasure, not from ye solid proof you have given me of recollection — but that I was anxious to learn ye welfare of one for whom I feel so deep an interest — we all deplore y'r loss — I feel it Believe me —

Petersham malgré pour-nous wrote to me to Day, saying that his month of 'Chamber-waiting' compelled him to invade ye 'Fumum et opes' of London & to relinquish both Aston & Doncaster for ye present — He desired to be highly commended to you —.

Again Webster is quoting from Horace, and lacks only the strepitum of the original to compare London fully with the smoke, the glitter, and the noise of old Rome.

He continues:

> Davies—ye immortal Scroope [sic] dined with us to Day & will tomorrow I believe. He was within 3 inches of Eternity yesterday in coming here—& bears at least evident symtoms [sic] of it in his visage if not in his body—
>
> My poor good lame friend Hawkins lost £200 to Day—strong symtoms of water on ye brain—Nettle is in 'statu quo'—I shall not follow ye attorney General's example in case of ye Hottentot Venus & I grant you a writ of 'Habeas Corpus'—you must come for him yourself—The assemblee [sic] of Beings here is only remarkable for having less women that [sic] men—

Saartjie Baartman was a young female brought over from Cape Town in 1810 so her steatopygian development and other anatomical peculiarities could be seen, admired, and studied by the mob. In the process the promoters made money. Under pressure from the black preacher Robert Wedderburn of Jamaica (a former slave of one of Bold Webster's close relatives and by this time a political agitator in England), the attorney general took her off the market.

> The Countess is inexorable, I in despair—ye ladies F. & C. [Frances and Catherine] desire their kind regards, & I looking with much anxiety to y'r return next Saturday am Dear B ever & anon y'r truly, JW. Doncaster. Sept.

We never know exactly who this countess was who was pursuing Bold Webster, and Byron is no help in his letters either.

There is a P.S.: "I am no beggar, but have you a gr't [i.e. great] penchant for our quondam friend Jack's picture now at Newstead?" He means Gentleman John Jackson, the pugilist.

The poet wrote a letter to Lady Melbourne on September 28, 1813, which contained the following:

> ... my time was passed pleasantly enough—& as innocently at Aston.... I have been observing & have made out one conclusion which is that my friend W will run his head against a wall of his own building. There are a Count & Countess—somebody—(I forget the name of the exiles)—the last of whom made a desperate attack on W. at Ld. Waterpark's a few weeks ago—and W. in gratitude invited them to his house—there I suppose they are now (they had not arrived when I set out)—to me it appears from W's own narrative—that he will be detected & bullied by the husband into some infernal compromise—& I told him as much—but like others of our acquaintance he is deaf as an adder. I have known him several years & really wish him well—for which reasons I overlooked his interference in some concerns of my own where he had no business—perhaps because also they had ceased to interest me ... but be that as it may—I wish he would not indulge in such freaks—for which he can have no excuse—& the example will turn out none of the best for Ly. Fy [Lady Fanny]. She seems pretty & intelligent—as far as I have observed which was very little.

Byron had suggested that his sister, Augusta, stay for a while at Aston Hall, and Lady Frances had then made the offer. On September 30, 1813, Byron wrote to James:

> My dear Webster—Thanks for your letter—I had answered it by anticipation last night—& this is but a postscript to my reply—my yesterdays contains some advice which I now see you dont want—& hope you never will—so—Petersham has not joined you—I pity the poor women—no one can properly repair such a deficiency—but rather than such a chasm should be left utterly unfathomable—I—even I—the most awkward of attendants—& deplorable of danglers [sic] would have been of your forlorn hope—on this expedition—nothing but business—& the notion of my being utterly superfluous in so numerous a party would have induced me to resign so soon my quiet apartments—never interrupted but by the sound of your swearing or the more harmonious barking of Nettle & clashing of billiard balls.—On Sunday I shall leave town & mean to join you immediately—I have not yet had my sister's answer to Lady Frances's very kind invitation, but expect it to-morrow—Pray assure Lady Frances that I never can forget the obligation

conferred upon me in this respect — and I trust that even Ly. Catherine will in this instance not question my 'stability' — I yesterday wrote you rather a long tirade about La Contesse [sic] — but you seem in no immediate peril. I will therefore burn it — yet I dont know why I should — as you may relapse — it shall een go — I have been passing my time with Rogers & Sir James Mackintosh — & once at Holland House I met Southey — he is a person of very epic appearance — & has a fine head as far as the outside goes — and wants nothing but taste to make the inside equally attractive, ever my dear W yours, Biron.

Augusta did not come to Aston Hall. She regarded Bold Webster as a silly, cantankerous fellow. Samuel Rogers was a patron of the arts, poet, and friend of Byron's. Sir James Mackintosh was a lawyer and former Indian administrator, and had just entered Parliament that July as MP for Nairn. Robert Southey was that year's new poet laureate, whom Byron had met on September 26, only four days before.

The poet's postscript to Bold Webster read:

P.S. I read your letter thus 'the Countess is miserable' — instead of which it is 'inexorable' — a very different thing — the best way is to let her alone — she must be a diablesse by what you told me — you have probably not bid high enough — now you are not perhaps of my opinion — but I would not give the tithe of a Birmingham farthing for a woman who could or would be purchased — nor indeed for any woman quoad mere woman — that is to say unless I loved her for something more than her sex. — If she loves — a little pique is not amiss — nor even if she dont — the next thing to a woman's love in a man's favour is her hatred — a seeming paradox but true — and circumstance & their fair passions will do wonders for a dasher which I suppose you are — though I seldom had the impudence or patience to follow them up.

Another letter to Lady Melbourne, written from London on October 1, 1813, says:

To-day I heard from my friend W again; his Countess is, he says, 'inexorable.' What a lucky fellow — happy in his obstacles. In his case I should think them very pleasant; but I don't lay this down as a general proposition. All my prospect of amusement is clouded, for Petersham has sent an excuse; and there will be no one to make him jealous of but the curate and the butler — and I have no thoughts of setting up for myself. I am not exactly cut out for the lady of the mansion; but I think a stray dandy would have a chance of preferment. She evidently expects to be attacked, and seems prepared for a brilliant defence; my character as a roué has gone before me, and my careless and quiet behaviour astonished her so much that I believe she began to think herself ugly, or me blind — if not worse [he meant homosexual]. They seemed surprised at my declining the races in particular; but for this I had good reasons; firstly: I wanted to go elsewhere; secondly: if I had gone, I must have paid some attention to some of them; which is troublesome, unless one has something in memory, or hope to induce it; and then mine host is so marvellous green-eyed that he might have included me in his calenture — which I don't deserve — and probably should not like it a bit better if I did. I have also reasons for returning there on Sunday, with which they have nothing to do; but if C. [Lady Caroline Lamb] takes a suspicious twist that way, let her — it will keep her in darkness; but I hope, however, she won't take a fit of scribbling, as she did to Lady Oxford [another of Byron's affairs] last year — though Webster's face on the occasion would be quite a comet, and delight me infinitely more than Oxford's, which was comic enough.

He continues, a little later in the same letter:

To return to the Ws. I am glad they amaze you; anything that confirms, or extends one's observations on life and character delights me, even when I don't know people — for this reason I would give the world to pass a month with Sheridan [the playwright, and lover of Lady Caroline Lamb's mother], or any lady or gentleman of the old school, and hear them talk every day, and all day of themselves, and acquaintance, and all they have heard and seen in their lives. W seems in no present peril. I believe the woman is mercenary; and I happen to know that he can't at present bribe her. I told him that it would be known, and that he must expect reprisals — and what do you think was his answer? 'I think any woman fair game, because I can depend upon Lady F.'s principles — she can't go wrong, and therefore I may.' 'Then, why are you jealous of her?' 'Because — because — zounds! I am not jealous. Why the devil do you suppose I am?' I then enumerated some very gross symptoms, which he had displayed, even before her face, and his servants, which he could not deny; but persisted in his determination to add to his 'bonnes fortunes';—it is a strange being! When I came home in 1811, he was always saying, 'B., do marry—it is the happiest,' etc. The first thing he said on my arrival at Aston was, 'B., whatever you do, don't marry'; which, considering he had an unmarried sister-in-law in the house, was a very unnecessary precaution. Every now and then he has a fit of fondness, and kisses her hand before his guests; which she receives with the most lifeless indifference, which struck me more than if she had appeared pleased, or annoyed. Her brother told me last year that she married to get rid of her family (who are ill-tempered), and had not been out two months; so that, to use a fox-hunting phrase, she was 'killed in covert.' You have enough of them, and me for ye present.

In his sixth unanswered letter to Thomas Moore, on October 2, 1813, Byron says, "On Sunday I return to Aston." He had had to leave the Websters for a short while, and returned to Aston on Sunday, October 3, 1813.

On October 5, 1813, Byron wrote a letter to Lady Melbourne, from Aston Hall: "W has lost his Countess, his time and his temper (I would advise anyone who finds the last to return it immediately; it is of no use to any but the owner). Lady F has lost Petersham, for the present at least; the other sister, as I have said before, has lost Lord Bury; and I have nobody to lose—here, at least—and am not very anxious to find one. Here be two friends of the family, besides your slave: a Mr Westcombe—very handsome, but silly—and a Mr Agar—frightful, but facetious."

The Mr. Westcombe, the single gentleman, and the curate who were all staying at Aston Hall are one and the same man—William Westcombe, who had just received his M.A. from Oxford but was still a curate, awaiting a rectorship which would soon come his way. Just that October his brother Nicholas, a canon in Winchester, had been murdered by a soldier of the 102nd Regiment. George Charles Agar (1780–1856) was a Guards captain, a distant relation of Lady Frances from the Irish family connected to Lord Normanton, and a good friend of Bold Webster's.

Byron continues:

> The whole party are out in carriages—a species of amusement from which I always avert; and, consequently, declined it to-day; it is very well with two, but not beyond a duet. I think being bumped about between two or more of one's acquaintances intolerable. W grows rather intolerable, too. He is out of humour with my Italian books (Dante and Alfieri, and some others as harmless as ever wrote), and requests that sa femme may not see them, because, forsooth, it is a language which doth infinite damage!! and because I enquired after the Stanhopes, our mutual acquaintance, he answers me by another question, 'Pray, do you enquire after my wife of others in the same way'—so that you see my Virtue is its own reward—for never, in word or deed, did I speculate upon his spouse; nor did I ever see much in her to encourage either hope, or much fulfillment of hope, supposing I had any. She is pretty, but not surpassing—too thin, and not very animated; good-tempered—and a something interesting enough in her manner and figure; but I never should think of her, nor anyone else, if left to my own cogitations, as I have neither the patience nor presumption to advance till met halfway. The other two pay her ten times more attention, and, of course, are more attended to. I really believe he is bilious, and suspects something extraordinary from my nonchalance; at all events, he has hit upon the wrong person. I can't help laughing to you, but he will soon make me very serious with him, and then he will come to his senses again. The oddest thing is, that he wants me to stay with him some time; which I am not much inclined to do, unless the gentleman transfers his fretfulness to someone else. I have written to you so much lately, you will be glad to be spared from any further account of the 'Blunderhead family.'

On October 8, 1813, from Aston Hall, he writes again to Lady Melbourne:

> I have volumes, but neither time nor space. I have already trusted too deeply to hesitate now; besides, for certain reasons, you will not be sorry to hear that I am anything but what I was. Well then, to begin, and first a word of mine host.—He has lately been talking at, rather than to, me

before the party (with the exception of the women) in a tone, which as I never use it myself, I am not particularly disposed to tolerate in others. What he may do with impunity, it seems, but not suffer, till at last I told him that the whole of his argument involved the interesting contradiction that 'he might love where he liked, but that no one else might like what he ever thought proper to love,' a doctrine which, as the learned Partridge observed, contains a 'non sequitur' from which I, for one, begged leave as a general proposition to dissent. This nearly produced a scene with me, as well as another guest, who seemed to admire my sophistry the most of the two; and as it was after dinner, and debating time, might have ended in more than wineshed, but that the devil, for some wise purpose of his own, thought proper to restore good humour, which has not as yet been further infringed. In these last few days I have had a good deal of conversation with an amiable person, whom (as we deal in letters and initials only) we will denominate Ph [i.e., Frances]. Well, these things are dull in detail. Take it once, I have made love, and if I am to believe mere words (for there we have hitherto stopped), it is returned. I must tell you the place of declaration, however, a billiard room. I did not, as C. says, 'kneel in the middle of the room,' but like Corporal Trim to the Nun [from *Tristram Shandy*], 'I made a speech,' which, as you might not listen to it with the same patience, I shall not transcribe. We were before on very amicable terms, and I remembered being asked an odd question, 'how a woman who liked a man could inform him of it when he did not perceive it.' I also observed that we went on with our game [of billiards] without counting the hazards; and supposed that, as mine certainly were not, the thoughts of the other party also were not exactly occupied by what was our ostensible pursuit. Not quite, though pretty well satisfied with my progress, I took a very imprudent step with pen and paper, in tender and tolerably turned prose periods (no poetry even when in earnest). Here were risks, certainly: first, how to convey, then how would it be received? It was received, however, and deposited not very far from the heart which I wished it to reach when, who should enter the room but the person who ought at that moment to have been in the Red Sea, if Satan had any civility. But she kept her countenance, and the paper; and I my composure as well as I could. It was a risk, and all had been lost by failure; but then recollect how much more I had to gain by the reception, if not declined, and how much one always hazards to obtain anything worth having. My billet prospered, it did more, it even (I am this moment interrupted by the Marito, and write this before him, he has brought me a political pamphlet in MS. to decypher and applaud, I shall content myself with the last; oh, he is gone again), my billet produced an answer, a very unequivocal one too, but a little too much about virtue, and indulgence of attachment in some sort of etherial [sic] process, in which the soul is principally concerned, which I don't very well understand, being a bad metaphysician; but one generally ends and begins with platonism, and, as my proselyte is only twenty, there is time enough to materialize. I hope nevertheless this spiritual system won't last long, and at any rate must make the experiment. I remember my last case was the reverse, as Major O'Flaherty recommends, 'we fought first and explained afterwards' [The major was a character in a couple of Richard Cumberland's plays]. This is the present state of things: much mutual profession, a good deal of melancholy, which, I am sorry to say, was remarked by 'the Moor,' and as much love as could well be made, considering the time, place and circumstances. I need not say that the folly and petulance of W has tended to all this. If a man is not contented with a pretty woman, and not only runs after any little country girl he meets with, but absolutely boasts of it; he must not be surprised if others admire that which he knows not how to value. Besides, he literally provoked, and goaded me into it, by something not unlike bullying, indirect to be sure, but tolerably obvious: 'he would do this, and he would do that,' 'if any man,' etc., etc., and he thought that every 'woman' was his lawful prize, nevertheless. Oons! who is this strange monopolist? It is odd enough, but on other subjects he is like other people, on this he seems infatuated. If he had been rational, and not prated of his pursuits, I should have gone on very well, as I did at Middleton. Even now, I shan't quarrel with him if I can help it; but one or two of his speeches have blackened the blood about my heart, and curdled the milk of kindness. If put to the proof, I shall behave like other people, I presume.

Byron would occasionally go and visit George Villiers, the 5th Earl of Jersey, at his home, Middleton Park, Oxfordshire. Jersey, although 15 years older than Byron, had in common with the poet from his past Harrow and Cambridge (Byron was at Trinity; the earl at St. John's).

Byron ends this letter with, "Good evening, I am now going to billiards." Then there is a P.S., written at 6 o'clock. "This business is growing serious, and I think Platonism is in some peril. There has been very nearly a scene, almost an hysteric, and really without cause, for I was conducting myself with (to me) very irksome decorum. Her expressions astonish me, so young and cold as she appeared. But these professions must end as usual, and would I think now, had 'l'occasion' been not wanting. Had anyone come in during the tears, and consequent consolation, all had been spoiled; we must be more cautious, or less larmoyante."

There is a second P.S. written at 10 o'clock, "Just escaped from claret and vocification on G-d knows what paper. My landlord is a rare gentleman. He has just proposed to me a bet that he, for a certain sum, 'wins any given woman, against any given homme including all friends present,' which I declined with becoming deference to him, and the rest of the company. Is not this, at the moment, a perfect comedy? I forgot to mention that on his entrance yesterday during the letter scene, it reminded me so much of an awkward passage in 'The Way to Keep Him' [Arthur Murphy's 1760 comedy] between Lovemore, Sir Bashful and my Lady, that, embarrassing as it was, I could hardly help laughing. I hear his voice in the passage; he wants me to go to a ball in Sheffield, and is talking to me as I write. Good night. I am in the act of praising his pamphlet."

Then Byron and Webster went to Newstead for a short trip. On October 10, 1813, from there, the poet to Lady Melbourne, "I write to you from the melancholy mansion of my fathers, where I am dull as the longest deceased of my progenitors. I hate reflection on irrevocable things, and won't now turn sentimentalist. W alone accompanied me here (I return tomorrow to Aston). He is now sitting opposite; and between us are red and white champagne, Burgundy, two sorts of Claret, and lighter vintages, the relics of my youthful cellar, which is yet in formidable number and famous order. But I leave the wine to him, and prefer conversing soberly with you."

He goes on to say:

> Mine guest (late host) has just been congratulating himself on possessing a partner without passion. I don't know, and cannot yet speak with certainty, but I never yet saw more decisive preliminary symptoms. As I am apt to take people at their word, on receiving my answer, that whatever the weakness of her heart might be, I should never derive further proof of it than the confession, instead of pressing the point, I told her that I was willing to be hers on her own terms, and should never attempt to infringe upon the conditions. I said this without pique, and believing her perfectly in earnest for the time; but in the midst of our mutual professions, or, to use her own expression, 'more than mutual,' she bursts into an agony of crying, and at such a time, and in such a place, as rendered such a scene particularly perilous to both — her sister in the next room, and — not far off. Of course I said and did almost everything proper on the occasion, and fortunately we restored sunshine in time to prevent anyone from perceiving the cloud that had darkened our horizon. She says she is convinced that my own declaration was produced solely because I perceived her previous penchant, which, by the bye, as I think I said to you before, I neither perceived nor expected. I really did not suspect her of a predilection for anyone, and even now in public, with the exception of those little indirect, yet mutually understood — I don't know how and it is unnecessary to name, or describe them — her conduct is as coldly correct as her still, fair, Mrs L-like aspect. She, however, managed to give me a note and to receive another, and a ring before W's very face, and yet she is a thorough devotee, and takes prayers morning and evening, besides being measured for a new Bible once a quarter. The only alarming thing is that W complains of her aversion from being beneficial to population and posterity. If this is an invariable maxim, I shall lose my labour. Be this as it may, she owns to more than I have ever heard from any woman within the time, and I shan't take W's word any more for her feelings than I did for that celestial comparison, which I once mentioned. I think her eye, her change of colour, and the trembling of her hand, and above all her devotion, tell a different tale. Good night. We return to-morrow.

That Lady Frances was not frigid — absolutely the opposite — can be judged from her later letters to Scrope Davies. A fire sometimes needs a skillful stoker, and Bold Webster, as nimble as he may have been as a pedestrian out on the open road, or with a pistol in his hand, was a slouch in the amour department whenever the object of his attentions was anyone but himself.

This ring that Byron smuggled to Lady Frances under the very nose of her husband was a tangible gesture to his new lover, and in return the lady would present him with a seal, and, as Paston and Quennell put it (supported by the earlier Maurois and others), "would [ask] for no other token than a miniature and an 'exchange of chevelure.' Among her letters are two curls of beautiful chestnut hair. One is wrapped in a little note—for they were still together."

About this time were written several undated letters from Lady Frances to Byron, as Paston and Quennell say, "while they were still under the same roof (Aston and/or Newstead)."

The first (actually dated 1813) from Lady Frances to the poet, is from this time, and reads,

> Think of you sometimes when absent—Great God—do not talk of absence. Would that my heart only dwelt upon the remembrance of you sometimes, but, alas! alas! My whole time is spent in meditation, & my meditation of him nearest and dearest to my heart—Had, indeed, that heart met some years ago with its beloved object it had not <u>perhaps</u> pined in secret. I say <u>perhaps</u>, not that I doubt your sincerity, no, had I <u>doubted</u> I should not have <u>trusted</u> as I have done, but I think you have deceived yourself into a regard you will upon consideration discover the object unworthy of, for <u>who can be worthy of your return</u>—However you may change never never, will time or place alter my affection—You have taken my heart, & with it my peace—Keep it—I will droop in silence, for <u>never</u> will I <u>swerve</u> from my <u>duty</u>—be still my beating heart, be still & break—I will endeavour from every eye so tender, so dangerous an attachment—will you forgive me for it? Can you regard me after betraying my weakness? Oh No! I fear you cannot—I am lost in my own eyes—I must be in yours—You ask me for—[she did not finish this sentence, but she may mean a lock of hair, or a miniature]. Shall I defer it till I can procure from London a <u>brilliant</u> heart to enclose it in, or will it be acceptable plain & simple, as it is. Do not again mention the word 'absence'; it breaks my heart. While near thee I feel an indescribable pleasure, a kind of delirium I tremble to have destroyed—Oh, do not destroy the fairy dream—You know what depends upon this being destroyed—I have committed myself to you—<u>Have you no other attachment</u>? Why should I presume to ask the question. Forgive me & punish my impertinence and this scrawl likewise forgive—Adieu, think of me &—I need not add what you can imagine—.

The second says:

> How gladly would I make any sacrifice, that would prove to you how dearly I regard, how sincerely—forgive me if I say—I love you—could I convince of the purity of my affection—and how it is absolutely winding itself, entwining round the thread of my existence, could I convince you of that, then, would you believe how much it costs me to say, never, never can I take the step you allude to, <u>never</u> will I involve him who possesses every particle of my tenderest affection in any unpleasant circumstances—I know you do not urge it—'tis the surest proof I have your regard—should I ever be happy again possessing a mind tortured with the recollection of guilt and receiving the object to whom my heart is joined by an eternal link—disappointed and despairing the wretch for whom he had sacrificed so much—Oh, forgive me—it is not a momentary resolve but the determination of four hours last night spent in <u>solemn meditation</u>—Oh! Forgive me—Do not judge of my affections and say they are cold—cold indeed they are to every body but <u>one</u>—and that <u>one</u> seems to doubt—Do not talk of parting—it wrings my heart—I cannot—and yet, it must, it must be—pity me when I make this sacrifice for better has been the struggle—Your two little

Lady Frances Webster-Wedderburn. From the author's collection.

pledges are sacred and never shall be separated from me, but pray, offer me no other — I do not want any token, but an exchange of la chevelure for, in case of your forming another, & a more happy, a more deserving attachment, the former you shall receive again — the latter <u>never</u> — It is not presumption my mentioning the word <u>attachment</u> — my classing it with you? Adieu — burn this & the other — I wish it — My whole, my last thoughts will be upon you — my last supplication — if the prayers of the guilty are received — will invoke every blessing upon him nearest & dearest to my heart.

This letter was one of the two at the Byron exhibition at London's Victoria and Albert Museum in 1974.

The third says:

Promise me to love me [sic] and not let my circumstances ever separate your heart from mine — I am ready to make any vows, to swear before God that nothing can alter me — Never can I change — I have given myself up to you, do not abuse my confidence — you have not — I am grateful, <u>very grateful</u>, for your forbearance, but I am resolute — I love dearly — I more than <u>love</u>, but <u>never</u> will <u>survive</u> my <u>fall</u> — I am <u>yours</u> in <u>every sense</u>, & untill some happy event makes my conduct not criminal, never will I look upon or think of any <u>other</u> person — by other, you know who I allude to — I wrote last night to you, but I was ashamed in the morning to have confessed a guilty passion, for learn, I am not so cold as you imagine me, and I invoked every blessing upon you for not having taken advantage of my <u>imprudent</u>, my <u>unguarded</u> situation.

I fear you must despise & hate me; for pity's sake do not, for till I knew you I knew not what it was to adore a person, & I could have appeared before my God perfectly pure and unspotted — Do not detest me — .

Another reads:

You fancy I was cold last night when I returned — unjust suspicion! Did you but know how my heart leaps when I see you after a separation of only one hour, you would not so unjustly & cruelly accuse. Sometimes my affection nearly outleaps my prudence. I call all my self-command into action, the struggle is hard, & perhaps it may bear a <u>cold construction</u>, but you have got to learn the <u>warmth</u> of my <u>affections</u> — they are cold to <u>every body</u> else — to you — I dare not say what they are — you ask me 'will I ever give you up'? — Never, never. 'Tis not in the power of man — neither sea or land can ever separate my heart from its beloved object — even should that object ever betray her for whom he professes so great an affection, and who is perfectly grateful for his regard, feeling conscious she is undeserving of it — I have committed myself to you — in every respect — You have not, I know, deceived me — remember, if at any time you alter, if at any time you change — you transfer your regard — if it promotes your welfare — I will bow, tho' it signs my death warrant — for I feel I <u>never</u> can <u>resign</u> you but with <u>life</u>, for believe me, my affection is <u>pure</u>. I would, at this moment, lay down my life for you, but be assured my love is <u>victorious</u>, my attachment is <u>strong</u>, is <u>unchangeable</u>, but not <u>guilty</u> — You say '<u>Farewell</u>.' I cannot utter the word — it destroys my existence — Oh! What a struggle between love and duty — never can I know happiness — Do not add censure to my misery — Do not pretend to suppose you have no pretensions to my regard — no <u>pretensions</u> — I have none to <u>yours</u> — How many more <u>worthy</u> than me do you know — <u>Never, never</u> will I give you up — If my love was of any other sort, I <u>might</u>, you see it is not. It is not a mad fancy of the moment; never should <u>you</u> have known it, had it not met with a return. <u>Do not deceive me</u>. I am interrupted — Adieu.

Quoting a letter via Paston and Quennell:

I enclose your request — Will you forget me? — Oh, no, I think you will not — at least you will pity her who suffers so much for you — What a heavenly disposition have you shewn to <u>him</u> [meaning Bold Webster] to-day — My heart is closer cemented to you every moment — Do not throw me off — my life is wrapped up in your good opinion — therefore preserve me — Adieu — We shall soon meet — Till then I cannot say farewell.

The Byron lock, one of the many that Lady Melbourne declared the poet set such a high value upon, was duly shorn and given Lady Frances (according to André Maurois and to Paston and Quennell). Maurois says, "Formerly, for Caroline Lamb, he had stopped short of this sacrifice and given her a lock from a manservant's head. That had greatly amused him, but to play such a trick on the delicate Lady Frances would have seemed monstrous."

On October 11, 1813, Byron was back at Aston Hall, writing another letter to Lady Melbourne:

> W is on the verge of a precious scrape, his quondam tutor! and ally [Campbell], who has done him some not very reputable services since his marriage, writing, I believe his billets, and assisting him to those to whom they were addressed, being now discarded, threatens a development, etc. W consults me on the subject! Of this I shall take no advantage in another quarter, however convenient; if I gain my point it shall be as fairly as such things will admit. It is odd enough that his name has never hitherto been taken in vain by her or me. I have told him that if the discovery is inevitable, his best way is to anticipate it, and sue for an act of indemnity: if she likes him she will forgive, and if she don't like him, it don't matter whether she does or no. From me she shall never hear of it.

Campbell had two very practical reasons, aside from old time's sake, for acting as his former student's letter writer and go-between. One was that, as an impoverished lawyer, he needed the money. Another was that he had fallen for Lady Frances, and was hoping for a divorce, so he could snap her up. Campbell was truly in love with the lady, and would have made her a wonderful husband, but she never even knew he existed, so to speak.

On Monday afternoon, Byron wrote again to Lady Melbourne:

> We shall be at Newstead again, the whole party for a week, in a few days. He haunts me — here he is again [i.e. Webster], and here are a party of purple stockings come to dine. Oh, that accursed pamphlet! I have not read it; what shall I say to the author, now in the room? Thank the stars which I yesterday abused, he is diverted by the mirror opposite, and is now surveying with great complacency himself — he is gone!
>
> ...My proselyte is so young a beginner that you won't wonder at these exchanges and mummeries. You are right, she is 'very pretty,' and not so inanimate as I imagined, and must at least be allowed an excellent taste!!

At ten o'clock he wrote:

> Nearly a scene (always nearly). There is a Lady Sitwell, a wit and blue; and, what is more to the purpose, a dark, tall, fierce-looking, conversable personage. As it is usual to separate the women at table, I was under the necessity of placing myself between her and the sister, and was seated, and in the agonies of conjecture whether the dish before me required carving, when my little Platonist exclaimed, 'Lord Byron, this is your place.' I stared, and before I had time to reply, she repeated, looking like C. when gentle (for she is very unlike that fair creature when angry), 'Lord Byron, change places with Catherine.' I did, and very willingly, though awkwardly; but 'the Moor' (mine host) roared out, 'B., that is the most ungallant thing I have ever beheld.' Lady Catherine, by way of mending matters, answered, 'Did you not hear Frances ask him?' He has looked like the Board of Green Cloth ever since, and is now mustering wine and spirits for a lecture to her, and a squabble with me; he had better let it alone, for I am in a pestilent humour at this present writing, and shall certainly disparage his eternal 'pamphlet.'

André Maurois re-creates a scene with very little resemblance to the original, writing in his book *Byron*, "Several times during dinner his [Webster's] coarse jesting provoked faint movements of impatience from his wife and sister-in-law, and Byron, in silent amusement, lost not one of their soft sighs, and savored them as a connoisseur."

Lady Sitwell was born in Yorkshire in 1779, as Sarah Caroline Stovin. She was the second wife and recent widow of Sir Sitwell Sitwell, 1st Bart. She married again in 1821, and died as late as 1860. Sitwell Sitwell hadn't been born thus, of course; there had been a name change when he was a child. The original last name was Hurt.

A few days later (October 1813) Lady Melbourne's approving letter inspired a return letter to her, in which the poet says, "Your approbation of my ethics on the subject gratifies me much. When we are happy, we are too much occupied to be aware of its extent; it is only during the subsequent repose, the 'abandon,' that you can discover, even to yourself, if you were really loved."

On October 13, 1813, the poet wrote John Hanson from his ancestral home of Newstead Abbey, "Dear Sir, I am disposed to advance a loan of 1000 [pounds] to James Wedderburn Webster, Esqre, of Aston Hall, York County — & request you will address there a bond & judgement to be signed by the said as soon as possible — of Claughton's payments I know nothing further — and the demands on myself I know also — but W is a very old friend of mine — & a man of property — & as far as I can command the money he shall have it."

Thomas Claughton bought Newstead Abbey from Byron in 1812 for £140,000, but was having difficulty making payments. He would sell it to Colonel Thomas Wildman three years later.

On October 13, 1813, Byron wrote to Lady Melbourne:

> I mentioned to you yesterday a laughable occurrence at dinner. This morning he [Webster] burst forth with a homily upon the subject to the two and myself, instead of taking us separately (like the last of the Horatii with the Curiatii). You will easily suppose with such odds he had the worst of it, and the satisfaction of being laughed at into the bargain. Serious as I am — or seem, — I really cannot frequently keep my countenance: yesterday, before my face, they disputed about their apartments at Newstead, she insisting that her sister should share her room, and he very properly, but heinously out of place, maintaining, and proving to his own satisfaction, that none but husbands have any legal claim to divide their spouse's pillow. You may suppose, notwithstanding the ludicrous effect of the scene, I felt and looked a little uncomfortable; this she must have seen — for, of course, I said not a word — and turning round at the close of the dialogue, she whispered, 'N'importe, this is all nothing,' an ambiguous sentence which I am puzzled to translate; but, as it was meant to console me, I was very glad to hear it, though quite unintelligible. As far as I can pretend to judge of her disposition and character — I will say, of course, I am partial — she is, you know, very handsome, and very gentle, though sometimes decisive; fearfully romantic, and singularly warm in her affections; but I should think of a cold temperament, yet I have my doubts on that point, too; accomplished (as all decently educated women are), and clever, though her style a little too German; no dashing nor desperate talker, but never — and I have watched in mixed conversation — saying a silly thing (duet dialogues in course between young and Platonic people must be varied with a little chequered absurdity); good tempered (always excepting Lady Oxford, which was, outwardly, the best I ever beheld), and jealous as myself — the ne plus ultra of green-eyed monstrosity; seldom abusing other people, but listening to it with great patience. These qualifications, with an unassuming and sweet voice, and very soft manner, constitute the bust (all I can yet pretend to model) of my present idol.
>
> ...I am totally absorbed in this passion — that I am even ready to take a flight if necessary, and as she says, 'We cannot part,' it is no impossible dénouement — though as yet one of us at least does not think of it. W will probably want to cut my throat, which would not be a difficult task, for I trust I should not return the fire of a man I had injured, though I could not refuse him the pleasure of trying me as a target. But I am not sure I shall not have more work in that way. There is a friend in the house who looks a little suspicious; he can only conjecture, but if he Iagonizes, or finds, or makes mischief, let him look to it. To W I am decidedly wrong, yet he almost provoked me into it — he loves other women; at least he follows them; she evidently did not love him, even before. I came here with no plan, no intention of the kind as my former letters will prove to you (the only person to whom I care about proving it) and have not yet been here ten days — a week yesterday, on recollection: you cannot be more astonished than I am how, and why all this has happened.

The seeming ingenuousness of the poet's claim to have arrived at Aston Hall with no preconceived notions of an amour with his hostess must have strained even the credulity of his correspondent.

Byron to Lady Melbourne, October 14, 1813:

> I believe little but 'l'occasion manque,' and to that many things are tending.... We have progressively improved into a less spiritual species of tenderness, but the seal is not yet fixed, though the wax is preparing for the impression.... He is a little indirect blusterer who neither knows what he would have, nor what he deserves. To-day at breakfast (I was too late for the scene) he attacked

> both the girls in such a manner, no one knew why, or wherefore, that one had left the room, and the other had half a mind to leave the house; this too before servants, and the other guest! On my appearance the storm blew over, but the narrative was detailed to me subsequently by one of the sufferers. You may be sure that I shall not 'consider self,' nor create a squabble while it can be avoided; on the contrary I have been endeavouring to serve him essentially (except on the one point, and there I was goaded into it by his own absurdities), and to extricate him from some difficulties of various descriptions. Of course all obligations are cancelled between two persons in our circumstances, but that I shall not dwell upon; of the other I shall try to make an 'affaire reglée'; if that don't succeed we shall probably go off together; but she only shall make me resign the hope. As for him he may convert his antlers into powder-horns and welcome, and such he has announced as his intention when 'any man at any time, etc. etc.,' 'he would not give him a chance, but exterminate him without suffering defence.' Do you know I was fool enough to lose my temper at this circuitous specimen of Bobadil jealousy [Bobadil is the braggart in Ben Jonson's *Every Man in His Humour*], and tell him and the other (there are a brace, lion and jackal) that I, not their roundabout he, desired no better than to put these 'epithets of war,' with which their sentences were 'horribly stuffed,' to the proof. This was silly and suspicious, but my liver could bear it no longer. My poor little Helen [i.e. Helen of Troy] tells me that there never was such a temper and talents, that the marriage was not one of attachment, that — in short, my descriptions fade before hers, all foolish fellows are alike, but this has a patent for his cap and bells. The scene between Sir B. and Lovemore I remember, but the one I alluded to was the letter of Lovemore to Lady Constant — there is no comedy after all like real life.... There ought to be an excellent occasion to-morrow; but who can command circumstances? The most we can do is to avail ourselves of them. Publicly I have been cautious enough, and actually declined a dinner where they went, because I thought something intelligible might be seen or suspected. I regretted, but regret it less, for I hear one of the Fosters was there, and they be cousins and gossips of our good friends the D.s [this must have been one of Lady Elizabeth Foster's relatives, who were connected (through her) to the Duke of Devonshire].

With Hanson having sent the necessary papers for James to sign, Byron loaned £500 to "Wedderburn & Co., for Fn" [Lady Frances] on the 15th of October, and six days later another £500 to "W Webster" [Sir James]. That is the way the loan was set up. The question is, would Byron have loaned the money to James if it hadn't been for Lady Frances? And did James know this? Was this all a plan to secure the loan from Byron? If so, it was a plan that, very definitely, went beyond expectations.

Byron was at Newstead Abbey when he wrote to Lady Melbourne on October 17, 1813:

> The whole party are here.... One day, left entirely to ourselves, was nearly fatal.... Was I wrong? I spared her. There was something so very peculiar in her manner — a kind of mild decision — no scene — not even a struggle; but still I know not what, that convinced me that she was serious. It was not the mere 'no' which one has heard forty times before, and always with the same accent; but the tone, and the aspect — yet I sacrificed much — the hour two in the morning ... she seems so very thankful for my forbearance — a proof, at least, that she was not playing merely the usual decorous reluctance, which is sometimes so tiresome on these occasions. You ask if I am prepared to go 'all lengths.' If you mean by 'all lengths' anything including duel, or divorce? I answer, Yes. I love her. If I did not, and much too, I should have been more selfish on the occasion before mentioned. I have offered to go away with her, and her answer, whether sincere or not, is 'that on my account she declines it.' In the meantime we are all as wretched as possible; he scolding on account of unaccountable melancholy; the sister very suspicious, but rather amused — the friend very suspicious too (why I know not), not at all amused — il Marito something like Lord Chesterfield in De Grammont [*The Memoirs of the Count de Grammont*, by Anthony Hamilton], putting on a marital physiognomy, prating with his worthy ally, swearing at servants, sermonizing both sisters; and buying sheep; but never quitting her side now; so that we are in despair. I am very feverish, restless, and silent, as indeed seems to be the tacit agreement of everyone else. In short I can foresee nothing — it may end in nothing; but here are half a dozen persons very much occupied, and two, if not three, in great perplexity; and, as far as I can judge, so we must continue. She don't and won't live with him, and they have been so far separate for a long time; therefore I have nothing to answer for on that point. Poor thing — she is either the most artful or artless of her age (20) I ever encountered. She owns to so much, and perpetually says, 'Rather

than you should be angry,' or 'Rather than you should like anyone else, I will do whatever you please'; 'I won't speak to this, that, or the other if you dislike it,' and throws, or seems to throw, herself so entirely upon my discretion in every respect, that it disarms me quite; but I am really wretched with the perpetual conflict with myself. Her health is so very delicate; she is so thin and pale, and seems to have lost her appetite so entirely, that I doubt her living much longer. This is also her own opinion. But these fancies are common to all who are not very happy; if she were once my wife, or likely to be so, a warm climate should be the first resort, nevertheless, for her recovery. The most perplexing — and yet I can't prevail upon myself to give it up — is the caressing system. In her it appears perfectly childish, and I do think innocent; but it really puzzles all the Scipio about me to confine myself to the laudable portion of these endearments. What a cursed situation I have thrown myself into! Potiphar (it used to be Oxford's name) putting some stupid question to me the other day, I told him that I rather admired the sister [Lady Catherine, who was then 18], and what does he? but tell her this; and his wife too, who a little too hastily asked him 'if he was mad?' which put him to demonstration that a man ought not to be asked if he was mad, for relating that a friend thought his wife's sister was a pretty woman. Upon this topic he held forth with great fervour for a customary period. I wish he had a quinsey!... I don't know where I am going — my mind is a chaos. I always am setting all upon single stakes, and this is one.

There is a P.S.: "My stay is quite uncertain — a moment may overturn everything; but you shall hear — happen what may — nothing or something."

James did not consider the possibility that Byron's expressed admiration for Lady Catherine was merely a ploy to throw him off the scent, and he started to play cupid. Byron says, "His marrying scheme, if premeditated, had been an excellent way of turning the tables; but it was done too abruptly and awkwardly to succeed — there was no foundation for his edifice, and if there had, I would have blown it about his ears. I prefer, if in the regular way, choosing my own moiety, though truth to tell, he recommended a woman of virtue; for I heard her say 'that she never was in a warm bath in her life,' a certain sign that the care of your truly good woman is always confined to her soul."

The day before Lady Frances and Byron were to part, he slipped her a note telling her it was all off, and blaming her for the mess they now found themselves in. She dashed off a letter and gave it to him. It read:

> If my feelings were like yours we should all be long separated — If I followed my own feelings I should say we never shall part, but Duty curbs my feelings—
> I trust we shall soon meet, but never will I swerve from my duty — My attachment is strong but never will be guilty — I feel I am wrong in having left my notes in your possession but I trust you will not betray me —
> I throw myself upon your mercy, but remember, what has passed is only known to us two. further [sic] communication — which I should be rue to hear — would instantly put an end to me — I do not say it as a threat, no, I scorn such a thing, gladly would I die for you — Remember, I follow Duty much as it may cost me so to do — no entwining arms can confine my heart which remains not after tomorrow — for it is yours and only yours—
> My heart has nearly broken reading your letter — I shall peruse & weep over it every night — would I had your picture — May I not have it — Depend upon it — You shall not have cause to repent your professions to me — I will not bring you into any unpleasant situation — I feel this moment ready to faint, for I must not cry before any body, but I will pine in secret —
> If ever you mean to betray or forsake me deal generously, deal candidly with me — I am bound to you (independent of my affection & attachment) by gratitude for your past conduct, let nobody dare say before me you have no principle — for you have proved it to me — I feel I shall betray myself at parting — save me as much as you can — I cannot utter the word 'Farewell' — Indeed I cannot — and yet I will for your sake — <u>I am yours</u> — you never can be separated from my heart, tho' you may be absent, yet night & day you will be present to my recollection —
> Do not despise me for my attachment, or give a wicked world the least room to talk — forgive me — do not speak lightly of me for an affection I cannot help — We may meet under <u>happier circumstances</u>. Till then. Adieu — Can I get your picture — I can contrive to receive it — My heart is bursting — then let it break & end — God bless you — .

This the first of her many pleas for a miniature of Lord Byron. Her desire for a picture would very soon become an obsession.

That evening, "Monday night, Oct. 18th," much disturbed, she sat down to write what became a monstrously long letter — five lengthy pages. As much as she may have wished to hand it to the poet the following day, she could only manage to complete the first part before morning, and so it would take a few days before he received the whole thing.

This exercise in prolixity opens: "Page 1. For two hours I have been sitting with my pen in my hand unable from the force of my 'cold' feelings' to form a letter — would that they were cold — but alas! all attempts are vain."

She continues:

> Did you but know the destruction my mind has endured since you settled to depart — Could you but see the agonizing sorrow & despair of her you professed to love since that fatal moment she internally murmur'd 'Farewell' to him most dear — you would not have written so <u>cold</u> a note — you would not have, you would not have <u>loaded</u> with <u>reproach</u> — at <u>such</u> a moment of <u>trial</u> — the heart <u>bursting</u> with <u>affection</u> — But I will not complain — I deserve it — I <u>merit</u> reproach — but I did not <u>expect</u> it from you — I have err'd — but do not despise me.
>
> I flew to my room to peruse the dear yet cruel paper you last put into my hands — how my heart sank within me at perusing the contents, but I know the heart which dictated it, I know it would never willingly inflict a wound upon one already bowed low indeed — Desperate has been the struggle between love and Duty — Duty appears triumphant aided by Reason but Love saps the foundation of the fabric you libel me — I cannot change — all attempts would prove fruitless — for affection has so entwined itself round the fibres of my heart — 'tis impossible to separate them — they must live and die together — I know not what 'tis to change — contemplate in imagination my feelings — judge of them by my too-evident altered appearance this morning — pause for a moment and then repeat, 'It is well. I shall not be surprised.' Reflect another moment, consider the risks I have run, the bounds I have o'erleaped in confessing an attachment I ought never to have breath'd — Consider, when I assure you at this solemn hour, in the most awful manner — with a heart depressed with grief, & breaking under the hours of separation — that I would make any sacrifice to secure your affections — Consider that I have sacrificed every claim to happiness, that I would not, in my state of mind, make any false professions — that I have given myself up a victim to a tender affection — that I have sacrificed every claim to happiness (which I could alone know on Earth by the profession — undivided profession of one object) to my God — my child — & my vows — to the breaking of which latter — God has denounced a curse to both parties — .

She wraps up Page 1 with "These are my feelings — Consider & weigh them — Then say — Is a mind thus strong to be doubted, to be suspected of change — Is it to be pronounced cold & incapable of Friendship — If I am in error, pity & forgive me for my heart is good — it has but one fault — If I am right, never again repeat — You think I may change — never again say 'Happiness I wish our love to be lowered to friendship.'"

Page 2:

> The accusation is unjust — Your affection is my life — yet even your <u>cold Friendship</u> would support me, and I should consider it with gratitude as an ample return for my attachment so unworthy of you — But I will be generous — I will make one last effort much as it may cost me to prove my affection is not selfish —
>
> I know the power of Man will be exerted to estrange my heart from yours (tho' as yet our attachment is unknown to any body [she had put 'every body,' but had changed it] — I know I shall have much to suffer on that account — yet again I say — the thing is impossible — I cannot change — I remember my former vows — I do not exact secrecy further than your own generosity dictates — I am yours — and yours you cannot prevent me from being — yet, stand firm my beating heart while I pronounce this struggling effort —
>
> I free you from all your vows — I release you from all professions you have made even from the 'one year' during which you promised to think of me [as Paston and Quennell interpret this, "Before Byron left Aston Hall" — although it was actually Newstead where they parted — "Lady Frances asked him to be faithful to her for one year"] — I leave you a free agent, unshaded, unfettered — I implore you to be happy — to think of some other — I could feel pleasure in your

happiness—I could smile and then I would—but the struggle is o'er, & I will not tarnish it by one word of reproach or threat—Be happy—A gleam of sunshine will brighten my thoughts, will for a moment enliven my heart, when the dreadful weight of having occasioned you the least uneasiness—of having been for an instant the cause of unhappiness [she had originally written 'happiness'] to you is removed—I am innocent, in fact, of the crime—for I feel unconscious—unworthy—so very undeserving even of your regard—much less of those professions so dear to my heart—I have now given you an opportunity—a bitter but generous opportunity to act your own part—one line will convince me of your feelings—Do not fear my reproaches—No—you shall not hear a murmur—but do not hate me—I cannot ask for that—be you happy—I look around, all is dark & gloomy—I have sacrificed all—but know, stern Duty, thou canst not enslave my thoughts, my heart—my soul—they are centered on one object—they ever will remain constant—even that adored object cannot change them—he cannot prevent them from loving even if so inclined he was—I can write no more—my head is giddy—my heart is sick & breaking—I am ill, very ill—I cannot help remarking myself the alteration so short a time has made upon my appearance—I am distracted—We shall meet—if not here—'twill be, I trust, in that place of everlasting peace where all sorrow shall be wiped from our eyes—and Sin & Death be no more—we shall meet—Be thou happy—I should imagine this to be no very difficult task did I believe all I hear, but I do not—Forgive me—bitter be my fate if I have willingly given you a moment's uneasiness—I have given you a generous opportunity—I again pronounce you free from those dearly remembered vows—I liberate you—in so doing—I strengthen my own attachment.

She finishes Page 2 with "It is four o'clock—Adieu—God—that sound wrings my heart—it tolls my fate—but you shall not hear a murmur—not one—may Heaven shower its most liberal stores upon you—I go to bed—but not to sleep—/4 o'clock."

She would continue this letter the next night, or rather, much later that day. But in the meantime, when dawn had broken, came the parting, the morning Byron was to leave. It was Tuesday, October 19, 1813. Byron left Newstead for London, accompanied by James Webster, who was traveling down to the capital so that the poet could put the final touches to the £1000 loan. The parting was more than sad for Byron and frighteningly so for Lady Frances. Fortunately, James just assumed that he—il marito himself—was the cause of his wife's emotion.

Later that day, on the way to London, Byron wrote to Lady Melbourne from Northampton:

W and I are thus far on our way to town—he was seized with a sudden fit of friendship, and would accompany me—or rather, finding that some business could not conveniently be done without me, he thought proper to assume ye appearance of it. He is not exactly the companion I wished to take; it is really laughable when you think of the other—a kind of pig in a poke. Nothing but squabbles between them for the last three days, and at last he rose up with a solemn and mysterious air, and spake, 'Lady Frances, you have at last rendered an explanation necessary between me and Lord Byron, which must take place.' I stared, and knowing that it is the custom of country gentlemen (if Farquhar is correct) [George Farquhar, playwright] to apprize their moieties of such intentions, and being also a little out of humour and conscience, I thought a crisis must ensue, and answered very quietly that 'he would find me in such a room at his leisure ready to hear, and reply.' 'Oh!,' says he, 'I shall choose my own time.' I wondered that he did not choose his own house, too, but walked away, and waited for him. All this mighty preluce led only to what he called an explanation for my satisfaction, that whatever appearances were, he and she were on the very best terms, that she loved him so much, and he her, it was impossible not to disagree upon tender points, and for fear a man who, etc., etc., should suppose that marriage was not the happiest of all possible estates, he had taken this resolution of never quarrelling without letting me know that he was the best husband, and most fortunate person in existence. I told him he had fully convinced me, that it was utterly impossible people who liked each other could behave with more interesting suavity—and so on. Yesterday morning, on our going (I pass over the scene, which shook me, I assure you), 'B.,' quoth he, 'I owe to you the most unhappy moments of my life.' I begged him to tell me how, that I might either sympathize, or put him out of his pain. 'Don't you see how the poor girl doats [sic] on me' (he replied); 'when I quit her but for a week, as you perceive, she is absolutely overwhelmed, and you stayed so long, and I necessarily for you, that she is in a worse state than I ever saw her in before, even before we were married!' Here we are — I could not return to Aston unless he had asked me — it is true he did, but in such a manner as I should not accept. What will be the end, I know not. I have left everything to her, and would have rendered all further plots superfluous by the most conclusive step; but she wavered, and escaped. Perhaps so have I — at least it is as well to think so — yet it is not over.

Benita Eisler maintains that this letter includes the words: "With her I am ready & willing to fly to the 'Green earth's end.' We are in despair." (The "Green earth's end" quote, which Byron uses often, is from Milton's *Comus*.)

Of this trip down to London, Thomas Moore wrote in his journal of April 16 to 20, 1820 (the opening lines are reproduced earlier in this book) that James "told me that, one day, travelling from Newstead to town with Lord Byron in his vis-à-vis [perhaps the same one Byron had exchanged with Webster in 1811] the latter kept his pistols beside him, and continued silent for hours, with the most ferocious expression possible on his countenance. 'For God's sake, my dear B,' said W-, at last, 'what are you thinking of? Are you about to commit murder? Or what other dreadful thing are you meditating?' To which Byron answered that he always had a sort of presentiment that his own life would be attacked some time or other; and that this was the reason of his always going armed, as it was the subject of his thoughts at that moment."

That evening Lady Frances began Page 3 of her long letter. (It is interestingly undiscerning of Paston and Quennell, in their book *To Lord Byron*, to call it an 18-page letter, and to guess that it was written "within a day or two of Byron leaving Aston." They do say, however, that it was written in the "neatest of tiny hands, without blot or erasure.")

Page 3.

> Tuesday night — rather Wednesday morng. 4 o'clock. Forgive the incoherent manner in which I wrote last night but I trust you will make <u>some</u> allowances for a distracted mind torn by the thoughts of separation — Forgive any hasty expressions torn from me by the <u>agony</u> of <u>despair</u>—
>
> "But indeed your note was cruel — however, a few kind words written afterwards fully reward me for all I have suffered — I am bound to you <u>for ever</u> by the <u>tenderest ties</u> of <u>gratitude</u> for your <u>kind expressions</u>— I again declare 'tis not in <u>human power</u> to turn the course of my love — of my <u>sincere attachment</u> to <u>you</u>— I am <u>yours</u> and <u>only yours</u> to <u>eternity</u>— I know 'tis <u>wrong</u> to avow it, but I hope I am not <u>wicked</u> — I hope you will not despise me — God grant you are well — and happy — Do you know I cannot yet discover what secret influence supported me under the agony of yesterday — For an hour I sate in the window — the tears trickling down my cheek — I felt Death would have been an acceptable visitor even then — but when you entered — when the moment of torture arrived — when I felt my hand lock in yours for the <u>last time</u>— and stole a look at that <u>too dearly cherished countenance</u>— when <u>necessity</u> forbade me throwing my arms around & <u>breathing</u> out my <u>soul</u> in <u>sorrow</u> on your <u>neck</u>—'Twas <u>then</u> I felt the <u>true horror</u> of <u>separation</u>—<u>desperation</u> marked my countenance which has now settled in <u>silent</u> despair — O God what I then endured words are inadequate to assess— I feel it now — and ever shall —
>
> My Byron, in all your writings you seem to accuse me and imagine our re-union is prevented by my caprice — Can you suppose I would fall a willing victim to my attachment — or is misery so charming that I would for a moment hesitate signing my happiness — was I not prompted by an all-seeing Providence who is alone capable of supporting us under all trials and afflictions — you will say that I am sermonising — but indeed I am not — believe me the greatest and only consolation under difficulty and trouble is communication with that Being who is capable of drawing us out of misery and has promis'd that what we ask faithfully we shall obtain effectually — I speak from experience and wish I could convince you what a load seems removed from the mind after Devotion — You will call it very presumptuous in me to include the above remark — I hope you will believe me sincere when I say it is the sincerity of my heart — and trust you will forgive me — I should like to have these foolish sheets burnt — It will oblige me much — also one I wrote the morning we took that <u>dearly</u> remembered, tho' eventually so <u>fatal</u> ride to Newstead — they are of no use to you —<u>you</u> are secure <u>without</u> them, & they are only mementos of <u>my</u> folly — At any rate burn the <u>scrap</u> alluded to if not these sheets — every thing else I leave to your honor — on which subject I must add a line in my defence — For you seem to be greatly hurt

with me — Forgive indeed you must — At the moment <u>she</u> [presumably her sister, Catherine] told me (unsuspicious) <u>they</u> had informed her you were apt to <u>triumph</u> in your <u>conquests</u> rather too publickly — I thought it better to beg of you not to betray <u>one</u> against whom the voice of slander never breathed — who <u>loves</u> you — and never <u>can</u> love another — you know the situation in which I wrote — therefore pardon my hasty remark —
    You are now <u>free</u> my Byron — be happy and think not of the <u>most wretched of beings</u> — .

So ends Page 3. Page 4 begins with the next mention of the miniature:

I must ask one favor upon certain conditions — will you give me your miniature to yourself — not the one you have promis'd to <u>him</u> [meaning James] — but another to <u>myself</u> — that I may be able to <u>indulge</u> my <u>sorrows</u>, contemplating <u>all</u> I love, and who I feel I have lost for ever — I have done my Duty — the recollection of that will cheer a moment <u>not very</u> far distant when an <u>awful</u> account will be required of me, of my <u>Acts</u> — I can answer firmly — of my <u>heart</u>, my <u>thoughts</u> — <u>every thing</u> else — they are wrapt up in <u>one object</u> which <u>nothing</u> but the <u>Grave</u> can <u>tear</u> from my <u>soul</u> — <u>Change</u> — Great God what a word — ask any <u>sacrifice</u> — name any <u>Bond</u> however dreadful to be put into effect when I change — and I will gladly enter it — I know no change but Death —
    But the conditions of the Picture — you will not refuse me? I am not surely asking in vain? I have liberated you from all <u>your</u> vows — I do not name myself — yet believe me mine is no <u>common love</u> — <u>ere long you will learn that</u> — You will be happy and then You may wish to reclaim the Gift — that will not do — if you comply it must be upon your promise I accept it that at <u>no future time</u> will you <u>demand</u> if [sic] <u>from</u> me — that <u>no change</u> will ever make you <u>reclaim</u> it — it shall never be known for my own sake — therefore you have nothing to fear from discovery — Whatever change may take place in your situation — of course I allude to your marriage — <u>no person in this world shall</u> if <u>once possessed</u> of it — wrest from me the image now stamped upon my heart — It will not harm your future wife — I will not indict you — but neither <u>she</u> or <u>you</u> can prevent me from loving — you <u>cannot</u> make me <u>revoke</u> my vows I again renew — You may despise me but cannot prevent my being yours and ever yours — <u>You</u> cannot prevent it — nor is it in the power of the <u>world</u> to do so — Pray let me have your picture — Do not refuse so humble a petition — but it <u>must</u> be upon my <u>own terms</u> — I will love and weep over it — it shall be my constant companion — & it will impart a gleam of pleasure to talk to the Image of that object for whom you are compell'd to pine — You know not what I suffer — and glad I am that you do not — You must answer this letter — and grant my request — Do not let it be a short one — write to me <u>once</u> — not one <u>unkind word</u> — and I will wear it with the Hair next my heart — Cruel Fate! Oh! bitter remembrance of our separation — Indeed you must write — I have need of it — fatal moment that parted me from him most dear, & left me heartless — for the little Irchin [sic, meaning her heart] went too. I could not detain him [i.e. the little irchin], you may throw him off but he will not return [i.e., to her] — he <u>will</u>, tho' unknown, still remain with you — you must not direct to me [at] Aston — it would fall into other hands —
    If you will think of me enclose your letter in a cover [she then deleted these last three words] directed for me in a cover addressed Miss Rawlence, 16 Green St — No, not Green Street, but 6 Caermarthern [sic] Street, Tottenham Court Road, it will be safer there — She will forward it to me — I shall not say who it is from — She will never guess, but would do anything for me — by being directed for her, your Servts will not know of your writing to me — Do not let Fletcher [Byron's valet] have the least hint for Heaven's sake —

Ah, the mysterious Miss Rawlence. Not exactly a go-between, but definitely Lady Frances' receiver and passer-on of illicit postal materials. Who knows what else she did for Lady Frances, or, indeed, for others. I have been quite unable to find out anything about her, except that she seems to have been a servant, based at 6 Carmarthen Street, just off Tottenham Court Road. Presumably she was loanable to Lady Frances on occasion, and perhaps to others. In late November or early December 1813 she seems to have taken a post with a family down in Devon, but it couldn't have been a posting of long duration, as by the beginning of 1814 she was with Thomas Bacon in Hampshire.

Lady Frances continues:

I know I am guilty, very guilty, not only in confessing my attachment but in beging [sic] of you to write to me — I hope you will forgive me and not think me very bad — Let your enclosed letter be well sealed — & directed for me — of course not franked — and let it be so folded that no eyes can penetrate — sealed at the ends — send it by the 2nd Post directed as above — she will then enclose it in a letter to me — If I obtain your picture, it can likewise be sent in the same manner.

Thus ended Page 4. Page 5 opens:

Only remember every thing must be done in a way to <u>prevent suspicion even there</u> — you will receive from her a small seal — it is very ugly — but you wished to have one, & I could not here get a better — no Engraver otherwise it should not take its flight destitute of some device <u>emblematic</u> of my <u>dismal attachment</u>. How I shall envy its visit — receive it — & remember it comes loaded with caresses, which it will deliver safe — will you allow me to have the feelings of my heart engraved upon the seal you gave me 'plus je suis séparé, plus m'attache' [the more I am separated, the more I am attached], or shall I send it to you to express your own — <u>I will</u> — I will enclose it tomorrow — if you object to so doing, return it directed to Miss R — inform me of it, and I will direct her concerning it — Hélas! quand te reverrai-je [Alas! When will I see you again?]

The long, drawn-out closing to the letter now begins:

I really must have tried your patience long ere this — but my heart is so full — and did you not tell me to pour it out to you? Did you not assure me you would forgive my foolish romance? You did — A word more, and I have done — I know there are other more deserving objects of your affection in Town — many who you may fancy love you better because they have yielded [again, definitive proof that she and Byron never consummated their relationship on a physical level] — many who have great influence over you — their jealousy is in all probability excited by your stay here — therefore be on your guard — and as you value me, do not give them the least ground for suspicion — do not drop a hint that there is any thing between us — rather on the contrary abuse me — I must not say I am jealous — for alas! You are nothing to me — tho' every thing that binds me to the world is centered in you — Do not therefore let them sift a word from you — you that might injure the till-then unsullied reputation of her whose heart & every affection, peace & joy — are fled with you — who has sacrificed every hope of happiness — who never knew mis'ry till she saw and loved — and who only now lives to think of and adore one object — and to weep o'er the remembrance of those happy hours we have passed together — but surely, tho' I have sacrificed thus far to Duty — we are not prevented from meeting — No — we shall meet in Town in winter — this thought, tho' distant, brightens for an instant my countenance — but I must not run on at this rate — I must endeavour and conceal the torture of my mind — I must, otherwise 'tis all over — I wear my Mask but badly — but I must mourn in silence, otherwise I shall involve you in what would render me everlastingly miserable and destroy any faint glimmering of hope that might exist — the consequences attending discovery — tho' they could not change my heart — tho' they could not perform what time, distance, force and the world cannot do — yet they would occasion you self-reproach — involve me & my infant in ruin — and render our meeting again impossible — I cannot profess to love him, that I cannot do — I am dead to all but one — my affections are settled — every body else totally indifferent to me — much depends upon your secrecy — I trust to your honour — and implore you not to deceive me — I have laid my heart and soul before you — I have put every thing in your power that would show implicit faith in your generosity — I have liberated you — you cannot me — for I am bound by an Eternal Chain — yet never could or would I survive the scorn of the world, which even the discovery of this letter would bring down upon me — I know I have acted wrong — You say so yourself in one of your notes, 'that you know you ought not to ask me to remember you' — I cannot forget you — never, never — receive this reassurance — you shall not again be troubled with my sorrows — you are free — Be you as happy, My Byron, as I am the contrary — forgive my follies — I cannot call them vices —

My whole heart is yours — is it very unworthy of you? — it is — I know it — but it will never injure you — Farewell — Farewell — May Heaven guard and protect you forever!!

That letter must have taken Byron a long time to read.
On Thursday, October 21, 1813, he wrote to Lady Melbourne:

Either W had taken it into his notable head, or wished to put it into mine, aye, and worse still, into ye girls, also; that I was a pretendant to the hand of the sister of 'the Lady' whom I had nearly — but no matter.... This brilliant notion, besides widening ye breach between him and me, did not add to the harmony of the two females; at least my idol was not pleased with the prospect of any transfer of incense to another altar. She was so unguarded, after telling me too fifty times to 'take care of Catherine,' 'that she could conceal nothing,' etc., etc., as to give me a very unequivocal proof of her own imprudence, in a carriage—(dusk to be sure) before her face—and yet with all this, and much more, she was the most tenacious personage either from fear, or weakness, or delicate health, or G-d knows what, that with the vigilance of no less than three Arguses in addition, it was utterly impossible, save once, to be decisive—and then—tears and tremors and prayers, which I am not yet old enough to find piquant in such cases, prevented me from making her wretched. I do detest everything which is not perfectly mutual, and any subsequent reproaches (as I know by one former long ago bitter experience) would heap coals of fire upon my head ... she had so much more dread of the devil, than gratitude for his kindness; and I am not yet sufficiently in his good graces to indulge my own passions at the certain misery of another. Perhaps after all, I was her dupe—if so—I am the dupe also of the few good feelings I could ever boast of, but here perhaps I am my own dupe too, in attributing to a good motive what may be quite otherwise. W is a most extraordinary person; he has just left me, and a snuff-box with a flaming inscription, after squabbling with me for these last ten days! and I too, have been of some real service to him [the £1000 Byron lent about this time], which I merely mention to mark the inconsistency of human nature. I have brought off a variety of foolish trophies (foolish indeed without victory), such as epistles, and lockets, which look as if she were in earnest; but she would not go off now, nor render going off unnecessary.

On October 22, 1813, Lady Frances wrote to the recently departed poet:

Friday Morng. 3 o'clock—6. After having written a letter to you, the length and contents of which I am ashamed of [sic], after having breathed every feeling of my soul in so unreserved a manner—I blush to find myself again with my pen in my hand, and still dedicating it to you—But I feel a kind of solemn peace when I am writing to you, as if we were not separated—I feel my pen (the only solace of absent friends) renders me independent of all <u>now</u> around me—I feel so ashamed of my scribbling—I do not think I shall give it wing, & yet I will—You must forgive every thing contained in those sheets & preserve in remembrance while perusing them the feelings of agony under which they were written—you must forgive, not despise, me for feelings you are the cause of—they were written under all the anguish of despair—under agony that seemed to rend my soul from its earthly tenement—they were pen'd by a distracted mind madden'd with the heart-sickening word 'Farewell'—ringing the death of peace—these were the circumstances under which they were written—then pardon—but do not despise or betray—I have received your note—Many, many thanks for it—it was a truly welcome visitor—I wish to answer it entirely, but alas! I am in as distracted state [sic] as I was on Monday—My bed has not received me since that day—till 4 in the morning, and then not to sleep, but to sigh & continue my thoughts—For our mutual Int. [i.e. interest], however, I must exist myself—I have shewn the necessity of mercy in my letter, indeed in <u>it</u>, every thing [this last added as a caret] contained in your note is already answered, and yet I will write—it relieves my mind—When you have glanced over the feelings of my mind, you will at once see how cruelly unjust is your doubt of me—Yes, my hand was cold and dead—I had not power to speak—nor <u>did</u> I live—but when I caught the last glimpse of him who possesses my every feeling I cannot describe what I felt, in the agony of my mind—I exclaimed, ''tis done'—'Great God, 'tis done'—'Great God, 'tis over'—Sister [Lady Catherine] attributed it to the recollection of all she had seen me suffer for the week previous—Had you seen me, pale, wan, trembling in the carriage, you would not have dared to doubt my feelings—I did not misconstrue yours—Had you seen me, and that others had not!—you would blame yourself for so unjust a suspicion—Is it not enough to be miserable, to be separated from your own heart—but must you be doubted?—Cannot I, tho' we are distant from each other, make you believe me sincere? 'Why have we parted at all?' and why my Biron [sic] ask that cruel question of me—Do you think it is pleasure to me to resign all earthly happiness and perhaps life? Consider this and do not reproach me—Consider the numerous, insurmountable barriers that separate us—One step of mine would involve us all in misery—guilt—and perhaps death—I cannot look on the consequences of such an act without horror—Forgive me speaking thus plain—I am bound to you by every tie of gratitude for your generous conduct in not urging a point, which for a momentary gratification w'd involve me in guilt & endless remorse, yourself in misery & self-accusation—Could you ever respect, could you ever place the least confidence or feel the least security in a woman who would thus fall?

Ask yourself these questions—not in the heat of the moment—but upon reflection worthy your [sic] mind—answer them—I know, when cool, how you will pronounce, tho' you may not acknowledge it—aware what must be the decision of every sensible mind upon that subject—Can you blame my consenting to sacrifice every hope of happiness and to drag on my remaining few days in misery?—But will you hate me because I fear I never shall call <u>you</u> mine, tho' yours I must ever be, even if separated by half the Globe—Will you not be my friend, and may I not adore my friend?—Yes, I may—You cannot refuse me your friendship—My Byron, I shall not live till I hear from you—for alas! I fear you will put a wrong construction upon what I have said—no, no, 'tis impossible—be kind to me, for I have need of kindness—I am distracted—one unkind word from you would make me—

I shudder at the idea—Do not accuse or despise me—but pity & forgive—forgive me if I have led you into an attachment, the recollection of which may give you a moment's uneasiness—But I have liberated you—and yet I do not know any person on Earth worthy of you—Dare I ask to whom you will turn—has Lady C. La [i.e. Caroline Lamb] any hopes of obtaining you? What presumption to hope these questions will be answered—and yet I could wish, presuming upon your promise of confidence, you would impart all your thoughts you may think me worthy of receiving—they shall be buried in that narrow, now deserted cell, the former inhabitant of which is flown forever—I could wish, notwithstanding all my resolutions, that in some of your hours of pleasure, one thought might be bestowed upon me—yet I do not desire that even, should the reflection afford you pain.

And now, My Byron, I must again say <u>Farewell</u>—that word awakes me to all my misery—I cannot stand it—If you regard my existence, write to me enclosed as I before observed—I will not insist upon it again—but, indeed, I must hear from you once granting my request—Pity me and (if you can) forgive me—If it is possible, assure me you do not quite hate me—Alas! I fear you can not [this last word was added in the form of a caret] forgive all I have said, have done, have written—I feel as a guilty wretch before you, a slave to an attachment I cannot conquer, and labouring under the agony of horror at having offended that beloved object—pardon & if possible forgive a true penitent—Adieu—Remember you have got your life in my hands—I trust you—Again, I repeat my vow I utter but with death—I am firm in <u>every</u> resolution—It is six o'clock and I am still up—6 cruel separation—Oh! My Byron—Forgive, forget, be happy—Think of <u>me</u>, but as one dead to every joy, to every person—Forgive my follies—& remember 'tis Duty that separates us—Duty, an insurmountable barrier—Make another happy—I will not complain—You shall not hear a word from me after this—Not one complaint—Farewell, Farewell.

She picks this letter up again a couple of hours later on "Fryday [sic] Morng. 8 o'clock," with the following post script: "I have been in bed, but could not sleep, and rise again to implore your forgiveness for all I have written—I am ashamed to read it. However, it shall go [i.e. in the mail]—You shall receive the involuntary effusions of my heart—if not acceptable—<u>brulez</u> [i.e. burn the letter]—a merited fate—not a line more."

Another, undated, "liberation" letter belongs to this time period:

Great God! What I shall suffer till I hear from you, my Byron, I cannot attempt to describe—The agony I endure while writing the dictates of duty is only known, is only felt by myself—Thank Heaven you do not know the full extent of my feelings—Many, many are the bitter pangs & struggles it costs me to pronounce your freedom—would to God I could fly to you with open arms and say receive & keep me forever—Be still—quiet this momentary transport—I must not hope—You cannot doubt my feelings—I should wrong you to suspect it—If you do, no words now can, but time must prove my sincerity—Give me your picture—I must have it—Let that favor being confer'd confirm me in the hope that you are not offended with me—I can stand any thing but your reproaches—Would to God I might cling to hope—I will—Oh! No, no, I must not—I have liberated you—I have liberated the being to whom I have united my soul—but I will watch in silent adoration <u>Him</u> to whom I have given 'that all which <u>tyranny</u> can ne'er enthrall' [again, a quote from Byron's *Giaour*]—

I do remember my vows—yours will I live & yours die—I again repeat them—You cannot release me from them—you cannot—I am bound to you by bonds which nothing can destroy—by every tie of gratitude for not urging a step that would have destroyed me [she means the physical consummation of their affair at Aston Hall and Newstead]—To you I owe my life and to you it shall be dedicated—even when I behold you happy with some then blest mortal I shall hold myself bound to my vows—I shall hold myself sacred to him for whom I now pine in silence and for whom I have given up and risked every thing—but I will not utter a word of complaint—I will be silent and calm—yes—I will be calm—Oh! My poor heart—I am dead to the world—I am dead to all but <u>one</u>—I will live in a cage, the key of which shall be attached to my <u>heart</u> and you know too well where that is—You never shall be jealous, for I will not look on another till we meet—we shall meet—persuade him [i.e. Bold Webster] to come to Town.

The speed of her transition in this last sentence from hopeless and self-indulgent sentiment to hard-hitting, gritty realistic scheming and take-charge attitude might reveal something very definitive about Lady Frances—that is, if her writing was not interrupted by even a short time span, and it's hard to say if it was or wasn't. If it wasn't, then we're either looking at someone with remarkable survival skills, or a fashionably insincere woman. One likes to suppose it is the former.

In any event, her letter continues in this harder mode:

Today's post brought me a letter from him, full of the most extravagant, fulsome language—my heart sickened—for I held at the time in my hand what is now pressed with my lips and bathed with my tears—it was full of cautions relative to you—he is suspicious and yet he is not—you must have seen thro' all that part at N[ewstead]—all occasioned by my melancholy—He said it would make you <u>fancy</u> I had no affection for him. My answer always the same—'It will <u>never</u> make him <u>fancy</u> such a thing'—Little does he know the state of my mind—nor must he—

My Byron, can you pardon this scrawl—these terrible but involuntary effusions of a soul wrapt up in you—I will not insult you by again urging secrecy—it would imply a doubt of your honor—upon which I have the greatest reliance—Otherwise I should not have committed myself in a manner I think to acknowledge—[she now proceeds, and it almost a joke to behold, to hammer him with the need for secrecy] do not be careless about this letter—indeed, I should like it to be burnt for fear of discovery—you might leave it about and, Great God—fatal would be the consequences—for I have determined never to outlive the publication of my shame—which can only take place thro' carelessness of leaving [this last word careted] writing about, therefore, if you regard me, be cautious—above all, beware of servts [servants]—.

In another letter to Lady Melbourne, written on October 25, 1813, Byron encloses one of Lady Frances's letters, saying, "I did (and it is no trifle) sacrifice the selfish consideration to spare her self reproach." One can tell that the poet is guilty about forwarding Lady Frances's letters to Lady Melbourne for inspection, but he sends this one anyway. It was not the only time he did this. It was a regular occurrence. He goes on to say, "if she is serious so am I—and as willing as ever to go through with the business ... my little white penitent appears rather more bewildered & uses two words—'effusions' and 'soul' rather oftener than befits out of the circulating library.... She mentions C [Lady Caroline Lamb]—but not one word of you—a proof at least—that she knows nothing of my extreme reliance & confidence in you.... I want your judgment about her—I cant be impartial."

On October 28, 1813 Lady Frances wrote to Byron:

Saturday. This morng again gladdened me—revived my drooping spirits—with the sight of your hand writing—A thousand times I prest to my heart those dear characters I now gaze on, traced by all I love. We expected—to day—thank God my mind was relieved from that idea by the receipt of a letter by to day's post—signifying his [i.e. James's; she cannot bring herself to say his name] intention of returning Monday next—it is couched in terms of great dissatisfaction at the receipt of my cold letter on Thursday morng, when he lived upon the hope of being assured of the continuance of what never existed—he beged [sic] of me to write again—I have, but no vows, no protestations of love—I avoided the point, by obscuring in terms of hauteur that I must beg no more of those questions to be put to me, as I had ever acted under the guidance of Duty and Principles in which I should ever continue, that I would rather sacrifice my life than deviate from the paths of Honor & Virtue—

> My letter, couched in these terms, has destroyed all suspicion, and at the same time left my sincerity unimpeached, as I only spoke sentiments you know to be true — Did you really see that paragraph the first thing? Would to God the names were united — It seems ominous, but I must not hope —
>
> Guilt must be the <u>errant courier</u> — and that I will never know — He will not, I know, be suspicious, yet remember, tho' it does not come to an open rupture between us, that I am not <u>his</u> — but <u>yours</u> — Remember that the world cannot alienate <u>me</u> from <u>you</u> — that no invention, art, or ingenuity, can estrange a particle of my feelings from you — <u>Remember this</u> — & only when <u>I change</u> do <u>you betray</u> — My Byron — he talks of going immediately to Scotland — Great God — what a distance would separate us — How many hundred miles will divide me from you — and yet I shall be present for I shall think of only you — not one other thought can <u>ever</u> separate my heart and soul from you — It is not absence, it is not time, nor change of scene, not even the <u>estrangement</u> of the beloved object itself — that can quench my affection — for it is a sacred flame, to which Death alone can be the extinguisher — Are you not tired of my vows? Indeed you are — But I will have done — Hasten, for Heavens sake, your picture, that I may receive it before we go — a thousand thousand thanks for the kind promise — I almost feared you would refuse — but stop — you have not received my letter wherein I mention the only terms upon which I will accept it — You have not received that letter, therefore I must still hope and fear — Grant you may not refuse — Cruel fate! How bitter to be obliged to rest all one's hopes of pleasure on the contemplation only of the picture of the beloved object, because the world and duty separate us — My Byron, I could ask you to write to me, but I will not, for we must not continue a clandestine correspondence long — but I will ask you to sometimes bestow a thought on me — Could you see me, could you behold the sorrow of my mind too visibly imprinted on my face, you would pity, you would forgive — You might even respect the mind that sacrifices every pleasure and gratification to the Law of God and preservation of others — Will you have the seal done for me and send it to Miss R [Miss Rawlence]? Every thing will be safe there, but I shall not [this last word careted] name what it is — No — We must be secret — Assure me of that — You are free — I am a wretched slave, bound by every tie of love, adoration, gratitude & respect — resolved to endure misery — since the only thing that could render life happy is unattainable — Adieu, mio caro — My heart bleeds — .

Bold Webster also wrote to Byron that very day, from "Aston Hall, Oct 28. 13":

> My Dear Byron, I intended to have written to you before braving ye <u>diligent inspection</u> I am persuaded private men's letters generally meet with, but I live in ye hope of seeing you so soon as <u>Wednesday</u> next that my only present difficulty is to excuse ye infliction of this scrawl upon you — I found ye Ladies F & C both vey [very] very well on ye point of despatching a courier to send me — They beg to be most kindly commended to y'r Lordship — To my comfort & surprise I found [George] Agar had not gone to Beverly as He intended — ye lovely Lady C. comes up with me & perhaps Lady Frances may be induced to pay her friend Lady Wedderburn [Margaret, wife of Sir David Wedderburn of Ballindean] a visit — I have lamented our separation daily — absence alone gives us a true estimation of what we value —
>
> As Ormond said He w'd not exchange his Dead Son Ossory for ye best living son in Europe neither w'd I exchange you absent for ye best present friend in Christendom [James here refers to the Cavalier James Butler, 1st Duke of Ormonde, and his son, Lord Ossory] —
>
> I hear of gr't changes when Parliam't meet — That hateful man of <u>Leather</u> has a demand enough on our friends to make a Patriot turn pale — poor England! — I despair unless we may have a Prince with capacity enough to read & sense enough to reflect on ye Roman history?

This reference to the "man of leather" is probably to Sir Nicholas Vansittart, Chancellor of the Exchequer, whose budget that year was shocking. The word budget comes from the French "bougette," meaning a leather wallet.

> Have you sent ye box to Gray — pray do — Have you seen ye Earl since? or has ye Countess's plurality of toasts scared you away?

The 2nd Earl Grey, the future prime minister and the man for whom the tea was named, was then leader of the opposition Whigs. Incidentally, the term "opposition" was to be coined by Hobhouse in 1826, during a speech in the House of Commons. Grey's countess was Mary Elizabeth Ponsonby, second cousin to Lady Caroline Lamb.

To render it <u>palatable</u>—try an episode of sage & brandy next time—I hope to see you gay & happy on Wednesday—cease to be a living proof that even in 'laughter ye heart is sorrowfull.'

If ye <u>Blue</u> or <u>Black</u> or <u>Green</u> Devils pursue you—ye '<u>Medicina Gymnastica</u>' on one so fond of (or used to be) will carry them off—

I have now tired you, My Dear Byron & exposed myself long enough—Tho' I am <u>bitter</u> bad in making <u>fine</u> speeches, I will only say of y'r extreme kindness to me 'manet et manebit alta mente repostum' [an improvised quote from Vergil's *Aeneid*, roughly translated as 'he remains and will remain deep within my mind']—

By ye bye—pray have this line engraved after ye last I wrote ye box—Poor <u>Gay</u>—! never exceeded 3 pages—<u>I</u>, who am ye Gay-est of all <u>Dull</u> things have ruined by writing 4!—[John Gay wrote *The Beggar's Opera* in 1728]

Write to me by Return of Post & so kindly furnish me with an excuse for writing to you—

It w'd be pushing ye joke m'ch too far to torture you thus—& thus—<u>often</u>

<u>Vale</u> et me ama, JW.

Another one, undated, from Lady Frances to the poet:

Business will, I believe, take <u>him</u> [James] up to Town next week with C, therefore be very cautious about every thing—my letters in particular—Do not say I sent you my seal to get cut for me, as they think it is gone elsewhere, but contrive to send it before Monday next to Miss Rawlence, 6 Caermarthen Street.

The picture, even if ready, do not send there till he is returned to Aston—You know not how grateful I feel for it—My feelings I cannot express—I must not—Oh! My Byron, My Byron! When shall I see you again? Shall I receive a letter from you? Shall I receive in it a confirmation of what I wish—that you have pardoned—have forgiven—the wretch—and will not hate her? But write your feelings uninfluenced by any fear of my compliments or reproaches—Is it true you think of going abroad? There you will forget me, indeed. I deserve it—I must say one thing—I will never stand your marriage with <u>near relations</u> of mine [she means her sister, Catherine]. <u>Remember</u> that—this arises from a hint that has been thrown out on the subject.

If you go abroad—how shall I contrive, even if you could allow me, to write or hear from you? My picture—my picture—I will talk to it—Cannot I? Yes.—I will talk to it and I shall fancy I see that benignant countenance smile upon me—unhappy! I long for Wednesday—perhaps on that day I shall hear from you—My heart trembles between hope & fear—the contents—if they are not kind—will make me—But not a word of complaint—Adieu—Adieu—he comes—Great God! I tremble still with the thoughts of discovery—It cannot be—I am yours—ever yours—for <u>ever</u> and <u>ever</u>—tho' the world separate us—Farewell! Farewell.

Again, an undated letter from Lady Frances to "The Lord Byron":

I write a line in great haste to day they do not leave this [place] till Saturday, therefore in case (tho' I have little room for hope) you might be tempted to think of me, do not let it be till Friday—when, if you write—I shall receive it on Sunday—I have been reading over your letter—I will not tell you how I behaved—Thank God! You cannot see me—Cruel! Cruel Biron—yet not a word of complaint will I utter—not a murmur in tone of reproach—Remember all I have said—Farewell—Wednesday.

A final undated one, from Lady Frances to Byron:

I am totally at a loss how to answer your letter, as I find all my efforts are ineffectual to convince you of the force and the truth of my feelings towards you—however as perhaps this is the last opportunity I shall have of addressing you without fear of discovery I shall endeavour to refute a few of your accusations as cruel as unjust, tho' your too-evident disbelief of all I say renders all of my exertions useless, towards impressing your mind with the firmness of my attachment, and assuring you that I am not the unprincipled Being which it is too-plain you imagine me to be— you fancy you can tell how all this will end—but surely you cannot have so despicable an opinion of me as really to mean what you have written!

I asked you to forget me, feeling unworthy of your remembrance, but oh! how will the reflection of being the subject of <u>one</u> of your thoughts gladden my heart—to fancy that while I am meditating upon the Image of all I love you may be bestowing a Thought upon her who is not vain enough to suppose you love her—is more than I dared expect—

We shall go to Scotland in about ten days — if it is possible let me have your picture by that time — I will not notice the cruel remark upon that subject in your note — nor descend to further explanation or vindication — I know not how long we shall remain there, but we are to be in Town [i.e. London] in the spring, till which time all before me is vacuum — I shall then see you? to that hope I cling, which perhaps may never be realised — .

She continues:

They are gone to Town today, at least left me — but will not arrive till Sunday — You will see him on Monday, perhaps before you receive this you may have seen him — as you value my life — as you regard me (and so I have reason to believe from a solitary expression in your Letter) Oh! My Byron! by every tie that unites me to you, be cautious, do not drop an expression that might tend to my undoing — he has not the slightest suspicion — nor is he the least jealous — therefore be prudent — reflect upon the consequences the contrary would produce — reflect upon my innocent smiling prattler [her young daughter, Lucy] — and be guided by your own feelings — We have had many & various conversations since that cruel separation at — — — [Newstead] and from what passed have strong reasons to believe our suspicions with regard to — — — [her sister Catherine] having played an intermeddling part are unjust — I was determined to be convinced — and am fully persuaded he did not influence the other's mind — In all our Dialogues Ar [Arthur, her brother] has reproached the other [Catherine] for every illiberal remark — both unanimous in their praise of you — And do you think I abused you or not? Oh! how my heart thanked them — — You will see — she went up with him to day — you wonder at my horror, at my fear of your marriage with my near relations — I feel I must ever love you — love is a poor word to convey what I feel — that love would be doubly criminal [i.e., the love between Byron and Lady Catherine] if its object was bound to another — and her a relation — I never could support the idea of injuring her in thought even — & I could not command my feelings — I could not sink them into cold Friendship as you mention — Alas! that is impossible — the frequency of Intercourse, the distracting thought of seeing you in the Arms of another — would make me burst the Barriers of Prudence — I fear it is any body — and yet you will marry — but a stranger I should not see — I should not have my wounded heart daily probed — Oh! Cruel Fate! What an insurmountable barrier separates us — it cannot be burst for Ignominy and Death stand at the other side — You do not know how deeply the steps I have already taken and fear of discovery prey upon my mind — so much so that I am quite altered — they perceive it, & plague me to death thinking I am in a consumption — — Miss R [Rawlence] comes to me on Sunday next, but you may still continue to enclose to her; all will be forwarded — He will not leave Town till Wednesday next, therefore may I beg one moment to be devoted to me before that time — do not write harshly to me — tell me you will not forget her whose existence is wrapt up in you — tell me you will not betray me, but if you find another more worthy of your affection — assure me you will not require me to yield up what I may possess — but that you will destroy all my writing — I will not complain — assure me of all that — give me your picture and you shall not hear from me again, you shall not be again molested — Adieu! Adieu! Remember me! Adieu till tomorrow —
    Friday night

She continued the letter the next morning:

Saturday morng — I have not been able to banish from my mind the terrifying opinion you entertain of me — I cannot remember one word ever drop'd that could give you the least ground for imagining me so depraved as to suppose I should ever fall a victim to any body — Have I not given you proofs — sufficient to convince any person — that my Resolutions are not to be shaken — then — when I assure you in 'no common terms' — of my indelible attachment — Do you judge me by yourself when you pronounce so hastily that 'I shall be ensnared by another'? I have already said too much —
    The idea of seeing me ruined by another possessing your mind distracts me — No! as long as I live I will stand before the world arrayed in the appearance of all my former virtue — yourself, the only person having the power to tarnish my name — You need not tell me not to destroy your letters — they are my constant companions — but I think the sentence in which you unite them with blood is rather ambiguous — no discovery can take place but thro' your own imprudence — and if any other idea enters your Head — apprise me of it — that you may receive the blot of my blood first instead of from circumstances which I do not regret — my affections became yours — and yours will they ever remain — my 'will' would have no effect upon subduing my attachment, was

I to exert it — 'Circumstances' shall not — & 'Time' cannot — 'When I form another attachment' — 'When I love another' —! Great God! Am I then fallen so low that the suspicion even should enter your mind — Do you imagine me so lost — You do not mean what you say — My fall is impossible — the sun must change its course first — never can that hour arrive to which you allude — I know not what to say, your suspicions distract me — 'I think my attachment to you is permanent' — and you shall know it — 'I am sensible my heart cannot exist without an object' — It <u>has</u> a beloved object — an object too tenderly and too dearly loved — and what can it desire more? Your 'will' cannot drive me from you — you may be cruel & unjust but nothing will alter my attachment —

These are not mere expressions — but deep rooted feelings & listen My Byron — may the vengeance & bitterest curses of Heaven fall upon me if ever I transfer one grain of my affections to another — if ever one day passes in which my thoughts are not yours —

You have acted generously, for which you have secured my gratitude — you cannot act otherwise — but do not be unjust — Do not treat me coolly or unjustly — do not let the horrible idea of seeing me another's again enter your mind — If I did not follow my heart shall I go without it —

You have desired me to deal candidly with you — I have — I must claim the same from you — and beg to be informed if ever you mean to betray my attachment — My Resolutions on that event are taken — for you have never given me one assurance of the secret remaining buried in your Breast forever —.

On October 29, 1813, Lady Frances wrote the famous "despairing letter" to Byron, who had been so enmeshed in *The Bride of Abydos* that he had neglected to reply to her letters as promptly as she required. This letter was also shown at the Byron Exhibition in 1974, and is one of the few Lady Frances letters ever to have come to light before now. It reads:

Great God, have I forfeited all claim to your regard even? I have — I must be forgotten — Three days have I anxiously, madly waited the arrival of the Post — but, alas! Three times have I been miserably disappointed — What can it mean? What will be the result of this deliberation? Oh! My Byron — I am dead between hope & fear — What can I imagine when I said when I candidly confessed how much depended upon my hearing from you, what can I imagine from your silence? That you have thrown me off — That you will betray me — No, it cannot be — I will banish the unjust, the illiberal, idea — But why have I not heard from you? I fear you are offended with me — I fear you hate me for opening my whole heart before you and pity me for the discovery you there made — <u>There</u> you discovered feelings that time or distance can never blunt — I have, you perceived, an attachment the endeavours of the world cannot change, an affection the art of man cannot cool or subdue — You saw there also the struggles between love & duty — You saw passion subdued by the voice of Reason — You saw happiness sacrificed to conscience — Beholding all these feelings — if you hate & despise, I will submit in silence.

But learn — You cannot change, you cannot alter me, you cannot absolve me from my vows, which I shall forever cherish, and which I renew daily — The more I think, the more I am distracted, at your silence.

I summon up all my courage but cannot chace [sic] fear from my mind — I will wait till tomorrow — if <u>it</u> brings disappointment also — I know not what I shall do — The person to whom I beged [sic] of you to enclose [i.e., Miss Rawlence] is coming down here to day till we go to Scotland — she will most likely leave Town the day after you receive this but you may still continue to enclose to me as I before directed you — they will be forwarded. But I must not write — I <u>will</u> not after I get your picture — It is wrong, very wrong, and makes me look guilty — Am I guilty? Be my friend and answer me — Consider me as your sister — Do not fear offending me — Write to me on that subject with sincerity & I will be as quiet as a Lamb — Advise me as you would if your sister flew to you under the same circumstances — condescend to give me advice and I will follow it whatever it may cost me — I will obey all you say, but do not tell me to forget or love you less — I cannot follow that — If you will give me your picture, How I will treasure it, May I call it my brother — It <u>shall</u> be my companion — However, do not forget how much depends upon secrecy — not only my life, but the happiness of my whole family — Do not forget how much mis'ry the publication of my shame would bring down upon innocent Heads! If you have any regard for me let that guide your Acts — and, Oh! beware of my letters — be careful! for if once seen, I [and here a word has been crossed out, and replaced with "am"] lost — for ever lost — I am undone for ever — They can be of no use, therefore destroy them — if not, assign your reasons — I cannot understand why you should keep them — why keep writings that will involve me in disgrace and ruin — I am lost in despair — I am bewildered and perplexed — My Mind is torn and distracted — My Heart and every tender feeling yours— pity me. Do not destroy the wretch yourself has made — Adieu, My Byron! Be happy and forget me — Farewell! Forget that I am miserable — Forget and betray not — Oct. 29th.

That same Friday, October 29, 1813, Bold Webster was writing his own letter to "Rt. Hon. Lord Byron, 4 Bennet St, St James, London," which he sent from Rotherham on the following Monday. It reads:

> My Dear Byron, on my way from Scotland to ye Continent I am hardly enabled to see you — tho' I very much wish it —
> I have parted with Rushton — having no use for him — his father is dead — & I really think it a pity — ye poor fellow has no better prospects than a return to ye farm promises—
> No one can want less stimulus to serve another than yourself & I hope you can do something for him.
> Pray let me have a line from you — & wishing you every happiness, I am ever y'r sincere & obliged f'nd [friend or fiend, it's hard to say], J. Wedderburn Webster. Fryday.

Rushton, and after all that fuss! This case is a perfect example of one of Bold Webster's less admirable facets— or simply, one of his facets, as they were mostly far from admirable. After all the energy expended on Rushton, Webster keeps him a couple of months then lets him go. Furthermore, he would soon take him on again!

Another short letter from Lady Frances from this period:

> 'Tis <u>when only</u> I ask you to remember her whose first sin originated in you — who you have deceived — But how dare <u>I</u> accuse — Have I not <u>deserved</u> it?— Have I not brought it upon myself? I bow in silence — He [James] leaves this [place] on Thursday next — He will see you, and I— miserable Being — shall remain in all the agony of fear, despair — and destruction —
> Forgive me, My Byron — and believe me, you have yet to learn the character of the woman who is not dead to virtue, and who (if not betrayed) will endeavour to atone for her follies— Adieu — You shall not hear — You shall not receive a line from me — You know what I wish and expect — I shall not repeat — I do not ask you to <u>think</u> of me even — but will it be any pleasure to you to be denied to read-over my letter — & to be assured that I <u>now</u> feel all & more than is there expressed? Alas! I cannot help it — Remember all I have written, & in pity consent to accord my request — or grant me some tie — even your word (which you have never yet done) that I am secure — I shall not encroach — believe me — for I am humbled — I am not what I was—<u>once</u>— I was gay and innocent—<u>Now</u> what am I? Oh! I will not say — But am <u>I</u> guilty? Oh! no— Farewell — Who has made me what I am? Who has rob'd me of health, peace & joy? He who I now petition not to expose me to the ridicule of the world, and who forces me to say farewell! forever, My Biron, farewell & oh! Remember me!

We have a letter from Lady Frances to Byron, dated "Monday," which must really be November 1, 1813:

> He is come —came last night — My heart sunk within me — he looks at me but not a word of reproach — he does not, I'm sure, suspect me — I hope I do not look guilty, therefore trust I shall avoid detection —
> Great God! From what a height I should fall did the world but know what has passed — Into what an abyss of misery should I be plunged by discovery — It should end in destruction — But it cannot be! No person can ruin my name but yourself— no person can involve me in ruin but him I now address— him for whom I am [sic] sacrificed every thing — and destroyed my peace of mind — and surely he will not betray me? Oh! No! he cannot — he will not — the secret remains buried in my bosom & never can be torn from it — I will brood over it for ever — but it is unknown and even unsuspected by every body — it is therefore in our power to conceal it — Do not plunge me so low — Do not make me destroy myself — Do not, Oh! Do not make me so bad to the world — that the humblest person — if innocent — may look upon me with pity — I shall not say a word more, Feeling secure in your principles of Honor — My Byron — he really is going to Scotland — Oh! How my heart sinks within me — Assure me that you have forgiven me, that you will not hate but sometimes think of me — Assure me of that & every thing else — & it will be my comfort in my days of solitude — among people not one of whom I care for — to gaze on the too pleasing assurance —

Last — Do not treat this warning with neglect — <u>I am firm in my resolutions of whatever nature</u>—

I do fear for you — for I fear for myself — I act not for my peace in this world but the next — I act — to be enabled a short time longer to indulge the remembrance of those happy hours I have spent in the society of him most dear who possesses my every thought & every feeling — In whom I feel a kind of sacred attachment & love that words cannot describe — I would not part with it for the mines of Peru — —

Act for my sake, and do not give me reason to repent the unlimited confidence placed in you — for believe me, tho' unfortunate, I never can act criminally — not even discovery would make me err in <u>deed</u> — Adieu! My Byron! Be you happy — I never can — — Hasten your picture — Adieu! Adieu!

Her letters to Byron went unanswered, so she wrote another [from sometime in Nov. 1813]:

It is as I expected — and I blush while I write — it is as I have deserved — Disappointments have succeeded each other with rapidity — All hope is fled, & I am content — I am satisfied — but I cannot banish the remembrance of those happy days I have passed in your society, when I have sate [i.e. sat] for hours lost in pleasing reflections, when I have watch'd — but no more, all is fled.

Perhaps you have even shown my letters, & oh! distracting thought, talked of me in a manner I tremble to think of — If you have, be candid, pronounce my doom at once — drive me into the arms of destruction, into the Gulph I wish to avoid — My Byron, if my suspicions are unjust, forgive me — and with sincerity allow I have ample room to exercise my torturing apprehensions— not a single line — not a solitary assurance that the secret shall remain buried in your own bosom —

Distracted with the fear of discovery, my mind torn with the dreadful idea of appearing before the world an object of contempt — and worn by these torturing fears— Can you be surprised at my suspicions, when I have not one tie upon which to form my grounds of security?

But it is impossible, it is a vague idea to imagine a man would behave in such a dishonorable manner — You have acted your part, and glad I am to have seen it so soon — I must implore you to return me my foolish letters wherein I poured out my whole heart before you — and would I could say those feelings discovered there were changed or capable of being changed — However I will not [this word was careted] complain — I will not give you so much room for triumph as to tell what I have suffered and what I now endure — I entreat you to return me my writings enclosed in a parcel.

It must be, for I can no longer endure the agony of uncertainty — better to know one's doom than to be under constant apprehension —

I am distracted, driven to desperation — he [James] is going to Town on Thursday, and perhaps may see some of my writing upon your Table, perhaps the first word that assails his Ear will be his wife's <u>folly</u> magnified into <u>Guilt</u>. Be it so, and I will bear it, I will even smile upon my destroyer — I will shield him from blame — I ever must —

Forgive the confession, My Byron — it forced its way — I wish to think you generous and honourable — I wish to think you devoid of treachery — and that you have not deceived me — <u>Let</u> me think so — and tho' I know your professions were only the effusions of a momentary warmth, yet you have nothing to fear from them. In mercy, then, be generous to me — I will not harm or molest you — You shall not hear of or from me again — but be sincere and warn me of the line of conduct you mean to pursue, that I may be prepared to meet the blow — 'Tis all I ask — and surely you cannot be so hard as to refuse this one request? Byron! Byron! You know not what you have to answer for — You cannot release <u>me</u> from my vows, for they are fast rooted, & never can they be torn up — You <u>may</u> hear of me, but <u>never from</u> me.

Remember your own lines [from *The Corsair*] — <u>I</u> now apply them —
Remember me — Oh! never pass my Grave
Without the <u>thought</u> whose relics there recline
The only pang <u>my bosom</u> dare not brave
Must be to find forgetfulness in thine

Byron's original lines were:

    Remember me — Oh! never pass my grave
    Without one thought whose relics there recline
    The only pang my bosom dare not brave
    Must be to find forgetfulness in thine

She was very close, and almost certainly did it from memory.

As has been seen already, James Webster's match-making efforts between Byron and Lady Catherine Annesley, although not seriously countenanced by Byron, had thrown her sister, Lady Frances, into a panic. That panic got worse, for she would soon write in a state of distraction to Byron, in early November:

> For God's sake, do not forget me — Never shall I forget you — never while I have the power of recollection — Forget me not — Forgive me, and remember <u>all</u> I have said, which I need not repeat — I wish the earth would open & receive me — I am dead to all but — Would I had seized the opportunity, but 'tis past — forgive me and pity me — I am yours— yours for evermore — believe me, you know me not yet — you do not know what I would go thro' for you — Oh, I feel I am going very fast. I shall not long endure the misery I feel. When you hear my fate, if you have forgotten me, at least drop the Tear of Pity for her who, Great God! save me —
>
> Remember! Never will I look upon another, never will any feeling warm my heart, till we meet again, but the fatal remembrance of hours that are passed, but which will be ever present to my mind — I feel half deranged, I have not closed my eyes since I came here, I feel I cannot endure the separation — you do not think so, but some day you will know it, some day you will know her heart who now writes, some day you will hear what she has suffered for you — Do not quite abandon me, <u>I am yours</u>— In mercy spare me — remember <u>my</u> vows, & <u>yours</u>— I am ill — What are you going to say to Catherine? —<u>Take care</u>— Do you know what? I am <u>desperate</u>, <u>very desperate</u>—
>
> Tomorrow — would tomorrow never was to come — O God! Support me under a trial I never before experienced — I fear I have already betrayed my feelings in part — tomorrow will accomplish, & yet I feel I shall be calm, a settled melancholy forever —<u>Remember my vows</u>— My heart is breaking, is bursting, and yet I will be calm, be very calm — Will you not say a word? Will you not write a line? Or will you say, 'Peace, wretch'? Do you throw me from you forever? Oh! horrible. Oh! distracting, torturing idea — Give me one kind word, one kind look — Your looks have shaken my head — Do not betray me — pity — save — and do not quite forget me — You must not write to me — Give me some slight proof that you do not quite hate me, and I will write to <u>you</u>— but be silent as the <u>Grave</u>— that word <u>brightens</u> my <u>thoughts</u>— In it all <u>sorrows</u> are <u>forgotten</u>—& <u>mine</u> will soon — Your <u>pledge</u> is worn <u>next</u> my heart, & never will be torn away — May Heaven preserve you.
>
> You just ask me, 'Can I change'? I again swear — never — may every misfortune await me the day I deviate from my vow — let this be registered in Heaven with my others— believe me — Give me one kind look — If ever you hear of my speaking to another person, thinking of another, pray that I may be annihilated [she had trouble spelling this word]— destroy me with your own hands— I should like to be destroyed by you — How sweet would be the blow — Adieu! I cannot say it — I shall betray myself, & then — Oh! bitter consequences fall upon me — I must away — Can you remember me, & not with honor? [she alternates in her spelling of 'honor,' as everyone did at that period of time when the 'u' was being added]. I think our separation will not cost you a great deal, will it? be generous, be kind — I have need of it — I am <u>ever</u> [underlined 3 times] and <u>eternally</u> [underlined 3 times] yours— Heaven guard you — Will you betray me? I have committed myself to you — to prove how fully I trust in you — I am not cold, my heart is not cold, my affection for you is pure but not guilty — Do not forsake me — If you do — but no threats — be silent — I will — .

Almost certainly from mid–November 1813, from Lady Frances at Aston Hall:

> Tuesday — you have ere this received two letters from me acknowledging receipt of your enclosed as I directed — I have now to thank you for one of the 5 just directed straight here — surely you could not imagine my suspicions as to the cause of your silence very unnatural, when for a whole week I did not receive an answer to one of my daily repeated letters—
>
> Dearest Byron!— Tho' that letter was <u>cold</u> & <u>explanatory</u>, one kind word contained in it and which I believe to be sincere, thrill'd to my heart — and made me feel pleasure foreign to my Mind — Are you really unchanged and unchangeably mine? The idea is too flattering — I will wear the dear assurance next my heart — & if delusion — why, I will still cherish the deception — and part with it never — My Byron, I will not write again since you think there is danger; even this — I will endeavour to form to yr wishes— it shall be very short — you <u>have</u> promised me your picture — do not retract so kind a favor — Miss R. [Rawlence] is here — but any thing sent there will be forwarded — I know I am bound to you by every tie of gratitude for your conduct to me —

but, alas! I am not worthy of the least portion of your regard — and perhaps you do not now care for my every other feeling which you possess, whether or not you never can affect what time, distance and Life will fail in, you never can estrange my heart from yours — Forgive me, I know not what I write. I am distracted and must not <u>hope</u>— My Byron — My Byron — sometimes think of me — I am unworthy — but still am yours — thro' life — of that you ought to be fully convinced by my former letters— Addio!— addio! I will not write again ——.

This next letter was written on or around November 14, 1813, by Lady Frances to Byron at Bennet Street, just before she was to go to Scotland:

Most truly gratifying & consoling to my feelings were the many kind expressions contained in your <u>last</u>, which I received yesterday morng.— Can there be a more transporting reward for all the sufferings affection must indulge when separated with scarce a hope of reunion — from the object of its choice — to find that dearly loved object — not as before, doubting, but sensible of the never-to-be-shaken constancy of her who lives but to love?

Indeed, My Byron, not <u>months</u>, but <u>years</u> will prove me as the magnet true, and you do me but justice to believe how dearly, how tenderly, I love you. I have put the most implicit confidence in you, and, believe me, not a doubt exists in my mind now as to my security — if ever your mind hesitates for an inst. upon my faith & constancy, and over my last letter, which cannot fail to reassure you, che sono a te quel che sei a me — fida e tenera [that I am to you what you are to me — faithful and tender].

The person to whom you enclosed your letter being here it was consequently forwarded and many were the looks of enquiry cast upon delivery — not a word, however, was said on either side — but, alas! you must no more enclose to her for she is going again into a situation with a family I believe in Devon [this was Miss Rawlence, her go-between] — mia vita, can I really not have your picture? Is it possible it can be finished [she means their relationship]? We go on the 23rd — Tuesday week — and still bitter will the journey be to me if I go unaccompanied by the image of all I love — if I could have it — but you will gratify my ardent wish, if you can, will you not?

If you thought it would not appear suspicious to your servts you might send it straight here, <u>well done up</u>, and directed for Miss R — it would come quite safe — I am sorry you have not sent the seal [She had given Byron her seal in exchange for a ring he had give her] — <u>he</u> [James] inquired for it yesterday — I said it was in town — questions arose — I framed answers — declared a lady had got it — and so it passed off — Pray send it <u>uncut</u>, or just as it is, directed for Miss—, but for l'amour de Dieu disguise your hand writing in direction [address] — you know not [this last word was careted] how the fear of discovery, tho' perhaps distant, alarms me — it disturbs my peace day & night — now you are going down to Middleton — pray be careful about my letters — After we leave this [place] I shall have no <u>Bags</u> to conceal my letters — I <u>must</u> not write — I <u>cannot</u> hear from you — and I am going —

My Byron, sometimes think of me with tender remembrance of those happy moments I have spent in your society — mio caro, si puo credere che m'amate teneramente [My dear, if you can believe that you love me tenderly] — You know not how I am bound to you by every tie — how eternally I am yours— Ah! Byron, consider how much depends upon your prudence and secrecy — Do not talk of going abroad — I cannot stand it — & yet, as you justly observe, if we must be separated (torturing, distracting idea) the distance matters not — We shall meet ere long, for <u>he</u> [she can never bring herself to say her husband's name — he is so odious, and will become much more so as time goes by] talks with the greatest regard of you, more than of any other person he knows — does that not prove the blindness of human nature & how easily mankind is deceived? May he always be deceived — and I — Great God! am the base instrument of deception, but in this instance, tho,' concealment is not a crime, for it preserves the peace and happiness <u>d'un marito</u> [of a husband] — the contrary would involve all in misery & woe —

I fear this is the last time you can hear from me — my writing becomes dangerous — I am so surrounded, even at this very inst.— Sometimes think of me — and feel happy in the conviction that I must ever remain constant and firmly attached to the object of my tenderest affections.

We really go on the day I mention [as it happens, they didn't — the date of the departure for Scotland would be postponed yet again]. Any parcel well <u>disguised</u> will arrive safe, directed as before. In it you can safely write — Farewell, My Byron — Never doubt the tender attachment of her who with sincerity is untill death, your affectionate & only yours.

Cannot I hear from you once more (tho' for the last) before I go? Your last letter, containing the transporting assurance of your affection, I have read over a thousand times with wild pleasure — every word spoke to my heart — to it I have pressed the dear characters and lost in meditation my thoughts have wandered, but far beyond whence they might — Farewell, detestable word — Ah! Byron — remember me. He is now writing to you [this would sometimes happen: Lady Frances and her husband, sitting across from each other, both writing letters to Byron] — Mio caro, never forget how much depends upon your Honour.

In Byron's journal of November 17, 1813, he starts off by saying, "No letter from **, but I must not complain." Later, in the same entry, he says, "Not a word from **. Have they set out from **? or has my last precious epistle fallen into the lion's jaws? If so — and this silence looks suspicious — I must clap on my 'musty morion' [a morion was a helmet] and 'hold out my iron.' I am out of practice — but I won't begin again at Manton's now. Besides, I would not return his shot."

About this time, in his diary, Byron also said, "If this had been begun ten years ago and faithfully kept!!! — heigh ho — there are too many things I wish never to have remembered, as it is."

Byron's questions about the whereabouts of the Websters were answered by James' letter to the poet from "Aston Hall Nov. 18. 13," just as Bold Webster was preparing to take Lady Frances up to Scotland to visit her Wedderburn relatives:

My Dear B, Tho' ay [i.e. any] communication with you gives me pleasure & interest at all times yet I am doubly interested at present under y'r promise of writing to me —

By dint of bad roads & good pay I reached this [place] in an incredible time after leaving you — My limner troubled me little — & his wardrobe less — I fancy 1 clean sheet, 2 cravats & 2 hands [handkerchiefs] form his Equipage — A Dressing Gown, w'd be Knavery in a Painter — since it is clear from Homer — than [sic] even Agamemnon rode without one —

Your poem [*The Bride of Abydos*] is printed I suppose ere this? — I am almost persuaded you must write by steam — W. [Walter] Scott's muse (tho' jaded to ye bone) goes a cart pace compared with yours — For myself, Rhymes are as scarce as Guineas — tho' blank paper meets with evy [i.e. every] encouragement that Bad Pens and Idleness can give it — so what with blotting & mending I generally raise two lines on ye ruins of Eight!!

On ye road down I heard of nothing but Napoleon's defeat & Lord Pomfret's Gaiety — ye latter excited infinitely more Interest among ye Orthodox folke here in Northampton — I am not likely to forget his [Pomfret's] revels, being stopped there by a lack of horses at 4 A.M.

This was William Thomas Fermor, 4th Earl of Pomfret, whose estate was Easton Neston, near Towcester, Notts. His was the only country mansion designed by Nicholas Hawksmoor. The title would die with his son in 1867. The 4th Earl's daughter would, many years later, marry Bold Webster's first cousin once removed, Thomas Wedderburn Ogilvy.

Are you going to Dwell in Hampshire? how are you now? I hope better than when I left you — Mind & choose a house as far from a Garrison, a pack of hounds, a lawyer & a Doctor as possible, & above all have a Parson that plays at Backgammon & holds his tongue.

As our own journey North is a sad tribute p'd [paid] to some melancholy relations, it gives me little interest — New faces are abominations in my sight — Bonaparte and Dr Busby [Thomas Busby, composer and author] are ye only two I yet wish to see — They are a pretty pair — ye Doctor — a Damnable Poet — ergo a Public Ennemy to Mankind — & I am credibly inform'd his spouting Son-is [this may refer to Busby's translation of Lucretius, just published] a sheer scandal to all lusty young fellows with healthy countenances —

To reconcile ye horrors of ye Hee-lands I shall read travels & histories from Mister Moses down to Master Hobhouse — A Truce to Bagatelle — have you call'd in Piccadilly — I hope so for may [i.e. many] reasons —

Lady F is vey [very] well — begs kind remembrance — When you see Lord V [Valentia] pray never mention ay [any] thing ab't me — he is equal to fishing in ye Deepest water — Pray take care for our sake — write to me, if possible immed'ly — remember y'r promise — If I lose y'r friendship I'll live extempore in future & if you forgive ye infliction of this scrawl you may well be a candidate for ye Philanthropic Society!

Ever y'r, JW.

9. Aston Hall

This next letter to Byron from Lady Frances is undated, but has to be Saturday, November 19, 1813:

> Dearest Byron, an opportunity now presents itself of writing a few lines to you, unsurrounded by inquisitive eyes—and—you may readily believe with what sincere pleasure I embrace it—I fear I shall have but few after we leave home, for it will be dangerous to attempt writing in the <u>presence</u> of Argus [she means her husband]—whose ocular powers augment instead of decrease.
>
> My whole thoughts are upon you, wrapt up in meditation upon him I really adore—I sit—insensible to all around me—day & night you are never absent from my mind—& never can be—Remember that—<u>He</u> [James] wrote to you on Thursday—pray answer his letter kindly, for I can assure you—you are, I believe, the only person who he truly regards—I almost fear (and still I do not banish Hope) that I shall not secure your picture—We are positively under orders for Thursday next—You will receive this on Monday [Nov. 21, 1813]—if you can possibly let me have your picture I can <u>only</u> receive it by return of Post. If not [you] may write to me, immediately upon receipt of this—and to prevent any danger of discovery, I enclose a cover directed for Miss R. [Rawlence] in an unknown hand—in which you may enclose a letter—<u>sealed</u> & <u>directed</u> for me in disguise—and send it by <u>Post</u>. The seal, if <u>not</u> cut, send to Caermarthen Street. I will direct them what to do, but do not write a line with it—Excuse my being so particular—did you but know all I have suffered & still suffer—from the fear of discovery—and at the same time, could you form an <u>idea</u> even, of the force of my affection—my real attachment to you—you would not be surprised at my caution & re-urgence of prudence & secrecy—Ah! Byron, I am dead to every body but you.
>
> Your rings have never been off my finger—night or day—Your other pledge—ah! it is too dear to me—Ere long, many hundred miles will separate us, but your assurances of unchanged regard (tho' undeserved, I feel) have produced comfort I never expected to feel—on my part—my former letters have breathed no common vows of constancy—to express my present feelings would only be a repetition [she struggled to spell this word] of them—of sentiments you well know.
>
> I must again implore you to be cautious at Middleton—Will you not write to <u>him</u> sometimes, it will delight me to hear <u>of</u> you, as I cannot continue to hear from you, except at home—even then, is it not very wrong? It is—I am intercepted—Adieu—M'aimez toujours & believe me, yr eternally attached, F.

A short postscript says, "Be very particular in enclosing—I shall anxiously look for Wednesday next—I am obliged to send a letter to C as a cover for this direction."

Perhaps from this time period is an undated letter from Webster to Byron:

> My Dear B, As an offering to your <u>vanity</u>—you may frank ye two letters to Lady Frances to day, as they contain <u>y'r ode</u>—by not doing it you will either insult her judgement or your own composition, so take y'r choice—
>
> I wish'd yesterday to have seen you—to make a very possible amatory representation concerning a certain lady we discours'd of ye other night—I may be how'r <u>mistaken</u>—
>
> There is no news but that a print is coming out of ye Cossacks putting Lord Sligo—<u>naked</u>—into his carriage again—This is of importance to a Princesses Gentleman—as earliest such I enable you to give her ye information thereof—
>
> Yrs at [?], WW.
>
> My name is—_____ths longer than a broad wheeled waggon in full motion—yet I dare not sign only W, for fear of being supposed a Copyist—& you are ye only man in ye Nation I w'd be ashamed to copy—<u>because</u> you are superior in wit & talents to all others—
>
> What is your nocturnal arrangement?
>
> If you confess ye ode too bad to be sent send ye letters back to me.

On November 22, 1813, Lady Frances wrote a letter to Byron:

> Monday night. As our journey is for a day postponed I cannot refrain from again writing a few lines to you—tho' all I could say would be but a repetition of what you so well know and which perhaps has not failed to 'weary' your patience—
>
> I yesterday morng. received your dear welcome letter, enclosed to—which I opened, imagining to be for me—I was not mistaken—Can you <u>imagine</u> with what joy—what delight—I perused the contents? All attempts at description are vain—Need I be told to preserve those lines traced

in the blood of him who is alone near & dear to my heart — or need I be desired to preserve the most insignificant thing connected with that object?

Oh! No! My Byron — as we are situated is not Mem'ry an enemy — & yet I cherish the 'fond deceiver' — and would not part with a particle of it for the universe — I wish I knew who that gentleman was to whom you allude in your letter — with regard to the play — I do not wish you to deny our acquaintance altogether — that would appear particular [In those days the English used this word as the Italians use it today, meaning 'peculiar'] — as the contrary is well known — I only mean — but you so well know my feelings upon that & every other subject, that repetition would argue absurdity, and indicate suspicion — if you for an instant considered how much depends upon your honor — what risks I have run, what agony I have & do still endure for you — you would think yourself bound to place a double guard upon every avenue leading to discovery — and consequently to the disgrace & ruin of her who is only yours — Do not by this think any doubts remain upon my mind as to your honor and secrecy — on the contrary — my confidence (as you well know) has been unbounded, and I trust you will forgive the unreserved manner in which I write to you —

L'amour d'une femme se mele [sic] toujours avec un tendre respect et un [sic] confiance sans bornes [the love of a woman always involves tender respect and a boundless confidence].

I cannot tell my sorrow at not receiving your picture before my departure — it is a bitter disappointment to me — You must not think of sending it after we leave home — I must await some more favourable opportunity. In the meantime your assurances of undiminished affection will console me under all trials — Tu est [sic] l'asile de mes espérances et le soutien de ma vie [you are the sanctuary of my hopes and the support of my life].

My vows — I can never forget, dearest Byron! All are contained in these words — I am yours till death — Love is a tender plant — in fact, an exotic — it requires care — let ours be sheltered by secrecy — and may it never fade with inconstancy —

Farewell! When shall we meet? To me you are ever present — your image is ever present to the heart of your eternally attached FW.

As a postscript she adds (something that was really on her mind, and the true reason for the letter):

Do not forget to send the seal — without a line — Truly I am yours — jusqu'au tombeau — et vous a [sic] moi? [to the grave — and you to me?] —
Too flattering idea — .

Two days later she followed this up with a brief note, undated:

I wrote in the fulness of my heart on Monday night a long letter to you which I cannot send till tomorrow pour des raisons.

I trust you are long ere this safe in Town — God grant you are well — would I could say that I was — but alas! Adieu — Heaven preserve you — Wednesday.

The dangers of a Byron letter to Lady Frances — or vice versa — going astray were always present and in the minds of the two participants, although how James would have reacted if such a letter had come to his attention is hard to say. His friendship with the poet was of such value to him, from the point of view of social standing, that he might very well have been willing to blind himself to his *jalousies* in order to maintain the status that came with being Byron's friend. Lady Frances was, at this time, as we have seen, particularly, at pains to point out to Byron that James had the greatest possible liking and regard for him — more so, in fact, than for any other person he knew.

Lady Frances's letter of or around November 14, for example, was a justification, perhaps, but, in any case, more of one than can be said of Byron's next letter to Lady Melbourne, of November 22, 1813, in which he lives up to one of the many reputations he had earned: not being able to keep a secret to save his life. Lady Blessington, the Irish novelist and wife of the Earl of Blessington, who got to know Byron in Genoa in the 1820s and who would write *Conversations with Lord Byron*, would later notice this trait with some alarm. The Byron letter reads, in part:

> The occasional oddity of Ph.'s [Frances's] letters has amused me much. The simplicity of her cunning, and her exquisite reasons. She vindicates her treachery to W thus: after condemning deceit in general, and hers in particular, she says, 'but then remember, it is to deceive un marito, and to prevent all the unpleasant consequences, etc., etc.,' and she says this in perfect persuasion that she has a full conception of the 'fitness of things,' and the 'beauty of virtue,' and 'the social compact,' as Philosopher Square has it [Byron was influenced by Fielding]. Again, she desires me to write to him kindly, for she believes he cares for nobody but me! Besides, she will then hear of when she can't hear from me. Is not all this a comedy. Next to Lord Ossulstone's voucher for her discretion, it has enlivened my ethical studies on the human mind beyond 50 volumes. How admirably we accommodate our reasons to our wishes!
>
> She concludes by denominating that respectable man Argus, a very irrelevant appellation. If we can both hold out till spring, perhaps he may have occasion for his optics. After all, it is to deceive 'un marito.' Does not this expression convey to you the strongest mixture of right and wrong? A really guilty person could not have used it, or rather they would, but in different words. I find she has not the but, and that makes much difference if you consider it. The experienced would have said it is 'only deceiving him,' thinking of themselves. She makes a merit of it on his account and mine.

This letter shows that Byron was trying to convince himself that Lady Frances had deceived him as well as her husband, and perhaps not her husband at all!

In the same letter to Lady Melbourne Byron discusses a rather strange episode. He had had some miniatures done of himself, one by James Holmes (Holmes later painted another, more famous miniature of the poet, in 1815), which Lady Caroline Lamb now had. Byron now asked for that miniature back, to give it to "a friend leaving England," as he put it to Lady Melbourne. That friend was Lady Frances, who was about to set out for Scotland.

In an undated fragment of a letter to Lady Melbourne, but clearly in the cold light of day, Byron says,

> .... pantomime. I don't think I laughed once, save in soliloquy, for ten days, which you, who know me won't believe (everyone else thinks me the most gloomy of existences). We used to sit and look at one another, except in duetto, and even then our serious nonsense was not fluent; to be sure our gestures were rather more sensible. The most amusing part was the interchange of notes, for we sat up all night scribbling to each other, and came down like ghosts in the morning. I shall never forget the quiet manner in which she would pass her epistles in a music-book, or any book, looking in W's face with great tranquillity the whole time, and taking mine in the same way. One she offered me as I was leading her to dinner at Newstead, all the servants before, and W and sister close behind. To take it was impossible, and how she was to retain it, without pockets, was equally perplexing. I had the cover of a letter from Claughton in mine, and gave it to her, saying, 'There is the frank for Lady Waterford you asked for'; she returned it with the note beneath, with, 'it is dated wrong, alter it to-morrow,' and W complaining that women did nothing but scribble — wondered how people could have the patience to frank and alter franks, and then happily digressed to the day of the month — fish sauce — good wine — and bad weather.

The next letter Bold Webster received from Lord Byron was dated November 22, 1813; it is now (in manuscript form) in the National Library of Scotland:

> My dear W — I have but time for a few words which shall be to the purpose — I have before told you & now repeat very sincerely — that when the time of your bond is up — I shall not enforce it — I consider ye security as merely nominal — & surely more for your own satisfaction than mine — even if my exigencies were pressing — I should not trouble you on the subject — and you know me well enough not to doubt me on such worldly matters — I have but one favour to ask you — if you feel any pressure for additional accommodation — always apply in the first instance — to me — if I can assist you further I will — & if I cannot — I may at least hit on some expedient to prevent you from taking the imprudent step you had otherwise adopted on the present occasion. So there is an end to the matter — until you revive the subject — I suppose you will at least prefer me to a Jew. — I meant to write you a long letter on lighter topics — but talking of money materializes one's thoughts and I must for the present close my dispatch with the satisfaction of having at least set you at rest on that head yrs ever Biron.

From Lady F to Byron, not dated precisely, but it was November 25, 1813:

Thursday. 10 o'clock. Dearest Byron, since the arrival of yesterday's post [this was the Wednesday post upon which she had placed her hopes] my mind has been perfectly distracted — your picture is gone & not arrived here — I suppose you sent it to C Street [she means 6 Carmarthen Street, just off Tottenham Court Road, in London, where her go-between, Miss Rawlence, had recently lived] — they have no directions to forward any thing to Miss—[Rawlence] but letters— Our journey was positively fixed for tomorrow — under all these circumstances think what must have been my feelings upon opening your letter and finding that your picture & upon which I had fixed all my hopes of comfort during our residence in 'the land of the mountain and the flood,' was absolutely sent to me and yet I could not receive it. I immediately made Miss— dispatch orders for any parcels <u>there</u> to be instantly sent off, & I have, I think, persuaded W [meaning her husband] to remain till Sunday — in which case I shall receive it before we go— You must, Dearest Byron, forgive this incoherent scrawl, for really, I know not what I write — I feel I love you more than ever, and words are wanting to express my sincere, my lasting attachment. Alas! You have no occasion to remind me of my vows, which I renew voluntarily too often [she and Byron, while in the heat of their intense affair at Aston Hall a few weeks earlier, had sworn to one another vows of eternal love] — have I not sworn to continue yours— & to <u>think</u> of no other— <u>Love</u> in that instance is out of the question — the greatest of impossibilities — I must now thank you for your — to me — invaluable present — I will not tell you how I shall receive it, or where place it, but what can be the history annexed to it — Surely there is nothing that renders it unfit for me to receive it, otherwise you would not, I'm sure, have sent it. However, it is too dear to me ever to return it and part with it to another. To who, Dearest Byron, would I give it? Remember, the possession of that portrait inforces [sic] doubly the necessity of secrecy — for God's sake do not give an <u>idea</u> even to any body who the possessor is— I shall let you know the instant I receive it, but only <u>one</u> line, as I fear you will be absent from Town — Miss L [possibly a temporary replacement for Miss Rawlence, although Miss L is definitely not a servant] thinks me deranged, & so I really think I am. I have never even hinted to her with whom I correspond — they say I am stupid — that nothing pleases me — I mentally exclaim, 'tout me plait quand j'etais avec <u>vous</u>' [all pleases me when I am with you] — Never shall I forget our journey — my heart even now throbs with the idea — Oh! Byron, l'absence me desole [the absence leaves me desolate] — and not to be able to lighten that terrible burthen, by imparting sorrow time can <u>never</u> cure, is too harsh, is almost insupportable.

Shall I find your new poem [*The Bride of Abydos*] in Edinbro'? How I long to see it — the Giaour (my dear companion) I have read till the book is no longer of use — it is imprinted on my memory — forgive my tortured, wild brain — rappelle-toi quelquefois de moi — forget my follies — and only remember that untill death I am yours — that you possess undivided my thoughts day & night — that I have renewed my vows before God — which can only be dissolved by your breaking the bond of secrecy —

Dearest Byron — Farewell — Love me, one half as I love you.

In Byron's journal of November 25, 1813, he writes, "Cribb [Tom Cribb, the pugilist] is the only man except *** [this means Webster] I ever heard harangue upon his wife's virtue."

That very morning Byron received from Lady Frances a lyric which she called "Concealed Griefs," which the great poet and gossip lost no time in sending on to Lady Melbourne. "I received them [the lyrics] this morning," he tells his confidante, "and I think them very pretty; pray tell me if they are, for, seriously, I am a very erring critic." What he meant was what anybody who ever read the lyric would know: that Lady Frances was as inept a poet as her husband.

This is "Concealed Griefs" in its entirety, not seen in 200 years:

> Amid gay Folly's thoughtless scene
> How hard to act a borrowed part,
> The careless ease of mind to feign
> While sorrow wrings the tortured heart.
> Faintly to force a languid smile —
> Perhaps it hides the starting tear,
> Or should a moment's mirth beguile
> The next brings anguish more severe.

> But Reason claims the arduous task,
> Why give fond friends a needless pain?
> And pity from the World to ask
> Would Grief's sad dignity profane?
> Come, Fortitude, with sturdy mien,
> And help these bleeding wounds to heal,
> Give me, at least, the look serene,
> And what thou canst not cure, Conceal
> But when from busy crowds withdrawn,
> Beneath the Sun's last trembling beam.
> Pensive I wander o'er the lawn
> Or move beside the murmuring stream
> How sweet to banish harsh controul
> While unconstrained the tear may flow,
> How sweet to yield the bursting soul
> To all the Lunacy of Woe —
> Then mem'ry comes with fatal power
> Oh! Might the fond delusion last!
> Recalls each gay, each blissful hour,
> For ever dear — for ever past

Finally the Holmes miniature of Byron that Lady Frances had so long and ardently waited for arrived in Thursday's mail, just after she had written her last letter to Byron. She wrote to the sender:

> I open my letter to say the picture is arrived, and safely in my possession, never to be separated from me — indeed it is like — Oh! Byron, how my heart thanks you for it — it seems to speak to me — it speaks comfort to my wounded mind — Oh! I will cherish thee, thou dear image of my absent Byron — I cannot put it out of my sight — & yet I must go down stairs — W has sent for me — I fear he will remark my agitation, & yet I must go — Thank Heaven you have not been an eye witness to the scene — indeed it is very like you — it is serious — it reminds me of that fatal morng. when I parted from all I love, & which is still as fresh in my Mem'ry — so fresh — one moment's recollection seems to break my heart.

A follow-up letter of thanks for the picture followed, undated precisely, but it was only a few hours after her previous one, and her third letter to the poet of Thursday, November 25.

> Byron, dearest Byron, never can I sufficiently thank you for it — You will not hear from me again. I shall have no opportunities of writing, but if I have, will you receive my letters? Yes, you will — for you promise me to love me — We shall meet in spring — to that I cling — on that I rest all my future comfort — Adieu — I must away — 'Thou art the cherished madness of my heart' [she is quoting from Byron's *Giaour*] —
> I feel, I feel it is not <u>love</u> it is adoration —
> I must be silent —
> Adieu! Adieu! Dearest Byron — let me know thro' W — I mean, by writing to him when you return to town ——
> Que ta vie soit douce
> Comme ton ame est belle —
> [May your life be as sweet as your soul is beautiful]
> My whole thoughts, heart & mind are wrapt up in you & you alone.
> Thursday, 2 o'clock.

On or around November 28, 1813, the Websters headed north, where James's Wedderburn relatives would make sure Lady Frances was properly sequestered.

The Bride of Abydos was written in this same November, and published on December 2. Zuleika, the heroine of this piece, was a composite of Augusta Leigh and Lady Frances Webster-Wedderburn.

On December 8, 1813, Byron wrote a letter to Thomas Moore, in which he recounts an episode at Aston Hall. The poet was in the habit of singing religious songs. James Webster came in one day, heard Byron singing, and with a grave voice, said, "Byron, I must request you won't sing any more, at least of those songs." Byron stared, and said, "Certainly, but why?" James said, "To tell you the truth, they make my wife cry, and so melancholy, that I wish her to hear no more of them."

Byron says, in another piece, "It has changed my views, my wishes, my hopes, my everything, and will furnish you with additional proof of my weakness."

G. Wilson Knight, in his book *Lord Byron's Marriage*, tells us that "Byron was first shocked by Wedderburn Webster's atrocious sense of values, and afterwards by his wife's easy principles." This is an interesting summation, and quite true, even though somewhat overstated. After all, Byron had known Webster for a long time, even by 1813, and women of easy principles were nothing at all new to Byron — or to Webster. Indeed, Peter Quennell accurately sums James up in his book *Byron in Italy* when he says that W was "an old friend, hopelessly improvident, and chronically hard up."

Unfortunately practically all of Byron's letters to Lady Frances were destroyed; certainly all of the ones from this time were. Byron stayed at Aston Hall on and off from the middle of September till the middle of October 1813. It was during this time and up till the end of November that the famous letters to the Wedderburns were written. Byron refers to Lady Frances also in his letters to Moore, but much more guardedly and less emotionally than in those to Lady Melbourne.

His journal also contains many references to the subject. He called Lady Frances "Genevra" and wrote two sonnets to her on December 17, 1813. It was only in the 20th century, with the publication of Byron's correspondence, that the literary world was able to figure out who Genevra was. Pre–1922 biographers drove themselves crazy trying to work out who she was and why she had caused him such misery.

> Thine eyes' blue tenderness, thy long fair hair,
> And the wan lustre of thy features — caught
> From contemplation — where serenely wrought,
> Seems Sorrow's softness charm'd from its despair —
> Have thrown such speaking sadness in thine air,
> That — but I know thy blessed bosom fraught
> With mines of unalloy'd and stainless thought —
> I should have deem'd thee doom'd to earthly care.
> With such an aspect, by his colours blent,
> When from his beauty-breathing pencil born,
> (Except that thou hast nothing to repent,)
> The Magdalen of Guido saw the morn —
> Such seems't thou — but how much more excellent!
> With naught Remorse can claim — nor Virtue scorn.

The second sonnet to Genevra ran thus:

> Thy cheek is pale with thought, but not from woe,
> And yet so lovely, that if Mirth could flush
> Its rose of whiteness with the brightest blush,
> My heart would wish away that ruder glow:
> And dazzle not thy deep-blue eyes — but, oh!
> While gazing on them sterner eyes will gush,
> And into mine my mother's weakness rush,
> Soft as the last drops round heaven's airy bow.
> For, through thy long dark lashes low depending,
> The soul of melancholy Gentleness
> Gleams like a seraph from the sky descending,
> Above all pain, yet pitying all distress;
> At once such majesty with sweetness blending,
> I worship more, but cannot love thee less.

It has been said that he probably wrote other sonnets to Lady Frances, but in his diary, after writing these two, Byron remarks, "Redde some Italian, and wrote two sonnets. I never wrote but one sonnet before, and that was not in earnest, and many years ago, as an exercise— and I will never write another. They are the most puling, petrifying, stupidly platonic compositions." If his sonnets are anything to go by, he was absolutely right.

From Scotland Bold Webster wrote an undated letter to "The Lord Byron," which reads:

> Dear B, Pray Send your yeomen to ye Post with ye enclosed—
> I am too ill to write all I have now to say—deaf! but never dumb & reduced to ye society of a few distant cousins with strong tenor voices—! near relations to me—all insupportable in sickness— They generally go hand in hand with undertakers—
> Let me know your plan—I have one to propose to you—Ever yours, JW.
> Royal Hotel, Edinbro'
> Write soon pray as I am on ye wing—.

It was some time before Lady Frances was next able to write to Byron. Her letter is headed, "Written at the foot of the Grampians—Decbr 28th [1813]." She starts out:

> At length the time is arrived for which I have unceasingly watched since the day I left home—I am now for one hour free—for that little space I may pour out the weight of grief which swells my almost bursting heart before you—who, if not changed—frightful idea—horrible—as I'm sure 'tis unjust—yet what claim have I to your constancy? Claim? only this—'That oath, tho' sworn by one, has bound us both.'
> Zuleika, perhaps thy fate may ere long be mine—Dearest Byron, art thou <u>my</u> Selim? [She refers to characters in Byron's *The Bride of Abydos*.] You know not the various torturing thoughts which tear my Mind—but did I not tell you my temper—did I not confess my weakness to you before we parted—Great God! So many terrifying thoughts rush upon my mind—I dare not continue lest I should betray my folly—and yet I will write—for if you are changed—if—Oh! If you are another's now—it matters little how I expose myself—still less what becomes of me— each other is alike indifferent to me—would that I could see you—but for one day—even for one hour—I could—Alas! What? Methinks I hear you say, 'Why Fanny wish to meet—is parting so sweet—that you wish for a pleasing repetition?'—I cannot answer you—I feel more than I can express—I am melancholy—and sullen—but did I not promise to forbear complaint—I did. They tell me I am to go to Edinbro' this winter for some time—gaiety has lost all charm for me—all places are alike indifferent to me but London—such are my constant answers—to my host of tormentors—<u>She</u> who was an eye witness to all that passed at home during that unfortunate tho' happy time we were together [she means Catherine]—writes me long lectures about my conduct to <u>him</u> [James]—little does she know—that I am dead to all but one—that I hate the whole sex—but one to whom my every feeling is devoted—Byron—will you not write to me once?—Yet how shall I receive it—I know not how I shall even be able to send this—for all letters there pass thro' the hands of—[James] and Mr and Mrs W [James's Wedderburn relatives]— therefore I can scarcely avoid the questions—and if they arise, I shall betray myself—for I am not quite dead to shame.

She continues:

> By a letter just now received from C. I am informed you think of visiting Holland—Is it true?— Dearest Byron, I must hear from you—Will you tell me if I still preserve a place in that heart you once flattered me I solely possesst [sic]—Oh! Tell me if you will carry with you the remembrance of her who cannot change, who is and ever must continue—how great so e'er the distance which separates us—constant to a spontaneous attachment—to an eternal affection—Your picture, dearest Byron, is my constant companion—I gaze upon it, till every feature seems to speak—It recalls to my mind many, many scenes, when we were together, when I was happy—in the looks of love.
> Will you tell me your real sentiments <u>now</u> towards me—I mean, will you candidly say if you still continue to love me—will you openly declare if you suspect any body is the least acquainted with what has passed between us, or if you have breathed it to a creature—My peace, happiness, all is lost—It wants but my character to make my destruction perfect—Yet, Byron, remember, whate'er be my fate, remember my last words are a repetition of my former vows—dearest Byron,

I am yours, and only yours—What do you do with my letters? How did you send those to Miss M? Beware of servts—Save me if possible for the sake of my family—

You have never given me one assurance that my secret is buried in your breast forever.

Another from Scotland, late December 1813:

It would fill volumes if I was to attempt to detail my mental sufferings—but to complain is useless—When shall we meet again? My Byron, my Byron, promise me sometimes to think of your Fanny—

It would be useless and unentaining [sic] to you to relate our adventures—we have made many visits, and consequently seen a variety of people—all equally insipid to me—for whatever company I am in, my thoughts are ever absent, ever fixed upon one subject—one dearly, tenderly loved object—Now for management, how to receive a letter from you, and avoid discovery—in which I shall expect all my queries answered—and say upon your Honor—have you any reason to believe my conduct is suspected by any body—forgive me if I beg of you to consider how much depends upon your honor and secrecy and prudence—forgive me for re-urging and at the same time remember the unlimited confidence I have placed in you argues that I have every dependance [sic] upon your generosity—you will receive this on Saturday next, the first day of the New Year [1814], which I trust is as loaded with as much happiness for you as I feel it contains misery for me—if you will write and enclose your letter directed for me in the cover I send directed for Miss R [Miss Rawlence]. I will write to her to night to beg of her to enclose it to me—and if she is not in C Street it will be forwarded to her in Hampshire [to where Miss R was, with Thomas Bacon, at Bagshot]—If you will let it be there on Monday the 3rd of Janry before night I shall just receive it before I leave this [place], but how will you get it conveyed there without employing an enemy either to take it to its place of destination, or to the Post?

I depend upon hearing from you—surely you cannot refuse me the favor?—I send a cover directed for myself—your hand is too uncommon to escape suspicion—enclose your writing so as no eye can penetrate and seal it with jusqu'au tombeau—Forgive this scrawl—it is the last you may receive from me—I have had one in my desk for 3 weeks without opportunity of sending—perhaps even this may never go—

She ends this letter with

My Byron Farewell, and believe the only pleasure I can feel will arise from the assurance that I am not totally indifferent to you—May Heaven guard you thro' life & to Eternity, and may we meet—Alas! I fear to hope—such bliss I feel would be too much—If you leave England I—God preserve you—

My last request is that then you will then sometimes write to W., that I may be relieved of my fears for your safety—My last words, that whatever clime contains My Byron, whatever distance separates us, still am I yours—faithful and true—Adieu—Ricordate mi [Remember me]—Excuse this incoherent letter—for I know not what I write—my feelings I cannot describe.

On January 6, 1814, Byron wrote a letter to Tom Moore, declaring, "Any thing is better than stagnation, and now, in the interregnum of my autumn and a strange summer adventure." The autumn one had been with Lady Frances, and the summer one with Augusta Leigh.

In a letter to Lady Melbourne on January 8, 1814, Byron says, "I have heard from Ph. [Phrances] who seems embarrassed with constancy—her date is the Grampian Hills—to be sure with that latitude & her precious époux, it must be a shuddering kind of existence." Of course, Byron enclosed Lady Frances's letter.

Byron's P.S. to Lady Melbourne in his letter of January 10, 1814, says:

Lady Mount[norris] was seized with a sudden penchant for [Augusta] and called on her at the Viler's [he means Villiers,' even though "Villiers" is pronounced "Villers"] and asked her to some party—in gratitude I presume for the Aston Rumour [the rumor of Byron's involvement with Lady Frances] of which I suppose the elder informed her—I am sure she could not refrain from saying something of her Sr Ph [he means sister Frances, although he really should have said daughter, of course] as both she & I saw that she was vigilant to plague us [this bears out the later tale told by Basil Jackson of Wellington and Lady Frances]. That business will never be renewed or rather never completed—I heard from Ph the other day as usual—but we shall not meet till Spring—by which time it is impossible she should not be altered—and even if not [I] shall not fool away my time on theories—and that stupid speculative reverie of Platonics—in which I was obliged to humour her fears or her coquetry—she will fall eventually (probably soon) into some less indulgent instructor's precepts—for whom I have been merely paving the way—it was not my fault that this will be the case—but she—no—I was the fool of her whimsical romance—.

The following day, January 11, 1814, Byron sent another letter to Lady Melbourne, which said that Mary Chaworth Musters "talks of coming to town in Spring—in that case I might have at least turned her friendship to some account by playing it off against Ph which from the disposition of the latter would have ensured her—but I have quite resigned my pretensions in that quarter and in every other."

Lady Melbourne did not take kindly to Lady Frances's treatment of the poet, and said so. But Byron, (almost) ever the gallant, replied, in a letter of January 13, 1814:

You are quite mistaken, however, as to her, and it must be from some misrepresentation of mine, that you throw the blame so completely on the side least deserving, and least able to bear it. I dare say I made the best of my own story, as one always does from natural selfishness without intending it, but it was not her fault, but my own folly (give it what name may suit it better) and her weakness, for the intentions of both were very different, and for some time adhered to, and when not, it was entirely my own—in short, I know no name for my conduct. Pray do not speak so harshly of her to me—the cause of it all.

A little later he continues,

So 'Ph. is out of my thoughts'—in the first place, if she were out of them, she had probably not found a place in my words—and in the next—She has no claim—if people will stop at the first tense of 'aimer' they must not be surprised if one finishes the conjugation with somebody else—'How soon I get the better of'—in the name of St. Francis and his wife of Snow—and Pygmalion & his statue what was there here to get the better of? A few kisses for which she was no worse—and I no better.—Had the event been different—so would my subsequent resolutions & feelings—for I am neither ungrateful nor at all disposed to be disappointed—on the contrary I do firmly believe—that I have often only begun to love—at the very time I have heard people say that some dispositions become indifferent.—Besides—her fool of a husband—and my own recent good resolutions—and a mixture of different piques and mental stimulants together with something not unlike encouragement on her part—led me into that foolish business—out of which the way is quite easy—and I really do not see that I have much to reproach myself with on her account—if you think differently pray say so.

The poet cannot leave the subject alone for long. In the same letter he comes back to the subject of Lady Frances: "As to Ph. she will end as all women in her situation do—it is impossible she can care about a man who acted so weakly as I did, with regard to herself—What a fool I am."

On January 15, 1814, Byron wrote a strange letter to Lady Melbourne, accompanying it with Lady Frances's last letter to him. "That you may judge exactly how far Ph & I are at present with regards to each other I send you her last epistle—the first part is girlish & romantic—& the whole not much to the purpose—as to the 'telling' I believe no one but yourself has any foundation but their own suspicions—and after all there is nothing to be told.—I had an odd dialogue lately with her sister—we were talking of passing time in the country—and I said that my usual & favourite method was to pass several hours of the day quietly and alone."

The next part of this letter is rather bizarre, and hard to follow. It is quoted word for word below, but for ease of reading is set out in a linear fashion, with the name of the speaker in brackets where necessary. Quote marks are not used in the letter.

    Alone, but not quietly—she answered
      [Byron:] What do you mean?
      [sister:] What I have said—I have seen you when you did not see me

Then Byron says to Lady Melbourne, "I asked as you may be sure for an explanation — which she gave me as follows — ." He continues:

> [sister:] The morning before we all left N[ewstead] I had been walking with Ph in the cloisters where I left her to go to my room — when I got to the hall door which was half open I stopped as I am short — sighted to look through my glass at a person leaning alone near the fire — & whom I could not at first distinguish — it was you — but I really did not know you immediately — you were perfectly convulsed
> [Byron:] Why did not you walk on & speak to me?
> [sister:] Because I was frightened & did not know what to do — but I turned back to Ph
> [Byron:] Did you mention this to her?
> [sister:] No, and I had reasons for keeping it to myself

Byron then tries to explain to Lady Melbourne (and possibly to himself as well, although he had definitely been caught crying quite violently over Lady Frances): "I perfectly recollect being where she describes — and some of my sensations — but I was not aware of betraying them to any one — the hall at N[ewstead] is in the Abbey part of that enormous mansion — & quite remote from any but my own rooms — and this was the last day but one we passed together. — You may perhaps judge from this that I do feel sometimes & that for her at that time I did feel enough — ."

On January 16, 1814, Byron wrote in his diary, "I am getting rather into admiration of Lady Catherine Annesley, the youngest [sic] sister of Lady Frances Webster. A wife would be my salvation. I am sure the wives of my acquaintances have hitherto done me little good. Catherine is beautiful, but very young, and, I think, a fool. But I have not seen enough to judge.... That she won't love me is very probable, nor shall I love her.... The business (if it came to business) would probably be arranged between papa and me. She would have her own way."

On the same day, January 16, 1814, Byron wrote a letter to Lady Melbourne, in which he wonders "why the abominable stories they circulate about Lady W., of which I can say no more." Later, in the same letter, he continues, "I wonder what your answer will be on Ph.'s letter. I am growing rather partial to her younger sister; who is very pretty, but fearfully young — and I think a fool. A wife, you say, would be my salvation. Now I could have but one motive for marrying into that family — and even that might possibly only produce a scene, and spoil everything; but at all events it would in some degree be a revenge, and in the very face of your compliment (ironical, I believe) on the want of selfishness, I must say that I never can quite get over the 'not' of last summer — no — though it were to become the 'yea' of to-morrow."

This letter crossed in the mail with one Lady Melbourne wrote to the poet, after having digested Lady Frances's letter from the Grampians. Paston and Quennell reprinted part of it in their book *To Lord Byron*:

> 'The oath, tho' sworn to one, hath bound us both' — rather wild even in theory, but it must be said by a person quite ignorant of the practice in such cases — how you might be bound without ever knowing it — and to what? — Really to be constant — does not that frighten you? — Don't you blush at the question? — 'Are you my Selim?' — In what manner could you answer this letter? — You could not even make use of your favourite basis — truth — not even swear to it — You must have given it up, or talked entirely of the past — perhaps that might have satisfied this poor little ignorant girl — There is much simplicity in many parts of her letter — I am very sorry for her, as I believe she is very sincere, and you must believe that she loves you dearly — though you will hardly own it to yourself — You have imbibed such ideas of the deceit practised by all women that you would never confess that you had any dependance [sic] on their constancy — And yet such things have come to pass, and from all I have heard of her character and actions, I am impressed with a belief that all that she says is true, and that she is not at all, as you expressed yourself, 'embarrassed with her constancy.' My opinion is that you were never so loved before, or you would know better how to appreciate her feelings — After all this I think her a little childish and now and then tiresome.

On January 18, 1814, in a letter to James, Byron says:

My dear W — Address your 'plan' to town where I shall return in a week — I like 'plans' of all things, particularly where they are likely never to be realized — I am on my way to the country on rather a melancholy expedition — a very old & early connection or rather friend of mine has desired to see me — and as now we never can be more than friends I have no objection — she is certainly unhappy & I fear ill — & the length & circumstances attending our acquaintance render her request & my visit neither singular nor improper — I mean to return to London in a few days unless prevented by the weather which is very impractical even at present — Your Papa & family are still in town [he means Papa-in-law, Arthur Annesley, 1st Earl of Mountnorris, who had two and a half years to live] — I see them occasionally and of the youngest [the younger of the two Juliana Lucys, who was then just 16] I should be glad to see more — but she is not yet out — & is generally — I dont exactly see why — kept out of sight — she will be very beautiful — as to more — I have never seen nor heard enough to judge. — It is said that you are coming to town in Spring — I shall be happy to see you — if I can be of any use to you in the mean time — the distance between us can make little difference — as business can be arranged without the parties meeting — I dont mean to press any offers of service upon you — but I hope you know already that I will at least treat you in a Christian like manner. — I wrote to you shortly before you left Aston on the subject you wished to hear upon — it is the last you shall hear upon it — till convenient to yourself. — If you are disposed to write — write — and if not I shall forgive your silence — and you will not quarrel with mine. believe me yrs very affectly, Bn. P.S. I presume your illness is merely the cold compliment of the New year — at all events I hope this will find you better.

Lady Melbourne again to Byron, on January 19, 1814:

I take some credit to myself for discovering that it would be difficult for you to answer PH's letter — Those who believe in C [Lady Caroline Lamb] think falsehood is so easy to you that you prefer it to truth — You see I judged otherwise — What another! — A young one coming up in succession! [she means Lady Catherine Annesley] — Not content with five or six I know of — and twenty I don't — You are looking after another — Well, be it so — And I only pray that this one may go on, as it will settle all the others in the best manner possible — What is she — fourteen or fifteen [actually, she was 18] — And you say a fool — How should you know? — Believe me, tho' so young, she is old enough to conceal a great deal of character — There is so much shyness at that age in general that it obscures all their ideas, and they can speak clearly on no subject — If she has no present unamiable qualities it is most likely she will turn out well — When these appear, it is hopeless, for living in the world generally increases them, and only softens them in appearance — witness C.

You estimate the force and truth of a person's liking by the correspondence they commit (C always told me so) — now I think it is a false way of judging, and that a person's conduct depends upon their character — A woman who respects <u>les bienséances</u> [proprieties], and is driven from them by a strong passion, gives you the greatest proof of attachment, but she still adheres to propriety and decorum in trifles when she has given it up in reality; and is much more to be relied on and believed than one of those whimsical ladies who defy the world and run headlong into every sort of imprudence, and call it Violent Love which cannot be controlled. I don't think Ph deserves that name. You differ from me, I know, because you have as yet only seen one sort of woman — or to express myself more clearly — women of one turn of mind — I think you understand what I mean, and your anger with Ph convinces me that I am right.

On January 21, 1814, Byron wrote Lady Melbourne, "Since I wrote last night I have received the 2 enclosed — what shall I do about Ph and her epistles? Since by her own account they run great hazard in their way to her. I am willing to give them up — but she says not a syllable about mine — no matter — ."

Byron's *The Corsair* was published on February 1, 1814, and one of the characters in it, Medora, was based on Lady Frances. Byron had begun the poem on December 18, 1813, and finished it a mere 13 days later. He states that it was written "con amore, and very much from existence." In the original manuscript the chief female character was called Francesca, in whose person the author meant to delineate one of his acquaintance (Lady Frances, of course); but, while the work was in progress he changed the name to Genevra (or Ginevra), and then finally, when the work was at press, he changed the name to Medora (the name given to Augusta Leigh's third child — whether Byron's or not — as a middle name).

The day *The Corsair* was published, February 1, 1814, Lady Frances wrote "The Lord Byron," despite her prior assurance to the poet that he would "never hear of or from" her again:

> Can you forgive my once more intruding a few, and but a few, lines upon your patience? Will you pardon me when I assure you they are the last you shall receive? I arrived here [Aston] last night, firm in the resolution of writing, contrary to my original determination, a letter of reproach to you, but the sight of the place, the very town in which I spent so many happy hours in the enjoyment of your society — every circumstance attending that fatal period — the recollection of scenes that I tremble to recall — rushed at once upon my mind, and drove every feeling from the field but love & tenderness — I hear from my sister that you are gone to yours, but I know better. I know where you are — happy happy woman in the sight of him I dare not hope to see — too happy woman — thy grief, tho' great, must appear as nothing when soothed by my Byron, and art thou <u>my</u> Byron, and dare I call you all I love on Earth? I will say no more — I will check my heart, it knows no bounds —
>
> Miss L is no longer in C Street, nor will they receive anything there. I enclose a letter for her, that is her direction, but do not frank it. Absent but ever present, as your dear self is to me — As to me — Memory beguiles me into happiness with her — delusion — and as I sit wrapt up in the chimeras of fancy which she presents to my mind I forget our distance from each other, our total separation from circumstances and connexion in Life — & I live only in retracing what can never be recalled — the time. I must not continue — I dare not hurt myself — I will not tell you my wicked wishes during a journey of 11 days thro' dangers of every description; you would hate me — tho' they were all for myself — 'tis you have made me what I am, therefore — but let your feelings towards me be voluntary — I will not bind you — nor will I mention my sufferings — I am the same, unchanged, & where is the power that can change me — Dearest Byron, Adieu — A word more — You know not how I love your sister — I never felt so great a regard for any other woman — do not make her despise me — perhaps I may know her some day — Can you imagine why I should love a person so much. I do not know? I will not tell you — do you think she <u>would</u> know me? Alas! Unanswered must my questions remain — Adieu.

Then, as a post script, but really intended to be the kernel of her message, she adds, "It may appear strange to you, but consider how I am situated, and do not be angry when I again request you to send my seal to Miss L [Bold Webster had been asking for the seal, say Paston and Quennell] — or, if you will not — for why I cannot tell — I must frame some excuse & get another like it, if I can — which will not be dear to me as the original you cruelly keep — direct to her, undirected to me."

From Bold Webster to Byron, dated Feb. 17, 1814:

> My Dear Byron, I had as much joy in dispatching a vassal to you at Newstead last week as I had afterwards disappointment in hearing you were <u>gone</u> — To say how <u>happy</u> we must have been to have seen you <u>here</u> w'd be saying <u>little</u>, but it w'd be <u>truth</u> —
> <u>I have heard of your journey</u> — — —
> Why won't you answer my letter? I wrote to you ten days ago [we do not have that letter] — remember I shall continue to expect to hear from you — untill you are <u>more candid</u> — or <u>less generous</u> —
> You will not marvel at ye incoherency of this servant — as I have just run thro' ye '*Corsair*' w'ch I confess has shaken off too much of my <u>mortality</u> to make me a decent correspondent — it is indeed a <u>sublime</u> poem — & proclaims ye author 'ye <u>favor'd child of taste & feeling</u>' — —
> I am to be in Town soon — en garcon [sic — 'like a bachelor'] for a time — ergo — w'd you allow Fletcher [Byron's valet] to look for a lodging for me — I must have 2 things in it — a clock & if a <u>The</u> — [sic] Landlord — He must not be <u>loquacious</u> —
> I repeat my entreaty to hear soon from you — accept my regards for every living thing near you & my envy for ye Dead! —
> Yours in this state, ever,
> JW, Aston Hall, Feb. 17.14
> I am serious abt ye Lodging — therefore you may oblige me by attend'g to my request.

Webster was looking for a discreet place to bring girls, and he was in a hurry, a state that would trickle over into the act that loosely represented the reality of his schemes, as, no doubt, any of his "conquests" would have been happy to confirm, if pressed. In addition to all that, Webster had developed a plan to tap Byron for more money, being broke again after the Scottish trip.

On February 20, 1814, Byron replied to Webster (in a letter which, in manuscript form, is now with the Historical Society of Pennsylvania):

> "My dear W — Your arrival at A[ston] was unknown to me till my own in London — & had it been otherwise — I could not have availed myself of your invitation from ye. state of the roads &c but I am equally indebted to your intended hospitality as if it had taken effect. — If you are serious in your intention of visiting London — Fletcher shall look out for ye. abode you require or I will do it myself if you think me more likely to obtain what will suit you — but you neither mention terms — time — nor place — & I shall wait your answer. — I have been again in ye. country but for a shorter time & distance — which has occasioned partly my delay in answering your first letter — you know that I am a very irregular correspondent & I have lately been a good deal occupied with business of one kind or another. — There is a new actor named Kean come out — he is a wonder — & we are yet wise enough to admire him — he is superior to Cooke certainly in many points — & will run Kemble hard — his style is quite new — or rather renewed — being that of Nature — .

Edmund Kean had just the month before opened as Shylock at Drury Lane. He was a sensation. John Philip Kemble, his predecessor as England's great tragedian, saw the writing on the wall, and quit the business, dying in Lausanne in 1823. George Frederick Cooke, Kemble's contemporary (and some say a better actor), had died only two years before, in 1812, a victim, like his career, of the bottle.

Byron continues:

> Nobody knows as yet what is to become of Bonaparte — the reports are various — but the war party have it hollow at home — a few days will probably see him all or nothing.
>
> Hobhouse is returned to England — full of health good humour & anecdote — I was most agreeably surprized by his arrival [John Cam Hobhouse had been gone eight months in Europe, returning on February 8, 1814]. — I have been living very quietly — & declined such invitations as have offered themselves — Ld [Mountnorris] or his family I have not lately seen — [Lady Juliana] seems to promise a splendid debut — & will perhaps be the finest pearl of the string — they are all very handsome but there is more of ye. youngest & her head is very Greek — I speak merely as a 'formarum spectator' [a term coined by Ovid, meaning "judge of forms,' i.e. human forms] for I have long passed the happy time when one's heart is turned by a pretty face, & can give my opinions as impartially as I would of a statue. — Believe me yrs very truly BIRON.

James's reply, although undated, must have been written about February 25, 1814. He was at his underlining best in this one:

> Aston Hall in <u>Worksop</u>—<u>Notts</u>. My Dear B, As ye precise time of my <u>advent</u> to ye Metropolis is uncertain to a <u>few days</u> I shall release you from ye <u>task</u>, w'ch your good nature <u>might</u> have imposed — I congratulate you on ye possession of <u>Hobhouse</u> — I have neither seen him or his father since ye <u>honors</u> of ye latter [that was December 22, 1812, when Ben Hobhouse was given a baronetcy] —
>
> I promise myself much — in seeing ye <u>multum</u> in <u>parvo</u> actor [much in little; he means Kean], tho' I but expect <u>a good copy</u> of that <u>great original Kemble</u> — with whom, in my humble opinion Shakespeare will <u>meet another Death</u> — — The <u>on dit</u> ("it is said," i.e., word on the street) of Notts is that ye Ex-<u>Connubiated</u> Mr. C-U'-L has <u>broke a leg</u> hunting — He may afford <u>one</u> however & then he must have <u>two</u> <u>redoubtable</u> ones left — as I hear he has been lately most successful in his <u>animal creations</u> — having already more <u>children</u> than <u>ideas</u> — this may be ye case with may [many] — <u>I</u> howe'r presume whilst I have but <u>one</u> [that was young Lucy, still the only Webster child at that point] — I may make ye remark with impunity — most men have one Idea — — — .

It is clear from this puerile joke about the unidentified gentleman that many of Webster's late night conversations with Byron and the other boys descended to where the interlocutors often found comfort, i.e., in the gutter; this they had in common with boys of all ages and of all generations.

He carries on:

> I have seen you lately <u>attacked</u> on <u>all sides</u> & defended by <u>a few</u> — & I am lost between disgust & surprise at ye impudent <u>impotency</u> of ye <u>former</u> — & ye inefficiency of ye <u>latter</u> — In a cause wherein so much may be said by loud facts that require <u>no champion</u> — I did indeed hope — if ye thing <u>was</u> attempted at all — it w'd have been marked with <u>strong features</u> — The bespattering of a Public Journal is how'r little worthy of notice & ceases to be of moment — <u>untill</u> dignified by a <u>defensive reply</u> — & tho' I cannot but <u>respect</u> ye motive & Design of those who undertook yt task I must lament it was not of another nature — Thus much for your <u>private perusal</u> of my zeal for y'r cause — & my <u>charity</u> to <u>others</u>! No one who ever knew <u>you</u> c'd accuse you of 'paddling <u>with ye silver oar</u>' — this is really ye <u>buffoonery</u> of <u>libell</u> — & you may well say to them with Chatterton
> 'Well, Burgum! Take thy laurel to thy brow'
> 'with a rich <u>saddle</u> — decorate a sow'
> [from Thomas Chatterton's mock will]
> To my surprise no one has yet visited you in ye <u>rough anticipation</u> of an <u>Epitaph</u> — but <u>myself</u> —! Those will ever be found to <u>laud</u> when there is life, hope & money, & but few <u>after</u> —
> <u>Scaliger</u> who c'd write 200 verses evry night during a <u>sleepless fit of ye Gout</u>, w'd have but 5 plain words upon his tomb & yet this <u>Gent'n</u> tho' no <u>minor wit</u> unwilling to be judged by a distich [a two-lined verse] left the task to more <u>credulous</u> hands — wisely shunning ye memorials to fatal to [sic] Dante, Ariosto & others — .

Webster was cheating a bit here. As he wrote he had in front of him Sir Thomas Browne's *Letter to a Friend* (1690), and quotes from it, first word for word, and then in paraphrase, the passage about 16th-century Italian scholar Julius Caesar Scaliger. Incidentally, the five words were "Julii Caesaris Scaligeri quod fuit."

> <u>Well</u> — I have taxed <u>you enough</u> & too long, I fear — <u>burn</u> this — when — or if — <u>never read</u> & believe me — ever yours in <u>this state</u>.
> I as much as <u>may be</u> in ye next, W.

There is an addendum, "P.S. w'd you send me a line to say whether Albemarle St, Dover St, or Bennet St has any good lodging — to what by ye week — rent to men of <u>my Estate</u> — is too trifling to mention!"

On February 28, 1814, the great poet dashed off another letter [which is now, in manuscript form, in the Stark Library, University of Texas] to Bold Webster, a reply to the latter's letter of (or around) February 25. It said:

> My dear W — I have but a few minutes to write to you. — Silence is the only answer to the things you mention — nor should I regard that man as my friend — who said a word more on the subject — I care little for attacks — but I will not submit to defences & I do hope & trust that you have never entertained a serious thought of engaging in so foolish a controversy — Dallas's letter was to his credit — merely as to facts which he had a right to state [Robert Charles Dallas was a friend and literary adviser to Byron] — I neither have nor shall take the least public notice — nor permit anyone else to do so. — If I discover the writer — then I may act in a different manner — but it will not be in writing. — An expression in your letter has induced me to write this to you — to entreat you not to interfere in any way in such a business — it is now nearly over — & depend on it — they are much more chagrined by my silence than they could be by the best defence in ye. world. — I do not know any thing that would vex me more — than any further reply to these things. ever yrs. in haste, B.

On March 3, 1814, Byron wrote to Tom Moore, "... and am besides embarrassed between three whom I know." The poet meant Lady Frances, Augusta Leigh, and Annabella Milbanke.

We know James called on Byron on Tuesday, March 15, 1814, but nothing else in Byron's diary is mentioned of the visit. "W W called" is all it says. Bold Webster had come to ask for money. We don't even know for sure if the two actually saw each other on that occasion, but they probably did, as the opening paragraph of the following letter from Byron is a reply to a request that never seems to have been made in writing. This letter, written on March 21, 1814, is in manuscript form in the Henry E. Huntington Library. It reads:

> Dear Webster/—I am sorry to say that in consequence of a disappointment for the present in the amount of the remittance I expected I am obliged to decline advancing the sum which I would readily have done had it been within my power.—With regard to joining you as a security—I should have no objection—but on the terms & with the persons to whom you have applied—I should only become instrumental in involving both without any permanent benefit to yourself.—I speak from experience—as my own difficulties have arisen from similar sources.—Your own agent could surely direct you to more reputable lenders—and better terms—and as you must have security to give on your own property—I should think the business might be arranged without your having recourse to the Advertisers in papers.—I regret very much that it is not now in my power to advance this myself—& I think you know that I would have done so had it been practicable. Very truly yrs, B.

By that time James and Lady Frances were on the Continent. On March 22, 1814, in Brussels, James's sister Mary married George Hawkins of Harnish House, Wilts, grandson of Sir Caesar Hawkins, of Kelston, Somerset.

At noon on "Wednesday," either March 30 or April 6, 1814, Byron wrote a letter (which is in manuscript form at the Carl H. Pforzheimer Library) to James. It says: "Dear W—I hear that you are in town & unwell—the last report I shall be very glad to have contradicted by yourself.—When you have nothing better to do I shall be happy to see you—if you are not disposed to stir in this weather I can call upon you when you like. yrs very truly B."

The Websters then returned to the Continent—this time to Paris.

So, did Lord Byron actually have a complete physical relationship with Lady Frances Webster? That question has occupied the thoughts and writings of many people. The answer is "certainly not." Her letter to Byron of October 3, 1813, makes that abundantly clear. A better question might be, "Did they love one another?" There can be little doubt that the answer is "yes."

10

Byron's Song

Sir John C. Fox, in his book *The Byron Mystery*, tells us, "It has been said there can be little doubt that 'The Song of the 4th of May,' and the Dedication to *Lara* were addressed to Lady Frances Wedderburn Webster, and, apparently, it is suggested that *Lara*, *The Corsair* and *The Bride of Abydos* were written under the influence of a passion for that lady."

Here Fox cites Coleridge's edition of *Byron's Poems*, volume iii, page 319. But what alarms the reader of this Fox passage is the mention of a new Byron work, "The Song of the 4th of May." Just as one has become comfortable in the belief that all the Byron works are known, here comes a new one. What is worse, no one else has heard of it either. It turns out that there is no such poem, not by that name, anyway. Fox simply made up this title, and wrote so dogmatically that for just a moment he succeeded in perpetrating a hoax, although one is sure that was not his intention.

The truth of the matter is that in May 1814 (the month Byron began work on *Lara*, which he warned that many people would regard as a continuation of *The Corsair*) the poet also wrote a song, which he sent to Tom Moore. Leslie Marchand says he sent it on the 4th of that month, and he was quoting from Tom Moore's *Letters and Journals of Lord Byron*, vol. 1, p. 554. However, *The Poetical Works of Lord Byron*, 1848, says the 10th. Anyway, this song was accompanied by the following note: "Thou hast asked me for a song, and I enclose you an experiment, which has cost me something more than trouble, and is, therefore, less likely to be worth your taking any in your proposed setting. Now, if it be so, throw it into the fire without phrase."

The song, in actual fact, was called *Stanzas for Music*. It goes like this:

> I speak not, I trace not, I breathe not thy name,
> There is grief in the sound, there is guilt in the fame;
> But the tear which now burns on my cheek may impart
> The deep thoughts that dwell in that silence of heart.
> Too brief for our passion, too long for our peace
> Were those hours—can their joy or their bitterness cease?
> We repent—we abjure—we will break from our chain,
> We will part,—we will fly to—unite it again?
> Oh! thine be the gladness, and mine be the guilt!
> Forgive me, adored one!—forsake, if thou wilt;—
> But the heart which is thine shall expire undebased,
> And *man* shall not break it—whatever *thou* mayst.
> And stern to the haughty, but humble to thee,
> This soul, in its bitterest blackness, shall be;
> And our days seem as swift, and our moments more sweet,
> With thee by my side, than with worlds at our feet.
> One sigh of thy sorrow, one look of thy love,
> Shall turn me or fix, shall reward or reprove;
> And the heartless may wonder at all I resign—
> Thy lip shall reply, not to them, but to *mine*.

Fox continues:

> But we know that when Byron visited the Wedderburn Websters at Aston in 1813 his relations with Lady Frances fell short of consummated guilt [here Fox cites Murray, volume i, pages 203, 204, 232. These are the *Byron Correspondences* published by Murray not long before Fox wrote his book, and Fox was still reeling, as was everyone else, over the truths revealed for the first time, especially about Lady Frances] and though the two corresponded afterwards, there is no reason to believe that the attachment was ever personally renewed. 'The Song of the 4th of May' is inapplicable to their case, and, for the reasons given above, *The Bride of Abydos* and *The Corsair* point to remorse far more than ordinary guilt. Beyond this, we have the unanswerable fact that Byron, frequently, in the presence of his wife and sister, identified the sister (Augusta) with the *Bride of Abydos*, and with the person addressed in 'The Song of the 4th of May.'

So, although Byron scholar E.H. Coleridge believed that the song was addressed to Lady Frances, Sir John Fox and most who came after him feel that it was to Byron's half-sister, Augusta. Fox himself has two reasons for his belief. One is that Lady Frances and Byron never consummated their relationship physically, and the other is the "unanswerable fact" that Byron, Augusta and Annabella often talked about Augusta being the addressee.

However, both premises rest on shaky ground. Just because Augusta, or Byron, or Annabella, says something does not necessarily make it true. And Fox's naiveté in the area of romance itself debunks his first premise. In addition to all this, Fox never had the advantage of seeing Lady Frances's letters to Byron.

Certain of Fox's august successors have come up with a risibly implausible angle to justify their champion: that the lady addressed in the song would have had to have been more hot-blooded than Frances Webster. As for blood temperature, a surface inspection of Lady Frances might, indeed, lead the unworldly to believe that she was of a somewhat frigid nature, but the truth is, like many glacial volcanoes, Lady Frances was as hot-blooded as they come.

After all is said and done, the critics who feel this is not Lady Frances may, of course, be right. It is impossible, at this remove, to know for sure, unless something new comes to light. But the question has to be asked: Was Lady Frances able to affect Byron in such a way as to inspire him to write this poem a few months after their affair? The answer is yes, without doubt. Byron's own evidence is overwhelming on this score. One small point, but worth noting, is his reference to "bitterest blackness." James Webster was the claimant to the Baronetcy of Blackness, his ancestral home. Of course, equating that "Blackness" with Byron's may be mere fancy, but Byron did know about Webster's claim, and took it seriously.

11

Vive l'Empereur

James wrote "To The Lord Byron, Albany, London" from Paris on May 5, 1814 (curiously, seven years to the day before Napoleon would die). It was Bold Webster's first taste of France, and he was entranced:

> My dear Byron, I should have written to you immediately to thank you for the Pistols, but I was a good deal hurried, & besides I thought you would like better to hear from me when I had reached the place of my destination — I can assure you that I value them very much, as I should value anything you allowed me to consider as a mark of your esteem and friendship, tho' perhaps I ought not quite to acquit you of a little malice in this heaping coals of fire upon my head by reminding me of the hard terms of the treaty of Lisbon—
>
> Since I saw you I have been constantly regretting that you could not get a furlough of a few days for this trip — and this not merely because I lost a companion whom I should (on the whole) have preferred to my worthy friend General Malthen [?] (with whom I fell in amgst others) but because Paris is certainly at this moment the most interesting spot in the world, from circumstances that can neither last, nor recur [Napoleon was in exile on Elba, and had been for precisely one day when James wrote this letter]—
>
> For the few last days my curiosity with objects of every sort, and those still remain [sic]— The mere sight of France & of Paris to a person that has never seen them before is quite delightful — then comes the Louvre filled with those great works of art that one has been hearing and thinking, and talking of all one's life — All this indeed will be the same at any other time, but the crowd of extraordinary persons now collected here will soon disperse — Two Emperors— two Kings— Blucher — Schwartzenburgh [Prince Schwartzenburg] — the English Minister (for so, in the most important functions of government, Lord Castlereagh must be considered) — all the Marshals of France — Talleyrand — and, to crown all, Lord Wellington, who arrived this morning [Arthur Wellesley had, only two days before, been created Duke of Wellington] — This is well worth coming to gaze at.
>
> As to Society I have not been here long enough to form any judgment — but the English till now there is none except what they speak among themselves — perhaps this may only mean that they are not admitted into it, which notwithstanding their many amiable qualities is not unlikely. However, one may very well concur that the French may be a little sulky and 'disorganised' at the present moment — Every thing here bears the appearance of conquest — The conquerors indeed are humane and politick, but still conquerors. Prussian guards keep the gates of Paris, Cossacks bivouac in the Place de Vendôme, and the day after Louis 18th rejected the constitution an immense body of foreign troops was paraded on the Boulevards and in the Tuileries and Lord Wellington arrived to swell the list of victorious enemies—
>
> The ceremony of the King's entry into Paris [this took place the day before James wrote this letter] was really magnificent — as fine a thing as a procession can be — the people shewed no enthusiasm whatever for the ancient line of their kings. They know well enough that they have had a Tartar congé d'élire [permission to elect], to chuse them again, and that if they had refused they must have incurred all the penalties of a 'premunire' from the Hetman Platow [Matvei Ivanovich Platov, the leader of the Don Cossacks fighting against Napoleon] — a venerable personage by the bye whom I saw last night, and who in his aspect (the sober) a good deal resembles the Duke of Richmond — I am inclined to believe, however, that the people really prefer the Bourbons— they think it is their best chance of a quiet life, but a great proportion of the soldiery,

Sir James Webster-Wedderburn, from a miniature. By kind permission of Tatton Hewetson.

I suspect, is attached to Buonaparte. At Lille they were not brought to submit to the new-old government without the greatest difficulty, and its [i.e., 'it was'] day before yesterday, I am told, that the Guards (late Imperial Guard) made a sad mistake in their acclamations and that many of them cried out 'Vive l'Empereur,' 'Vive Napoleon,' but then I am also given to understand that this is only a bad habit, and that in a little while (not longer, I suppose, than it would take to educate a parrot) they will be quite perfect in a new lesson —

In the mean while your poor friend Buonaparte, is cutting a deplorable figure [Byron had been, and still was, an unabashed admirer of the French emperor, and this became more embarrassing as time went by] — at one place (Lyons, I believe), he was pelted by the mob, and forced to cry out 'Vive le Roi' — at Avignon he was still worse treated. The people rose upon him and he fled for his life — first disguised in an Austrian uniform — then in an English one, calling himself Lord Burghersh —

This is wretched and for a man who has played so great a part, but to say the truth it is not very creditable either to the Allies. They may not be able to restrain the clamour, but they ought to protect him from the violence of the mob —

If you find leisure to write a few lines (directed to me 'chez Messrs Perregeaux') [the French bank]) you will do me a kindness by letting me hear from you —

Ever most sincerely yours, JWW.

James ends with "6th [i.e., May 6]. P.S. I find upon enquiry that it was Buonaparte's own choice to travel without any escort from the Allies, so they an't to blame — Talleyrand has just been declared Prime Minister."

Patrick Laforce, in his book *Wellington the Beau*, which devotes Chapter 11 to Lady Frances, describes Paris at this time as "a curious mixture." He quotes the painter B.R. Haydon as saying that the city "had an air of mortified vanity and suppressed exasperation which was natural." Mr. Laforce says, "Thousands of wounded French veterans mingled with the returning émigrés, who, after twenty years absence living on their wits and charm in London, were delighted to be back. High-waisted coats and tall feather-trimmed hats were the rage that summer. The centre of Paris was full of the occupying armies. The Cossacks were camped out in the Champs de Mars, the English in the Champs Élysées, and the rough, boisterous Prussians who annoyed and terrified the Parisians, were stationed in Luxembourg, Tuileries and the Concorde."

The few mentions James Webster gets in Laforce's book is as a captain. A writer of a generation one earlier than Laforce, Elizabeth Longford, gave James a promotion the Army never did, and many writers who followed Miss Longford chose to subscribe to her rather than to the facts.

12

Master Shallow

In June 1814 Webster was back in London, looking for yet another loan from the poet. Byron refused, calling him Master Shallow (though not to his face, of course; Byron was as two-faced as all the others, if not more so).

On June 8, 1814, Bold Webster wrote to the poet:

> Aston Hall, Worksop, June 8. 14. My Dear <u>Byron</u>, Being aware of your aversion to <u>consistency</u> I have some reason to hope I may hear from you—for as you never answer <u>notes</u> in London you may not always treat letters from ye country in ye same manner—
> Can you still give me leave to sport on ye <u>Newstead Manor</u>? as we propose visiting that <u>pious ruin</u> en masse from this [place] as before—if you <u>can</u>—or <u>may</u> come here—or if we are not m'ch out of y'r way (going elsewhere) I assure you most sincerely ye pleasure we sh'd have in seeing you w'd be great—in propisition to that regard with w'ch I shall ever be, Dear B, yours—.

Later that day James dashed off another letter, undated, to "Lord Byron":

> Dear Biron, Tho' I send daily for [postal] franks I shall be equally obliged by y'r returning them un-franked whver it is <u>inconvenient</u> [sic] without any ceremony—Has lady Sitwell asked you for Saturday eng [evening]?
> Ever y'r truly, J. Wedderburne Webster.

There is a P.S.:

> "If you ever love a woman with one eye—say in defence—with that—she sets ye world on fire—if she'd another she'd reduce it to ashes!
> Pray send ye seal I gave you to be engraved with this device—a tombstone & a shatter'd skull laying upon it—motto 'Ne plus ultra'
> I think it a memorable thought—Don't reject it because it is mine—
> I have never seen or heard of ye vater—were you serious
> Write soon pray & remember our last conversation.

On June 11, 1814, Byron replied to James's letters of June 8:

> Dear W—My arrangements with Mr Claughton are still so undefined—that I am not sure whether I can comply with your request or not—however—I will enquire—and if I have the power you may depend upon the permission.—I did but receive one note from you during your last visit to town and I had been up all night for a week together—& being at ye. same time in expectation of seeing you here or meeting you somewhere I delayed answering till you were gone—our avocations seem to have led in different ways—& yet at that time I was a good deal out—as it is called.—I thank you for your invitation—which you may repeat with great safety—and ever am very truly yours. B.
> P.S.—I hope you settled every thing to your wish with your M.P.—and that if you go over to N[ewstead] you will pass your time pleasantly.—I shall always be happy to hear that you are doing well.—Your Lady Sitwell has sent me a card for tonight, but I shan't go. I have had enough of parties—for this summer at least.

However, that night Webster arrived and dragged Byron, against his will, to the party at Lady Sitwell's. Webster later wrote a manuscript note on Byron's letter of that date:

> I did take him to Lady Sitwell's party in Seymour Road. He there for the first time saw his cousin, the beautiful Mrs. Wilmot [born Anne Horton, she was the wife of Byron's cousin, Robert John Wilmot]. When we returned to his rooms in Albany, he said little, but desired Fletcher [Byron's valet, who had a gargantuan propensity for ladies of the evening, and who, much to Byron's dismay, introduced Robert Rushton to that form of entertainment] to give him a tumbler of Brandy, which he drank at once to Mrs. Wilmot's health, then retired to rest, and was, I heard afterwards, in a sad state all night. The next day he wrote those charming lines upon her — She walks in beauty like the Night…

Lady Sitwell's soirée was the last occasion on which the two old friends, Byron and Webster, were to see each other for many years.

Lady Frances's first letter to Byron since February 1, 1814, was taken up with trying to get her letters back from the poet. It was written on June 17, 1814:

> Will not the sight of this well-known hand astonish you?—Nay, start not—You have nothing to fear.
>
> I feel I cannot much longer support the recollection of some events which for many months past has embittered every moment—and as I am sensible the time is not far distant when all will be alike to me [she means that her death is imminent]—I do not wish to leave a single memento in existence of my past—my <u>only</u> folly—therefore, by every power of Heaven and Earth—by ye recollection of—Stop! they must be buried in oblivion by your every hope hereafter—I implore you to return every letter of mine in your possession—I implore you on my knees—I beseech you with uplifted hands to grant my petition.
>
> If for one Inst. you hesitate in acceding to my <u>last</u> request—consider ye crime of keeping by <u>force</u> in your possession one line—one word—that might hereafter tarnish my honor, which I thank God is unsullied—at least I trust so—for unless, by you, it is unblighted—you may think ill of me—but I solemnly assert—and without vanity—that untill I knew you I was innocent as my child—you know ye conflicts I sustained—you also know my triumph over myself—If again you hesitate—Oh! Byron, remember your sacred promise to restore each line if I wished—Now I claim ye fulfillment of that promise—not because I am changed—Alas—No! Do not drive me to a state of desperation by your refusal—You will perhaps say that I ought to have compleat confidence in you—I have every dependance [sic] on yr honor—I have given sufficient proof—In every sentiment I am unchanged, as the <u>picture</u> will show—but I will not explain—till I have destroyed <u>every line</u> relating to my folly, that might [these last two words she crossed out] which I am determined to do—till I have proved whether your former professions of affection were sincere or not—Ah! I am leaving home for a time but not <u>all</u> [she and James were off to the Continent]—I beseech you to enclose them, I mean my letters—<u>every line</u>—not even excepting this letter—<u>well sealed</u> & directed for me in a parcel directed for Miss Rawlence, Thos. Bacon, Esq, Farnboro' Place, Bagshot, Hants—She has directions to forward them, to me <u>immediately</u>, unconscious of her charge—by return of Post—You will hear from me—I expect your immediate compliance, else all opportunity is lost—I will not at present say more—Should you be careless in sealing & directing I am ruined—I shall consider that I receive every line secured by yr Honour—my head turns round—I cannot now write more—but, Oh Byron, I depend upon you—do not betray—do not deceive me—May every happiness attend you—Adieu. Adieu.
>
> Again I beseech you to be careful in enclosing to Miss R—as I shall be absent from home—June 17th, 1814.

A short letter from Byron to Lady Melbourne, on June 21, 1814, went like this: "Since I wrote last night I have received the two enclosed. What shall I do about Ph. and her epistles? since by her own account they run great hazard in their way to her. I am willing to give them up, but she says not a syllable about mine; no matter."

What he means by this and what he actually did are two different things. He means that he was willing to send her letters back to her, as she requested, but claimed to be worried about his letters to her. In any event, he never acceded to her request. Knowing how desperate she was, and how much it would hurt her if he didn't send them—he didn't send them.

"Dear Byron," wrote James on July 31, 1814:

> I have not troubled you in this way for some time — being ye last opportunity I can have in <u>this</u> land at least for some time —
>
> We leave this [place] for Ostend next Saturday. I shall travel thro' most parts of France, but our inter-mediate <u>reste</u> will be Brussels — where our family are all assembled in full divan — <u>This</u> you will allow <u>must</u> be always a strong <u>inducement</u> — I hear Parnassus is moved to Hastings — or in other words that you have taken a house there — what is ye place famous or agreeable for? [Byron had, indeed, taken a month's lease on Hastings House].
>
> I sh'd be much gratified in hearing from you before we go — but it must be by return of Post, and nothing can give me more pleasure than to hear you are in possession of ye <u>little</u> enjoyment that I can believe most things in this day capable of conferring on a mind like yours — If you want a House — this will be at your service — & a neighbourhood I sh'd imagine not unsuited to your arrangement —
>
> I since went to Newstead not having heard from you & by taking the other road when we leave this [place] I shall avoid ye only charm of seeing it, w'ch in your absence I would never wish to do — will Rushton, who is a part of my Establishment, forfeit y'r <u>good will</u> — as they term it — by going out? I ask the question at this regard — if so — If so, I shall not stand in his way — Adieu, Dear B — Let me hear from you — now — if ever —
>
> Yours very truly, JWW
>
> Aston Hall, Worksop, July 31. 14.

It is fascinating to note that Rushton was now back with the Websters.

For August 3, 1814, there is a forged Byron letter supposedly written from Hastings to W. Webster, Esq., of Long's Hotel, Bond Street, London. This letter was reproduced by Schultess-Young, Letter IV, pp 159–160. This is chronologically the first of the five Major Byron forgeries that Ehrsam, in his biography of the major, has listed as being to Webster:

> My dear Webster, — To-morrow, probably, I shall take leave of my old friend Ocean and proceed to Notts. The review you sent me is one of the dullest. It begins with the striking and new axiom, that 'there is nothing new under the sun'; and, in order to exemplify it, rambles into one of those prosy <u>nil ad rem</u> ramifications from the main branch of enquiry, with which the fields of modern criticism, to the infinity joy of the amateurs of siestas and day-dreams, have been exquisitely tangled and prolifically overgrown. For this purpose illustrations of romance, drawn from Pegasus, Perseus, Bellerophon, &c. &c., and as old as the Ark, according to Bryant, are resorted to by way of novelty; and the <u>oracula decies recocta</u> of Charlemagne, Bradamonta, Amadis de Gaul, King Arthur, &c. &c., is hashed up for the loathing palate of the public. The scribe of this article, whoever he may be, tells no such truths as that 'false rhymes are a blemish.' He might himself take a respectable canon of criticism from the medical proverb of "physician cure thyself.' The second ponderous article may suit the taste of some half-dozen shovel-hats; but the public, who cares little for any 'justification' but that of getting money's worth for their six shillings, will gape over the first two pages. The rest I leave to the 'antediluvian whales,' and remain, Yours affectionately, Byron.

In August 1814 James's other sister, Anne, married Archibald Murray Douglas, captain in the 52nd Foot, and brother to James's stepfather, Robert Douglas of Brigton. They would have three children: William, Elizabeth, and Mary. It was about this time, 1814, when James's stepfather's father died, that his mother, Elizabeth Read Wedderburn Douglas, and her husband left Aldeburgh for the north.

Lady Frances's sister, Catherine, married one of the Duke of Beaufort's sons, Lord John Somerset, on December 4, 1814. She was 19.

On January 26, 1815, Byron wrote to Hobhouse, from Seaham, the little Durham harbor village where Annabella Milbanke came from: "You know I have paid off Scrope; that is 6000 pounds and more; nearly 3000 pounds to Hans. *Carnal*; then I lent rather more than 1600 pounds to Hodgson, 1000 pounds to 'bold' Webster, and nearly 3000 pounds to George L, or rather Augusta. The last sum I never wish to see again, and the others I may wish. I have W's bond, which is worth a damn or two, but from Hodg. I neither asked nor wanted security...."

The arcane reference to Hans. Carnal ('Carnal' alone being italicized) is to Hanson, and an in-joke connected somehow to legend of Hans Carvel. The George L is, of course, Augusta's husband, George Leigh. The fact that Byron had given, rather than lent, Hodgson £1000 in 1813 to pay off his debts, lends a troubling aspect to Byron's character, always recognized as duplicitous yet never ungenerous— unless he happened to be in dire straits, in which case his famous generousness was able to mutate with ease into everything as Shylockian as he pretended to despise. Hodgson had given a bond to the poet in exchange for the extraordinary gift, and Byron had "forgotten" to destroy it. The money was never paid back, not by Byron's death in 1824 anyway, when his executors came after the unfortunate Hodgson for the outstanding monies.

Incidentally, the Websters are not mentioned in *Memoir of the Rev. Francis Hodgson, with Numerous Letters from Lord Byron and Others*, compiled by James T. Hodgson, and published in 1878.

13

Waterloo: Ball, Battle and Poem

On June 15, 1815, on the eve of Waterloo, Mr. and Lady Frances Webster were present at the Duchess of Richmond's ball, probably the most famous event of its type in history, thrown in the ballroom of the Richmonds' rented house on rue de la Blanchisserie, Brussels. Also present that evening were Countess Mountnorris (Lady Frances's mother), Lady Juliana Annesley (Lady Frances's youngest sister), Lord John Somerset and his wife, Lady Catherine Annesley (Lady Frances's sister; Lord John's brother, Fitzroy, later Lord Raglan, commander of the Allied forces during the Crimean War, was invited but couldn't make it), the Capels (Lady Caroline Capel—a resident of Brussels since 1814 when she was forced into exile due to her husband's gambling debts—and her adult daughters), Arthur Shakespear of the Light Dragoons (actually, despite his billing, of the 10th Hussars), Capt. Pakenham of the Royal Artillery, Sir Charles Stuart (grandson of the Earl of Bute, and ambassador to Paris, 1815 — 30, he will play a considerable role in our story), the Misses Ord (the six step-daughters of Thomas Creevey, who had married William Ord's widow in 1802), General Don Miguel de Alava (Wellington's Spanish aide-de-camp), the Grevilles, Mrs. Pole, la Comtesse Assche (Belgian noblewoman), and Dr. John Hume (Wellington's personal physician). And finally, but not least, the Duke of Wellington himself, who had met Lady Frances not long before, and had been truly smitten with her, despite the fact that she was seven months pregnant (and notoriously neglected by her husband) at the time of Waterloo. The Duchess of Richmond's invitation list for the ball was given by the Duchess to Lord Verulam, and by him to Lady de Ros, who published it in *Murray's Magazine*, 1889, volume 5, No. 25, in an article entitled "Personal Recollections of the Great Duke of Wellington," by the [at that stage] Dowager Lady de Ros.

Lord Mountnorris had a house in Brussels, which made it convenient for everyone. Incidentally, the shawl Lady Frances wore at the ball is now in the possession of her great-great-great-grandson, Simon Heneage.

Elizabeth Longford, in her 1969 book, says, "Lady Frances Wedderburn-Webster was another of the 'Loose Characters' on whom Brussels society cast an alert but disparaging eye." This is such a facile comment as to be considered unresearched. Brussels may have cast an alert eye on Lady F., but a disparaging one? Hardly likely, given the rest of the cast list.

The last letter Wellington wrote before the battle was at 3 o'clock on that Sunday morning:

> My Dear Lady Frances, As I am sending a message to Bruxelles I write to you one line to tell you that I think you ought to make your preparations, as should Lord Mountnorris, to remove from Bruxelles to Antwerp in case such a measure should be necessary.
>
> We fought a desperate battle on Friday, in which I was successful, though I had but very few troops. The Prussians were very roughly handled, and retired in the night, which obliged me to do the same to this place yesterday. The course of the operations may oblige me to uncover Bruxelles for a moment, and may expose that town to the enemy; for which reason I recommend that you and your family should be prepared to move to Antwerp at a moment's notice.
>
> I will give you the earliest intimation of any danger that may come to my knowledge; at

present I know of none. Believe me, etc. Wellington. Present my best compliments to Lord and Lady Mountnorris [no compliments, it will be noticed, to her husband].

Wellington, as soon as the battle was over, tore a page from his pocket book and wrote a note to Lady Frances, assuring her of "James's safety" (this note was later sold by auction at Sotheby's for a considerable sum). Later, whenever he suffered from an ailment, James had a tendency to lead people to believe it was from a wound at Waterloo.

It is these two factors—the brief "James's safety" note, and the later ailment-induced fabrications on the part of Bold Webster—that have inclined many to the belief that James Webster was on the field at Waterloo. But he was not. He was, in fact, an aide-de-camp to Lord Uxbridge, and serving with the 9th Dragoons at that time. Elizabeth Longford, in her book *Years of the Sword*, wrongly describes James as a captain, whereas he was, in fact, a mere lieutenant. She also (in the same book) says that "Lady Frances had married a Hussar officer in 1810—James Wedderburn-Webster, who turned out to be the worst kind of sexual braggart." She was right about that.

Perhaps more damaging, because of the Wellington letters to Lady Frances, it was rumored (a rumor started by Lady Caroline Lamb) that the duke was late to the battle due to a dalliance with the lady in question. Highly unlikely, however.

On June 16, 1815, the day after the battle, Lady Caroline Lamb wrote to Lady Melbourne about the trips the gentry were making out to the field to pick up mementoes:

> Lady F. Webster most affected and Lady Mountnorris who stuck her parasol yesterday into a skull at Waterloo. Perhaps a certain rivalship makes me see her less favourably, but indeed, Lady F. Webster is too ridiculous. Mr Bradshaw an amiable Dandy close to me, says it makes him ill for 2 hours after he has seen her. I conclude that you have heard that the Duke of Wellington fell desperately in love with her and 2 others, which was the cause of his not being at the battle in time.

This rumor would persist, forever. Dorothea, Princess Lieven (wife of the Russian ambassador in London, lover of Metternich, and preeminent gossip monger) in her diary entry of April 18, 1821 (six years after the event), wrote, "Let me introduce the characters of my story. Lady Frances Webster, married to a jealous husband who has reason to be jealous. She is a young and rather pretty woman although she is a little too washed-out for my taste [she was a fine one to talk about being washed-out]. But my taste has nothing to do with it and other people admire her: for instance the Duke of Wellington five or six years ago and nearly forgot in her company that he had the battle of Waterloo to win. There was talk of a lawsuit, but he avoided the scandal by paying down some thousands of guineas.... That is my first character."

At half past eight in the morning of the 19th, the day after the Battle of Waterloo, Wellington again wrote a letter to Lady Frances from Brussels:

> My Dear Lady Frances, Lord Mountnorris may remain in Bruxelles in perfect safety. I, yesterday, after a most severe and bloody contest, gained a complete victory, and pursued the French till after dark. They are in complete confusion; and I have, I believe, 150 pieces of cannon; and Blücher, who continued the pursuit all night, my soldiers being tired to death, sent me word this morning that he had got 60 more. My loss is immense. Lord Uxbridge, Lord FitzRoy [sic] Somerset, General Cooke, General Barnes, and Colonel Berkeley are wounded; Colonel De Lancey, Canning, Gordon, General Picton killed. The finger of Providence was upon me, and I escaped unhurt. Believe me, etc. Wellington.

A popular verse of the time reads:

> Uxbridge: By God, Sir, I've lost my leg
> Wellington: By God, Sir, you have

Another victim of the battle was Hobhouse's brother.

A potentially misleading (for scholars, that is) letter from the King of the Netherlands to Field Marshal the Duke of Wellington, from Le Haye, on June 24, 1815, mentions that he has received the duke's letter of 19 June. Interestingly, he recognizes the service of a Lieutenant Webster, aide-de-camp of the Prince of Orange. (The Prince of Orange commanded I Corps of the Infantry.) But this was not James but a certain Lt. Henry Webster, no relation.

On July 7, 1815, Lady Caroline Capel wrote to her mother from the Continent, "Lady Frances Wedderburne Webster is gone for the purpose of being confined here." What she meant was that Lady Frances, eight months pregnant, was now in Paris, ready to go into labor.

The two Wellington letters to Lady Frances were not deemed publishable until the Duke's son, the 2nd Duke of Wellington, included them in the *Supplementary Despatches* in 1858 (the *Despatches* and their follow-up, the *Supplementary Despatches*, are a multi-volume book of the letters written by the Duke of Wellington at this time). Indeed, in 1838, when Colonel Gurwood (while he was editing Volume XII of the original *Despatches*) asked Wellington about the Lady Frances letters, the Iron Duke replied, "I think it best not to insert these letters to Lady F. Webster. The Gentleman [Webster] who is selling them was in the King's Bench or one of the Prisons for debt; & offered them there for sale for thirty pounds. If they are published without the Names some of those who have seen them will certainly recollect to whom they were addressed; & will add the Names. That would create a nine days' wonder; which ... it is the object to avoid by omitting the Names. It is best therefore upon the whole not to publish the Letters; as they contain nothing of publick or military interest."

According to Richard Ford, artist, writer, and close friend of the 2nd Duke, Wellington exclaimed, on receiving them back, "What a fool I must have been when I wrote those letters." This is to be found in a note written by Ford in the margin of his *Apsley House & Walmer Castle* (1853, 2nd Duke's copy).

There was a third letter to Lady Frances in Brussels, which was written in answer to her inquiry about the fate of Napoleon. This third Wellington letter was dated July 14, 1815, Paris, and Lady Frances received it on the 17th. It gives Lady Frances a factual account of Napoleon, and ends with "I hope to see you soon."

Here it was, in Brussels, that the Lamb met Lady Frances Webster, who was now one of Wellington's favorites. Caroline Lamb flirted outrageously with the Iron Duke. "No woman can resist Wellington," it was often said, and with reason. The great man was irresistible. A notorious womanizer, he carried himself with the confidence of a rake who had never failed. He did not know how to lose the game, so he won instead, every time — except, perhaps, in the case of Lady Frances, and then there were heavily mitigating circumstances, the most notable being her advanced stage of pregnancy.

Bold Webster couldn't wait to tell Byron he'd just received a letter from the Iron Duke himself (or rather his wife had — "we," he says, by way of enormous self-deception). The day after receipt of the letter, he wrote:

> My Dear Byron, I felt every regret in leaving England once more — without seeing you — but it was impossible in ye time I had — I am told by those perhaps less interested in your welfare than myself — that you are gay & happy — I wished to have witness'd this — you certainly possess every <u>worldly</u> means of being so — & I know no one to whom I wish it more sincerely [except himself, of course] — — We are all (for Lord M'tNorris' family & ours are now united) going to Paris in a few days — in regard to myself I have nothing to say that would give ay [any] of my friends <u>pleasure</u> — more than this I need not say now — but if ye recollection of former years is not entirely effaced, let me hear from you & you shall hear more fully from me —
>
> We heard from ye Duke of Wellington last night & his letter dated ye 14th from Paris gives promise of another battle — w'ch you may hourly expect to hear of, as the french [sic] army still hold out obstinately on ye Loire & are from 80 to 100.000 men strong — he says he is to march after them immed'ly —
>
> Napoleon is on the L'isle D'aix [sic] — waiting untill the weather blows our Cruizers off ye coasts — before he decamps for America — you have no idea of ye enthusiasm with w'ch ye french fought at Waterloo — ye wounded officer refused to be carried from ye field, but desired only to

die on ye spot where ye Emperor had fought — one man was seen whose left arm was shatter'd by a cannonball to wrench it off with his other & throwing it up in ye air exclaimed to his comrades—'Vive l'Empereur jusqu'à la mort.' There were many other instances of ye like. This you may depend on however as true.

One of the above mentioned "other instances of ye like" could not have failed to escape the notice of Bold Webster. His wife's fairly new brother-in-law, Lord John Somerset, who had married Lady Catherine Annesley the previous December, had a brother, Lord Fitzroy Somerset (they were both the sons of Henry Somerset, the 5th Duke of Beaufort). Fitzroy, who was Wellington's aide at Waterloo and also the great man's nephew by marriage, got into an argument with a bullet on the field of that battle, and lost not only the argument, but his right arm. While the surgeon was carrying the arm away Somerset yelled out, "Hallo! don't carry away that arm till I have taken off my ring." His wife had given the ring to him.

Actually the Emperor Napoleon had already left the little island off the Atlantic coast of France when Webster wrote his letter. It was a month after Waterloo and Napoleon was trying to get to America. However, the odds were stacked against him, and he surrendered to the British on July 15.

Webster continued:

> The Hollands and Besboroughs [sic] &c are here — & the <u>Lamb</u> — if I mistake not — it will be long before the <u>shepherd</u> is forgot — you will understand me.

Frederick Ponsonby, 3rd Earl of Bessborough, and his wife, Lady Henrietta Spencer, were the parents of Caroline Lamb.

> We meet frequently in society & you are not <u>infrequently</u> ye subject of conversation.
> Direct to me 'Poste restante — Paris' — & believe me Dear B, <u>ever yours</u>, J Wedderburn Webster. Bruxelles. July 18. 1815.

Then there is, as usual, a P.S:

> We are amused here with a ludicrous report — at our expense tho' — that a <u>conspiracy</u> is discover'd in <u>London</u>! That Lord Grey is in ye Tower & Ponsonby cut his throat — Whitbread having done so for ye same reason!!
> Pray write to me at Paris.

The references here are to George Ponsonby who, with Grey, led the opposition in Britain, and to Samuel Whitbread, unstable English brewer and politician and fanatical supporter of Napoleon, who had, indeed, slit his throat on June 6.

(Paston and Quennell transcribed part of this letter, with no date ascribed, but their transcription is so shockingly sloppy and full of errors that it is as if one is reading a different letter altogether.)

So, the Wedderburns moved to Paris, preceded and followed closely and with great enthusiasm by the Lambs and everyone else in and out of the great man's retinue, every hanger-on who wanted to be glimpsed with illuminati.

Rumor was flying about the Duke and Lady Frances. It was the gossip item of the day. And people assumed it to be true because the rumor was ubiquitous. On July 28, 1815, Robert Pemberton Milnes (of Fryston Hall, Yorks) wrote a letter to Scrope Davies, the postscript of which says, "Lady F Webster you may have heard was at Paris — the avowed mistress of the D of Wellington." Tim Burnett, in his book *The Rise and Fall of a Regency Dandy*, says, "In September of the same year Webster even wrote to Byron on the subject."

All was not a bed of roses for these gentrified folks. And all did not run smooth for the Iron Duke after Waterloo. In the August 5, 1815, edition (among other editions) of a Brussels newspaper appeared a sensational story about Wellington. The *St James's Chronicle* in London picked it up, the offending *Chronicle* editions being August 3, 5 and 8. They then put in:

> Fashionable alliteration:
> In the letter W, there is charm half divine —
> War, Wellington, W ... W ... and Wine!"

It also said, "The cessation of warfare has, in Paris, enabled scandal to resume her usual influence on the public mind. A report is very prevalent in the first Parisian circles that a distinguished commander has surrendered himself captive to the beautiful wife of a military officer of high rank, in a manner to make a very serious investigation of this offence indispensable." The amour, the *Chronicle* said, would lead to a "Crim.Con. case," meaning a criminal conversation piece, the legal grounds for divorce before the 1857 Marriage Act. The *Chronicle*, however, appeared to translate it as "Criminal Connection" (an alternate and equally valid interpretation of "Crim.Con"].

It was said that Wellington had flirted with Lady Frances during the Duchess of Richmond's ball on the 15th of June, and afterwards walked alone with her in the park. The Countess Assche, a Belgian aristocrat with a notorious inability to handle English names, wrote in her notebook of her evening at the ball, "I would willingly have throttled him [Wellington], from the impatience which his phlegm caused me, and the ease of his conversation with Lady Withesburne to whom he paid ardent court."

Wellington's game was to be as phlegmatically normal as possible on the eve of the great battle, in order to unnerve his opponent. This was standard psychological warfare of the day.

"She was pretty," continues the Belgian gossip, "and pious, and Wellington was very much attracted to her, and he may have walked alone with her in the Park, if alone it can be called in such a popular night spot. Wellington's wife had left Paris with the first wave of refugees, so he was alone on the Continent."

There is, however, an illuminating if very unsubstantiated report by Basil Jackson, which was first brought to public attention in his book *Notes and Reminiscences of a Staff Officer* in 1903. Elizabeth Longford covers this well in her 1969 book *Wellington: The Years of the Sword*: "One incident in her [Lady Frances's] much-discussed relationship with Wellington was witnessed by a 20-year old subaltern on the Royal Staff Corps, Basil Jackson."

In the words of Mr. Jackson himself,

> I shall now vary my tale by introducing a bit of gossip. I was sitting one afternoon in the Park with an elderly Belgian lady when a very great man walked past us, and immediately after a carriage drew up at an entrance on the opposite side of the park, and a lady alighted, who was joined by the great man. My friend and I, prompted by curiosity, arose to see the result of the junction, following with our eyes the lady and gentleman until they descended into a hollow, where the trees completely screened them. We then perceived another carriage arrive, from which an old lady descended, whom I recognised as Lady M.N. [described by Miss Longford as an agitated female sleuth], who went peering about as if looking for some one or something [Miss Longford erroneously transcribed this as 'who was peeking about'], but was completely baffled by the tactics of the lady and gentleman, and left the park re infecta [unfinished business]. She was clearly in search of her daughter, Lady F.W., of whom 'busy fame' whispered light things. But I must proceed to matters of more moment.

The green hollow, however, kept its secret. Posterity must be grateful to Jackson as no doubt Jackson was grateful to providence for this glimpse of Restoration comedy. Imagination would, no doubt, fill the blank in the story with the seduction of Lady Frances by the Duke of Wellington under the nose of her mother Lady Mountnorris — but for the inconvenient fact that Lady Frances was expecting a baby in a few weeks. Doubtless, to ease the imminent labor pains, her mother would lend her a box of Ching's Patent Worm Lozenges. The Countess Mountnorris never went anywhere without her 5/6 box of Ching's.

Patrick Laforce, in his book *Wellington the Beau*, has assembled a bunch of tributes, or testimonials, from that time — gossip, merely — to illustrate Lady Frances's Wellingtonian standing at that period of her (and the world's) history. He (Mr. Laforce) quotes James Simpson, a lawyer in Paris at that time, on his (Simpson's) entering Marshal Junot's house on the occasion of the Duke of Wellington's first victory ball: "[T]here sat [in a salon off the main ballroom] two very beautiful Englishwomen of high fashion, Lady Webster Wedderburn and Lady Caroline Lamb keeping a chair vacant between them. In a few minutes the Duke of Wellington himself looked into the room, when the ladies called to him that they had kept a place for him."

Apparently Wellington joined the ladies, and Simpson continues, "The two ladies were then joined by Walter Scott, the poet, and the four formed a very merry supper party. Lady Caroline Lamb startled us by an occasional scream."

Laforce quotes Simpson again, who was at the Duke's review of 10,000 troops on the Plain de Clichy the following day. According to Laforce, Simpson wrote: "The Duke, beside him rode a very pretty woman whom I recognised to be Lady Frances Webster whom I had seen at the Ball. The Duke was on a white horse, a conspicuous object. After receiving the salute of the line he cantered forward, followed by ADCs, servants, and Lady Frances to pass along the line. The Russian Emperor Alexander was a spectator at this review."

The difficulty here is not so much with Advocate Simpson, but with Laforce, who does not give exact dates in his book; nor does he give sources, notes, or references. To illustrate the dangers of his reportage, here is the original of the Simpson passage he attempts to quote, from *Paris After Waterloo*, written by Simpson and published by William Blackwood of Edinburgh in 1853:

> Beside him [the Duke] rode a very pretty woman, whom I recognised to be Lady F.W., whom I had seen at the ball. The Duke rode a white horse, which is always a conspicuous object. After receiving the salute of the line, he cantered forward, followed by his aides-de-camp and servants, and Lady F., to pass along the line.

However, as Laforce quite rightly says (referring to Lady Frances), "Lady Charlotte Greville was a more serious contender for the Duke's heart. If he did not see her each day, he wrote to her."

Then a quote by Laforce from Lady Frances Shelley's diary: "On Friday I would not go to the opera for fear of being in the Duke's way, as I guessed Lady Frances Annesley would be there." This reference to "Lady Frances Annesley" is odd, in that she was never referred to in that manner.

And one from Harriet Arbuthnot, one of the Duke's many amours: "At the time of the battle of Waterloo Lady Frances Webster was 'regnante.'"

The *Chronicle* continued, "The husband has laid his damages of 50,000 pounds which it is said the fortunate lover offered to pay; but this affair was too notorious for composition or the party injured had too much sensibility to be content with wearing 'gilded' horns."

Two days later the paper followed up with, "Several of the public prints have in some particulars gone too far in their insinuations ... and have blamed a 'crim.con.' and magnified damages in their usual sweeping way.... We may moreover ask, if the rumour of a criminal connection at an antecedent period, while subsequent to it the wedded parties lived & appeared together ... be sufficient grounds for an action at law?"

What the paper was getting at here is only what was going around, that Wellington and Lady Frances had been doing this (whatever it was, or wasn't) for some time prior to the explosion, and that, notwithstanding, James had continued to live with her as if he accepted, if not necessarily approved, her actions (if offensive actions existed). So, was a legal action really appropriate?

A denial followed: "We are rejoiced to learn from good authority that there is not the least foundation for a story of criminal intercourse on the Continent." However, a later paragraph in the same *Chronicle* article says: "A very beautiful woman of Irish extraction is said to be a party in the amour at Brussels which has made so great a noise on the Continent." The lady of Irish extraction was Lady Frances, and the *Chronicle*'s aforementioned rejoicing seems to have extended only as far as gleeful irony.

This libel had a great effect on Wellington, to name but one. William Lennox, his aide, describes a conversation with the Duke in his book *Three Years with the Duke of Wellington in Private Life*. As Lennox tells it, he was writing out letters of invitation to a ball when the Duke came in with his Spanish friend, General Alava. "Have you the newspaper?" the Duke asked Lennox. "I suppose it is the usual style of attack?" After examining the article, the Duke added, "That's too bad—the writer's a walking lie—never saw her alone in my life—this must be checked." This excessive protestation by the great man could only mean one of two things: Either the rumors were not true, or they were spot on.

Lady Frances Shelley considered the relationship between Lady Frances Webster and Wellington to be purely platonic. However right she might have been, she had a vested interest in so regarding it, as she, too, had adhered herself as if with glue to the Duke's coat-tails. In *The Diary of Frances Lady Shelley*, edited by her grandson Richard Edgecumbe, volume 1, page 135, she says "he was simple and kind to" Lady Frances Webster "in public, but nothing more" (although the words "in public" may be telling here).

By the early autumn of 1815 Wellington seems to have convinced James Webster that there was no truth to the rumor of his relationship with Lady Frances, and it seems equally evident that James believed him, otherwise he might well have sued for a divorce. However, this is not taking into account the possibility of the little game James and Frances might have been playing, a profitable game.

James Webster, deprived of his wife's physical attentions now for too many months, was feeling the itch, and was attracted to Caroline Lamb. He was, however, a little wary, probably because his instincts, however much he tended to override them, were still functioning and sending him warning signals, but also because he would have had competitors, including Byron, already long into the game.

Nevertheless, he wanted an all-clear from Byron before he decided one way or the other. He wrote the poet from "14 Place Vendôme, Paris—31 Aug [1815]":

> My Dear Byron, I had hoped to have heard from you ere this—having written from Bruxelles, but it seems you have a just sense of ye <u>value</u> y'r friends have for every thing pertaining to you———
> The papers will announce my <u>son</u> to you—heir to his father's foibles & his———
> You were to have been <u>Godfather</u> to ye <u>last</u> [i.e. Lucy, Bold Webster's eldest child]—we agreed 'Byron Wedderburn' w'd be a vey [very] heroic name—but <u>seriously</u>—I <u>now wish you to stand for this</u>—

What this meant was that he wanted Byron to stand as godfather to this new child. On August 28, 1815, James and Lady Frances's eldest son, Charles Byron Wedderburn Webster, was born in Paris, an event that was covered in *Scots' Magazine*, 1815, p. 873, and in the *Annual Register*, volume 57, page 115. The child had yet to be named however, until Byron's agreement.

Webster went on:

> Laying aside every feeling—that I hope you believe me to possess feelings founded upon our intimacy in former years—ye recollection of w'ch serves but to embitter ye present, as they never

can recur — laying these aside, I sh'd wish a son to bear ye name that must ever be held dear to Talent & ye ornament of ye day in w'ch he lived —
Shall it be so — or not? — Send me a few lines as soon as you can — I have seen a good deal of 'The Lamb' here — & thought more — She possesses an infant manner & naiveté of expression that might be fatal to ay [any] sentimentalist who was much in her society — her weapons tho' light, easily reach ye heart — [he wrote a whole sentence next, but obliterated it] Is all cold with you? — [what he means is, 'Byron, are you finished with her?'] I presume so now — y'r flock has no Lamb —
Tho' 'gentle dulness ever loves a joke' [from Alexander Pope] this is fact — She was taken for Hobhouse's mother by one of ye first restaurateurs in Paris —!!!
There is no incredible report here but that you admire Lucien's Poem to a Proverb — Walter Scott is here — a truly pastoral figure in this city — to tell ye french [sic] 'that man is a poet'! is at once to tell them all is possible with us [meaning the Scotch race, or more probably, the British in general; Webster was toadying to Byron here, knowing well the great Romantic Poet's worry that Scott might be considered the greater of the two] —
There is no new plot in agitation — ye opposition are in Despair — Creevey, who is here, walks ye Tuilleries [sic] in vain — & is in ye last stage of a consumption — .

Thomas Creevey, who regularly plied places such as the Tuileries looking for gossip, would actually live another 23 years.

The Milky Dandy (W-W fecit) Sir W de B — — the — is here — & points ye toe to ye admiration of evy [every] maitre des graces in Paris — ! — 'Parvos, Parva — decant!' —

Who this Milky Dandy was I have been unable to determine. His name seems to have been Sir W de B — the, and Webster owns that he himself coined the nickname for this fellow. Anyway, again as Bold W misquotes from Horace, Parvum, Parva, Decent — "little things please little minds."
His next words are more than interesting: "We hear you are writing 'Poems by a Gentleman and his Lady' — is it so — ." It is difficult to know what James is referring to here; he himself does not seem to know, as we shall see in Byron's September 4 reply to this letter.
He continues, "I hear m'ch of Lady Biron — is there a chance of our seeing you & her Ladyship in Paris — remember you will defer the Christening of my heir — ."
On September 4, 1815, Byron replied to Webster's August 31 letter (in a letter that is now, in manuscript form, in the Art Gallery, Museums, and Royal Pavilion, Brighton), from Piccadilly Terrace, saying:

My dear W. — certainly — if Lady Frances has no objection — & you are disposed to be so complimentary — I cannot but be accordant with your wish; I give you joy of the event & hope the name will be fortunate. Lady B. is very well & expects to lie in December — I wish a boy of course — they are less trouble in every point of view — both in education & after life. — You are misinformed — I am writing nothing — nor even dreaming of repeating that folly — & as to Lady B. she has too much good sense to be a scribbler — Your informant is therefore more facetious than accurate — .
    A word to you of Lady [Caroline] [Lamb] [on the original manuscript there is an attempt, by another hand, to obliterate the name which appears on the manuscript copy of this letter. The copy indicates that this letter was addressed to Place Vendôme, Paris] — I speak from experience — keep clear of her — (I do not mean as a woman — that is all fair). She is a villainous intriguante — in every sense of the word — mad & malignant — capable of all & every mischief — above all — guard your connections from her society — with all her apparent absurdity there is an indefatigable & active spirit of meanness & destruction about her — which delights & often succeeds in inflicting misery — once more — I tell you keep her from all that you value — as for yourself — do as you please — no human being but myself knows the thorough baseness of that wretched woman — & now I have done. —
    I believe I can guess the 'important subject' on which you wish to write — but I would rather decline hearing or speaking of it — for many reasons — the most obvious & proper of which is that

however false — it is too delicate for discussion even with your most intimate friends — to copy your own words I 'believe nothing I hear' on this point & advise you to follow the example. —
I write in the greatest hurry — just returned to London — if you answer I will write again — in the interim Yrs ever B.

Belonging to 1815 (inasmuch as a forgery can belong to any supposed date), there is an undated forged Byron letter from Piccadilly Terrace to W. Webster, Esq. This was reproduced by Schultess-Young in 1872, letter V, pp 161–162. Ehrsam credits it to the forger Major Byron and adds that it was probably meant to be dated between June 1 and October 31, 1815:

Monday morning. My dear W, — Pray, where did you get that Phoenix of a butler? 'The pimple of his purple nose/Exceeds the royal ruby.' He is a perambulating epitome of your wine cellar, and does you honour. If the superintendent of the culinary department is a counterpart of the man, you need fear no refusal on my part to dine with you. But, as I am a follower of old Prynne, as regards his *'manner of studie,'* I do not dine — *'which breaks off one's fancy, which will not presently be regained,'* like your *'common mortals'*; but I will try your claret, and may be some fish, or any other light preparation of your subterranean 'savant.' If that stammering 'peer of the realm' dines with you, pray put 'a *furlong*' between his lordship and my 'counterfeit.' He reminds me of Dr. Darwin, a most notorious stammerer, who used to splutter forth with a sort of triumphant smile, that 'every b-b-b-body might sp-sp-sp-speak p-p-plainly if he w-w-w-would.' Ever yours very truly, Byron.

In a follow up letter to one that her husband had written to Byron from Brussels, Lady Frances wrote from "Paris. Sept. 5th, 1815":

My dear Lord Biron, I have partaken in Mr. Webster's disappointment that we have not heard from, or indeed scarcely of you — since an event that, as it has fixed your destiny so will it, I trust, insure you every happiness this world can afford [she means his marriage to Annabella].
I have heard much of the amabilité of Lady Biron and I believe her every way worthy of that name, and I conceive this to be no common compliment — I fear our sojourn here, and the little chance of your visiting France will give me no opportunity of ye pleasure of her [meaning Annabella's] acquaintance for a long time to come.
Mr W. has a great wish, that what was talked of with my little girl should be realised with my boy — that of his being christened after you — He tells me he has written to you on ye subject, but I thought it necessary I should be a party to the request — I hope the name (if he bears it) which has given so many beauties to the age — may in maturer years, at least, impel him with the Desire to be a Pupil in the school of so great a Master —
I was concerned to hear poor Newstead was to be again sold — I had hoped it would again revert to you — as it is — it has in a degree deprived your friends of the grateful memory of the happy hours they may have passed there during your time. I feel much interest in my old friend [Joe] Murray and trust that he is not a part of the purchase —
I hope you will let us hear from you soon — and believe me, My dear Lord Biron, ever truly yours, F. Wedderburn Webster.

On September 10, 1815, Bold Webster wrote to Byron a letter broaching the subject of the Wellington scandal, something the poet (and everyone else) knew about already anyway:

My Dear Byron, Thanks for y'r <u>letter</u> & your <u>concurrence</u> — Charles Byron [the latest Webster, upon whose nomenclature and god-paternalism much rested] sends his Duty, & is in a flourishing state —
I have seen much of ye Lady in question & an évènement [event] that took place between us ye <u>very</u> day I heard from you confirm'd <u>partly</u> what you say — but to do her justice it was contrived by ye pious exertions of that good Christian Lady M'tnorris — When we meet again if <u>that</u> may ever be — more on this subject — I know you too well to believe ay [any] thing said ag'st you even [at the beginning of the new page the word 'confidential' is written at the top and underlined] were it possible that one who once — — — you to madness [for some reason Webster substitutes the verb he had in mind with a long dash] c'd attempt it — you are seldom named — & never <u>wronged</u>, when you are —
In regard to another & more important matter, did my feelings want either <u>evidence</u> or

conviction on ye subject — I sh'd be silent even to you — but as they are fully assured, I may allude to this infernal calumny, as a man w'd to a suspected assassin, who has wounded him in ye Dark, & to find this wretch out shall occupy me in evy [every] way — No man — dare — or would be base enough to invent such a thing —& the only remedy is to endeavor to drag ye author to light & bring an immede action ag'st ye most ostensible paper — which I have order'd to be done — I had thought ye person in question above all detraction even in this bad world, but there are times in w'ch virtue's self cannot walk ye Earth with impunity — Will you be ye friend in one way —

Tell me the real opinion of the world — and how my conduct is canvass'd, if there is a man entitled to respect who thinks that I ought to act otherwise, feeling as I do on the subject — I entreat you to tell me — you have been my friend. Be so in this essential point —

The Spanish army have enter'd france [sic]. Ney [Marshal Ney, one of Napoleon's generals], it is thought, will be pardon'd —

It is generally thought the winter will produce a few plots that will end in a massacre of certain people —

Talma [François-Joseph Talma, 1763–1826, great French actor and friend of Napoleon] is all that is worth hearing or seeing — he is very grand in Nero but he loses ye actor in affecting ye Napoleon, who he is uncommonly like in form & manner —

W'd you like a beautiful miniature of ye Emperor? I have been offer'd ye best likeness in Paris for 25 louis — they are very rare now — if so I'll send it to you — nothing can be finer, either as a painting or a likeness — untill I hear from you on ye subject — adieu! if you write to me — as formerly — w'ch, if you are still ye same Byron — I want to correspond with you on a very important matter — You know what I mean — believe nothing you hear, but that I am ever yours, Js.WedderburneWebster.

A long P.S. reads:

Do you mean to keep Rushton — I shall have [then he mentions a name, presumably his page, but the name, which would have been difficult to read at the best of times, has been crossed through. It looks as if it may be something like 'Lysoman'] — but Pages are awkward elves sometimes —.

Pray give me a sketch of W'm Lamb [he then crossed out the word 'Lamb'] — the Protector — I cannot make him out —& I look in vain for ay [any] precedent —

I hope you will have a boy —! With y'r double Barony, it w'd be hard to want a head to bear ye Crown — Dou you stay long in Town? I think I shall have to go there soon — Let me hear from you —& believe me yours ever.

14 Place Vendôme, Paris, Sept. 10th. 15

Byron had evidently taken Rushton back into his fold, after Webster's flight to the Continent had left the servant once more without a billet.

Finally, yielding to the bombardment, the poet wrote back, from "13 terrace Pic[cadilly]," on September 18. This reply, which is now to be found in the same place as the September 4 letter, says:

My dear W. — Your letter of the 10th is before me. — Since your last I received a note from Lady Frances containing a repetition of your request — which was already answered in my reply to you — I am obliged by her politeness & regret that she should have taken the trouble of which I presume you were the occasion. —

With regard to Lady C.L. [Caroline Lamb] — I wrote rather hurriedly & probably said more than I intended or than she deserved — but I fear the main points are correct — She is such a mixture of good & bad — of talent & absurdity — in short — an exaggerated woman — that — that — in fact I have no right to abuse her — and did love her very well — till she took abundant pains to cure me of it —& there's an end — You will deliver her the enclosed note from me — if you please — it contains my thanks for a cross of the 'Legion of Honour' which she sent me some time ago from Waterloo — I never received it till yesterday —.

The poet continues:

You may have seen 'much' but not enough to know her thoroughly in this time — She is a good study for a couple of years at least. — I will give you one bit of advice which may be of use — She is most dangerous when humblest — like a Centipede she crawls and stings. —

As for 'him' [William Lamb] — we have not spoken these three years — so that I can hardly answer your question — but he is a handsome man as you see — and a clever man as you may see — of his temper I know nothing — I never heard of any prominent faults that he possesses — and indeed she has enough for both — In short his good qualities are his own — and his misfortune is having her — if the woman was quiet & like the rest of the amatory world it would not so much signify — but no — everything she says — does — or imagines — must be public — which is exceedingly inconvenient in the end however piquant at the beginning. —

And now to the serious part of your epistle — Humph — what the devil can I say? — as your mind is so divided upon the subject — I wonder you should ask me to say anything — it is thrusting poor dear innocent me into the part of Iago — from whom however I shall only take one sentence —

'Long live she so — & long live you to think so!'

I must repeat however that it is not a topic for discussion — You must know & judge for yourself — and as to the 'real opinion of the World' which you wish to hear — you may surely discover that without my turning it's [sic] speaking trumpet — one thing you may be sure of — if there is any thing bad you will always as Sheridan says 'find some damned good natured friend or other to tell it to you' —

Pray are the Rawdons [Francis Rawdon, 2nd Earl of Moira, and his wife] in Paris? — if they are — I wish you could remember me to Miss R — & tell her that Lady B. has not heard from her since she wrote from Rome — if you come to England — you will easily find me — probably in London — ever yrs most truly B.

In some real ways James Webster was Byron's foreign correspondent during those tumultuous autumn days in Paris following Napoleon's final downfall. His letter to the poet of "Sept. 28 18 — [meaning 1815]," from "56 Rue St Lazare Paris," is a reply to the poet's letter of September 18, and begins with a thought he'd had after he had sealed the letter: "P.S. I have open'd this to tell you — 400 1/2 pay officers were last night arrested by ye Duc de Richlieu [sic] — a general insurrection is evy [every] where apprehended" [Richelieu was prime minister of France, and of the same family as the great Cardinal of Louis XIV's time].

The letter proper begins, "My Dear Biron, I received y'r letter with much pleasure — & deliver'd ye enclosure [i.e. to Lady Caroline Lamb] with some reluctance — not from ay [any] way connected with myself—"

Bold Webster had verily aimed for the Lamb, and it looks good that the lad's bolt went home true; however, now it was all over. He continues:

In regard to ye Lady our intimacy is on ye wane — — I have no goût [taste] for ye kind of Beings she is surrounded with — & I never could presume to rival Officers of Horse — on a peace Establishment far less — when protestations are sent forth from ye protecting shade of over-grown mustachios — her feelings towards you — resemble an intermittent fever —

I think it almost incurable — beware — & I think half her absurdities now arise from a wish to fly to ay [any] thing — from the memory of that [meaning her memory of Byron, rather than, say, her memory of Bold Webster; therefore this is Webster at his most obsequious] — or from a wish to make consistent past events by acting systematically upon ye same principle —

In regard to myself, I have done [a presumed double entendre] — She wish'd much to know ye contents of y'r first letter — She can only injure me by sheer invention & I concur she will hardly provoke me to act a part — I certainly never shall unless she first throws ye glove — as to William L——b — you don't know him — and ye world knows him less — He is neither tame or [sic] good temper'd — Clever, he may be — but it is that kind of negative talent that is of little use to himself — & of none to others — Son extérieur est assez bon — but I can assure you, he is a pertinacious gentleman — on home affairs — I owe him for a compliment at least — I am told 'he says W is ye best I have seen of that sett' — I presume he means your friends — I have done with ye couple for ever — With you, I fear, it may be otherwise — your letter writing &c &c may awaken what evy [i.e. every] interest sh'd suppress —

The Treaty of Peace, they say, was rejec'd yesterday — They have taken off the million for Louis — all Paris is in an uproar — Fouché & Talleyrand told him — if he rejec'd that treaty ye Allies first proposed, they c'd not answer for his life 6 hours —

The fact is — there is not one voice in 5 throughout France in their [i.e. the Bourbons'] favor —

Paris to a man dislikes ye Tribe — There is not a stone that does not echo Le Pauvre Empereur!—
Seriously I w'd not give ye tythe of a Birmingham farthing for ye head of one of them — as— to
the Pictures— after <u>Bombarding</u> poor Dear Old D'Enon, we have got them —& by way of making
his Peace with ye Devil, ye Pope is to send y'r Regent ye Apollo!!—

The interesting expression "tithe of a Birmingham farthing" is one Byron used in a September 30, 1813, letter to Webster. Whether Webster got it from the poet, or whether they both got it from someone else, it is not, and never has been a standard British expression.

This business about the pictures: Hitler wasn't the first to raid art galleries throughout Europe. Napoleon did the same thing, through his agent Vivant Denon, director of the Louvre. It is said that after the Emperor's defeat in 1815, Pope Pius VII offered to send the Prince Regent (the future George IV) the Apollo Belvedere if Britain would help the Italians restore to their rightful places the captured objets d'art. However, in the end, the Apollo went back to Rome.

In 1814 Sir Thomas Lawrence was commissioned by the Prince Regent to paint the portraits of 25 of the leading European statesmen who could be said to be responsible for the downfall of Buonaparte. Pope Pius VII was one of them, his sitting finally taking place in 1819. The Pope is Lawrence's masterpiece.

Webster's letter continues:

You are right in saying that all Car —_____Lamb's acts must be public — She now amuses Paris by breaking busts of L'd Wellington. He asked me to dinner last Sunday — in his own words 'to see her break another bust just arrived from Bordeaux'— I declined ye festival having seen it perform'd before—.

It is difficult — nay, impossible — to imagine Bold Webster, or anyone else, turning down an invitation from the Duke of Wellington, especially at that point in history.

Of Lady Caroline Lamb he continues:

I hear tho' it was done in her <u>best</u> style — It amuses ye Gothamites— and as it is only at her expense, is harmless enough, ye french [sic] can't understand it, & suppose in horror that it is a <u>rehearsal</u> in plaster of Paris— of some winter night's massacre we are plotting ag'st them —.

In this last letter he had forgotten to answer some of Byron's questions, so wrote another to "The Rt Hon, Lord Byron, Piccadilly terrace, London." It was franked on "2 Oct 1815." It reads:

The Rawdons are not in Paris— Tell Petersham all ye women breathe but upon ye report of his r'ed [rumored] entrée here —& assure him that a Deputation from ye Company of Master tailors will present him with an address on ye Pont Neuf—
Have you seen Mrs Erskine's Spanish Tale — I saw ye MSS [manuscripts] — N.B. a good soporific "To one canto of Busby's Lucretius— take 5 verses of ye above s'd [said] 'Spanish Tale'"— The faculty no longer use opium — or laudanum — where there [sic] patients <u>can</u> & <u>will</u> read — I admire ye melodies much — ye motive under w'ch I hear they were written — more — Scott admires— the first most whether from itself — Mrs W — or your — Taste — I shall not determine — but to my feelings nothing can exceed ye beauty of ye 3rd verse of 'Oh weep for those'— this with — ye sun of ye Sleepless & Herod's Lament — are worth ye whole book ———.

If James was not under the influence of opium at the time, he should have been. Rarely has such gibberish been committed to paper by such a fool and sent to such an august personage.

Eliza B. Norton, writing as Esme Stuart Erskine, had had *Alcon Malanzore: A Moorish Tale* printed in Brussels in 1815.

The letter (if it can be called that) continues:

Do you know what Lord Erskine said after reading ye Corsair?—— What a mass you must hear — of what never was said — Lady Frances is offended at y'r not answering her epistle —<u>Mine</u>—(if you get so far) you will say — is — Thank God —<u>finished</u>—! if you find time or inclination — let me hear from you — if no other theme — something 'worthy ye Lamb that's slain'— added — y'rs ever truly, J. Wedderburne Webster.

Oh, but he hasn't finished!

Since closing my letter, it occurs to me you may be ignorant of ye fate of my Berwickshire purchase & of ye embarrassment w'ch its connection has thrown upon me —

My Trustees refused to complete ye purchase, — ye consequence has been ye re-sale of ye estate to my prejudice some thousand pounds & with ye usual continence of ill luck other misfortunes have followed in harmonious succession!

Pray don't leave my letter abt —

Lord Kennedy has been fined 1500£ by ye C't [i.e. Court] of Session, for calling an attorney by his proper-name!

This is new — but no enigma —.

In 1815 and 1816 James published several *Miscellaneous* poems, as well as the notorious *Waterloo and Other Poems*, which was reviewed in the *Quarterly Review* of January 1816 (volume 15, pages 345–350), and not to Webster's satisfaction.

It all started with Walter Scott. Not long after the event the great Scotch poet had visited the battlefield and written *The Field of Waterloo, and Other Poems*. Six thousand copies were run off in mid-August 1815, and the book sold well despite awful reviews, the best-remembered of which is this anonymous quatrain:

> On the ensanguined plain
> Full many a gallant man was slain
> But none, by sabre or by shot,
> Fell half so flat as Walter Scott

Undaunted by his hero's critical reception, with a copy of Scott's new work in hand Bold Webster proceeded diligently to contrive his own *Waterloo and Other Poems*. Perhaps an unsuspecting public might buy his, thinking it was Scott's.

Then came the letter to "John Murray, Esq., 46 Albemarle St, London," in which Webster tried to cash in on Byron's friendship to win a contract with his publisher. "Webster W" wrote the letter on "Dec. 18.15 [December 18, 1815]," from "35 Rue de la Madeleine, Paris," and it reads:

Sir, I have written a poem on 'Waterloo' which I intend publishing, with many other pieces of a miscellaneous nature —& I am desirous it sh'd be edited by you — You will oblige me by stating ye terms on which you will undertake it —

Waterloo is nearly 500 lines & ye other pieces in all between 4 & 500 —

I believe my friend Lord Byron, who sees a good deal of you, is not in town, else I sh'd have requested him to speak to you upon it —

I wish them to form a vol. a'ut [about] ye size & type of ye Giaour, ye poem being written in stanzas will well admit of this—

Favor me with yr early reply & Believe me D. Sir, Yrs faithfully, J. Wedderburne Webster.

This approach didn't go over too well with John Murray, probably in part because of the style of the letter and in part because Murray, like everyone else, knew what an idiot Bold Webster was. There was also the fact that the poems were shockingly bad. No one in England would have touched *Waterloo and Other Poems*, and Webster didn't bother trying beyond Murray. He went straight to Paris, to Didot.

It was all knocked off very quickly, indeed, quicker than even James expected, as is to be seen from a letter he wrote Byron on January 15, 1816. In this letter James seems disingenuous, trying to secure his own miserable moment in the sun before Byron's next work swept aside all competitors in the marketplace:

My Dear Byron! You never answer one's letters without they speak of <u>marriages</u>—<u>Deaths</u>!—or <u>christenings</u>!!—therefore my perseverance is either a proof of my Christianity, or my persecution—I have been of late preciously afflicted with ye metromania—as a cure I am about being stuck in <u>print</u>—Query—w'ch is worse—ye <u>remedy</u> or ye <u>disease</u>—?—Seriously tho,' I wish to know when y'r new poem comes out—as it would be madness added to folly did I suppose mine c'd <u>breathe</u> 2 days ye same atmosphere with it—therefore pray tell me—if you have ay [any] charity—Defer it untill ye beginning of March, as there are reasons w'ch prevent ye publication of mine untill ye end of next month—In regard to ye <u>circulation</u> of such matter be it foul or fair—I have little fear, as I divide the world in those cases under two heads—half read from <u>mischief</u>, ye rest from vacant curiosity——

I may have reason to regret severely—certainly shall—that in ye progress of my malady I had not ye benefit of such a Physician as y'rself—shall I send you a proof copy?—If I do, what will you do with it——One word of dedication—I have a cordial hate to them [i.e. book dedications] in any event above ye condition of a Garrett-author [sic], tho' y'r own is ye only name that c'd grace any page (good or bad) that might appear, as you stand responsible for my child in this world. I think it c'd be hardly fair to make you so for my Poems in ye next [i.e. in the next world]—

Sir Robert Wilson—ye Dandy of ye Desert—& Col. Hutchinson—are in prison here by arrêt of ye French Government—for ye escape of Lavallette [sic]—

Rely on it, this step w'd not have been taken upon slight grounds—I believe they are in possession of evidence to prove ye fact—

Lord Th—____t [Thanet] I hear will shortly receive an order to quit this capital—

Remember me kindly to Scrope—ask him to shew you ye lines by a relation of Ney's—

If you will write direct here before ye first of next month—after—'Poste restante, Tours'—

Joy & greeting for y'r Daughter!—Tho' ye Dutchess [sic] of [regrettably, her name has been crossed out] assur'd me it was a Boy—Transubstantiation is ye only un-natural operation I sh'd doubt her d—____'s capability of performing—

Write pray & Believe me Dear Byron—ever yours—J. WedderburneWebster. 35 Rue de la Madeleine, Paris, Jan. 15.16.

Count Marie Lavalette, a deluded Napoleoniste, had, in the brief period between Elba and Waterloo, seized the Post Office in Paris, and after Napoleon's final surrender found himself on trial for something akin to war crimes. In December he escaped, with the aid of some Englishmen, including Wilson. "Dandy of the Desert" was an epithet due to Wilson's service in the army in Egypt, bestowed upon him ad hoc by Webster.

The *Quarterly Review*, founded by Byron's publisher John Murray in 1809 with William Gifford as editor (the same writer of the *Baviad* in 1794), was a hugely successful periodical, thanks largely to Gifford's violent attacks on new writers who dared put forth their works on the market.

Roy Benjamin Clark, in *William Gifford: Tory Satirist, Critic and Editor*, says that Gifford "snapped his fingers contemptuously under the nose of the author [i.e. Webster].... He ended by observing that Didot [that is Firmin Didot, of the French publishing house of Didot], with his stereotype machine, had used the device of verse to make the pretended Englishman 'write himself down an ass.' This review elicited Webster's reply to the *Quarterly* through the pages of the *Morning Chronicle*." Here is said review, in biting full:

ART. II.—*Waterloo, and other Poems*. By J. Wedderburne Webster, Esq. Paris, printed by Didot, Sen. 1816. pp. 72.

The subject of this article belongs rather to mechanics than literature: what Dean Swift ridiculed as a visionary scheme has been reduced, by modern ingenuity, into actual practice; and the fancy of the Laputan philosopher to make a machine for grinding the vocabulary into treatises has been, it seems, realized by our ingenious neighbours the French.

Everybody knows that M. Didot is not only a celebrated printer, but a great mechanist, and, if not the inventor, at least the introducer of that mode of printing called Stereotype, in which the lines and words are not made up of separate letters as heretofore, but are cast at once into permanent forms ready for use. Having words, and even lines, thus prepared, it was a natural yet ingenious thought to endeavour to apply some moving power by which they might be disposed in proper places and forms, without the delay, expense, and uncertainty of human labour.

This moving power M. Didot seems to have acquired; and in the little work before us he exhibits a complete specimen of his success. It was not, indeed, to be expected that the machine, however ingenious, could always place the words in intelligible order, or work out any thing like sense or meaning; but as to the mechanical part it has succeeded surprizingly, and, to the eye, the lines of this pamphlet look as like real bona fide verses, as if they had been written by the hand of man, and printed by the ordinary process of the press. It occasionally, indeed, happens, (we suppose from the accidental breaking of a pully [sic] or a spindle,) that some of the lines want a foot, and that there are little flaws in different parts of the work; but errors of this kind in so new an invention are inevitable. We know that Sir Richard Arkwright's cotton machine, improved as it has been by long experience, will sometimes make a flaw in a piece of goods; we are therefore not to be surprized if M. Didot's verse-engine should be, at its first setting off, liable to similar accidents.

But while we do full justice to M. Didot's ingenuity, we cannot but lament the ill-temper and hostile feeling towards England, which has induced him to announce the fortuitous produce of his engine as an English poem, and to affix to it a name, which, if not the name of an Englishman, is at least a union of English names: very probably there may be no individual of the double name of Wedderburne-Webster; still, however, the names are so notoriously British, that all foreigners, and even some of our own countrymen, will, we doubt not, believe that there is really such an author as J. Wedderburne-Webster, Esq. to the no small disparagement of our literary, and even of our national character.

But that which shews at once the depth and source of the malice of the French printer and his associates, is, that they have selected the immortal day of Waterloo as the subject of their experiment, and that the nonsense which their machine a vapeurs (so they call their steam-engine) has ground, is represented by them as a song of triumph on that great victory.

We are ready to admit, that the French nation can never look back on that day without some emotions of sorrow, and that even the existing government may feel some slight twinges on the score of national vanity; but we think that the Royalist Police would have shewn no more than a becoming gratitude to this country if it had prevented a publication which — under the colour of a new mechanical discovery — is evidently intended to throw ridicule on the battle of Waterloo and the British language and nation. What would be thought if we were to collect all the French exercises of a ladies' boarding-school, print them on fine paper with Bulmer's best types, and circulate them in France under the title of Éloges de Sa Majesté Louis XVIII, par le Comte de la Grenouilliere? Doubtless the French ambassador would not be slow to complain of such an indignity; yet these French exercises would certainly be as much an éloge of his Majesty, as the verses of the pseudo-Wedderburne-Webster are an éloge on Waterloo.

But our readers will be, by this time, curious to see some patterns of this curious workmanship — it is our duty to give them, but we do so, not without regret that the names of Soignies, Hougoumont, Waterloo, and Wellington, should be thus degraded. That we, however, may not be in any degree 'participes crimines,' we shall give out extracts verbatim, literatim, and, if we may use the expression, punctatim.

The following, we suppose, may pass for the invocation —

> Oh! that the Muse, should dare essay,
> To sing in such an humble lay
> The hottest field beneath the sun,
> Since warring man in strife begun:
> But might his lowly, feeble lyre,
> In others, wake th'heroic fire —
> Like a bright beacon on the steep,
> 'Twould cheer his lonely vessel o'er the deep.—p. 7.

Our readers will observe what pleasant confusion the machine has made here. The Muse is of the masculine gender, and has a lyre, which lyre is a bellows, which bellows is to wake a fire, which fire is to be a light-house, by which light-house his (the Muse's) lyre or bellows (now become a ship) is to be cheer'd o'er the deep! What must the French think of us when they are told that these are English verses!

Again —

> Bear witness, Soignies' darkling bowers,
> And Hougoumont! thy shatter'd towers—

> Tho' each, by war — not tempest rent —
> Thou yet can boast — one battlement!
> That long shall speak to other times,
> And mock the pow'r of despot crimes;
> For well thy rude unhallow'd fane,
> ath mark'd the downfall of the rebel train! — p. 10.

This whole stanza is a curious piece of verbal Mosaic; but the most wonderful of all is that line in which a wood and a house are jointly apostrophised with a singular pronoun and a plural verb, on the subject of a talkative battlement common to both.

In fact, M. Didot himself appears so pleased with the effect of his machinery in this instance, that he grows quite wanton upon it, and in a strain of no great courtesy or grammar, adds, 'Whether this is the case, I really do not know, but if any person is inclined to dispute the point, I have no possible objection to their going to Hougoumont to ascertain it.' — p. 75.

But we have a further complaint against our ingenious persecutor. Having apparently collected from the conduct of our countrymen who literally swarm around every penny-show-box in Paris, that John Bull is somewhat muddy-headed, he has taken an insidious advantage of the circumstance to propound a riddle to him, which would have puzzled Sphynx herself.

> ———the vulture shriek'd aloud,
> And the red traveller sought his shroud. — p. 9.

'Now riddle-my-ree, what is this?' After a hundred conjectures, we ended with determining that it was One of the Foot-guards, going on the forlorn hope. No such thing. It is the rising sun! The peculiar malice of the question lies in this, that whereas the 'red traveller' of Ossian (from whom the word is taken) is 'broad and bright and glowing,' the red traveller of the poem is first black, and then of no colour at all, for he never makes his appearance!

The battle itself could hardly be darker than the following riddles which, we presume, pretend to describe it.

> Impell'd with fury to the shock,
> Th'Imperial Eagles left the rock;
> And rushing in distended line,
> Sent quickly from destruction's mine,
> A shower of varied shot and steel,
> Which few were there who did not feel. — p. 16.
> 'Twas then, two hundred cannons roar,
> Loud heralds of the guilty shore —
> Tore up the surface of the ground,
> Whose very CENTRE TREMBLED at the sound!
> And quick, like meteor of the night,
> The bright cuirassiers join'd the fight;
> And gave their curses to the wind,
> With speed once urg'd, no arm could bind. — p. 11.
> 'On to the charge!' he loudly cried —
> As forward to the steep he hied;
> *Stand to your guns! — point them well —*
> That each may some dread mission tell —
> Spare not the foes — nor sue for life —
> *But hunt victory — 'even to the knife!* — p. 12.

In this last extract our readers will observe that the two lines distinguished by italics have been a little damaged in the weaving. The latter of them, a note informs us, is a touch at Palafox's [the Spanish general Palafox, who resisted Napoleon in 1808] famous cry at Saragossa, War to the knife! which meant a struggle so long, so close, and so deadly as to reduce the combatants to the use of their daggers; but war being only of one syllable, and the space requiring a word of three, the machine put in 'victory' — Wedderburne, or Nincompoop, would have done just as well.

Another instance of the glorious cross-readings inseparable from a poem fabricated by a steam-engine, occurs in page 15 —

> None sued for life,
> And those who were compelled to yield
> Rush'd headlong on their broken———

sword a human being would have said; and it would have been thought an illusion to the incident so frequent in Roman history, in which the defeated hero rushes on his own sword, but the machine immediately happened to grind up another word, and that other word happened still more unluckily to be one of the most opposite meaning which the whole box could furnish:—

> Rush'd headlong on their broken----SHIELD!'—p. 15.

How the boys at the French Lycées, who will probably be perfidiously taught to read this as English, will stare at our classical knowledge!

The following wonderful passage would seem to imply that, in our English creed, souls can never be crushed TILL they have died.

> Then Albion's banners tower'd on high,
> And ev'ry horror rent the sky;
> Man rush'd on man—'till death had hush'd
> Those souls, that else had ne'er been crush'd.—p. 20.

And the poem goes on to say the battle was so tremendous, that when the ghosts of the dead men came back in the night to look for their bodies, they were not able to find them.

> -----------there the spirits of the slain
> Might seek to find their earthly forms in vain.—p. 21.

And this is the trash which M. Didot has the perfidy to palm on the French public as the exultation of an English gentleman on the battle of Waterloo!

In the poems which follow [he means the other, shorter poems which appear in Webster's book] we suspect that M. Didot has not trusted even to his engine to make nonsense; for these appear to be put together with a degree of ingenious malice against us, of which we cannot conceive a mere machine, however well made, to be capable. For instance, the four following French lines are very correctly given:—

> J'abandonne l'exactitude
> Aux gens qui riment par métier;
> D'autres font des vers par étude,
> J'en fais pour me desennuyer.—GRESSET.

Now mark the difference!—the following are subjoined as an English translation of these lines.

> Willing I yield all rhyming rules,
> To hireling bards, and pedant schools;
> May fancy guide my careless lay—
> And pleasure wing my hours away.—p. 39.

This is evidently a burlesque on our supposed ignorance of the French language, as absurd and offensive as if we were to quote that famous passage in Shakespeare—

> I'd rather be a kitten, and cry mew,
> Than one of those same metre ballad-mongers.

And then give the following as a Frenchman's translation of it:—

> Maudit soit l'auteur dur, dont l'apre et rude verve
> Son cerveau tenaillant, rima malgré Minerve,
> Et de son lourd marteau, martellant le bon sens,
> A fait de mechans vers a-peu-pres onze cents.

All this is sufficiently atrocious on the part of M. Didot; but we have kept for the last the cruellest insult of all, one which we have no doubt is levelled at the supposed disposition to blunder of our Irish brethren:—this outrageous libel is called The Wish, and the unfortunate Wedderburne Webster, in his new character, is thus made to express himself:—

> A WISH
>
> When hence my spirit wings its aerial flight—
> And life is fled into the realms of night!
> When, as some bird sits lonely on the mast,
> My form may ride upon the desert blast—
> Be my sole monument the moss-clad sod,
> Raised on the spot where man hath never trod—
> By the lone rock, upon my native hill,
> Where the grey thistle holds dominion still!—p. 40.

> Here then the air and the realms of night are the same thing; and when life flies, it flies to the realms of night; and when that comes to pass, the body rides just as a bird sits; and then there is to be a monument — not for the soul, for it is flying, nor over the form, for it is riding — but a monument to be raised, Jove knows why, where, or by whom; for it is to be built in some extraordinary desert where man has never trod; and yet this desert, where man has never trod, is the very place where Wedderburne Webster represents himself to have been born ('silice in nuda') amid a grove of thistles! — a paltry device of M. Didot to make our pretended countryman 'write himself down an ASS.'

In actual fact, Gifford may not have written this review. Certainly John Wilson Croker, a freelance reviewer, wrote the notorious condemnation of Keats's *Endymion* in 1818, so Webster could, after smarting for two years, finally console himself with being in good company. Gifford, or Croker, or whoever actually wrote the "Waterloo" review, did, of course know Wedderburne Webster well, as witness the reviewer's mentions of pamphlets and treatises for which James was well-known, even then. In addition, James was a literary aspirant, and would have come to the attention of the staff of the *Review*, especially socially. Gifford and his crew were simply satirists.

As for the review itself, it is unquestionably just. But it is devastating also. James was only 27 at this time, and one wonders why he continued writing after such an attack. His thick skin must have seen him through. The poetry is absolutely dreadful, and it was foolish of James to think he could put it out to the world and expect anything less harsh from the critics. It fully deserved the attack launched by the *QR*. Of course, this rubbish is no less tedious than any of the rubbish written by Byron or Shelley, but that perhaps, is a view through a magnifying glass two centuries old. Judged by his peers, James Webster certainly fell short of Byron, whom he was trying to imitate.

One sleepless night in March 1817, Byron wrote a few versicles that he later enjoyed sending to friends. They went like this:

> I read the "Christabel,"
> Very well:
> I read the "Missionary";
> Pretty — very:
> I tried at "Ilderim";
> Ahem!
> I read a sheet of "Marg'ret of Anjou";
> Can you?
> I turn'd a page of Webster's "Waterloo";
> Pooh! Pooh!
> I look'd at Wordsworth's milk-white "Rylstone Doe":
> Hillo!
> I read "Glenarvon," too, by Caro. Lamb —
> God damn!

Christabel was Coleridge; *The Missionary of the Andes*, from 1815, by William Lisle Bowles; *Ilderim, a Syrian Tale*, just released, was the work of Henry Gally Knight, the same Knight to whom Bold Webster would reply in a pamphlet 13 years later; Miss Holford's poem "Margaret of Anjou" had also just come out, in 10 cantos; "The White Doe of Rylstone," by William Wordsworth, had been around for a decade or more; *Glenarvon* was Lady Caroline Lamb's novel, also just published.

Bernard Grebanier writes in *The Uninhibited Byron*:

> Webster decided to burst upon the public as a poet himself with a volume published in Paris, 'Waterloo, and other Poems.' In the past he had contented himself with scribbling political pamphlets, much to the embarrassment of all connected with him, and to the foolishness of which Byron had been captive audience at Aston. It is not at all beyond possibility that the title of this

volume and the long poem itself were an attempt to capitalize on the scandal connecting his wife with Wellington. That would have been quite consistent with this ridiculous man's character. The book bore a motto from 'Childe Harold' and the 'Advertisement' apologized for the contents while at the same time trying to win distinction for Webster by dragging in his friendship with Byron. It spoke of the 'Beauties, which the Gigantic Talents and Mighty Genius of my friend Lord Byron have given to the World — which the present age have — never can equal [sic].' An idea of the quality of Webster's verse may be gleaned from a concluding passage after many stanzas denouncing Napoleon and gloating over his exile to his 'Ocean Rock':

> Insects of a Day! Creatures of an Hour!
> Dare ye deem other of your short liv'd pow'r?
> E'en the dull Bat that flits on leathern wings
> Is privileg'd [sic] beyond ye mortal things!
> It still may flit — and buz [sic] away its day...

Webster provided a note here: "Day is of course used here to express the date of existence — for in point of fact the Bat's Day is the Night"

Among the shorter pieces are "To Phoela," "To Corinne," "A Wish," "The Parting," "On Love," and "Lines on Lord B — ns Portrait." This last includes the lines

> Such thy form, o! B — n, but say what art,
> May paint the colours of thy noble heart...

Early in 1816 James warned Wellington verbally and in writing against the scandal-mongering Lady Mountnorris, mother of Lady Frances. A written reply was sent by Wellington to Webster on January 6, 1816:

> Dear Sir, I was out when your note came here, and am but just now returned.
> I consider what passed between you & me the other day as entirely confidential; and I will have no communication upon it with any body; I am very little inclined to hear family disputes, and am very indifferent as to what is said or may be said about myself, excepting as far as these scandalous stories are turned to affect an innocent person. Even in that case when I hear them they serve only to put me on my guard for her sake; and I don't feel the slightest inclination to discuss them with any body whatever.
> You may depend upon it that I shall decline to have any communication with Lady Mountnorris excepting that which as a gentleman I am liable to have with any Lady I meet in society. Ever Your's most faithfully, Wellington.

On January 24, 1816, Augusta Leigh wrote to Annabella, Lady Byron, about Lord Byron, "His temper good, but he is much perplexed by a letter from Ly F. Webster again! & I'm to copy it for you & send it for yr opinion & advice if possible!!!" We are not privileged to have this letter.

In a letter written later that night, again to Annabella, Augusta says:

> This letter from Paris has set his brain into a sad ferment. He has begun an answer which is civil & cool enough, but whether he will send it or not I don't know. In ye present state of things I think it rather desirable he should, because any change respecting you may induce him to do some mad thing or other on that subject. He has already mentioned going with Hobhouse to Paris to see what she means. Is it not (hers) the most barefaced impudence you ever heard of? I had not time to tell you the handwriting this time is her own I mean not disguised & the seal the Dove returning to the Ark with ye olive leaf motto, 'La Fidelité mérite la Confiance.' B's first idea was 'had she heard you had left Town?' or any reports about you & him — in short his poor head is quite off on this subject & I should like to knock hers agst the wall....

On January 25, 1816, Augusta again wrote to Annabella about Byron. "He is certainly very unpleasant tonight. Says he will go off with ye first woman who will go with him — & constant allusions to Ly F to whom he has written a most improper answer. I don't know if it is actually gone, but it must do mischief if it does go & if by chance her Spouse gets hold of it I think will cause an uproar."

The upshot of all this scandal was that James and Lady Frances sued Mr. Charles Baldwin, the proprietor and editor of the *St. James's Morning Chronicle*, on this account. On February 16, 1816, Chief Justice Vicary Gibbs—known as "Vinegar" Gibbs because of his acid tongue—heard the case of "Wedderburn Webster, Esq. and Frances Caroline Webster, his wife, v. Baldwin, proprietor of the *Chronicle*," in the Court of Common Pleas. Wellington was in France during the trial, but it was obvious during the case that he was right behind James and Frances in their suit. Wellington's name certainly came to the fore during the trial. John Campbell, in court, said that Lady Frances "had always preserved an unsullied reputation" until Baldwin had printed his "false, scandalous and malicious libels charging her with having been guilty of adultery."

Counsel for the plaintiffs, Serjeant Best, stated the case. As reported in the press, he explained that a nobleman of rank, like Wellington, would naturally visit, when in Brussels, families of corresponding quality, though "he was never in his life alone with Lady Webster." Counsel dwelt on the lady's approaching confinement (at the time of the scandal) and the Duke's exalted character as "the saviour of Europe and the greatest commander of any age & country," etc. Best then called the Duke of Richmond, who pronounced Lady Frances "a lady of singularly amiable & decorous manner." Even after reading the libels, neither the Duke nor Duchess of Richmond had seen fit to lessen the intimacy between Lady Frances and their unmarried daughters.

Best also said, "Mr W. Webster was a gentleman of fortune, and was allied to many noble families; his wife, twenty-four, the daughter of the Earl of Mountnorris, was endued [i.e., endowed] with great beauty—but her beauty was lost sight of by those who knew the virtues she possessed." He also mentioned the August 3, 1815, edition of the *Chronicle* which said that when, after the battle of Waterloo, Wellington "came to visit the wounded—perhaps the wounded heart was meant." Best said the meaning of this obviously was "all he went back to Brussels for, after the victory, was to indulge in adulterous intercourse."

In the face of not only a well-presented case for the prosecution, but also common sense, Mr. Serjeant Lens, for the defense, could come up with nothing but an admission that he was utterly bested, and how much to pay for damages, etc. The case was a complete triumph for the Websters. £50,000 damages was asked, but Justice Gibbs awarded £2000 to the offended parties, allowing that to award less might be an indication of less innocence.

In a letter to his brother, written on the day of the trial, James Webster's former tutor, John Campbell, still a struggling young lawyer, wrote in a very excited state over Lady Frances:

> I have not been recently engaged in any cause of public interest except that tried on Friday, of which you will find an account in the newspapers, Webster and Lady Frances against the 'St James's Chronicle.' Two thousand pounds damages! I was exceedingly anxious, indeed. The whole responsibility rested on my shoulders. I had little to do in public. I will just give you a specimen of the way in which juniors at the bar are kept down. It was my business to open the pleadings, as we call it, and I ought naturally to have stated all the libels to the jury. When I was getting up to do so, Best said, 'Don't you say more than it is an action for a libel.' Well, then Vaughan [Mr. Serjeant Vaughan] ought to have examined the first witness as to the publication, which would have left the Duke of Richmond to me, in examining whom respecting the Duke of Wellington and Lady Frances some éclat was to be expected. As Best was concluding his speech, Vaughan said, 'Campbell, do you take the first witness to prove the publication, and I will go on with the Duke of Richmond.' In both instances I was compelled to comply. There is an invariable and systematic conspiracy among the leaders to depress a junior, and to cut him off from all opportunity of gaining distinction.
>
> Webster and his wife have been a week in London, and I have seen a good deal of them. She is the most fascinating creature that ever lived, and I believe in my conscience most perfectly virtuous. I really am quite in love with her. She may well be the conqueror of the conqueror of the world. Although she has certainly met with more flattering attention during the last twelve months than any other woman in Europe, her manners remain a perfect model of simplicity as well as of elegance. It is whimsical enough that she is going to reside in the parish of Cupar [which is where Campbell was from]. There is a house called Cairnie Lodge, at present inhabited

by a brother-in-law of Webster's. There they are going on a visit, and they leave London for that destination this morning. James, at his own request, carries down a letter of introduction to our father. I wish to heaven she would remain in Fife till the autumn. Having been the idol of Brussels and Paris during the last twelve months, she is personally acquainted with almost all the distinguished characters in Europe. Then as to the battle of Waterloo she may be said to have been present at it. I rather think she was not forgotten in the Duke's visit to Brussels the next day. And at any rate she had intelligence from the field every hour. What she has seen she tells with as much naiveté as a country girl. I was five hours in conversation with her on Friday evening, and it seemed but a moment. James insisted on giving me as an acknowledgment ten small bronze busts of the Greek and Latin poets which he had brought with him from Paris, and which now ornament my mantel-piece....

John Murray wrote to Byron that W had been successful. Byron replied ironically, in a letter to Murray on February 16, 1816, "Dear Sir — I thank you for the account of Mr. and Lady F.W.'s triumph — you see by it — the exceeding advantage of unimpeachable virtue & uniform correctness of conduct &c &c." Byron also told a friend that he would have had Lady Frances himself rather than leave her to Wellington. It was just after this case that Byron wrote his "Then fare thee well, Fanny" poem.

Much of this material on the Wellington period comes from Elizabeth Longford's classic books *Wellington: The Years of the Sword* and *Wellington: Vol. II.*

The scandal continues to be reported, even to this day. For example, in the February 3, 1995, edition of the *Wall Street Journal*, Edward B. Furey Jr. of Woodhaven, N.Y., wrote a letter about the Duke of Wellington, in which he says that the Iron Duke was "linked ... with Lady Shelley, Mrs. Harriet Arbuthnot, Lady Frances Wedderburn-Webster, Lady Caroline Lamb, Lady Charlotte Greville, Madame de Stael and assorted singers."

Byron wrote a letter to Webster on April 16, 1816. That letter, in manuscript form, is now in the Beinecke Library, at Yale University. It says:

Dear Webster/— I have no desire to dun or to distress you — but I was surprized at your silence — more specially hearing that you were purchasing lands & tenements. — Hearing this I naturally thought you were in a state of disentanglement — & my own affairs being at present in a very poetical posture — I stated to you my expectation that you would take steps towards the payment — for which I can hardly be considered as very importunate — as it is now the third year without allusion to the subject — nor had it been made now — were I not about to leave England — & anxious to settle my affairs previously. — I now write to mention — that it being inconvenient to you — I will say no more on the subject — You must be aware that it could be no pleasure to me to receive that which it would be disturbing to you to pay: — & as I lent it with a view to prevent difficulties I shall not now render any little advantage it may have been to you useless by plunging you into new ones. — I should & shall of course neither take nor authorize any measure that may be disagreeable to you. — Kinnaird (the Honble Ds) is kind enough to act for me while I am abroad & I will direct him not to molest you. — I write in the greatest hurry with packages — passports — &c — but shall not be off for a day or two. ever Yrs. most truly BYRON.

Douglas Kinnaird, Byron's banker at Messrs Ransom, Morland & Co., London, and a tangential player in the story of the Websters, was a month younger than his friend Byron. The fifth son of the 7th Baron Kinnaird, he was a product of Eton, Trinity, and the Continent. Byron called him "my trusty and trustworthy trustee and banker, and crown and sheet anchor." Later a politician, Kinnaird died unmarried at the age of 42.

This matter of the loan did, indeed, rankle with Byron. It annoyed him that Webster, recently come into a lot of money via the *Morning Chronicle*, went out and splurged instead of paying Byron back. Even the ever generous Byron, notwithstanding his eager-not-to-offend letter, could not forget that insult — and he wouldn't.

On April 25, 1816, Byron left England for good (nothing to do with the loan, though). Just four days had passed since he had signed his separation agreement with Annabella.

In May 1816 James Webster began to effect the purchase from William Sibbald of a house in Roxburghshire, in Scotland. There he and Lady Frances would be neighbors of Walter Scott, the novelist, then 44 and only a couple of years away from a baronetcy and enormous fame.

In early May 1816 Scott gossiped to J.B.S. Morritt in a letter, "We are told Mr Wedderburn Webster is to be our neighbour at a large house now for sale in the neighbourhood of Melrose — in that case we may hope to see the D. of Wellington for despite the verdict of the jury agt. the St. James Chronicle man he had greatly the appearance of L'Ami de maison."

Traveler, classical scholar and politician John Bacon Sawrey Morritt (ca. 1772–1843) had been a friend of Scott's for almost a decade, and only that year, 1816, had been to visit the poet at Abbotsford, Scott's impressive house.

On May 16, 1816, Scott wrote to Charles Erskine from Edinburgh, "I hear Sibbald & Wedderburn are sparring about their bargain already."

In June 1816 Lady Frances had had enough and walked out — but only temporarily. Byron wrote on the leaf of his "Argument," addressed to the Right Hon. Frances Wedderburne Webster on leaving home June 1816, commencing, "Go, Volume of the Wintry Blast." Signed "B." This book went for 15 guineas at Sotheby's on February 21, 1908.

On July 4, 1816, Lady Frances's father, the Earl of Mountnorris, died, aged 72. Ten days later, on July 14, Bold Webster's younger brother, David, died at Brigton, aged 14.

In the afternoon of August 2, 1816, Walter Scott wrote to the Duke of Buccleuch, "Your Grace will have heard that the Duke of Wellington comes to Scarborough perhaps further north — 'How shall we pay him honours due?' — I had this from good authority; Mr Wedderburn Webster (who is a whipper-snapper) now by the grace of God a neighbour in place of plain honest William Sibbald — he is you know the husband of Lady Frances Webster though I give no credit to the scandal."

On August 21, 1816, Scott wrote again to Morritt, from Abbotsford, "For your further encouragement we have got in our neighbourhood my Parisian acquaintances Mr Wedderburn Webster by nature a fool and by art a coxcomb and pest of the first water and his wife Lady Frances a very pleasant woman in manners as well as young and pretty but who has certainly fallen into bad hands in the breaking and looks melancholy & speaks sentiment when no better discourse is to be had."

There had to be, given all the fuss, a British edition of J. Wedderburne Webster's *Waterloo and Other Poems*, and indeed, it was published on August 24, 1816, in octavo, printed for Longman, Hunt, Rees, Orme & Brown, of Paternoster-row; J. Ridgway, Piccadilly; E. Kerby, Stafford-street; and A. Constable & Co., Edinburgh. The cost: 5/6 (5 shillings and sixpence).

James Webster wrote to "The Lord Byron, London" on "Sep. 20. 16" from "Cairney Lodge, Cupar, Fife." This was presumably a reply to Byron's "dunning" letter of five months before, and by September the poet had long left England. In fact, he was in Switzerland as Webster wrote his letter, a fact that Webster would have known but pretended not to.

> Dear Biron, I have received your letter — & am very sensible of ye kind manner in w'ch you have terminated my bondage — Depend on it, whenever it is in my power, I will do that w'ch is proper — & what your interest demands —
> If you have 5 minutes to spare let me know if Rushton is still on your Establishment — & how you mean to dispose of him? — —
> Do you go via Paris?
> Your 'fare-well' is admirable — Depend upon it — a better alternative c'd not have been administer'd to ye poison'd mind of ye world —
> God bless you, ever y'r sincerely J Wedderburne Webster.

On September 22, 1816, Byron wrote in his *Alpine Journal* (a diary of his trip in Europe), "Girl with fruit — very pretty — blue eyes — good teeth — very fair — long but good features — reminded me of Fy."

There is a forgery of a letter supposedly written by Byron in Milan, to W. Webster, Esq., on November 1, 1816, which is to be found in Schultess-Young, Letter VI, pages 162–4. Again, Ehrsam claims this as a forgery perpetrated by Major Byron:

> My dear Webster, — Your letter addressed to the care of Mons. Heutsch [Swiss banker] at Geneva reached me at Milan. I have some remembrance of the circumstances you mention. The whole matter appeared to me a species of diseased consciousness; ay, as Dr. Johnson would have said, <u>scrupulosity</u>. About this same marriage ritual, both on the part of the couples and the clergymen, the scene was laughable enough, at any rate to an unconcerned spectator like <u>mysen</u> [sic]. The parson screwed his face into a gloomy smile, cast off his holy garb, withheld the pious benediction and amen; and so, unwedded, left the melancholy pair. The declaration of the husband to the wife, '<u>with my body I thee worship</u>,' as the marriage ceremony of the Church of England runs, seems to border closely upon idolatry. Had I met such language in the works of Tom Paine, I should have inferred that Tom was at his gibes. But there is a faculty in some persons 'Who can ease/Twist words and meanings as they please.' And I have been told by some of this tribe, that 'worship,' in a canonical sense, may either import <u>adoration of the Supreme being</u>, or <u>civility</u> and <u>respect to a wife</u>. If the term has so equivocal a meaning, applicable in a different sense to the Almighty and to a frail creature, ought it not to be expunged from the marriage ritual, to ease the conscience of those who may not, in all instances, have quite refinement enough or subtilty [sic] to understand a canonical <u>double entendre</u>? In addition to this worship of the lady, she must have a dowry <u>ad libitum</u>; that is to say, for so the saying is, she shall be '<u>endowed with all his worldly goods</u>,' notwithstanding that the lawyer, a few hours before churching time, may have taken pretty good care to reserve the most part of such goods for the said husband's use. Don't you think that this is, with a witness, 'Playing the changes upon cases/As plain as noses upon faces'? I shall set out in a few days for Verona and Venice in company with Hobhouse; therefore direct your letters to Geneva; they will be forwarded. Believe me, Ever yours very affectionately, Byron.

Lady Frances's sister, Lady Catherine Somerset, gave birth to her first child, Frances Georgiana Elizabeth, on November 7, 1816.

Webster's reply to the review of his original French edition of *Waterloo and Other Poems* in the *Quarterly Review* of January 1816 was published in the *Morning Chronicle* on December 19, 1816. It was severely critical of Gifford, the editor of the *Quarterly*, even though, as mentioned above, it may have been the reviewer Croker, and not Gifford, who had attacked Webster's piece.

On February 15, 1817, Byron wrote to John Murray, "Of Mr H[obhouse]'s quarrel with the Quarterly R[eview] — I know very little — except Barrow's article itself — which was certainly harsh enough — but I quite agree that it would have been better not to answer — particularly after Mr W.W. who never more will trouble you — trouble you."

Hobhouse, too, had been blasted for his article in the January 1816 edition of the *QR* about life in Paris during the last days of Napoleon.

On February 24, 1817 (although Byron erred, dating the letter 1816; he was not yet used to the new year) Byron wrote to Douglas Kinnaird from Venice, "Hobhouse's epistle to the Quarterly — I have not seen — but I suppose it to be a wrathful composition — He will not be pleased to hear that Wedderburne Webster was his precursor in reply to the Quarterly — Murray tells me that W.W. answered it in the Mg [Morning] Chronicle — in a new style of controversy — I saw in Switzerland in the autumn — the poems of Webster and I suspect that he made more by the prose of the St. James's Ledger — than he will by his own poetry — Amongst the ingredients of his volume I was not a little astonished to find an epitaph upon myself — the desert of which I would postpone for a few years at least — just to see out the row which is beginning amongst you."

In a letter from Byron in Venice, to Thomas Moore, on February 28, 1817, he writes, "I hear that W.W. has been publishing and responding to the attacks of the Quarterly, in the learned Perry's Chronicle [James Perry was owner of the *Morning Chronicle*]. I read his poesies last autumn, and amongst them found an epitaph on his bull-dog, and another on myself. But I beg to assure him (like the astrologer Partridge) that I am not only alive now but was alive also at the time he wrote it."

On March 7, 1817, Byron wrote to John Cam Hobhouse from Venice, "Wedderburne Webster having been quizzed in a former Quarterly—has replied to the Editor in a letter to the learned Perry—which he concludes by leaving him (the Editor of the Quarterly) with 'feelings of contempt and oblivion'—I am afraid it will not please you—that this same evil genius W.W. should be also a respondent to the Critics—as I recollect in Switzerland you gave him & his preface to the devil for having taken in vain with his awkward compliments the name of a friend of yours [Byron is subtly referring here to James Webster's toadying plaudits in the preface of *Waterloo and Other Poems*]—not so much for the sake of your friend—as of a projected preface in which you were pleased to be gracious." (In other words, Hobhouse was annoyed that Webster had beaten him to the punch in using the Byron friendship in a preface. One up for Bold Webster here, one feels.)

On the same day, March 7, 1817, Byron wrote to Scrope Davies, "I should be glad to know your opinion between the respective answers to the Quarterly of Wedderburne Webster & Hobhouse—I have not yet seen neither—but my friendship for Hobhouse would naturally balance in his favour—now you are impartial—or I fear rather inclining to Webster—but pray let me know—Hobhouse will not be pleased to hear that W.W. has been running the same career of respondency—so pray don't tell him—at least till I am present to hear you & mediate."

On March 9, 1817, Byron wrote to John Murray from Venice, "I saw in Mr Wedderburne Webster's poetry that he had written my epitaph—I would rather have written his."

On March 20, 1817, John Murray wrote to Byron (Memoir 1, 383), "Wedderburn Webster is again at work; he is composing a pamphlet on the subject of the recent suspension of the Habeas Corpus Act."

Byron, replying to John Murray from Venice, on April 9, 1817, writes, "So—Webster is writing again—is there no Bedlam in Scotland?—nor thumb-screw?—no Gag?—nor handcuff?—I went upon my knees to him almost some years ago to prevent him from publishing a political pamphlet which would have given him a livelier idea of 'Habeas Corpus' than the world will derive from his present production upon that suspended subject—which will doubtless be followed by the suspension of other (his Majesty's) subjects."

On April 10, 1817, Byron wrote to Scrope Davies from Venice, "Is it true that W. Webster is writing upon the suspension of the 'Habeas Corpus'?"

There is a forged letter, purportedly from Byron to James, written on June 17, 1817, from La Mira, near Venice, which, in manuscript form, is now in the Library of the Royal College of Surgeons, London. Ehrsam claims this a forgery written by Major Byron. It reads:

> Dear Webster, The honourable Member and his suite—consisting of four sons—Madonna and her nine daughters—the Gazette des Étrangers registers the names of all the big & little Eves—passed through Venice a month ago—I met them one night in the Piazza—not a seat was to be had—and I was going to ascend to an upper room at the Gran Bretagna—when a voice by my side exclaimed—'Voila—Monsieur Bifsteck et sa grande famille'—and I turned to observe.—There they were contentedly—a round dozen filling the longest table—the father with a plump face—savoury and sober as the steak he was named after—his wife—so fat and chuckling—nine girls with short waists [?] bonnets—and looks so ruddy and modest—and four young men—most stupid—'Oh—my good God! I shall sink under the weight'—and the waiter behind—as he advanced with a large tray of ices—and such a pile of cakes—Could cakes create the sense—I had enjoyed a good notion of sublimity.—The glasses contained every variety of colour and quality inscribed upon the bill—The mother took two—a red a white one [sic]—three of the youths followed the hint—and it was worth payment to see the shrewd face & true with which the waiter shewed—as he set them before her—Voila—Madame—votre blanc et votre rouge!'—This was all very well—in the gamine spirit of fullism and abundance—the air of the party—&

the smiles of the company — proved the thing decidedly. — However, the load had scarcely disappeared — and no extraordinary time was lost on the change when the good man [?] out ''twas very good — to be sure — but we would like something after — to warm it.' 'Eh — Betsy — my dear —(he says to the youngest girl) suppose we have some coffee —& some nice cakes?'— The waiter was summoned — the coffee ordered — and the Mercury was about to vanish towards quick service — when the honble M. J. cries— and some brandy —'I'll have some brandy!'— as I supposed to cool the coffee —'Fie! dear (exclaimed his easy nib) no brandy here — ye say"—& the girls added 'Oh!' with altered looks. 'Yes— but I will though — I tell you — dear —'tis the fashion here. Why — look there that gentleman with the black mustaches— don't you see — that's brandy he's got'—'But he calls that a <u>petty vere</u>, love.' —'Well — then — let me have a petty vere!'— I left 'Mons. Bifsteck et sa grande famille' over coffee after ice — Heigho!— at home habitually we do not look at half that comes before us— have we set our eyes at a double stare on every thing we meet — The contrarities of life — though not greater — are at best more humorously displayed on this side of the water. I have been at Rome (a few weeks ago) — where I admired the Coliseum — and the red stockings of the Cardinals— and sat to Torwaltzen [Byron's friend Hobhouse had persuaded Byron to sit for the great Danish sculptor Berthel Thorwaldsen] for my first — Pray — let me hear from you — at your time & leisure — believing me ever and Truly & affectionately [?] BYRON.

14

Monument to a Dead Son

On October 6, 1817, James's son, Charles, after a long and distressing illness, died at Nantes, in France, aged 2. The *Times* of October 16, 1817, mentioned the death of Byron's godson and namesake. The little lad was buried in Caen Cathedral, where there is a monument to him. On this monument are the following poetic lines written by James:

> What though no heraldry or pomp of woe
> Proclaim the tenant of the space below,
> Yet tears of love and piety combine
> To bless and consecrate thy humble shrine.
> Too loved, too lovely, thou art called away
> To the blest regions of eternal day,
> As some bright meteor bursts on human eyes,
> Gleams o'er the deep, then mingles with the skies
> So thy pure spirit winged its heavenly flight,
> And rose triumphant o'er this world of night.
> Peace to thy narrow bed and infant grave,
> Oh! had the hearts that bleed the power to save,
> Thy future years had gladdened other times,
> Or now, thy form reposed in other climes,
> But vain the struggle in the parent's breast
> Else Caledon had been thy place of rest.
> Land of my sires! Oh, when I tread thy shore
> And think of one who ne'er can see thee more,
> Then busy memory, with a sad alloy,
> Shall dim they eye that else had filled with joy,
> And dwell with sorrow on the lovely bier
> Far from the Caledon where all is dear!

It is just as well that Gifford or Croker did not get their hands on this piece!

After the death of Charles Byron Wedderburn Webster, James wrote a manuscript note on Byron's letter of September 2, 1813, "My eldest son — now dead! was christened 'Byron Wedderburn,' and when I afterward mentioned the loss to Lord Byron he almost chuckled with joy or irony." Byron had told James, "Well, I cautioned you, and told you that my name would almost damn any thing or creature."

This from Lady Frances to Byron, from "Paris, Janry 18th, 1818":

> My dear Lord, you will oblige me very much by franking the enclosed letter to Wr Wedderburn [i.e. her husband] and I trust your Lordship will excuse the liberty I have taken in troubling you — I wrote to you some months ago thanking you for accepting the office of God Father to my little Boy — and must confess I felt hurt at the silent manner with which it was received [the words 'my letter' were written above these last three words] — It sprang wholly from myself — Allow me to congratulate you on Lady Biron's safety and the Birth of your daughter and with all the sincerity of reality — Believe me as ever, Frances W. Webster.

Byron wrote a letter to Webster from Venice, on May 31, 1818:

> Dear Webster, I [am] truly sorry to hear of yr. domestic misfortune—and as I know the inefficacy of words—shall turn from the subject—I was not even aware of yr. return from France—where I presume that you are a resident.—For my own part, after going down to Florence & Rome last year, I returned to Venice where I have since remained—& may probably continue to remain for some years—being partial to the people the language & the habits of life—there are few English here—& those mostly birds of passage,—excepting the one or two who are domesticated like myself.—I have the Palazzo Mocenigo on the Canal' Grande for three years to come—& [a] pretty villa in the Euganean hills [a group of hills not far from Venice] for the summer for nearly the same term.—While I remain in the city itself—I keep my horses on an Island with a good beach, about half a mile from the town, so that I get a gallup [sic] of some miles along the shore of the Adriatic daily—the Stables belong to the Fortress—but are let on fair terms.—I was always very partial to Venice—and it has not hitherto disappointed me—but I am not sure that the English in general would like it—I am sure that I should not, if they did—but by the benevolence of God—they prefer Florence & Naples—and do not infest us greatly here.—In other respects it is very agreeable for Gentlemen of desultory habits—women—wine—and wassail being all extremely fair & reasonable—theatres &c. good—& Society (after a time—) as pleasant as anywhere else (at least to my mind) if you will live with them in their own way—which is different of course from the Ultramontane in some degree.—The Climate is Italian & that's enough—& the Gondolas &c. &c. & habits of the place make it like a romance for it is by no means even now the most regular & correct moral city in the universe—Young and old—pretty & ugly—high and low—are employed in the laudable practice of Lovemaking—and though most beauty is found amongst the middling & lower classes—this of course only renders their amatory habits more universally diffused.—I shall be very glad to hear from or of you when you are so disposed—& with my best regards to Lady Frances.—believe me very truly yrs B. P.S. If ever you come this way—let me have a letter before hand—in case I can be of use—.

Mail could take ages in those days, at the best of times, but when it was addressed to a peripatetic such as Bold Webster, it might not ever reach him at all. Byron's letter of May 31, 1818, finally caught up with James in mid-July in Havre, in Normandy, where he was residing for a few days until his English creditors lost a bit of interest. Lady Frances had fled to her mother's. James dashed off a letter to the poet from "Havre 25 July 18"; he meant 1818, but presumably, despite the occasional custom of the day, was so harried he couldn't remember the year.

> Dear Byron, I had ye pleasure of receiving your <u>illegible</u> epistle only a few days ago—as it had travelled to London & sundry other places—
>
> I had not heard of your temporal arrangements at Venice & I had little imagined that they embraced a determination of remaining so long in Italy—away from a country where malgré <u>all</u> that <u>may</u>—or <u>can</u> be, no man can have in himself, or can excite in others, more interest in England as she <u>is</u>—is poor indeed in ye possession of names, whose acts <u>might</u> dignify—& whose works <u>will</u> adorn ye brightest Page of her future History—& it is lamentable to think that <u>any such</u>—particularly those who have identified themselves with her existence sh'd assume a voluntary exile—
>
> I merely express what I feel to you, remember as a public character—but am far from entering ye Temple of private feelings & considerations, to each I have no title—I confess I was, & am anxious to hear a little from you of what one never hears from others—I mean <u>Truth</u> of yourself—
>
> Dallas & Trevanion are both living near this town, ye former permanently I believe. He is book-making comme ordinaire, & desires me with many kind remembrances to say 'That you appear to have given him up—w'ch he feels he does not deserve'—The latter is as good a creature as ever, but I presume like others, a little ye worse for wear—.

Robert Charles Dallas was a writer, born in Jamaica in 1754. His sister married Byron's uncle, George Anson Byron, and Byron dedicated parts of *Childe Harold* to Dallas, who had been the first to see *Childe Harold* and had waxed enthusiastic. He died the same year as Byron, 1824, at his home at Ste.-Adresse, Normandy, and was buried in Havre.

Henry Trevanion was inextricably and almost—if not downright—incestuously involved with the Byron family. He was married to Augusta Leigh's daughter Georgiana, but ran off with

Medora, his sister-in-law (who was possibly Byron's daughter). Medora had a daughter, Marie, by Trevanion, and later a son by a Frenchman. The son would become a Catholic priest in France. Medora died in 1849, aged 35.

Webster continues his news:

> I saw Hobhouse last week where I don't think he is seen to most advantage, in ye column of a <u>ministerial</u> paper—
> His speech at Burdett's Dinner was well season'd & consequently tolerably indigestible to ye M's [members, i.e. of Parliament]. I hear they lose a considerable majority this Parliament—

Sir Francis Burdett, long-time M.P. for Westminster and leader of the radicals in the House, had just won his seat again in a tight fight with Murray Maxwell. That night (July 13, 1818), at the Crown and Anchor Tavern, was held the victory dinner, attended by such notables as Douglas Kinnaird, Michael Bruce (who had been involved with Lavalette, in France, and, also in Paris, but in a different way entirely, with Lady Caroline Lamb) and, of course, Hobhouse.

> Young Valentia has lost ye co. of Wexford (I fear) after a long & what is worse an expensive contest [that very month in fact]— His facetious father, with all due deference to connectionship [the father in question was Webster's father-in-law] is not [sic] greater favorite of mine than formerly—
> Lady Frances is at present with her mother in London— So I am <u>B:A</u>: here in ye mean time— our affairs & pecuniary entanglements required ye presence of one of us & my own was impossible as you may know—.

This "B:A:" is almost certainly a "fecit W-W," i.e., a nonce term coined by Bold Webster, probably Baccalaureate Amoris (Bachelor of Love) or some such.

He continues:

> I wish m'ch it were in my power to say any thing <u>satisfactory</u> far more to <u>act effectively</u> in a certain matter, on w'ch we corresponded before we either left G. Britain— But what can I say?— Since <u>action</u> is more than ever out of my power. I trust you are assured of this.
> In order that I may live where I can only enjoy life (permanently) in England I am now endeavoring to arrange with those who w'd otherwise render it impracticable— Now for <u>yourself</u> I feel no doubt but it is natural I sh'd wish some assurance as to ye custody of ye Bond &c, as you may have unintentionally left it in ye hands of some one who might possess both ye power & ye will to annoy me, altho' in opposition to your wishes. Pray let me hear from you fully on this (to me) distressing matter, as soon as possible & address me 'Poste restate, Le Havre de Grace'—
> What is your Nottingham news? I hear Mrs C is recover'd. Her fate was truly tragical. On dit que Mr. <u>Wildman</u> has bought your estate. I once knew him & never thought he possessed either money or taste to become ye proprietor of Newstead— I hear he is embellishing ye house with ye spolia of <u>such</u> Projectors— magnificence & absurdity—"

Colonel Tom Wildman, a former hussar who had served as aide-de-camp to Lord Uxbridge at Waterloo, had indeed bought Newstead that year with money he had inherited from a Jamaican fortune. He acquired Newstead for a song, £95,000; Claughton, the previous owner, took a loss of at least £50,000.

> What is ye price of a decent Pallazzo [sic] at Venice? I am far too material a Being for ye Euganean Hills & I apprehend few w'd disturb your possession of ye Throne of Ortis [this is a reference to Ugo Foscolo's literary masterpiece *The Letters of Jacopo Ortis*. Foscolo was a friend of Lady Caroline Lamb]—
> Believe me Dear Byron, ever yrs most truly, Wedderburne Webster.

The inevitable postscript:

> P.S. I heard that <u>your friend</u> & <u>my enemy</u> Giffard [he means Gifford, the critic] was <u>dead</u> but it turns out to be a more harmless man— to literary delinquents at least— <u>Old Bailey</u> Giffard [John Gifford, the police magistrate, who had died on March 6]—.

Lady Frances's brother, Henry Arthur Annesley, known as Arthur, married Sarah Ainsworth on August 14, 1818, and died six days later.

James got another letter from Byron on September 8, 1818, written from Venice, Byron's reply to James's letter of July 25, 1818:

> Dear Webster—[12 lines crossed out] It is not agreeable to me to hear that you are still in difficulties—but as every one has to go through a certain portion of sufferance in this world—the earlier it happens perhaps the better—and in all cases one is better able to battle up in one's youth than in the decline of life.—My own worldly affairs have had leisure to improve during my residence abroad—Newstead has been sold—& well sold I am given to understand—my debts are in the prospect of being paid—and I have still a large Capital from the residue—besides Rochdale—which ought to sell well—& my reversionary prospects which are considerable in the event of death of Miss Milbanke's mother [who would die in 1822].—There is (as is usually said) a great advantage in getting the water between a man and his embarrassments—for things with time and a little prudence insensibly reestablish themselves—and I have spent less money—and had more for it—within the two years and a half since my absence from England—than I have ever done within the same time before—and my literary speculations allowed me to do it more easily—leaving my own property to liquidate some of the claims, till the sale enables me to discharge the whole;—out of England I have no debts whatever.—You ask about Venice;—I tell you as before that I do not think you would like it—at least few English do—& still fewer remain there—Florence & Naples are their Lazarettoes where they carry the infection of their society—indeed if there were as many of them in Venice as residents—as Lot begged might be permitted to be the Salvation of Sodom,—it would not be my abode a week longer—for the reverse of the proposition I should be sure that they would be the damnation of all pleasant or sensible society;—I never see any of them when I can avoid it—& when occasionally they arrive with letters of recommendation—I do what I can for them—if they are sick—and if they are well I return my card for theirs—but little more.—Venice is not an expensive residence—(unless a man chooses it) it has theatres—society—and profligacy rather more than enough—I keep four horses on one of the Islands where there is a beach of some miles along the Adriatic—so that I have daily exercise—I have my Gondola—about fourteen servants including the nurse (for a little girl—a natural daughter of mine) and I reside in one of the Mocenigo palaces on the Grand Canal—the rent of the whole house which is very large & furnished with linen &c. &c. inclusive is two hundred a year—(& I gave more than I need have done) in the two years I have been at Venice—I have spent about five thousand pounds—& I needed not have spent one third of this—had it not been that I have a passion for women which is expensive in it's [sic] variety every where but less so in Venice than in other cities.—You may suppose that in two years—with a large establishment—horses—houses—box at the opera—Gondola—journeys—women—and Charity—(for I have not laid out all upon my pleasures—but have bought occasionally a shillings-worth of Salvation) villas in the country—another carriage & horses purchased for the country—books bought &c. &c.—in short every thing I wanted—& more than I ought to have wanted—that the sum of five thousand pounds sterling is no great deal—particularly when I tell you that more than half was laid out on the Sex—to be sure I have had plenty for the money—that's certain—I think at least two hundred of one sort or another—perhaps more—for I have not lately kept the recount [he means women].—If you are disposed to come this way—you might live very comfortably—and even splendidly for less than a thousand a year—& find a palace for the rent of one hundred—that is to say—an Italian palace—you know that all houses with a particular front are called so—in short an enormous house,—but as I said—I do not think you would like it—or rather that Lady Frances would not—it is not so gay as it has been—and there is a monotony to many people in it's Canals & the comparative silence of it's streets—to me who have been always passionate for Venice—and delight in the dialect & naiveté of the people—and the romance of it's old history & institutions & appearance all it's disadvantages are more than compensated by the sight of a single Gondola.—The view of the Rialto—of the piazza—& the Chaunt of Tasso (though less frequent than of old) are to me worth all the cities on earth—save Rome & Athens.—Good even yrs. ever & most truly B.

From Venice, Byron wrote a letter to Augusta Leigh, on September 21, 1818:

> Dearest Augusta—I particularly beg that you will contrive to get the enclosed letter safely to Lady Frances—& if there is an answer to let me have it.—You can write to her first—& state that you have such a letter—at my request—for there is no occasion for any concealment at least with her—& pray oblige me so far—for many reasons.

15

The Sucking Salamander

In the autumn of 1818 James and Lady Frances separated. He went to his house in Nantes, and she stayed in England and that October embarked on a monumental affair with Scrope Davies.

John Cam Hobhouse wrote to Byron on November 4, 1818, "SBD [Scrope Berdmore Davies] is got into the hands of Lady C L [Caroline Lamb] and is in deep with Lady F W. As they [the two women] are in some measure *de tiennes* ["yours"], I suppose he makes love to one and hate to the other with your poetry."

The two women were very friendly at that time. Lady Frances conducted her affair with Davies with considerably more discretion than some of her other affairs, as rumor did not come down in history until 1976, when Scrope Davies's trunk was opened. But obviously Hobhouse knew, and now Byron knew. Which really means everyone and his uncle knew.

This Scrope Davies trunk has a history. It was in 1820 that Davies—no wife, no children, no apparent heirs—finally fled England, bound for the Continent, one step ahead of the creditors, a fate that befell a predictable number of dandies. Before he left, however, Scrope went to his London bank, Ransom, Morland & Co., and deposited in a vault — unknown to anyone else except the bankers—a trunk. There the trunk reposed, undisturbed, until 1976, when it was finally opened by Barclays, who had long ago bought Ransom, Morland & Co., and were now custodians of said trunk by virtue of its residing within a building at Number 1 Pall Mall East, a building owned and at that point in time under alteration by Barclay's. This trunk was found to contain literary gems—Scrope's letters, bills and receipts, school memorabilia, and invitations; betting records; copies of Canto III of Byron's *Childe Harold*, and of *The Prisoner of Chillon*; several Shelley poems; letters from Byron and many other personages, including no fewer than 21 by Lady Frances to Scrope, and (it has been rumored) a lock of her hair.

Barclay's loaned the trunk and its contents permanently to the British Library, and it was catalogued and preserved, the loose papers arranged into volumes and then bound. In the wake of this find, much publicized at the time, Tim Burnett, for one, gained access to the trunk, and from the raw material was able to compose a book titled *The Rise and Fall of a Regency Dandy*, which was Scrope Davies' first biography. Lady Frances and Sir James are mentioned.

Unfortunately not one of the 21 trunk-letters from Lady Frances to Scrope Davies contains a reasonable date, so there must be some conjecture in their arrangement. It appears, however, that the correspondence begins with a very short note addressed to Scrope Davies, Esq.: "I shall be most happy to see you this morning at half past 11 o'clock."

It was common in those days to send a letter to someone saying that one was on one's way up. The next, addressed to Scrope Davies, Esq., 11 Ryder Rd, says:

> Lady Frances W. Webster in offering her best regards and Compts [Compliments] to Mr Scrope Davies begs him to believe how much she laments having been from home yesterday when he was so good as to call in Edward Street, and assure him of the pleasure she shall feel in seeing him.

> If Lady F mistakes not, Mr Davies is but lately returned from Venice [she did mistake, says Tim Burnett]. If so — how fares that favoured child of Trust and Genius [she means Byron] from whom an anxious & admiring World now vainly asks fresh drops of Etherial [sic] Essence but anxiety & Care [added as an afterthought] withers the stem of Genius & while they hover o'er the mind blight the buds with the mildew they are created in. Thursday morning.

The third carried the date "Friday," and said: "I shall knock at your Door in ½ an hour — When I shall claim a rehearsal of ye Conjugal tragedy wch you promised me & ye line wch B. [Byron] addressed to that She-Salamander."

The line she is obviously referring to, in the seventh canto of Byron's *Don Juan*, reads:

> Just as you'd break a sucking salamander
> To swallow flame, and never take it ill

Only a few people have ever seen these letters, Tim Burnett and Martin Davies being two of them. Both have long been baffled by the remark about the "Conjugal tragedy." Unfortunately we will all continue to be so. The meaning was understood by the writer and by the receiver of the letter, but by no one else.

She ends the letter with "I quit this City, thank God, & my Lawyers at 2 — But indeed I am now reconciled to any thing since I found that archbishop Sheldon once offer'd 1000 [pounds] for ye Gout — Yrs very much. F. Wedderburn Webster."

These first three letters are all, evidently, happy letters, addressed to Scrope and/or signed by Lady Frances; they are bold, and written testimony of the first, exciting flush of a new romance. All goes well. But it does not last.

In the next letter things are still fine between Lady F and Scrope, but events are now conspiring to thwart and frustrate her and the relationship. It is very definitely a foreshadowing that some things are not meant to be.

> Your letter is this Inst put into my hand and the postman waits for an answer — I have only time to thank you for it deeply & sincerely & to assure you that my prayers are ever for yr happiness & that wherever or when you are — yr wishes shall be mine — Adieu. They tear me from my pen — Adieu. Thursday. You never sent me anything for my album — Pray do — How goes on ye Election.

On January 4, 1819, Tom Moore was at a function where he met Lady Frances. In his *Memoirs, Journals, etc.* he says, in Vol. 2, page 249 (Diary entry for January 5, 1819):

> Devizes ball in the evening; Lady Frances W. there. Introduced to her, and had much conversation, chiefly about our friend Lord B., whom she talked of, as if nothing had happened — and (if I may believe Scroope [sic] Davies) nothing ever did — but B. certainly gave me to think otherwise, and her letters (which I saw) showed, at least, that she was (or fancied herself) much in love with him — His head was full of her, when he wrote the Bride [of Abydos] — I remember his describing to me her hand falling dead out of the hand of her husband's very much in the way it is described there — Several of these beautiful things, published (if I remember right) with The Bride were addressed to her. She must have been very pretty when she had more of the freshness of youth, though she is still but five or six and twenty; but she looks faded already. I should pronounce her cold-blooded and vain to an excess — & I believe her great ambition is to attract people of celebrity — if so, she must have been gratified — as the first Poet & first Captain of the age have been among her lovers — the latter liaison was, at all events, not altogether spiritual — at least the character of the man makes such platonism not very probable — her manner to me very flattering & the eyes played off most skillfully — but this is evidently her habit — the fishing always going on, whether whales or sprats are to be caught. — She told me she had an Album, which was begun & nearly half written through by Lord B. (the first thing in it, 'When from the brow where Sorrow sits'), and she had another which was as yet blank, & which she had resolved still to keep blank, till an introduction to Mr. M [Moore] should enable her to ask him to begin it for her — I fought this off as well as I could — said I must know her better before I could have the tête montée sufficiently for such an undertaking, &c, &c. She spoke of Godwin's daughter (the sister of Byshe [sic] Shelley's wife) by whom B. had had the child he wrote to me about lately, christened Allegra — said that the woman was hideous....

The Byronic quote by Moore is in fact a misquote. It is the first line of "Impromptu, in reply to a Friend," first published in the 7th edition of *Childe Harold's Pilgrimage*, 1814, and should actually read, "When from the heart Where sorrow sits." But this piece by Moore is tremendously revealing, if not conclusive in any way. First, we learn that Byron had bragged to Moore about consummating his relationship with Lady Frances. However, we know that there was no physical consummation of the relationship. We also know that Byron was quite honest with other people, including Scrope, on this score ("I spared her"), so why he would have lied to Moore is unclear — unless, of course, it is Moore who is lying.

Moore's diary entry also adds a lot of weight to the argument that Lady Frances was the one addressed by the Byron versicle that Fox called "The Song of the 4th of May." And, of course, according to Moore anyway, Lady Frances had set her sights on him (Moore), an offer he refused.

From now on it is clear that Scrope is two-timing Lady Frances and she knows that he is toying with her. That may not have been his intention, but the effect was the same.

Addressed to Scrope Davies, Esq.:

> This whole day I have looked to see you — I am soon going out — Adieu — May Heaven bless you — Thee and thee alone — you will know me — know what I have to combat with — and read my heart — how it [?] — Adieu! I must ever remain unchanged & unchangeable tho' circumstances & your present resolutions conspire to separate us for ever — but I will say no more — Adieu — Adieu

The next goes:

> Every circumstance has conspired to defeat my plans so well formed for this day — & fate seems determined to trifle with my happiness — blame me not — if you knew how my heart was fixed on to-day you would pity me — I returned last night — found some of my family remained home — no Carriage and am unable to walk — a friend has promised to take me out — if she does I will make her leave me at Mrs----- at about 4 o'clock & walk home — tho' in fact I am ill — if she does not I wont [sic] despair — but nothing — Oh! nothing can or will alter me or my work to accomplish ye plan — can I leave this — You ought to believe & feel this. Could you see me at this moment you would [word crossed out] I know not how to send this note — for I have not one servt. in ye house of any kind — They are all sent out — I must wait till one returns — Adieu! God bless you. 12 o'clock.

Then, apparently, Scrope told her something startling. She responded:

> Your note — I have just received — it astonishes me — The carriage is at this Inst at the Door — Half past one — I am to be at Mrs Leigh's at 2. I have 7 visits to pay and dine at [the hour is obliterated] at Lady Ashbrook's — & am to be with ye Dss [Duchess] of Wellington at 4. Judge then how I can see you to-day but I will put off my going tomorrow till 12 o'clock and see you at 10 if you like to come — I make no comment — You know me well!

Another:

> I received your letter a few days back — its contents went deep to my heart — in defiance of all the expressions in yr former letters — this one proved you were not indifferent to me — it breathes a language dear, very dear — but it breathes ye breath of madness — like a Hot house of forces — Despair to a premature perfection — you are unhappy — and I ye Cause — detested wretch that I am — I wither & curse what I would culture & bless — yesterday brought me another letter — I will not tell you whether want of will or illness prevented me so many days writing to you — ask yr own heart — let it speak — & 'twill tell you which — Ah! Could you see me — you would not have cause to ask why. I did not write — nor can I now write much — Forgive you! what have you done that requires forgiveness? Ah! Well do you know, nothing! I have volumes at heart, but cannot write to-day. I have destroyed your letters and do you also destroy mine — 'Your letters produce me pain.' Unfeeling! Too well you know ye contrary — but they do, yes! They do produce me pain & agony — because they breathe ye language of grief — & I have not power to wash that grief away which I w'd die to purchase — I will but that they form my all — you write in irony

> when you talk of being ye loser by ye correspondence — ye only loser — Ah! well you know that if there is Talent in Great Britain, in you it has found its abode — & you well know what your letters must become to an indifferent — but to one — to me! — Well you know all I would say — why — why this mock humility — you make me proud of my own ignorance — it makes me sincere — No, write — why deprive me of any — all of my comfort — I have need of yr letters — you are happy — and life is not wholly cursed — Tell me you do not doubt me & I will cease to curse my fate — to be ye cause of grief to you is ye greatest crime I could commit — Adieu! — I must not write more — forgive me — I am in a state you must not know — but tell me — I have not injured you by my feelings — & I care not for their effects upon my self — Adieu!

Then she goes to Bath, and every effort is made to fix the broken relationship. There are three letters to Scrope from Bath, and then she went to Southampton to set sail for (presumably) France.

The first to Scrope from Bath:

> Health to my friend! I do accept you as a friend and promise that ye past shall be forgotten as much as in my power to forget — I rejoice that your plans are changed — I rejoice that all is so changed since it contributes so much to your comfort — I rejoice that you remain in England — your ambiguous expressions filled me with horror — but now all is well — and my mind is relieved — may you be happy! happier than you have been — it will give me always pleasure to hear from you — Thank you — I have no Commissions too acute — and besides your time is fully employed — Music, Poetry, Elections & digging midst dead men's bones must amply fill your time — Perhaps you would ask at Twinings [the tea shop] for a little bill I left unpaid and send it down when you next write to me — I thank you for your wishes respecting my happiness — I thank you so much — but wishes seldom have any effect! I went to Bath on Friday last! — I am very anxious to hear how poor Mrs Leigh goes thro' her trial — I love her — dearly love her — and I believe her my friend — My request for my bill was founded on yr promise and you leave nothing — promises are thin — Adieu! my head aches to madness — my brain is on fire and writing maddens me — I have a friend! — Health & happiness to that friend! — Peace — joy — happiness and all forever & age — Adieu & whenever you welcome ye hour — Enough — Adieu — I await yr reply. Yr Friend

The second to Scrope from Bath:

> Your letter arrived yesterday but I was away — Of my wish to see you — you have not — you cannot have — You dare not have a doubt — but you write as if I was ye disponer of events and wishes of myself instead of a slave — surrounded — questioned — maddened — a continual espionage — even on my thoughts — and I am ill — I leave this [place] on Monday — Shall be at Southampton at night — 'tis all I know — nor can I find out if I am to be accompanied save by my servts — I think not — You have not forgotten me! I thank you even for the words and drink them as the Cup of Life. Adieu — If you will write to me by tomorrow's Post direct — Post Office Bath I go there tomorrow for the Baths & return Friday — but if you write & require an answer direct Bath for on Saturday no Post goes to London — Adieu — May you be happy — happier than me you must be. Oh! I have suffered much on yr account — but 'tis just — God tempers the wind to the shorn lamb — I will be firm — Wednesday.

The third to Scrope from Bath:

> Saturday. Your letter reached me at Bath on Friday but surrounded by observation, questioned and maddened — I did not dare to write to you — and to-day there is no Post, but this will go tomorrow —
>
> Tis you alone can make me repent any promises made — My fecund spirit has never bent but to you [Scrope must have recognized the duplicitous intent of this statement, even though the intent was kind] — Prudence leads one way Inclination points the other — I curse ye one — & sacrifice to the latter — Oh! if you knew ye once proud & stern spirit for the Being bow'd down before you — tho' you might set less value upon my affection — you w'd never dare to doubt it —
>
> I shall be at Southampton on Tuesday at one o'clock at the Inn above the Dolphin — the same side of the street — sign unknown — my stay or hours or days will depend on the Vessel & Wind — I rule neither — Oh! that I could turn the hand of fate — then would I fill it up for me — you know well what I wish — The Sea may be my grave — but if it gives up its victim — remember the passage is short — & our separation need not be of long duration —

You will see me depart—but we shall meet again—'Tho' familiar with that which would destroy many' do not use yr power too much on one who cannot bear so much—Adieu—Adieu.

Another, which seems to follow on from the Bath letters, and may have been written from the Dolphin, in Southampton:

Tho' millions of Angels or Demons stood watching over me, yet I will write to you—I am observed, watched—& yet I will write a line—Never can I give you an idea of my feelings at leaving English ground without seeing you—you did not receive my letter—I looked, but looked in vain—Oh! why am I cursed, for indeed I am—and why is my life a chain of misery—alternate, hope—despair & promise.—Good God! when shall we meet—& you no more care for me—But I know not what I say—I prayed for an end—but return of morn but brightened misery—why did I live—and where art thou—Ah! what can I?—I go tomorrow to our destination—I know not for how long but I know well with what feelings—however, 'tis done—I have quaffed the Cup to the Dregs—but little remains and there Adieu to all—in writing Adieu the wounds of my heart burst open afresh and present a ghastly picture of the triumph of feelings over ye mind—What a wreck! I must draw the curtains!—May you be happy—Happier than me you must be—from you I cannot rest—I go—I am in a state of mind you must not know—Adieu—

Mrs Leigh will tell you implicitly that my voyage was horrific!
March 7th.

Another:

I have now two letters before me addressed to you, neither of which I dare send—I commence a third with ye same resolution—& will endeavour to command myself as far as to write a letter I ought to send—thank you for the example—there are some points explained in these two letters I should wish to touch upon but I must not trust myself—They will again hurry me beyond my depths—I only returned home last night from my sister's in Gloucestershire & found yr letter which I conclude was written on Saturday. I lament not having had it in my power to reply to it by Sunday Post—tho' perhaps had I remained here I might not have been able for I was (something quite new to me) confined to my bed both Sunday & Monday the greatest part of ye day & wholly to my room by delirious headaches—I wrote to you during my absence but <u>reasons</u> prevented my trusting my letter into the hands of others—& my Epistles are little worthy yr denial at any time much less when perhaps ye subjects they contain have altogether escaped recollection—Your letter perplexes me a little—It commences with a contradiction which I [?]—

Believe me I never doubted your wish to serve your friends—I well know you can be a <u>real friend</u> for myself—My happiness is beyond all human power—I am sorry my letters are [?] but I suspect I am not in the habit of writing what I do not myself understand & my letters are perhaps quite intelligible to all who wish to comprehend them—.

The preceding paragraph is overlaid with a good example of cross-writing, i.e. writing horizontally on the page as opposed to vertically, and over the top of the previously written letter. This was quite common in letter-writing of the day. The cross writing says, "I am ill—am to bed—miserable—Oh! Why these cruel, indifferent letters! but I must be silent—Adieu! Adieu!"

The main letter continues:

What a strange being is Man—how inconsistent & uncertain—he walks the Earth & when he finds a flower, plucks it—wears it in his bosom for a time—its [?] gone he throws it from him, treads upon it & without one pang turns away & whistles on—passing from flower to flow'r—he forgets that every rose is not without a thorn—I must not continue—my letters seem to afford you so little satisfaction that I hardly know on what subject to write—I can hardly write to you on trifling ones & all I can now say to you on others seems to weary you—I would be gay & merry—I want to amuse you—but I cannot—for in my heart & in my brain—there wakes the worm that cannot die—the thought that ne'er will sleep again.

I am delighted to hear such good accounts of Mrs Leigh—she promised them from herself—mais, hélas! les promesses ne valent pas beaucoup [promises are not worth much]—I imagine your [half a line destroyed at this point]—should this reach you & [you have] [again, part of a line obliterated] to spare — I claim its devotion — I have much to say & all to think — but my heart sinks within me & I turn from all connected with a secret you are in possession of — the effects of which must in time destroy me since no time can work a change — Adieu! Continue to direct as before — & I will now release you from that insufferable little constant intruder — I — my egotism shall briefly and in my beging [sic] you to believe me as ever your sincere Friend [then a scrawled signature]. My best wishes attend Mr Hobhouse.

Another, a note merely, very short:

Tho' cruel, my blessing — prayers — hopes & wishes follow you. May God forgive you! Adieu — Adieu! You know not what you have done — Adieu.

Another:

It is given up but from no fears of B [i.e. Byron] or thought of <u>his</u> opinion — no care of <u>his</u> wishes — I have sought health but cannot find it — I have called peace — My call remains unanswered — I thank you for your anxious wish but men's wishes are generally vain — I have always heard Mrs M was a delightful person — but with you all are delightful — Why do you not go down to their home & come here — the syren [sic] of St James' is then blessed with what I once possessed & with what I also was also to possess — happy — happy Being! Mrs L. [Leigh] is to me delightful. I had a letter from her yesterday — she mentions <u>my friend</u> — God grant her well thro' her dreadful undertaking — Adieu! I am unable to write more — I have [you] always at heart — Do not get your letters franked & write, pray, write — I do owe Murray [John Murray, the publisher] for some books — Adieu — God bless you! Sunday night.

Another:

Now I am indeed unfortunate! I have read ye truth and am miserable —
  You called yesterday, I found, and because I gave orders for nobody to come to me till I rung [sic] my bell — being really ill — they denied me everybody — my friend ye Dss [Duchess] of Richmond called three times & they would not admit her — They have made her angry but all my anger can avail me nothing — I have but ye happiness in which my heart was fixed — Adieu — Adieu — May you never know what I am now suffering.

Another:

I know not what to say or think — in a letter I received on my return home & to which I replied you wish me to understand that you were then indifferent to me — on Saturday morng I received another which seems to restore me all I had lost — it breathes a real feeling — but its language distresses & makes me miserable — but oh! what words can speak my feelings at the contents of your letter this day received — What have I done to deserve this — Have you studied the Catalogue of Cruelty to select yr most bitter words and twist them with gall into a string of accusations — the most unjust & cruel — and against whom? Oh! blush when I write — that poisoned shaft is aimed — those deadly wounds planted in the breast of one whose only fault has been betraying her weakness — I did not expect this of you — you read my heart — you saw its struggles — Oh! I thought you generous — and I believed you just — my feelings can never change — there are sentences in your last letter which I shall not quote — but in the midst of <u>all</u> — 'I can lift up my hands to that high power,' bow & say 'Not guilty' — Ah! proudly bow — When did I seek happiness thro' your misery — ? Cruel, cruel Being! But I will not reproach you — I will not complain since my Image pursues you & shrieks, <u>be wretched</u> — why not seize the Traitor — and try thy utmost act — for by Heavens thy dagger's point would be far less painful than thy scorpioned words — you would then see my blood flow free from its fountain — & in its last & warmest drop you w'd read ye only sentiment it has ever traced — Why use torture when one kind stroke would end all — you know me not, you will one day know me & then perhaps you will remember & regret the agony you have occasioned me, which, tho' buried, is not without its effect — A fire, tho' hidden — not smothered — conceal'd it burns — slow but sure — your letter of yesterday received gave me pleasure — its words were more congenial to my feelings — but today — Oh! — I must not think — for my brain's on fire — it will not stand much more — the chords of my heart are almost overstretch'd — Oh! wrap them gently — it does not need a giant's strength to break ye vital string — I trusted to you ye secret of my heart — in mercy spare your power — Tell me, after having read [?] how have you dared to write this letter? — Perhaps you did not mean it — Oh! Can you tell me so — and I will indeed bless you — Thank you for wishing my happiness — It is a Phantom I seek — I have long been indifferent to my fate — & I have now to thank you for making me more so — you fly from happiness — there are some people who court misery & indulge in gloom — I almost think you are one determined to view [life] thro' the mirror of a distempered mind — & to be [end of line obliterated here] and [?] ye wretchedness of a being who w'd die for you, because every principle of Duty — Honour & Virtue forbid her to bless you — See her you still may — you have the power — you have — No! She will never break yr heart — hers is almost gone — but tho' the thread is weak it may still weave a <u>blessing</u> for you — Adieu! I destroy yr letters & in Honour you ought to do ye same by mine — our situations demand this — assure me you do & I shall feel more confidence in writing — I have a husband & child! [Lucy, the only one surviving at that point of time, was then six] — my letters might injure them — Adieu! Forgive the letter — I believed myself stronger — & my feelings less strong — Oh God! Oh God!

An undated and very short note, reads, "Read your note — You do not know me — You will one day know and believe and perhaps remember me — Adieu."

One of the later letters, just after Scrope had dumped her, contains this:

I have nothing to say — 'tis past — 'tis done — the bitter Cup has been long held to my lips — I have tasted it — but 'tis now — now — ah! now I am to drink its poisoned Draught — the gates of misery are opened wide to receive me — Destruction sits enthroned — Come fast — come sure & throw thine arms round me — I am ready to die — come Death — Oh! I have long been indifferent to my fate — and I have to thank your kind liberation for making me more so — 'Our will cannot alter our feelings' — and mine will burn an unconsumed fire — you cannot quench it — but it will never reach you more — how it will burn — Eternal — its progress is sure — & would it were more quick — I will not complain — I will not reproach you — No! I will persuade myself you are right — 'twas my own fault — I cherished the fatal spark — & gently fan'd it till it burst into an Eternal flame — Oh God! what shall I do — forget you do you say — smile & forget you! — there is madness — madness — fever in the thought — forget you! Listen to me, I charge you — listen to me while I have power to write — for there is something stirs within me — my brain's on fire — Listen to me — would you have me forget — would you know ye time when your Image will leave my heart — go to Heaven — There I cannot tell what may be — I can only answer to ye last moments of my life — Never! entwined — madly were — It cannot be — my feelings will descend to yr Tomb — I will go beyond — if in another world we are permitted to pursue a recollection of what passes in this — here, tear open my heart & the deepest steel will not inflict so bitter a wound as you have done this day — Oh! that some being w'd [would] rid me of life — a detested life — and shorten ye pangs of a lingering Death — there are daggers in my heart that have stab'd deeper than ye assassin's steel — the sun of my life is set — & life without a sun — Oh! Cold, cold chamber — Why did I dream of happiness? Why did I sleep — & when ye gentle Vision played before me — I smiled — & slept again — Mad fool! Thy punishment is just! — I was a dream [sic] — but, Oh! Why did I sleep? I wake? — to curse this withered heart that will not break — Adieu — you told me not to write — forgive me forgive me — my mind is in agony — Forgive me — I know not what I do — I am in a state you must not know — Forgive me — No! I will not open yr wounds — they shall remain closed — I would not open them, I — who would lay down ten thousand lives to make you happy — I have murdered you — Oh! I have murdered you — I have sacrificed my own peace, happiness forever! Forget me — forget ye wretch who has caused you unhappiness — forget me — I <u>am</u> a wretch but I w'd have loved thee, have fondled thee in my heart — in to its very core — & now I cannot throw thy image out — it festers there — Oh! I am indeed a wretch — Remember my fate is interwoven with yours — <u>all</u> is in yr hands — where'er you go — my spirit will hover over you — tho' absent I shall be with you — & my last breath will waft thy name to heaven — Adieu — Adieu — forgive me! Adieu! I believed myself stronger — I was not aware of ye force of my feelings — they have injured you & I curse myself — Adieu! if you will go — let me bless you first — be happy — happier than me you must be — Oh God! Oh God! Oh God! Heaven bless you — you have preserved me from ye agonies of guilt — my Child may now look upon me without a blush — Remember my life is in yr hands — Farewell — I am going — I know not where — I shall go the Theatre — & when my Carriage is dismissed — I shall leave ye house & go — God knows where — I know where you dine Yes! & I will see you — tho' unseen I will! I am calm for ye moment I will dismiss my Carriage & pretend anything — anything — so as I see you but unseen — Yes! I shall do something — Oh! I tremble for myself —

Take yr letters which I loved next to my heart's God — take them — you have my life — but the last—Never! I will wear it on my heart—till it Crumbles to Nothing—& If my life goes first—there it will remain—you cannot fear then, in Death I cannot harm you—In Death I shall be yours—mention it no more—Never shall you have it—God bless you. I give you my hair—torn from my head by that which shall drink my life—if you do not preserve yours—I am firm—a demon's firmness has this day ta'en possession of me & now I feel a mad fool—& my mind is big with ye idea of seeing you tonight—I will walk—nobody will see me—& return to ye Play—Adieu—I can no more—My God My God—assist me—Save me—Oh! save my head—it turns—it maddens—Oh! thou but adored—Forgive me my many faults—<u>All</u>—for I have loved thee to madness—to destruction—till Death—You have given me your heart—I will never part with it—till the Life Drop springs from my own—Heaven preserve you—I am lost—lost—undone [and now] you are gone.

Another, clearly subsequential—and it seems to be the last—says,

I cannot resist the desire I feel stirring within me to communicate with you once more, especially as it may be my fate never again to have the opportunity of doing so—Between the hours of two and three to morrow [sic] I may perhaps be what the chymists call 'decomposed'—If such should be my lot, remember me with affection for I have loved you to madness—if I should survive then, I pray you, destroy this letter—My mind is quite calm nor can anything make it otherwise—Of all the pangs which I shall feel, that of separating from you will be the greatest—There is at this moment a Demon urging me on, and I cannot resist—But where will this end? If there be existence in another world, and if our Spirits may revisit these scenes mine shall most assuredly do so. Dear Creature adieu—I have destroyed all your letters—The time approaches and I am resolved—Farewell—I am giddy, giddy even to death—it is—the hand that now writes this will soon be cold—It is done—Conceal this letter as you value your soul's health—as you dread the vengeance of an angry Spirit—All is deadly—Farewell—Farewell—your hair is in my bosom—When you see Byron tell him that you heard from me in my last hour—but tell no one else—.

The 21st letter (not necessarily chronologically) seems to have a date, Dec. 24, 1818, and begins, "There are moments when the heart triumphs over tribulations."

Scrope, as weak and fearful of life as he was, was remarkably unfit to be a paramour of Lady Frances, and probably of anyone else. One may wonder why she even bothered with him. But, he was there, he was available, he was willing—at the beginning, anyway—and he had certain assets that appealed to her, assets that, of course, would eventually turn into liabilities and sting them both. Scrope was far, far from stupid, and, indeed, realized his inadequacies better than anyone, better even than Lady Frances herself—and she saw his failings only too well.

Another failing Scrope shared with all other dandies—all of them perforce narcissistic—was his overwhelming and uncontrollable desire to blab about his sexual escapades. They all did it, those dandies, in detail. Discretion was not part of their makeup. The fun was not in the boudoir antics per se but rather in the talking about it to others, the preen, the peacock, the adulation.

They would get down to the nitty gritty in these braggadocci. Scrope got down there. Miss Frances Williams Wynn, in her 1864 book *Diaries of a Lady of Quality*, wrote: "Lady Frances has a double claim to immortality for at least one letter from the hero of Waterloo was addressed to her from the battle-field. Scrope Davies, who took the credit of being high in her favour, told me her peculiar mode of manifesting preference, which I suppress."

So, we know for sure that Scrope talked about the "sucking salamander" to some of his friends, but he did not brag about her openly, otherwise it would have become a scandal in its own day, and it did not. So, all in all, Scrope seems to have done a remarkable job in keeping the whole thing quiet. His comparative silence, combined with Lady Frances's almost uncharacteristic discretion, leads one in the direction of amazement and wonder that this affair was never made public until 1976.

16

Nantes

An undated (but 1819) letter from Webster to Byron, written from London about May 20 of that year, was the first (extant) communication between the two in a long time. It reads:

> My Dear Byron, I received your <u>verbosa epistola</u> some months ago & have delayed answering it under a hope that now ceases to exist, that I should have seen you at Venice this summer —
>
> I thank you very sincerely for ye manner in w'ch you express yourself in regard to ye Bond — in allusion to this, pray inform me when you <u>will</u> be in England — or how long you remain where you are —
>
> In Prosperity, our <u>feelings dictate</u> ye <u>events</u> of life — so far at least as they depend on self will — but they become our <u>Preceptors</u> & Guide on ye contrary side of ye question —<u>your</u> Sun is now in its meridian — may it remain so — — —
>
> Newstead has been prodigiously well sold I hear — J'espere vraiment que l'acquéreur n'a pas vous payé à la Claughton [I really hope the purchaser hasn't paid you like Claughton did] — — I still think what I told you on ye spot many years ago, — that you never sh'd have sold ye abbey itself & ye Park around it —
>
> <u>Posterity</u> will give too sure a verdict in favor of my opinion Depend upon it — — — Lady Frances hears occasionally from your sister Mrs Leigh with whom she was extremely happy to become intimate with [he correctly deleted this last word] in London last winter — where is my old soi-disant friend ye <u>colonel</u>? — There is nothing new in our world. My friend Fife expects ye vacant Green ribband [the insignia of an aide-de-camp] — My relation, Mr Wedderburn [James Wedderburn] ye present Solicitor General, will be ye new Lord advocate (for himself) & Scotland [this promotion never happened] —
>
> You may be surprised to see ye majority still ag'st ye Catholics — I am not — agreeing decidedly with one Mr. Locke upon ye subject — Mr. Horace Twiss has succeeded with his 'Carib Chief' at Drury Lane if not beyond the expectation of others certainly far beyond his own — & malgré le moine [despite the monk] P. Moore Maturin has carried Covent Garden completely by his Fredolpho —

Carib Chief, a play by writer and politician Horace Twiss, opened at the Theatre Royal, Drury Lane, on May 13. Charles Robert Maturin, 1782–1824, Irish novelist and dramatist, and curate of St. Peter's, Dublin, was noted for his tragedies, including *Fredolfo*, which opened at the Covent Garden Theatre on May 12. Peter Moore was an elderly politician, a great friend of Sheridan, and had made his fortune as a young man in India. He was the moving spirit behind the re-building of the Drury Lane Theatre. He was the last wearer of a pigtail in London society, and (not for that reason) died an exile in France in 1828. Why Webster refers to him as a monk is unclear.

"Is ye Vampire by you?" demands Webster, in the same letter, continuing:

> If not you sh'd send one to ye Galignani who libels you upon ye occasion — Pray send me all ye news and scandalum you can — Tho' I have a bad nose at an inuendo [sic] as Addison said — having always had an abhorrence of what ye world are too fond [sic] — the detraction of others, a school w'ch has ever too many Disciples, at least among Idiots & Devils — .

What Webster means here is the short story published in the *New Monthly Magazine* on April 7, 1819, written anonymously (but actually by John William Polidori), and falsely attributed to

Byron. It caused quite a stir—a supposedly new work by Byron—and by May the great poet was denying it. Giovanni Antonio Galignani was an Italian publisher of the English-language *Messenger* in Paris.

> How is your child? [he means Allegra] & all your establishment? I hear you are strangely alter'd, what I don't [sic] credit—grown stupendously corpulent—if this is ye case we can only say 'Nil fuit unquam tam dispar sibi'—

This last Latin phrase is from Webster's (and everyone else's at that time) literary hero, Horace, in his *Satires*. It was re-used by another of Webster's favorites, Addison, as the opening quote in his March 28, 1712, essay for the *Spectator*. Addison's story and quote were remarkably appropriate, and it was (not untypically) erudite of Bold Webster to have used it. The phrase means "Nothing has ever been more unlike itself."

> Direct to me 'Poste restante à Nantes, Loire Nif'—& believe me ever yours Truly, Wedderburne Webster—
> Lady Frances begs to be most kindly remember'd—

By the summer of 1819 the short but meaningful affair with Scrope Davies was over, and Lady Frances rejoined her husband, who was still living in Nantes. There he had a small private printing press, on which, in June 1819, he printed a book of 40 pages entitled *A Genealogical Account of the Wedderburn Family*. The author is listed as James Wedderburn Webster, Esq. The motto on the title page is "Virtus sola nobilitas" (virtue is the only nobility), and there is a dedicatory letter, dated "Nantes, June 1819," to Sir David Wedderburn of Ballendean (sic), in which the principal of the motto is by way of being enforced. There are copies of this little book in the libraries at Birkhill and Meredith; in 1902 a copy was in the possession of Charles Webster-Wedderburn, James's grandson. The present author has another.

In 1819 James gave up the name Webster and became simply James Wedderburn, his original name. It took some time for the world to catch up on this news, partly because he had been changing his name with some frequency over the last decade and no one cared, or even knew. They called him Webster, Wedderburn Webster, or Wedderburne Webster, depending on what had lodged in their memory. However, by 1821 he had changed it to Webster Wedderburne (no hyphen), and before 1827 he finally changed it to Webster-Wedderburn (with a hyphen); except for a few aberrations, this last is the version that has stuck, not only for him, but for his descendants.

There is an amusing article written in the February 1946 edition of the *Month at Goodspeed's Bookshop* (Boston, volume XVII, no. 5), which says: "In a document which has survived, the gentleman is addressed as James Webster Wedderburn Webster; if this was really his name, we are afraid we shall confuse him with James James Morrison Morrison Weatherby George Dupree [this refers to the protagonist of the A.A. Milne poem "Disobedience"]. All this seems unkind to a man who had enough sense to preserve a rare book for posterity and the taste to enjoy the amenity of a private press, on which he printed poems and a couple of epitaphs—one on his bulldog and one on Byron (who was alive at the time). We could have avoided this cattiness by saying that Webster was the husband of one of Byron's sweater-girls before girls wore sweaters."

The rare book they refer to is the copy of *Childe Harold* that Byron presented to WW on March 1, 1812. The article is inaccurate in saying that James printed the epitaphs—of course, Didot had printed these. However, overall, this (perhaps rather reluctant) 1940s defense of James has its points.

On July 2, 1819, Byron replied from Ravenna to James's May 1819 letter:

> Dear Webster—Your letter followed me to this city—where I have been some time.—A friend of mine—the young Countess Guiccioli [this is Teresa, another of his amours]—is very unwell—and I came down from Venice to see her about a month ago.—The poor Girl—who is but twenty

years old [she was more like 18] — and has been married about fifteen months to a very rich nobleman of Ravenna — (She is his third wife — & he is sixty) has had a bad miscarriage — and her symptoms threaten Consumption — but I hope better. — If you write to me address to Venice — my letters will be forwarded. — I answered you before about the bond — and do not know that I need say more upon the subject. — I presume nobody has called upon you on my part for payment. — Newstead was sold and the purchase money paid. — I regret that the tone of your letter is so desponding — and my own spirits at this moment are not in a state to reply to you very cheerfully. — The accounts you have heard of the alteration which has taken place in my appearance may be true — it would be odd indeed if some change had not occurred. — Mine has not been the most regular — nor the most tranquil of lives. — At thirty I feel there is no more to look forward to. — With regard to the imputed 'Corpulence' — my size is certainly increased considerably — but I am not aware that it amounts to that 'stupendous' degree which you enquire after. — At eight and twenty I was as thin as most men — and I believe that hitherto I have not exceeded the decent standard — of my time of life. — However — my personal charms have by no means increased — my hair is half grey — and the Crow's-foot has been rather lavish of it's [sic] indelible steps. — My hair though not gone seems going — and my teeth remain by way of courtesy — but I suppose they will follow — having been too good to last. — I have now been as candid as any thing but a too faithful mirror can be — I shall not venture to look in mine — for fear of adding to the list of that which Time has [added] — and is adding. — I regret that you do not pass into Italy — for my sake — because we should meet — and for yours — because it must be better than a provincial town of France. — Here all the cities are capitals — and have not that provincial tone of the secondary towns of other kingdoms. — If you were on this side of the Alps I would go a good way to meet you. — Why don't you come? — I really wish that you would, or could. — yrs. ever & truly B. Tomorrow I have to undergo a presentation to the Cardinal Legate of the district, and I am not fond of introductions. — P.S. — My best remembrances to Lady Frances — .

On July 5, 1819, Byron wrote to Lord Kinnaird, from Ravenna, the letter saying, "I had a letter from W. Webster the other day — he is at Nantes Loire Nif — and I have half a mind to go back in search of La Fanchette [Lady Frances] — but I know nothing of the geography of the place — Where the devil is Nantes? — and what is Loire Nif — a river I suppose — an't it?"

From Bold Webster at "21 Piccadilly, London" to Byron, dated "23 Sept. 19 [September 23, 1819]":

My Dear <u>Byron</u>, I believe I have a letter from you [this was Byron's July 2 letter] laying at Nantes where my family still are — I find it necessary again to recur to our <u>Bond</u> & since I am unable to pay it I am sorry I have to do so — but of one fact I reflect with much satisfaction, that <u>your own</u> affairs are now too prosperous to make it of any comparative moment —

I am about mak'g a general assign't in favor of my creditors & ye am't I have at present to give up, will barely pay interest upon my <u>common debts</u>, without calculating my private & friendly ones — w'ch are yourself, George Agar & my Brother in law Geo. Hawkins. I hope you, with them, will therefore enable me to settle with ye before named persons (viz — The Common Creditor) by waiving <u>your</u> claim to <u>interest</u> in ye mean time, w'ch indeed my income is inadequate to pay — & I am sure you w'd not wish <u>your name</u> incorporated in <u>such</u> a <u>deed</u> as that in question; let me know as soon as possible whether you <u>do</u> or <u>not</u> — Of course I conclude that if it is ever in my power you will naturally expect to receive ye am't of ye Bond with interest, but untill it is, & particularly at this moment, I am sure you w'd not wish to distress one of your oldest friends —

I was last week at Tunbridge where I saw some part of your family & friends — & you are far, very far from being so widely separated from ye wishes & thoughts of either, as yourself perhaps — or others might imagine — I forbear & ever have done my [this last word he crossed out] so, treading on uninvited & that, such private ground — but it is difficult to reconcile silence with regard & ye hazard of those suggestions, that I think (perhaps vainly) w'd ensure your happiness ultimately — let me hear from you soon — & if I can do any thing to serve you in — or out of London, rely on ye pleasure & fidelity of ye agent —

Ever Dear B. yours sincerely, JW.

From Venice, on October 5, 1819, Byron's reply to James's September 23 letter reflects a confusion over parts of Webster's letter that are as great as any other reader's would be:

> Dear Webster [then 11 lines crossed out] The latter part of your letter which I presume refers to some communication you may have held with Lady B's family — I do not quite understand; — if you imagine that there is any prospect of a reconciliation, you are deceived either by your own good wishes for such an event — or by some ambiguity in their expressions on the subject which must naturally be an awkward one. — I feel naturally curious to know what could have led you for a moment into such a notion — and I ask you from curiosity to tell me more explicitly. — Did you see my daughter — and how is she? —

He is referring here to Ada, his only legitimate child — by Annabella Milbanke — who would marry the future Earl of Lovelace and die in 1852, aged 37, having had three children of her own.

> I have another here (by a different mother) who is three years old nearly — and a pretty child —.

This child is Allegra, daughter of Mary Shelley's stepsister, Claire Clairmont.

> Whatever you have to say — You may speak out — it is a subject too public long ago — and too remote now — to require any delicacy between old acquaintances further than politeness requires. — I have some idea of going with my natural daughter Allegra to settle in South America — provided a colonizing plan which I have heard of — as about to be proposed by some Commissioners from Venezuela now on their way to England — be put in execution. — On this last subject my letter to Mr. Hobhouse has explained my ideas. — If you are in communication with the Noel family [formerly the Milbanke family — they changed their name in 1815 in order to acquire money through a legacy] or Lady B — I wish you would request them to aid me in getting my settled property — transferred from the funds to other & (what I think) safer security. — Mortgage or any thing would be preferable to the funds. — pray write soon — and believe me, yrs very truly BYRON.

There is another forgery of a letter by Byron to W. Webster, Esq., purportedly written from Venice on November 9, 1819, which is in Schultess-Young, letter VII, 164–166, again perpetrated by Major Byron. That this letter is indeed a forgery can be seen by, if no other evidence, only a cursory reading of the sequence of letters between Byron and Webster, i.e. Webster's of September 23, Byron's reply of October 5, and Webster's reply to that, on November 19, the very period when Byron's "Donny Johnny" was coming out. This exchange of letters does not permit of a genuine Byron letter of November 9. Besides — and this is a trait that runs through the Major Byron forgeries — this is too clever and thought-out a letter for Byron to have written to Webster. Not that Byron wasn't capable of writing such a letter; he just would not have done so to Webster. Anyway, the fake reads:

> My dear W., — I am glad you like 'Donny Johnny.' Murray says the poem has *not sold well*; so Murray says; Galignani tells a different tale. Of all my works 'D. Juan' is the most popular in Paris, and sells doubly in proportion, especially among the women, who send for it the more it is abused. The Don is a sore subject with the *moral* readers of your island, and has been the cause of a great row amongst the Philistines of the '*modern Athens*,' viz. briefless barristers, priests without parishes, physicians without fees, &c. &c. The canting raskals of the '*northern metropolis*' [he means Edinburgh] have constituted themselves into a sort of Upper House in the republic of letters. Latterly, however, it would seem, that, under the dingy banner of '*the Man of Ebony*,' an attempt is making to control this self-assured superiority; and that there are now two literary parties in the 'intellectual city,' opposed to each other in politics, parts, poetry, and presumption. The origin of the contest between the *Blues* of High Street and the *Olives* of Princes Street, as I understand they affect to consider themselves, in *apery* no doubt, for they have no originality of the *blue* and *green* factions of Constantinople in the decline of the empire, is exceedingly diverting. Like man and wife, rail however much they may against each other at home, they make a common cause on the community out of Edinburgh. The *Blues*, the aristocratic Whigs of the Review, with the watchwords *gentility* and *genius*, affect great style and fashion in their '*walk and conversation*,' and 'boast a splendid banquet once a year,' at which the talk is all about *tea-cups* and *Tokay*. For, on these occasions, they are determined '*to sink the shop.*' The *Olives*, who, being Tories by profession, and of course in immediate connection with '*the Archons*' of the modern

Athens, are the cocks of the dunghill, whose sweet voices would have thrown Queen Christina into ecstasy. I read the other day a capital story about the '*she-king*' of Sweden, whose *virginity* was probably of the same stamp as that of our own Elizabeth.... Christina, instead of a nightcap, always enveloped her head with a towel. One night, being unable to sleep, she ordered music in her chamber, and had the curtains drawn over her bed; but, enchanted with some part of the performance, she thrust her head through the curtains and screamed, '*Mort diable! qu'ils chantent bien.*' The musicians, and especially the eunuchs, were so terrified at her head and nose, that they ran away. My *captain of the horses* is waiting, and I must be off to the Lido, and snuff the Adriatic *breezes* amongst the *treees*. Believe me, ever yours affectionately, Byron.

To Byron's October 5 letter Bold Webster replied from "21 Piccadilly, 11 Nov 19 [November 11, 1819]":

> My D'r Byron, As we are become almost a nation of 'Jews & Infidels' your surprise sh'd be less at my Shylockonian [sic] reference to 'my Bond'—to be serious tho' I have not & never c'd have any apprehensions on that subject from you, but it is a necessary part of ye arrang't with all my creditors, that ye Deed sh'd be executed by you, or your Deputy as well as others—if therefore you have given any person here a power of attorney for such purposes Pray let me know—
>
> I am not acquainted with Lady B—& the channel through w'ch I acquired ye conviction under w'ch I wrote & now write to you in allusion to a certain subject, was a remote tho' infallible one—& I am quite persuaded all is in your own power—it is out of all reason to think otherwise—Nature found you great—but remember she is unequal alone to preserve her own works—This is the Crisis of your life, & you will be the architect of your own happiness or remorse—Glory or oblivion—your hand alone can wither those laurels w'ch your country has so liberally offer'd to ye Shrine of Genius—return then to that country & to ye society of those friends, who are only capable of conferring ye value we ought to attach to life & its distinctions—
>
> The plan of S. America I can't suppose you serious in—That w'd indeed be an immolation of ye brightest hopes & w'd at once throw ye ignoble mantle of oblivion over ye proudest memorials of your past days—.

Webster wasn't wrong, but it is mildly interesting to speculate upon what might—or might not—have happened if the poet had wound up living in Buenos Aires.

> I write as I feel warily upon ye subject. Remember you invited me to 'speak out,' & if I give offence, I shall not sacrifice an old & such valued friendship at ye expence [sic] of my sincerity—
>
> Your Daughter I hear is vey [very] well & promises m'ch—her mother I fear may not be equally if at least ye Depression of ye mind be such there as is represented—
>
> How is ye young Countess G. at Ravenna? [He means Teresa, Countess Guiccioli] If ye sex were ever admitted into ye Church, I sh'd not Despair of seeing you with a Cardinal's hat.
>
> You know of old, ladies were made Deaconesses when baptism was performed by immersion—I suppose you w'd say—for im—read—sub [i.e., "for 'immersion,' read 'submersion'"]—
>
> I had ye honor of being made acquainted with Mrs Leigh some time ago, but not being an importune visitant I have only met her once—pray say is Don Juan your work or not?

Don Juan was published anonymously in July 1819, or at least the first two cantos were. There would be 16 all told, and the poem was still unfinished at Byron's death.

> Let me hear from you soon, & let me entreat you at all events to abandon S. America—ye idea is really too aronautical for you [what he means by this is unclear, as is much of what James says. He has a job spelling the word that could be argonautical, or aeronautical, i.e., 'up in the air']—
>
> Ever y'r truly, J Wedderburne Webster.

Presumably Webster, like everyone else, knew that the two primary reasons Byron had fled England two or three years before—creditors and the growing concern of certain persons over his incestual habits—still applied. In addition, he had, by now, made a life for himself in Italy.

Anyway, Webster waited for a reply from Byron, hoping he hadn't gone too far in his outspokenness, but he waited in vain. Byron never replied. And it would be months before James would take up his pen again to write to the poet.

John Cam Hobhouse, in his diary of January 29, 1820, wrote: "Webster Wedderburne (as he now calls himself) walked on the top with me — a very strange creature, miraculously blind to his own defects. He said he should like to be a barrister, and thought he would gain great reputation by opening on a crim con case. This from the greatest ass and cuckold in London."

That same day, January 29, George III died, and Prinnie succeeded him at last. The Regency period was officially over, although for lack of a new name the ten-year reign of George IV and the reign of his obscure successor, William IV, have been incorporated by careless history under that label. It was not until the arrival of a plump and pretty eighteen-year-old girl in 1837 that the Victorian era dawned, a very, very different kettle of fish.

In March 1820 James Webster and Lady Frances were living at 132 Piccadilly, in London. They had been there certainly since February. However, in March James was obliged once more to flee England and his creditors, and set up a temporary residence in France — another forced exile. A very pregnant Lady Frances stayed on at Piccadilly, where her son, a second Charles, would be born on July 1.

On April 5 or 6, 1820, Thomas Moore wrote in his journal (he was in Paris), "Nothing that I remember except that Wedderburn Webster called upon me & left a request that I could let him know Lord Byron's present address."

In a letter to John Cam Hobhouse, written from Ravenna on April 6, 1820, Lord Byron said,

> There is a bond of Mr W Webster's dated 1813 — with a judgment — principle [sic] 1000 — interest 500 — total 1500 — will you get it sold — that is desire Hanson to do so; — I will take any discount — but it must be in monies — and not on Mr Hanson's account.— Messrs Dawson — Capron — and Rowley — of Saville Row [sic] — Attorneos are not unlikely to treat for it — as they are already in W's affairs [Dawson, Capron & Rowley, solicitors, actually of Savile Place].— I really cannot afford to lose the whole — and prefer this method to awaken him — which otherwise I must have done — whenever he returns to England — I know that Dawson and Capron &c. have lent him money — and are therefore of opinion that he is payable — and would be likely to buy his bond — though [for ?] but a trifle.— Put Hanson on the scent — he likes it.—

On April 13, 1820, Tom Moore wrote in his famous journal, "Called upon Wedderburn Webster — told me [when] he [last] heard from Lord Byron (about two months since) he was at Ravenna — fear from this [that] he has got into the clutches of the Guiccioli's husband."

This meeting between Moore and Webster took place in Paris. Moore erred in that Webster hadn't hear from Byron since October of the previous year. Anyway, a few days later, his journal entry reads: "April 16 — 19 — Lost two of these days at very stupid dinners; one with a Leicestershire squire, Jack Story, and the other with Wedderburn Webster at the Trois Frères Provençaux; Douglas of the latter party. Meant to go to the "Barbiere di Seviglia," but was too late, so adjourned to the Café de la Paix, drank punch, listened to nonsense from — — — [meaning Webster], and was heartily sick of both." Then he tells of the story Webster recounts relating to his (Webster's) trip from Newstead to London in the vis-à-vis, which is reproduced in this book at October 19, 1813.

In a letter to John Cam Hobhouse, from Byron, written from Ravenna on May 11, 1820, the poet says, "... in 1808 — you put me in to prose at Brighthelmstone [Brighton] about Jackson [Gentleman John Jackson, the pugilist] — & WW & Debathe" (James Wynn De Bathe, an old friend from Byron's Harrow days).

Finally, from "Paris" on "16 mai — 1820," James could stand the Byronic silence no longer, and dashed off a letter to "The Lord Byron, Poste Restante, a Vénice, en Italie":

> My Dear Byron — Your long silence after ye rec'pt of my last letter (in Nov.) is too unequivocal a proof that ye subject matter was disagreeable, if not offensive to you, for me to doubt — at any

rate you must admit you provoked me to a sincerity, wh I did not hesitate & never will refuse to bestow, where I conceive ye interest & happiness of those I value & esteem is involved — my opinions & convictions remain unalter'd, but y'r silence has effectually repelled ye discussion of that wh was only dictated by a sincere friendship & ye renewal of wh w'd be unwelcome & (I fear) unavailing —

I have been here two months — w'd it were sure to be my last exile! — at ye moment I thought I had subdued my Briareus of ye North (y'r friend Mr. Sibbald) I rec'd information of his hostile intentions wh I deemed prudent to evade by watching his operations on ye other — from this side of ye Channel — .

Webster had purchased the house in Scotland from William Sibbald, but, like Claughton in the case of Byron and Newstead, was having a problem coming up with the payment, and the 100-handed, 50-headed character of Greek mythology (Sibbald) was coming after him.

I am howe'r ab't to cast the die, as I expect Lady Frances to be confined next month & I therefore return immed'ly [he means to London] as no personal sacrifice w'd induce me to be absent under such circumstances — if you will write — Direct 132 Piccadilly — your acc'ts are always refreshing, to say ye least of them — to y'r friends they have a double interest — As you must hear frequently from [Tom] Moore, I need not harrass [sic] you with ye Dull & Improbable 'on dits' of this place — Our Ministers I heard had resigned on ye Divorce question, — wh you may know ye Chancellor is so orthodoxically violent upon — but it was a Salisbury-house report & like most others confounded I have heard since, tho' certainly neither impossible or [sic] improbable before ye session closes here — The 'Amyclas vivere' has long been ye maxim & in such time it is a wise one — where heads are easier struck off than subdued —

The soirées [i.e., the evening papers in Paris] how'r teem with ye reported advent of 'Lord Byron — et la Reine' — I wish they w'd place you in better company — Moore, as you may b'le [believe] 'goes out' as ye saying is, but little — Tho' like Lucifer I occasionally peep in upon his Paradise (but unfortunately happiness & content are not infectious) & he has indeed apparent cause for both — She is beautiful — in my opinion [i.e. Moore's Paradise] — a tragick beauty, which is very taking in ye suburbs of Paris — has he announced your 'Laureat' here? His name it is impossible I sh'd remember & w'd to God I c'd forget his [this next word is cut off, but is presumably 'face'] also — but among may [i.e. many] worse, there is a most sanguinary épître addressed to y'r L'dship, to wh succeeds a most facetious ode to — ye almighty — This is a day of mourning with me — & a fast — for ye memory of half a dozen teeth, whose loss I had yesterday to deplore —

Mr Jackson [the pugilist] w'd beg to know I suppose if I lost them 'by my own consent' — purely so, I assure you — tho' not with ye Dentist — as he was — as he was unused to such a specimen of English nerve — but as those wh remain are pronounced infallible, I hope it is ye last occasion upon wh such a requiem will be required — .

Again, strange that such a self-promoting Scotsman should proclaim himself an Englishman — ah well, a sign of the times, perhaps.

How is Allegra? — Is Scrope Davies with you for he is not in ye world, or [sic] has he been lately — I hope how'r he can still be gay & witty at ye expense of his friends — Badinage apart, I like him much, he was always a favority [sic] of mine — Hobhouse made or rather said his debût [May 9, 1820] in ye house last week & gave that elder Brother of ye Trinity — Bankes — a most classical set-down, wh was vey [i.e. very] salutary, as old Bankes was always a most inordinate retailer of ye Dead — & a very Dull tho' innoxious [sic] practioner [sic] in a living language — .

Bold Webster wouldn't have been so fond of Scrope if he had known that Scrope had had an affair with Lady Frances! The Bankes referred to is Sir Henry Bankes, senior M.P. for Corfe Castle; the junior member being his second surviving son, George Bankes; his oldest surviving son was none other than William John Bankes, the previously mentioned and unfortunate Egyptologist; Trinity was a reference not only to the three of them, but to their college at Cambridge.

Pray let me hear soon 132 Piccadilly & believe ever, Dear Byron, yours, Webster Wedderburn.

On June 1, 1820, Byron wrote to Tom Moore from Ravenna:

I have received a Parisian letter from WW [Webster's May 16 letter] which I prefer answering through you, if that worthy be still at Paris, and, as he says, an occasional visitor of yours. In

November last he wrote to me a well-meaning letter, stating, for some reasons of his own, his belief that a reunion might be effected between Lady B. and myself. To this I answered as usual, and he sent me a second letter, repeating his notions, which letter I have never answered, having had a thousand other things to think of. He now writes as if he believed that he had offended me by touching on the topic; and I wish you to assure him that I am not at all so!, — but on the contrary, obliged by his good nature. At the same time acquaint him the thing is impossible. You know this, as well as I, — and there let it end.

I believe that I showed you his epistle in autumn last. He asks me if I have heard of my 'laureat' at Paris, — somebody who has written 'a most sanguinary Épître' against me, but whether in French, or Dutch, or on what score, I know not, and he dont say, — except that (for my satisfaction) he says it is the best thing in the fellow's volume. If there is anything of the kind that I ought to know, you will doubtless tell me. I suppose it to be something of the usual sort; — he says, he don't remember the author's name [Lamartine was the man].

On July 1, 1820, James's third child and second son, Charles Francis Webster Wedderburn, was born in Piccadilly, London (where James and Frances were then living, and had been on and off — when they weren't in French exile — certainly since February of that year). That year J. Webster Wedderburne, Esq.'s, political tracts, *The King's Case Stated: an appeal to both Houses of Parliament on the proceedings pending against the Queen* (73 pages, printed on September 28 by Bowdery & Kerby, of 190 Oxford Street, London) and *The Queen's Defence; Remarks on Her Majesty's Defence. Addressed to the House of Lords* (28 pages, printed on November 2, 1820 by Ed. Kerby of Stafford-street, Bond-street; and by Ballantyne & Co., Edinburgh) were published, as was his 14-page pamphlet *General Sir Robert Wilson, M.P. on his conduct at the late meeting in Southwark*, also printed by Kerby. James said of the first two that they were both written with ease and plausibility; neither, however, strengthened the King's case by any argument not already exhausted by the newspapers of the day. In 1821 Rivington's of London published *A defence of Sir Robert Wilson's dismissal from the King's service*, a political tract by James.

On November 9, 1820, Byron wrote to John Murray from Ravenna, concerning John Cam Hobhouse, "... why he lampooned me at Brighton in 1808 — about Jackson the boxer and bold Webster &c."

The year 1820, though, was most sadly signal for the death of old Joe Murray, and the departure of Scrope Davies, his "exile," as Tim Burnett puts it in *Rise and Fall of a Regency Dandy*. "Money wherewith to gamble, and society wherein to shine, had been the twin pillars of his life, and from henceforward he was to have little enough of either." An insightful comment, and ineffably sad. For a while Scrope's whereabouts were unknown. Lady Frances spread the rumor that he had gone to South America (letter from John Murray to Byron on August 15, 1820).

Charles Francis Webster-Wedderburn, eldest surviving son of Sir James and Lady Frances Webster-Wedderburn. By kind permission of Tatton Hewetson.

17

The Duel

At Coombe Wood, Kingston, just outside London, on April 21, 1821, a farcical duel took place between Mr. James Wedderburn Webster and Lord Petersham. Charles Stanhope, Viscount Petersham (1780–1851), one of the foremost dandies of his day (who would, in 1829, succeed his father as Earl Harrington), had been flirting with Lady Frances. This was nothing new for Petersham, of course, as he had been flirting with the good lady (and every other pretty lady) for years. This time, however, he had gone too far, and James took exception, thrashing Petersham with a riding whip up and down St. James's Street. The duel was the natural result.

The whole episode is well covered in various caricatures of the time, now held by the Department of Prints and Drawings of the British Museum. Each cartoon is thoroughly described, with notes, in Dorothy George's *British Museum Catalogue of Political and Personal Satires*, volume x, 1820–27, reference numbers 14278–14285.

No. 14278 (the one shown in this book, courtesy Simon Heneage), an engraving (colored impression) by I.R. Cruickshank, and published in April 1821 by G. Humphrey, of St. James's Street, London, is headed: "By St Peter, this is no sham! or, A new cut for the groom of the stool." It shows a contretemps on St. James's Street, in front of a corner-house. Webster Wedderburn grabs Petersham by the collar and, with raised horse-whip in hand, says: "What I have caught you have I Master Sham Peter how dare you attempt to injure my Wife's character by saying you could play my part as well as I can, you boasting lying Dandy. take that! and that! and that!!!—." Petersham, protesting, exclaims: "Me Sir! you labour under a Mistake I am a Gentleman and will resent this Insult some other time." A lady (l.) [at left] exclaims: "Oh! my dear Lord, I am afraid will be killed." An officer and civilian at right, arms linked, say: "he shews the white feather again." A boy with a hoop grins at Petersham and says: "what a Dandy oh ah." Note the maid and girl at upper window, the child saying: "La! Betty he has been naughty!"

A paragraph appeared in the *British Press*, April 5, headed, "Extraordinary fracas in High Life," stating that in a rencontre between Mr. W.W. and Lord P., Mr. W. used his cane and the most opprobrious epithets. A correspondence between Lord Foley (the 3rd Baron Foley, Petersham's cousin), acting for Petersham, demanding an explicit and public denial, and Colonel Charles Palmer, for Wedderburn, assenting to a modified denial, was sent by the latter to the *Morning Post* on April 17 (Palmer was no stranger to duels). The article stated that Petersham had been paying attentions to Lady Frances Wedderburn. Charles Cavendish Fulke Greville, the diarist, wrote on April 15: "I know that P. was cudgelled..." (*Memoirs*, 1938, volume i, page 116). The Princesse de Lieven gives the story (*Letters to Metternich*, 1937, page 132). The article went on to say that the duel followed, on April 21. Petersham, "the superlative roué of the age" (Westmacott, *London Spy*, volume i, page 232), it says, was a Lord of the Bedchamber, and James Webster-Wedderburn (1789–1840) [sic] was an officer of the 10th Hussars. 12½ × 9⅜ inches. With border 14⅛ × 10⅛ inches.

Caricature by kind permission of Simon Heneage.

17. The Duel

No. 14279, an engraving (colored impression) by I.R. Cruickshank, and published in April 1821 by John Fairburn, of Broadway, Ludgate Hill, is headed "Peter Sham-Peter Shampood; or, The Consequence of Kissing and Telling," and below the title: "taken from Life, in St James's Street." On St James's Street, Webster Wedderburn grabs Petersham by the collar, exclaiming: "How dare you, you d—n'd Scoundrel, make use of scandalous reports of my Wife—You libel on all that is either noble or fashionable—You Ape—you infernal Puppy—take this horse-whipping as a proper reward for your insolence." Petersham, with bent knees, responds with: "Sir, Sir, What the Devil, sir eh Sir—Damn me what d'ye mean Sir—you know my rank Sir—privilege, Sir—Oh the Devil—I never said I Kissed your Wife, but if I had Sir, 'tis truth Sir—Chalk Farm Sir, Mantons and a Saw-pit for this Sir by the blood of the Stand-ups I will have satisfaction." A dandy looks on, amused, a lady on each side. One lady says: "As I live it is Lord P. and Wed. Web. What can be the meaning of the Rencontre?" He replies: "O nothing in the world your Ladyship—a mere trifle, a bagatelle, only a hoax that's all His Lordship whispered at Almack's that he had been a little too intimate with a certain lady—that's all my lady, that's all pon honor." The second lady offers: "I think he deserves to be horse-whipped for not keeping the secret." Petersham's groom (a tiger in the caricature) in the curricle, exclaims: "Damn that Jealous Humbug how he's Shampooing my Master in the public Street." A little chimney-sweep at right foreground says: "Here's a Mill! go it, go it, my noble—serve him out—Sweep! Sweep!"

This print is advertised, *Examiner*, April 15, as "A New Caricature. Just published, price 1s coloured...." It is depicted in No. 14282. 8⅝ × 13⅛ inches.

No. 14280, an engraving (colored impression) by J.L. Marks of 163 Piccadilly, and published ca. April 1821 by Marks, is headed "One of Lord Sham-Peter's Night Scenes, Brought to Light." The scene is a cobble-stoned area between two dwellings in London. At left is a coach and pair. The door of the coach is open, and a lady sits inside. In the foreground, Wedderburn, wearing footman's livery, is attacking the much bigger Petersham, who, alarmed, says: "Im struck with surprise! what little low-bred fellow are you—ho—ho—I have some faint idea of you, but, but y-y-your L-L-L-Lady your Lady Sir." Wedderburn replies: "Peter—shame on your conduct it matters not Whether-born in a Palace or a Stable-yard I can feel an affront Sir, and revenge it too." A dandy behind Wedderburn says: "Web! Web! What the Devil are you about, if you dont resist 'so help me god' it shall be our last meeting, after this I shall not be able to get up to morrow I shall be so infernally ill." The lady in the coach says: "Now for Wellington to protect me." Looking on, the coachman says: "Ay! Ay! I thought it would be found out." A man dressed similarly to Wedderburn watches. Stable Yard, St James's, was Lord Harrington's town house. 8 9/16 × 12⅞ inches. With border, 8 13/16 × 13⅛ inches.

No. 14281, an engraving (colored impression) by J.L. Marks of 163 Piccadilly, and published ca. April 1821 by Marks, is headed "Peter Sham Love's Duel." At left, Petersham, knees bent, holds a pistol, and puts a bottle of Bergamot to his nose. Crying, he says to the determined Wedderburn: "Stop! Stop! Stop! (Pray Sir) Do not kill me yet—let me take one smell or, I shall swoon before I'm dead,—O! the impolite Bow-Street officer: not to come to appointment.—If I should escape, I'll never go after Married Women again if I do D—- me." He has tied his hat to his head with a scarf. Lord Foley (his second in the duel), skulks behind a bush. Standing behind Wedderburn is Colonel Palmer with a pistol. 6⅛ × 9 5/16 inches. With border, 7 3/16 × 9 13/16 inches. *Caricatures*, xii, 190.

No. 14282, an engraving (colored impression) by "Crook" [I.R. Cruickshank], and published in April 1821, by J. Fairburn, of Broadway, Ludgate Hill, is headed "Peter Sham—Abraham!!!—or, The Dandy Jew, the Crack'd Colonel, and the Horn-Boy." Colonel Palmer sits at left, in full hussar uniform and holding a busby. Petersham faces him holding a caricature in his left hand. Colonel Palmer replies with a sardonic smile: "Ha! ha! ha! all a Mistake my Lord—

all a rediculous [sic] mistake by heaven — ha! ha! ha! Web declares upon his honor it was all a mistake he took you for Abraham the Jew Broker, the greatest rascal in Town and the horse-whipping was meant for him, not you — Damn'd Droll, my Lord — Damn'd droll — ha! ha! ha!" Petersham answers: "Why D — n me Sir, no such excuse shall be Palm'd off on me — this is worse and worse first horse-whip me, and then call me Abraham the Jew Broker — my honor is undone Sir — look here, Sir, they have commenced Caricaturing me already — is there no way of settling it without a gun shot wound — I am ruined, do you hear that rascal of a horn-boy in the Street, what a noise he makes about me." We can see through a French window a newspaper boy running with papers under his arm, the papers reading "Duel." The boy blows his horn, and a speech bubble appears, saying: "Here's a true and particular account of the Duel that was fought at Coombe Wood, when a noble Lord was shot through the brains with Paper Pellats from a Pop-Gun!! but as his Soul was impenetrable, he is recovering — This most Curious-est Duel, all for one ha'penny." Above Petersham's head, on the wall, is a pair of pistols with the inscription "Peace Establishment." At his feet lies an open box full of letters, with "Letters from Lady Frances" written on the box. Lying at Palmer's feet is a paper: "Anecdotes of the late 10th." Lying on the table between the two men are papers and writing materials. The paper next to Petersham says: "Notice of an Action for Crim. Con."; "Challenge to fight W — — with Pop-Guns"; "Taylors Bill £250." The one next to Palmer: "Dear W — I am infernally ill so help me Bob [signed] Pal — r." On the wall hang two pictures covered by speech bubbles from the mouths of the two men. The picture frames bear the inscriptions (at left) "Mail Coach Adv[entu]res"; and (at right) "Watch House Adventures." For the duel see No. 14283.

It is alleged that Petersham induced Palmer to withdraw the bullets from the pistols. To "sham-Abraham" is to feign illness. Petersham's profile, the whiskers which frame his chin and resemble a beard, and his exotic dress give him a Jewish appearance. Colonel Charles Palmer was the son of the projector of mail-coaches. The allusion to the "late 10th" is to the 10th Hussars and to Palmer's removal from the regiment in 1814 (over the Colonel Quentin court-martial). For his letters to the Press over the duel see *Journal of H.E. Fox*, 1923, pages 63, 67.

No. 14283, an engraving (colored and uncolored impressions) by I.R. Cruickshank, and published in April 1821 by G. Humphrey of St James's Street, London, is headed "Peter's Sham Duel, or A Dunghill Cock Endeavouring to Show Game." Wedderburn, at right, stunted and unprepossessing, fires his pistol at the bigger, more elegant Petersham, whose pantaloon seat takes the blast. Petersham, on fire, hops about, exclaiming: "Pray do'nt [sic] fire at me, my dear Fellow, it may injure my Whiskers pon honor. — such a shocking Idea to look at a nasty Pistol. Oh! I shall faint where is my Lavender? I wish I was at home Oh! Oh!!" Wedderburn has a powderhorn over his shoulder. He exclaims: "Take that for my Wife, you Liar! you contemptible puppy, you Cur. look how his hand shakes I'll blow him to St James's, Damm'me, he's nothing when screw'd to the stcking [sic] place." Colonel Palmer, his amused second, stands behind him, hands in pockets. At his feet are a bottle and an empty dueling-pistol box. A signpost next to him points to Combe [sic] Wood. He says: "That is a prime joke, ah! ah! I have drawn the balls out of the pistols, so it's all a Flash that's the way to give every Body Satisfaction..ah! ah! ah!" Lord Foley, Petersham's second, steps back, saying: "Oh daisy me! his Lordship Is hit in the Seat of his Honor I mus [sic] get behind a bush or I shall be in danger, and smell of Powder for a Month. O la!!" An equally amused coach postilion stands by, saying "ah! ah! ah!" Behind the tree is a coach painted with a coronet, signifying nobility. A surgeon sits in the tree, holding shears and examining a plaster spread across his branch. He says: "I must cut a plaster to cover the part all over; then Phlebotomize and keep him in a Stable Yard" (see No. 14280 for this reference). Petersham's second pistol lies at his feet, next to it a bellows inscribed "Hair Powder" and papers inscribed "Don Juan, court Plaster" and "Almacks." Wedderburn holds his second pistol. At his feet lie a blunderbuss with attached bayonet and a paper inscribed "Satisfaction."

The duel was fought on 21 April, at Coombe Wood, Kingston; shots were harmlessly exchanged and the parties reconciled. While it was pending there were bets that Petersham would not be a principal. *Journal of H.E. Fox*, 1923, pages 63, 67, 69; Greville, *Memoirs*, 1938, volume i, page 116. 9¼ × 13¼ inches. With border, 10⁵⁄₁₆ × 13¼ inches.

No. 14284, an engraving (colored impression) by W. Heath, and published on May 9, 1821 by S.W. Forbes, of 50 Piccadilly, is headed "Peters Sham Gallantry, or Stable Yard Discipline No Joke to a Delicate Dandy." Wedderburn, looking as he does in No. 14278, has just exited a carriage and crossed to grab Petersham by the collar and raise his horse-whip (again, much like 14278). Lady Frances is standing behind Petersham, who says: "Now my dearest Angel we shall have a luxurious Feast in the absence of—what ho the Devil D—n unlucky Mistake this spare my delicate sensibility pray!!! I meant no harm indeed." Wedderburn replies: "Your delicate sensibility of Countenance renders it doubtfull to which Sex you belong, however your attire allows me to treat you as a Male so take that & that & then to breakfast with what appetite you may." Lady Frances says: "Oh my poor Peter I hope your Tender frame will not be completely destroyed by this rude attack, & unfortunate disapointment [sic], poor dear thing." 12 × 8½ inches.

No. 14285, an engraving (colored impression), by I.R. Cruickshank, and published in May 1821 by J. Fairburn, of Broadway, Ludgate Hill, is headed "The Duel between Web and Sham-Peter—or, Most Horrobly [sic] Frightened!!" After the title: "Scene, Coombe Wood." Wedderburn, at left, fires a blunderbuss with "Egg's Hair Trigger" inscribed on it, and is thrust backwards by the recoil, his hat flying off, hit by a blast of flame from a pistol fired by Petersham from behind a tree. Petersham sniffs eau de cologne from a bottle. An awkward-looking weapon stands against the tree, bearing the words, "Rifle Barrel." Wedderburn says: "O, Lud! how cursedly My Piece kicks—She has'nt [sic] been Ram'd home enough enough [sic]—She was always a Rum-one, and though I once got Thirty Thousand by her, she has upset me at last." Next to him is a case of bottles containing spirits, inscribed "Restorative Cordials. From Waterloo," and a cannon on a gun-carriage with the inscription: "To be used if necessary." Petersham says: "O, dear, O! My head twirls round like a Whipping-Top—If it wasn't for this Smelling Bottle of Lady Francis's [sic] sweet Water, I couldn't stand." Beside him is a box labeled "Parfait Amour. Fribourg and Pontet's. Tabac en Poudre." Petersham's groom, at right, in the curricle, says excitedly: "If he hits my Master's Napper that's impenetrable If anywhere else I shall lose my Place." Colonel Palmer, Wedderburn's second, shouts: "Murder! Murder!! Peter has shot Web's head off, and we shall all be hang'd—What shall I do? What shall I do?"—At background right, Foley, Petersham's second, runs off, with hair on end and hat flying off, says: "I don't like the Smell of Powder so, d—n me I'm off." 8¾ × 13¼ inches.

The *Times* of April 23, 1821 (page 3) has an article entitled "Correspondence and Meeting Between Lord Petersham and Mr Webst. Wedderburne. We give the following correspondence, on the joint authority of the parties interested:—

No. I

Sir.—Upon my return home, at 6 o'clock this evening, I first saw your publication in this day's morning paper, and, in consequence, lost no time in despatching an express to Lord Petersham, at Brighton, who will instantly, upon receiving my letter, return to town; and that moment you shall hear from me. I write this, Sir, to account for what may appear a delay on the part of Lord Petersham, in not writing to you the moment your publication appeared. From yours, Sir, &c. Foley.

Hamilton-place, 7 o'clock, Thursday evening, April 19.

P.S. Lord Petersham cannot return before 7 or 8 o'clock to-morrow.

No. II

My Lord.—I have this instant received your lordship's letter, and beg to state that I shall be at home at all hours to-morrow, and ready to answer all communications. I am, & c. T. Webster Wedderburne [sic].
April 19, 8 o'clock P.M.

No. III

Sir.—Owing to a mistake, Lord Petersham did not receive my letter till late this morning, consequently is only just arrived. He now desires me to say that it is absolutely necessary you should either send a friend to me, or fix a time and place of meeting to-morrow morning. I shall be at home till 11 this evening, to receive your reply. From your humble servant, Foley.
Hamilton-place, Friday evening, 7 o'clock, April 20.

No. IV

My Lord.—It was with much surprise, after having been detained at home the whole day, in consequence of your Lordship's note of last night, that I have received one from you this evening, desiring me either to send a friend to you, or to fix a time and place for meeting Lord Petersham to-morrow morning.

Let Lord Petersham distinctly state the grounds on which he calls upon me, and my friend will then be ready to receive your Lordship, or any communication on the part of Lord Petersham. I am your Lordship's, &c. (signed) T. Webster Wedderburne [sic].
Friday evening, April 20, 1821.

No. V

Hamilton-place, Friday evening, half past 10.

Sir.—It is with astonishment that I read your letter demanding an explanation of the ground upon which Lord Petersham now calls upon you for satisfaction. You have not contradicted, but encouraged, a most scandalous and prejudicial report against his personal honour: he calls upon you positively to contradict it, or give him that satisfaction which is due to a gentleman falsely accused. The cause of your having been kept waiting during the day has clearly been explained; I must, therefore, now repeat the necessity of your immediately fixing upon the time and place of meeting to-morrow, or giving, under your hand, for publication, a contradiction of that scandalous and false report before alluded to. Too much time has already been lost to attend to explanations, that may, under some pretence, be withdrawn. From yours, &c. Foley.

P.S. An immediate answer is expected to the above, directed to Brooks's Club House, St James's-street.

No. VI

To Lord Foley.

I am perfectly of Lord Foley's opinion that too much time has been lost in this affair; but I beg to ask to whom is that delay to be ascribed?

Since every circumstance has been made public, and since so much has passed between the parties, I considered it necessary on that account alone to demand "the distinct grounds on which Lord Petersham calls upon me."

Lord Foley presents me with an alternative which is wholly out of the question.

I am aware of no "false report" in currency against Lord Petersham, and if Lord Foley means that I could be capable of withdrawing any explanation I had once given, I must repel such an insinuation with indignation; and I will not permit any person to dictate that line of conduct to me which is alone consistent with my own honour to point out.

I now, therefore, name three o'clock P.M., at Coombe Wood, near Kingston, where I shall expect to meet Lord Petersham. (signed). T Webster Wedderburne [sic].

No. VII

Sir.— I have received your letter, appointing 3 o'clock to-morrow afternoon, to meet Lord Petersham at Coombe Wood, near Kingston, which shall be punctually complied with. From yours, Foley.
Brooks's, Friday night.

A meeting, in consequence of the above correspondence, took place between the parties Saturday afternoon, at three P.M., attended by Lord Foley and Mr. Kerr, the former as the friend of Lord Petersham, the latter that of Mr. Webster Wedderburne, when, after exchanging two shots each without effect, the seconds interfered, and the affair terminated.— Observer.

The most absurd leap of faith was made by one John Gideon Millingen, who wrote a book called *The History of Duelling*, published in 1841. Because the *Times* had misread Bold Webster's initial as a "T" instead of a "J," Mr. Millingen guessed at the most likely completion of this name, filling in the blank as "homas," and thus his recounted episode is titled, "Between Viscount Petersham and Thomas Webster Wedderburne, Esq., April 21, 1821." There never was a Thomas Webster Wedderburne, and that that author did not know Bold Webster is astounding.

It is almost comforting to speculate that James might well have used the pistols Byron gave him as a gift exactly seven years before.

After the duel the Websters moved to Boulogne, in France, in yet another attempt at reconciliation. Frances was pregnant again. If they could escape England, they might escape themselves and each other.

On September 20, 1821, Byron wrote a letter to John Murray from Ravenna, in which he says, "All my loves too make a point of calling upon her [Augusta Leigh].... [T]he year before last I think Lady F W W marched in upon her—& Lady O [Oxford] a few years ago spoke to her at a party—and these and such like calamities have made her afraid of her shadow."

On September 28, 1821, Byron wrote to Murray again, in relation to letters from Byron, "As to those other correspondents (female &c.) there are plenty scattered about in the world—but how to direct you to recover them—I know not—most of them have kept them, I hear at least that Lady O & F W have kept theirs—but these letters are of course inaccessible—(& perhaps not desirable) as well as those of some others."

In September 1821 Tom Moore ran into James in Paris, and it soon came out that Bold Webster still owed Byron the 1000 pounds. Indeed, he never paid it back. Moore's journal entry for September 30, 1821 says, "Dined at Tegart's— WW there—owes Lord Byron, he says, a thousand pounds and does not seem to have the slightest intention of paying him." And, although one can and should despise Webster for such shocking behavior, one must also blame Byron for being so open-handed with his debtor (see the letter written to Webster on November 22, 1813, which tells James never to worry about the debt, and that Byron would never press him for it, no matter how hard he himself was pressed).

On September 30, 1821, Lady Frances wrote to her husband (this letter Byron having received a copy of and kept, thus its continuing presence in the Murray Archives):

> Your letter dated the 20th only reached this [place] the same day with others to other people bearing date the 26th. It was contrary to my intention, after the dreadful past, to have trusted my

self to write, but the solemn appeal you make to my feelings, coupled with my children's name, forces me to break this my resolution, and I will endeavour to answer your letter, tho' not in <u>fine</u> language, at least as moderate as wounded feelings will allow, and as most probably it may be the last communication, I shall try to make my language as clearly understood as possible — To pretend to recall to your mind the whole of your conduct towards me since a very short time after our arrival at Calais would be absurd — it must, tho' <u>unallowed</u> by yourself — be fully present to your mind, & if it does not now fall surely it <u>will</u> ere long rush to your recollection with many a bitter pang, too well you <u>must</u> feel all —

However, as your letter to me is couched in language that would imply I was the aggressor, I feel a few words necessary — I landed at Calais resolved <u>if</u> in human power to make you happy, and if possible to be happy myself, and in every hour since that time my mind can rest with the greatest delight — I feel I have not one single moment even to reproach myself for — you know the conduct pursued towards me after we had been here 5 weeks occasioned, I am sorry to say, by my firmness in paying money for our children's common expences [sic] in Engld instead of giving it to you, and urging you to follow my mother's advice & remain near the coast, instead of going to Paris, where inevitable ruin awaited us — You know the manner in which (I will not say you leagued with your servant) you allowed that butchered servant to speak of your wife — you witnessed my astonishment at your extraordinary and unintelligible language until accident opened my eyes by allowing me to hear a conversation between you and the servant couched in words about your wife. I think to repeat — did I not repeat some sentence to you that made you exclaim in the name of God who told you — you know the scene that followed — you saw me phrensied at hearing from the common tradespeople the manner in which your servant Lake, as the organ of your sentiments, spoke of me in the <u>common Brandy shops</u> — you know how often before I was aware of the extent of your infamy —

I begged to come to Boulogne, to the Bradshaws' and under various excuses you begged me to remain, and asked it as a favor the 2 or 3 first times of your leaving me at Calais [she had first written the word 'there,' but substituted it with the name of the French port town] that when I had heard what was going on, I have immediately ordered the carriage to seek Mr Bradshaw's protection, and you have <u>gone upon your knees</u>, and swore you would never rise till I promise to remain, that a repetition of such language should never occur, and that we would endeavour to be happy! — I have then counter-ordered the carriage, and also my permit of embarkation, which I had ordered, when feeling I was bound to seek the protection of the laws of my country against the moral assassination I was hourly experiencing from my husband's servant, and which he [her husband] quietly allowed — after those promises, did I not quietly allow you to go to Boulogne alone in your carriage (tho' the expence was constantly urged as a reason for <u>my</u> not going) and for what purpose —

Oh God! to labour to prejudice my relations against me, to use language of me that you would not dare apply to the commonest wretch — to talk of me as 'a woman of gross appetites,' <u>ready to rush into the arms of any man</u>, as a creature living in open prostitution with God knows who at Calais, and this was the woman who 12 hours or less before you had knelt to — had implored her not to make a public business of what had passed — had assured her you never could live 'happy without her,' &c &c — <u>This</u> was the proud wife whose character you laboured to blacken in the eyes of those she respected, the woman you spoke of as going into gardens & houses with men at Calais, the woman whose movements were subject to a continued espionage, who you desired that wretch to follow, thereby justifying his most villainous inventions, that you actually sent back to Calais to remain unknown, to afford ample scope for his invention & profligacy, knowing the key to the husband's favor — when you found out I was resolved to leave Calais, you return and go to a hotel, to which I, by chance, go to [sic] take rooms for a couple of days previous to my departure & getting money, the time of our house being up — the first thing I am informed of by the waiter is that WW & his servant are there — I return home again to see Mr Pike Carew [I have been quite unable to find out who this man is] to settle with the ruffian in whose house I lodged — he is good enough to come and suddenly you enter, you wish him to go, as <u>your</u> friend (for I had never seen him but once before), I insist on his remaining, and before him enter on the whole of your behaviour to me since my landing — you remember the scene that there passed — you hurry about me, confessed you had acted wrong, that you had been inflamed against me, by whom! by a man who millions of times you called a perfect villain, you then asked me if I would answer some questions, which I answered with my hand on my heart, but <u>all</u> your questions were put under a solemn promise from Mr C [i.e. Pike Carew] & I not to breathe a word to the man himself. He could easily make you the promises, having no taste for the society of servants—you then begg'd me to think no more of any thing, that the valet should be sent off and we should be happy & should go to Boulogne together—under these feelings we went to the Hotel, but the vow could not rest—the next day you remained closetted with Lake till 9 o'clock!! the consequence was fresh infamy and a revival of the same scenes, for the valet, finding his plot for a moment defeated, exerted villainy to secure your favor, and by a nod made you again insult your wife! I then declared before Mr Carew I would not go with that man to Boulogne, and so it was settled. You afterwards ordered your own cabriolet for you & him—that I might remain if I liked & ended by entreating me to let the man go with us for his month under your honor, he should then go—I, like a fool, yielded—

We came to Boulogne, and from that moment I never heard you say a civil word—you were scarcely at home, not one Evening but when with company, and never entered my room but to insult—Have I not heard you use the worst language to me at dinner and turn around to that man and laugh—at Calais, if for a moment you have taken my hand, if that man entered your home did you not throw it [her hand] from you, to prevent his seeing you, afraid to let him see you kind to your wife—Did you not one day in your most insulting way at dinner desire him to prepare another room for you, and in a few days beg to return to mine which I proudly rejected—you know the conduct you pursued to me down to the day of your leaving Boulogne, the affray with your servant took place, with that very man, who that very morning because I would not wait for you to go out with me to buy some dishes, I believe actually followed Lucy & I [sic] down every street!!

Upon that business thank God I feel I did all that could be done for your good—if you do not know it, all in this town do, and but for those gentlemen you since would have such a different punishment—although you kindly said that we all had endeavoured to throw you into prison & that all your friends in England said it was a praiseworthy act—By your absence I discerned you had been favoring your friends by letters of abuse about me, one from Mr Bullen who must have had a sad tale told him before he would say 'if yr wife is really what you describe, then you should take the most determined steps, if you are sure you have proof'—These words prove yr accusation was of the present moment—I then heard all the villifying [sic] language you had used about me, & having settled as far as possible the affair of Lake, I resolved it was impossible to live with you, and that you should be made to prove your words—On your return you remember the scene that passed before Col. Knight, who was a witness to all—how often did you say it was your wish to separate from me, that I was the most wicked person in the [this last word crossed out; she was presumably going to say 'the world'] existence, that no power on Earth should tempt you to live with me—but that you wished me to remain quiet till after the trial—in the mean time fresh villainy reaches my ears daily, and after the trial before Col. Knight & Mr Grady, I gave you an occasion of justifying yourself in the presence of that wretch & that the past should be forgotten—but you did not dare face him—After repeated scenes which are unnecessary to repeat to you finding you wished to continue defaming me yourself & not daring to give me the least protection against a drunken ruffian who was hourly destroying my character in his master's name, in every shape—even in the lobby of my own house—When he actually declared it was his master's intention to swear the child was with him, and instead of you being maddened by supposing you an accomplice of such a creature, you proclaimed yourself his partner & abettor, by not saying a word to him of reproach, on the contrary, he & his friend the nurse were closetted with you by the hour together from which interviews you used to come forth to insult me & your servants to use, as they called it, their master's language about your wife—and when forced by an open exposure to send the man away, the wretch who for amusement or on account of a china bowl you had not hesitated to [?] was, for [?] your wife's character quietly asked to leave the house—but his departure only increased your enormous persecution of me—you insulted me for every thing—because I allowed Lucy to go to Mrs Bradshaw's because I refused to dine at home (when any of the Canaille by whom you were surrounded dined with you) the only day a gentleman dined with you, I was told at every turn to get out of the house, that I had better go to the Blackguards who were my friends—that you never desired to see my face again, that you were going to bring actions against me & had brought over the lawyer (who from your former character of him I refused to associate with) to take down evidence and God knows I cannot repeat a hundredth part of all you said—After all this, after you had attempted to seize my child, in concert with that poor wretch Lake's successor

Mr Courtney better knn [known] in England under the name of Currie & Co. the advertising quacks—and after your villainous & atrocious but thank Heaven unsuccessful attempt to injure me in the opinion of the person who you know I valued, who you had heard me so often speak of with delight — Mr St John — I resolved to save my girl from your grasp, and seek the protection which my uncle's home offered — I felt it due to all my family, to all who had shewn kindness to me, particularly after what passed in England to prove I was not the polluted creature who you had laboured to save — but the unfortunate one you had laboured to destroy — I have endeavoured to give an outline, the detail would fill volumes, as I before said I cannot accuse myself of a single movement against you, and all are aware of your atrocities against me — and yet your letters & conversation speak of me as the aggressor — of <u>you</u> as the injured. What has been the conduct of yourself & companions since I left the house — you know what I was — you know what my heart was capable of — had you shewn the slightest inclination to reform, avow yourself the offender to your wife, and instead of contriving to abuse me, had said 'I am sorry' — I would have returned — 'tis true you sent me word, my home was open to me & you would leave it — so I was to return to it as a culprit — as one ashamed and afraid — as the victim of caprice — it was impossible! — I have argued with my own mind, but it would not stand the blackening horror you would stamp upon it — I felt I would rather die than return to play away my reputation — you know what I was, you knew this proud spirit could never brook the loss of society's good opinion — I should have soon stood an outcast, and have owed the kindness of an individual to toleration & good nature, as if I was bad — I was perfectly aware of all I should bring up myself, but I felt I should be happy in a cottage for the remainder of my days, giving the world a proof that I was not what <u>my husband</u> said I was — Did you not continue to tell of the actions against me and your Divorce of me as a wicked wretch — Did you not tell Mr Jefferys that had you seen one spark of good in my mind you would have worked to improve it, but that all was bad — 'tis true you always ended by saying 'do not think I mean to say any harm of her, or to injure her honor' — so it was <u>nothing</u> in your eyes to have a wife more abandoned than the wretches in the street — sunk so low that the proud beggar, if innocent, might point at her with pity — <u>you</u> could keep the opinion of the world & be contented to live with <u>such</u> a creature — but <u>your</u> wife preferred leaving the world feeling innocent than submit to the suspicion of guilt, submit to the unjust, cruel, destructive conduct of him who had sworn at the altar of God to protect me — and now you talk of doing all in your power to save me from the dreadful situation in which I have placed myself — let all who read these pages speak & think for themselves — you 'wish to arouse me to something like a sense of what I owe myself and children' — You speak of me as an object of pity & condemnation to the well thinking part of society — you urge me to a home of my own when you have left me none, but <u>that</u> which is not in your power to deprive me of — You talk of your affection, of your interest in my welfare — of your anxiety to serve me in any way — to all who have known me the <u>sequel</u> proves <u>how sincere you have been</u> — you found me young & happy — I now stand wretched and alone — you leave the most infamous orders at the house — you prohibit me from seeing my boy — and the grossest insult is offered to any body I send to see him — the cook, the only respectable person in your set, was forced by the atrocities to leave the house & my baby to a set of miscreants who neglect him to a fearful degree — the very shop people cry <u>shame</u>, actually without Good, and the house turned into a noisy alehouse — my poor child left to the mercy of providence and trusted to a nurse who <u>I</u> had sent out of the house for bad conduct — I am forced to exile my other poor child from me, as I find the espionage still continues by your clan, now you have retreated from the scene of action — I trust she is beyond your reach, but I tell you now candidly, and you know I am firm, that I will wade thro' death & destruction to save <u>that</u> child from the hands of those mauvais <u>your</u> mother & sister — no barrier shall restrain me. You urge me to leave this [place] — for why? — because here I am safe, under the protection of kind friends and my most trifling action has a witness, and here I will remain, unless Mama, my brother, Sir James [Cockburn] and Mr Bradshaw [her uncle] decide to the contrary, until your action, so loudly vaunted [she had spelled it the old way — vanted — but had corrected it] by yourself and the incipient conversation of your process in the Consistorial Court is brought against me for bad conduct <u>here</u> & at Calais with person or persons unknown, the result will then decide our future conduct, and if you get a Divorce, we shall both be free — What! Shall I [?] a step that [?], when I find the very baker & butcher talking of the actions you are to bring against me, <u>your wife</u> — my blood boils at the manner in which you have sought to degrade me — Bring your actions, & let the world know what I am & what I am not, do this, or at once proclaim yourself the destroyer of your wife — till then your adieu and professions of friendship and affection are insulting to me, and a degradation to yourself — I bear you no ill will — nay, I can forgive you, your conduct to me, so long as I possess my children — they are my only heir and for their sakes I ask for vindication — In regard to my going to Engld — you know well you would then take my babes untill I went into Chancery, which you know I have no funds for — 'tis very simple the talking and providing them, but I know you have them not, and lawyers are not contented with words— you urge Nantes or Bruxelles— I am willing to do whatever my family advises, but not to live alone exposed to the machinations of my enemies— but even had I the inclination, I have not the means, as you well know, you left no money, and the money from Sir James [Cockburn], to which you allude, having opened his letters, you must have seen was a bill to Nantes which nobody but Madame de la [?] could touch — the remainder you contrived to get from me by Charles's pretending the nurse would lose her passage, if not paid. I paid her and you had actually refused her permit & denied her wish to go! — Do not let these remarks tempt you to send any money, for I shall return it — I never have taken yours & never will — In regard to your being naturalized here, undeceive yourself, it is impossible — Besides, what object could you have living with a woman of whom you have spoken such dreadful language, but one — but fear not, you have never known me do an unhandsome thing, when no eye witnessed my acts, and now I stand before the God I trust I shall not be wanting — I will not praise myself, but well you know what my conduct has been to you thro' 10 long years— and what it would again have been from my landing [at Calais, that is] but for yourself. Did I adore you I would now act the same — I only ask for what will keep those dear children — I wish for nothing more — I shall write to Sir James [Cockburn] to appoint 2 trustees— I know nobody — I have heard the manner in which you have gone alone to my relations and friends— I who could have spoken truth have been silent to all —

There remains nothing for me to say further — indeed all I have written is mere repetition of what I have said & written to you — again, I repeat, I bear no malice — I will seek in no way to [?] you from this moment I will never mention the past — and the time will come when you will look back with regret to the time when you might have been perfectly happy and have made me so— had you not yielded to the low villainy of servants— you have destroyed my happiness— but I shall still live in peace & believe me in whatever situation I shall hail your sense of error with joy — and with a joyful heart see my children's father regain his place in society — for God's sake leave me quick possession of them — the contrary can do no good, for I swear to baffle your every attempt — why act unhandsomely — why persecute me further — what could you do with them — Adieu — I shall always hope for your happiness & hope you may find in others as sincere a friend as thro' every storm you have found me. Adieu, Frances Wedderburn.

A revealing letter in many ways, bringing more into focus not so much the recipient as the sender. For example, Lady Frances clearly has a good grasp of the mentality of her husband's type — the aristocrat more at home with servants than with his own class, at least on certain occasions— and one can't help wondering where she gained such an insight. Was it from her own father? We know her brother, the 2nd Earl of Mountnorris, was more than a little strange, and we more than suspect that something lurked inkily horrible within the mind of her recently departed brother Arthur, so it may well be that Fanny had a genuine inside knowledge of the darkness of men's souls, and had had it since childhood.

Byron must, somehow, in between reading Lady Frances's letters (the ones she wrote him, and the ones she wrote to James of which she sent copies) have found time to write, for *Heaven and Earth* came out in 1821. Bold Webster wanted a copy, or more specifically the inscription it would carry. An undated letter reads,

Dear Byron, I return 2 of the books you sent me with many thanks—
You will hardly recognize in ye enclosed ye person & friend of former years but tho' totally unlike when painted in 1819, I hear it is now a perfect & melancholy resemblance of all that was— or ever — — dear to me —
You will return me ye picture sealed — send me yr letters back & let me know if you wrote to Paris [i.e. to Lady Frances] & as to what effect I shall inquire when we meet — but ye late sepulchral weather defied all egress except for those who are never to return —
Ever your JWW.

The P.S. reads, "Send me 'Heaven & Earth' if you have it & ay [i.e. any] other book you please—"

In October 1821 James wrote a letter to his cousin John Wedderburn (which is in the John Wedderburn collection) as to his uses of the names Webster and Wedderburn.

In November 1821 his next son, Augustus George Henry Desire, was born in Boulogne, in France. The child was baptized at the British Embassy Chapel in Paris on January 18 of the following year. This baptism is entered at the Bishop of London's office, Doctor's Commons. His name is given as above except omitting the "Henry," and his parents are named as Wedderburn Webster, Esq., and Lady Frances Webster.

On December 28, 1821, James wrote another letter to John Wedderburn (which is also in the John Wedderburn collection), enclosing (i) a copy of the case submitted to counsel (Mr. Horne) and counsel's opinion on it with regard to his use of the names Webster and Wedderburn, dated 30 Oct. 1819; (ii) an extract thereanent from James Webster's will; and (iii) the following family register:

> David Wedderburn of Shenley Hill Co. of Herts, Esq., born in 1759 [he errs here; it should say 1757], the third son of Robert Wedderburn of Pearsie in Angus, Esq., married in 1787 [he errs again. It should say 1785] Miss Eliza Read [although his mother was known as Eliza, James really should have written Elizabeth here], daur of Alex. Read of Logie, Esq., and Miss Fletcher, daur of Robert Fletcher of Ballinshoe, Esq., & Brother to Colonel Sir Robert Fletcher, Commander in Chief at Madras.
>
> In 1790 David pursuant to the will of his great uncle James Webster of Clapham, Esq, & by Royal Licence, assumed the name and arms of Webster for himself & his heirs in lieu of that of Wedderburn. He was for many years partner in the house of Wedderburn, Webster & Co. By & under the will of his uncle aforesaid he acquired a considerable property & died aged 42 [he was actually 43], at Bath of a decline, in 1801, leaving issue of his marriage three sons and two daughters, James Webster, born in May 1789 [he did not err but simply lied here; it was 1788], Charles, born in 1799, a Cornet in H.M. 6th dragoon Guards [it was actually the 12th Light Dragoons, and he would retire from the 31st Foot in 1828], David, born in 1801, died at Brigton aged 14 yrs. Anne born in 1790 [actually 1791]. Mary do. in 1788 [she was born in 1793; James was way out here, accuracy not being his forte].
>
> The eldest son James Webster Wedderburn of Clapham aforesaid, for some years a lieutt in H.M. 10th and 11th Regts of Lt Dragoons married in Oct. 1810 Rt. Hon. Lady Frances Caroline Annesley, 2nd [sic] dau of Arthur, later Earl of MtMorres [he errs almost tragically here, given that the gentleman in question was his father-in-law; it was not Mountmorres, but another peer, Mountnorris] by the Hon. Sarah Cavendish his second Conntess [sic] & has issue two sons & a daur, Lucy Sarah Anne, born 2nd March 1812, Charles Byron Wedderburn, born Sept. 1815 [this should be Aug. 1815] & died & is buried at Nantes in 1817 [he did

Augustus George Henry Desire Webster-Wedderburn, son of James and Lady Frances Webster-Wedderburn. Painting attributed to William Joy. By kind permission of Tatton Hewetson.

die in Nantes, but is not buried there; Caen Cathedral is his resting place], Charles Francis Webster, born in Piccadilly 1st July 1820.

Of David Webster's daughters Annie, the elder, married in 1815 [this should be 1814] Captain Archibald Murray Douglas of H.M. 82nd Regt [this should be 52nd Foot] & has issue. Mary m. at Brussels in 1816 [this should be 1815] George Hawkins of Harnish House, Co. Wilts, Esq., 2nd son of the late Sir Jno Caesar Hawkins, of Kelstone House [this should be Kelston House], Somerset, & as yet have no issue. [James is his usual pretentious and inaccurate self here; George Hawkins was the son of John (not John Caesar) Hawkins, who was never a knight, being the third son of Sir Caesar Hawkins, 1st Bart. This John predeceased his father, and therefore, even if he were the first son, which he wasn't, would not have been Sir John.]

Mrs Eliza Webster the widow of David aforesaid, remarried in 1803 [it was actually 1802], Robert Douglas of Brigton in Angus, Brother of the late Colonel Sir William Douglas, C.B., of H.M. 91st Regt & next heir in remainder to the Baronetcy of Glenbervie after his cousin, the Hon. Sylvester Douglas, Lord Glenbervie, who has no issue. Of this marriage there is issue one son: — William, younger of Brigton. November 10th, 1821. J.W. Wedderburn [signed].

This last paragraph is typical Bold Webster doubletalk. There was indeed a baronetcy of Douglas of Glenbervie, which had become dormant in 1812, when Sir Alexander, the 7th Baronet, died without issue. The matter was settled in 1831 when Kenneth Mackenzie, son-in-law of the 6th Baronet, became the 1st Baronet Douglas of Glenbervie, of the second creation, he having changed his name to Douglas. James is putting forth his own claimant, another James failure.

18

Sir James

In 1822 James was summoned to the King's levee, where he was knighted. What had caused the new King to look so benevolently on Webster was that James had composed a short genealogical account of the royal family, a compilation remorselessly plagiarized from other sources. The King could well have done without this compilation, and indeed it is highly doubtful that he ever saw it. But, as James was one of the inner circle, and didn't yet have any major honor, it seemed expedient to award him one for something—anything—and this idea was cooked up while the regal sun still shown upon him. The almost official excuse given was James's tract, *King's Case Stated*, written a couple of years before.

Paston and Quennell say that in 1821 "the long-suffering Lady Frances left her husband and took her children (two girls and a boy) [should be two boys and a girl] to the house of a relation in Paris." James went back to England. After a while both parties wrote at great length to Byron, the wife appealing for sympathy, the husband for help toward a reconciliation. "The poet seems to have been genuinely anxious to bring the pair together again," say Paston and Quennell, "and a friendly correspondence was carried on between Lady Frances and himself."

In July 1822 James's sister Anne, wife of Capt. Archibald Murray Douglas, died.

The *Times* of October 29, 1822, reported: "Geneva, Oct. 8 (from a correspondent). An affair of honour took place at Ferney [a town in France just across the border from Geneva] on the 5th instant, between Sir Francis Vincent, Bart., and J.H. Felix, Esq., the former accompanied by Sir J.W. Wedderburne and the latter by Captain de Maryn. After an exchange of two shots each the parties left the field on amicable terms. Morning paper."

The very rich Vincent, 10th Baronet since the age of 6, was Webster's best friend at this time, despite being only 19 years old. He would marry in 1824 and five years later be forced to sell his family home, the magnificent Debden Hall in Essex, for a phenomenal 94,800 guineas. He would survive, duels and Wedderburn, until 1880. Curiously he was the fourth great uncle of Simon Heneage, cousin of the author of this book.

19

Kiss Me, Hardy

Webster was in Genoa between October 22 and sometime shortly before November 10, 1822, in order to see Lady Anne Hardy, wife of Nelson's Admiral Hardy. Bold W was paying a persistent and unwished-for court to Lady Hardy (whose famous husband was away in South America as commander-in-chief of the squadron there), and in fact intended to marry her, even though both he and she were already married. Lady Hardy told Byron of this ludicrous suit which W was forcing on her.

Edward Trelawny, who was present when W called on Byron, reports, "I remember one of his old friends saying, 'Byron, how well you are looking!' if he had stopped there, it had been well, but when he added, 'You are getting fat,' Byron brow reddened, and his eyes flashed — 'Do you call getting fat looking well, as if I were a hog?' and turning to me he muttered, 'The beast, I can hardly keep my hands off him.' The man who thus offended him was the husband of the lady addressed as 'Genevra,' and the original of his 'Zuleika' in the *Bride of Abydos*. I don't think he had much appetite for his dinner than day, and never forgave the man who, so far from wishing to offend, intended to pay him a compliment."

However, W's comments may have been partly responsible for the poet's going on a diet during the fall and winter.

Trelawny was an absolute character who has been the subject of several biographies. This unique and unalloyed remittance man, part of Byron's set during the great poet's last days, wrote, among other works, *Recollections of Shelley and Byron* (1858; upon later publication, it became known as *Records of Shelley, Byron, and the Author*).

In that book Trelawny writes of how, around this time also (probably on October 25, 1822), he and Byron called on W at the Croce di Malta Hotel in Genoa (also known as the Croix de Malthe, the famous inn down by the harbor), and looked up his name in the guest book. "Damn the fellow's presumption," yelled Byron, "look, here he is, booked Baronet and aged 32 [Webster was a year younger than Byron, and thus 34]. Why, he is much older than I am!" Byron then took a pen and wrote Knight aged 40, and said, "Does he think to hum — us with his black wig?" [According to John Gore's book on the Hardys, Webster's hair was originally fair, and Byron himself refers to it as once having been flaxen].

On October 26, 1822, Byron wrote a letter to Webster from Albaro:

> Dear W.— Any time from two till three, and if you like to ride, I can have you mounted on one of my horses. I called at three precisely, and asked thrice distinctly for the Cavalier Webster, in much better Italian than is spoken at Genoa; but the name seemed incomprehensible, tho' not ye title. The answer was— Do you mean the 'nobile Inglese' who came here two days ago? I replied — I mean the Gentleman who called on me yesterday. 'He is gone out and returns at 5 — to dinner' was the reply. I left no card, as it was not impossible that they w'd have left it with a Stranger. It is provoking enough that you should have been detained by their stupidity, for such it was as Count Gamba [brother of Teresa Guiccioli], who was with me, not only heard my inquiries, but repeated the name himself — as well as an Italian can repeat a name with four

consonants in it. Believe me, yours ever and very truly, NB." [Byron had in April 1815, in order to benefit from his wife's maternal uncle's generosity, added Noel to his surname, thus becoming George Gordon Noel-Byron.]

In another letter, from Genoa, to Lord Kinnaird, Byron says, on December 1, 1822,

> I have just seen the illustrious James Wedderburne Webster [although the name has been asterisked out in some copies of the letter] — who came to visitate me here — I had not seen him these ten years [ten years is a slight exaggeration] — He had a black wig on — and has been made a knight for writing against the Queen. — He wants a diplomatic situation — and seems likely to want it — He found me thinner even than in 1813, for since my late illness — (at Lerici on my way here) I have subsided into my more meagre outline — and am obliged to be very abstinent by medical advice — on account of liver & what not. — I found him increased rather — but not much; — looking redder — but tolerably fresh — and no wiser than heretofore. — He talked a good deal of skimble skamble stuff [i.e., meaningless rubbish] — and is gone to Florence. — But to the point — or at least my point in mentioning this new chevalier our old acquaintance. — Ten years ago I lent him a thousand pounds on bond, on condition that he would not go to the Jews — He took the money and went to the Jews. — Hanson [Byron's lawyer] has his bond — and there is ten years interest due upon it. — I have never dunned him — but I think that he might at least have paid some of the interest. — The Bond (though a good bond) is — I presume — valuable according to the possibility or probability of recovering said monies. — Now a Mr C. Hanson is a purchaser of bonds — (it hath a judgement probably to it) will he purchase this of me? or will anybody else at a discount — somewhat considerable? What effects the Grantor of said bond may now have I know not — but I presume — some still — though he has parted with his wife who was the best of them. — He had (besides her) a considerable property at one time.... He might have repaid me out of Wellington's money [the £2000 won by Webster at the *Chronicle* trial of 1816] — or Petersham's [Viscount Petersham, Bold Webster's recent dueling partner, had too, presumably, had to wind up paying some sort of considerable damages. If so, it was settled out of court, and did not make the papers]. Now what shall I take for said bond? or rather what is to be got? — Perpend — pronounce — Hanson will perhaps want it as 'part of his account' — but he shan't have it — nor shall he have any more 'parts' till we know the whole. — I have never pressed Webster — but to say truth — he has behaved shabbily about it — and had the impudence to ask me the other day — whether 'my heirs could act upon it.' — I feel disposed to save them the trouble — but should I not — I trust they will require their due — I am sure that all my creditors have been a good deal less patient.

Austin Gray, in his book *Teresa*, describes this event, or rather puts his own erroneous interpretation on it, and also confuses the date on which it happened: "Webster scratched his black wig and looked dubiously into his friend's face — would it be convenient, he mumbled, if he left all arrangements about that loan for his 'heirs' to settle?"

In fact, Byron had not even had the money at the time he lent it to Webster back in 1813. He had sent to Hanson from Nottingham a request for an advance of that sum against Claughton's expected payments. James's ideas about money and the responsibilities attached to it were vague, to say the least. But, as his granddaughter, Maude, says, "He wasn't a drunkard, and that has to be to his credit."

On the same day, December 1, 1822, but this time from Albaro, Byron wrote to Lady Hardy:

> ... in the interim yr. Chevalier arrived — and calling upon me had not been two minutes in the room (though I had not seen him for these nine years) before he began a long story about you — which I cut short as well as I could by telling him that I knew you — and was a relative and was not desirous of his confidence on the subject. — He — however, persisted in declaring himself an illused Gentleman — and describing you — as a kind of cold Calypso — who leads astray people of an amatory disposition — without giving them any sort of compensation — contenting yourself it seems — with only making one fool — instead of two — which is the more approved method of proceeding on such occasions.... He (the Chevalier) bored me so upon the subject that I greatly fear (heaven forgive me for you wont [sic]) that I said something about the 'transmutation of hair' but I was surprized into it — by his wanting to [swear ?] me out that his black wig — was the shock (or shocking) flaxen poodle with which Nature had decorated his head ten years ago....

Paston and Quennell comment that "it was the sort of wig that no one else would have ventured to wear."

Byron carried on, in the same letter, "He is gone post to Leghorn in pursuit of you — having (I presume in consequence of your disappearance) actually — (no jest I assure you) advertised 'for an agreeable companion in a post-chaise' in the *Genoa Gazette*. — I enclose you the paragraph."

While all this was going on, Sir James Webster's brother, Lt. Charles Wedderburn Webster, married on December 11, 1822, at Douglas Church, in County Cork, to Rebecca, daughter of Sir James Chatterton, Baronet, of Castle Mahon, County Cork.

On December 14, 1822, Byron wrote a letter to John Cam Hobhouse, from Genoa, which says, in part, "Since I have been here — I have seen Dick Fitzgibbon [Richard Hobart Fitzgibbon, later 3rd and last Earl of Clare] ... Lady Hardy ... and lastly that little and insane James Wedderburne Webster — now conceited into a knight (but of no order — a regular Address and City knight) yclept Sir James Wedderburn. I saw little change in him — except that his countenance rather more resembled his backside than heretofore — and that he had gotten a new wig — and says he means to marry — having a wife living — from whom he cannot get divorced."

But the matter of the outstanding Webster debt was pressing hard on the mind of the poet, who was himself always pressed, and more so now. In a December 16, 1822, letter to Douglas Kinnaird, written from Genoa, he reiterates, "Can't you sell — Webster's bond — (Hanson has it) with ten years interest due — (an excellent recommendation!) principle [sic] a thousand, interest five hundred pounds. — It hath a judgement — or a 'Vision of Judgement' to it — I would take almost anything for it."

Byron's latest work, *Vision of Judgement*, had just come out, hence the play on words.

On January 12, 1823, Byron wrote to Webster (in a letter that in manuscript form is now in the Carl H. Pforzheimer Library), inviting his old friend down to Genoa to hear in person his side of the squabble with Lady Frances:

> Dear W. — I have not been unwell seriously — but I am at present so tormented with chilblains — as to be nearly unable to move — None of the books you wish are in my possession or they should be at your service — but I have two of your own (the translation of O'Meara [*Historical Memoirs of Napoleon, 1815*; translated from the original manuscript by B.E. O'Meara, 1820]), which after a month's delay and three livres expence (for the binding — and not dear — for they are decently bound) your Genoese Abbé or whatever he was at length forwarded — I suppose that he handed them to his friends till tired — & then condescended to direct them to their owner's temporary destination — I should be glad to detain them a little longer, for they are in great request with all natives of my acquaintance — although all the principal part is omitted in the translation. — I will send down for you if you are disposed to venture into this Arctic region — my own chilblains (fact I assure you) defy Opodeldoc and Turpentine — and seem f [i.e., for the] moment as effectual as [the paper is torn here] in making me a fixture [here?]. However, the first practicable day — I shall essay to mount on horseback — believe me, very truly, yours, NB.

20

Reconciliation

Having failed in his pursuit of Lady Hardy, and now bent on reconciliation with his wife, who remained at Paris with her children, Bold Webster did indeed decide to venture out from Chambéry, where he was then living, to see Byron during that most notorious of Alpine winters, 1822–23. Byron regarded his friend's ludicrous libertinism flavored with sentiment with mingled cynicism and kindly tolerance. It was ironic that Byron should be called on as mediator, but he acquiesced and entered into the business with all the tact he could muster. James sent another letter to Byron and a miniature of Lady Frances, as she was now.

On February 2, 1823, Byron wrote to Sir James:

> My dear W—the picture which you sent will accompany this note—it is indeed a sad remembrance and I can with difficulty trace any resemblance—at least to my memory of the Original. The letters will be also enclosed—which are still more melancholy—but I see nothing in them to prevent a reconciliation if both parties would but condescend a little to their own eventual happiness—and to that of their children. By Thursday's post I wrote to Paris—and my letter was sealed before I had received your packet.—I trust that I have said nothing that can offend—or militate against the interests of either party—I think the painter's is the greatest calumny against her hitherto—which is unpardonable—for the infant in the same miniature is much better done, though I am no great judge of such matters. I send you some books—but the one you mention is not in my present possession—nor have I had, nor am likely to have any copy for some time to come.—The works of that Author [he means himself] are not often in my library [James had asked for some volumes of Byron's poems]—nor have I read many of them—indeed hardly any—since their publication.—'Werner' came to me in a parcel from London—without my direction—and escept [sic] the French translation (required by Me G [Madame Guiccioli]) and a scurvy ten-franc English Edition published at Paris—and sent as an index of Piracy—by the indignant Galignani (to persuade me to let him have a copyright) I have not a line—but—I err—there are two or three stray volumes—but they are of an old date—and scattered, I believe, amongst my other books—and I know not their place.—You have no great loss—however—I believe,—for the poem is not of great repute—nor is likely to be so.—So much for scribbling—but it is your own blame—since you entered upon the subject. I hope that my negociation [sic] will be more successful—it at least deserves to be so.—yrs. always & affectly. NB.

Webster had not yet received this latest Byron letter when he wrote one of his own (undated, though written on or about February 4, 1823) to "The Lord Noel Byron." He was preparing to set off for Genoa to stay with Byron for a while.

The letter reads:

> My Dear B, I have had a letter from my little Girl [Lucy] with bad news as to poor Lady F. & wh fills me with ye worst forebodings—She is confined with a severe inflammation on ye chest—That complaint has always been ye rock, on wh we all feared—her all—(poor thing!) w'd be wrecked—as it is not new to her & has always attacked her in a severe & determined manner—
>
> I shall see you on Friday & yet there is no letter [if he had waited, which he couldn't, there would have been]—something must be done—Sir F. Vincent has written me a letter—as to my having told his mother that he was in Paris—of (not) an equivocal Description, & tho' I have no

desire to break more lances I shall put his epistle in your hands & expect y're [sic] candid opinion—I shall then also shew you copies of ye letter or business wh I shall write tomorrow anent. The proceeds & proceedings of this Day, although my fears for F. put me in a horrible state of mind before wh all other matters give way—Ever y'rs, JW.

Making his way through Turin and Asti, Sir James Webster-Wedderburn arrived in Genoa on Friday, February 7, 1823. Austin K. Gray, in his book *Teresa*, tells it like this: "A ghost from that far-off English past rose in the shadowy form of Lady Frances Webster—the unhappy wife who had shrunk from his [Byron's] caresses in hopeless tears. She had left her husband now and was living in Paris with her children. Bouncible James, her egregious spouse, came bumbling into Genoa and pestered Byron with his confidences. In the name of friendship—as a fellow-poet—as the godfather of his son—he begged the one-time wooer of his wife to write to her—plead with her—to come back to her husband's longing arms."

Mr. Gray was one of the few authors who ever looked at the Lady Frances letters—not that it seems to have done him much good. He refers to James on one interesting occasion as Jimmy Webster. Although this may be Mr. Gray's name for Sir James, it is not one that was ever applied to Bold Webster in his own lifetime, or indeed since. This sets the tone for the acceptance level of Mr. Gray's interpretations, if not for his facts. For example, Lady Frances certainly didn't shrink from Byron's caresses; quite the reverse.

Anyway, he goes on to say, "By a miracle of last-minute virtue he had not lost his wife—then—that was left for the Duke of Wellington to accomplish—and he had obtained a thousand pounds from her lover. He wrote to Lady Frances and she answered, gratefully and tenderly—if he bade her return to her husband, she would obey."

None of this makes sense at all. In addition to the grotesqueries of his writing and sequences, Mr. Gray's facts are wrong concerning the settlement.

As for his next passage ... "To urge him on in the good cause, Webster sent his intermediary a miniature of his wife. The timorous child that Byron had known was a woman now, long-nosed, handsome, with smiling lips and mournful eyes. A sad remembrance, he told Webster when he sent the token back, and he wrote to Lady Frances again. She gave him a thousand reasons why she would never go back to her husband—beginning with his cruelty and ending with her own infidelity. Be my friend, she implored, but not in friendship as the world understands that feeling—'No, that lovely passion which Byron alone can understand—Byron alone can feel.'"

The piece about the miniature; this is an unwitting insight by Austin Gray into what may well have been the modus operandi of the Websters—high class prostitution, without ever going all the way. Lady F as the flame, the prominenti as the moths, and Bold Webster as the pimp. They certainly made a lot of money following this course, whether they planned it or not. If this is indeed the thrust—unwitting or not—behind Mr. Gray's statement, then Lady Frances could hardly have been timorous in 1813.

Coincidentally on that same day, February 7, 1823, Lady Frances wrote to Byron (who was then in Genoa):

Paris 7 Febry 1823. My dear Lord Byron, I have this hour received your kind letter of the 28th ult., and can assure you that it has given me heartfelt pleasure, every feeling comes grateful for your kind recollection & still kinder interests which you appear to take in my unhappy fate, I feel it deeply & from the bottom of my heart. I thank you—Your wish to affect a reconciliation between my husband & myself is the offspring of a generous, noble mind, but you are, I suspect, totally unacquainted with the cruel circumstances that forced me to abandon my home, & rescue my unhappy infants from the grasp of one who had violated every tie, & proved himself divested of the most common feelings of human nature.

Your friendly interference will oblige me to intrude a long, long explanation upon you, a long statement of <u>public</u> facts (for my whole conduct has been public), and if, after a patient perusal, which your friendship seems to assure me, if, after that, Lord Byron says, 'Lady Frances, live with yr husband' — it shall be done — but oh! how changed must that noble mind be if it does not start in horror at the conduct of a <u>man</u> who laboured to destroy the character of a woman, & that woman his wife — Did I even adore him, did I feel the agony of separation to my soul — <u>My Duty</u> to myself — to my children — to all society — demands that I cld never see him again. I left him, not from caprice, not from the passion of the moment, No! I writhed under his horrible accusations for months, till almost crushed to death, & urged on by <u>every</u> friend, I started from his grasp and said — then I defy you — & swore never to see him again till in a public court he proved me to be the worst, or himself the most diabolically depraved on Earth — I will send you the copy of ye letter I wrote to him after our separation. It is long, but it will explain more than I could now do — I have never since looked at it — he has the letter — the copy you will keep, it may hereafter be of use, tho' I wish to forget all — him — all — but one happy part of my life, which I never can cease to dwell upon.

Still in the same letter, she says:

How cruelly has he destroyed his own happiness & my peace, for even when I came from Engld with him in 1821 he was more sure of all that I could bestow — for regret for a moment's égarement [mental distraction] which the misery of a pained heart hurried me into — I resolved to devote myself to him — & to <u>you</u> I declare I would have sacrificed every feeling to perfect his happiness — but he was resolved — my ruin was his aim — <u>he had not got rid of me to his own advantage</u>!!! After I left him he went to England — & to all my relations, to everybody into whose house he could <u>force</u> admission — the horrors he spoke of me were such I dare not repeat — He came to Paris — he desired to see his children — I declined till he had retracted his words, 'that they were not his' — He did, & in writing — <u>retracted</u> upon his <u>honor</u> — what in the public street of Cheltenham he had asserted to Lord John Somerset — He requested to see me — This I positively refused — He desired to have his letter back, & upon my declining he wrote me a most insolent letter, that he was now convinced I was staying in Paris for some bad purpose, that I ought to go to Switzerland. I declined further communication — He sent a Mrs Hutchinson to me, who I was then acquainted with, to beg I would see him & she used all human eloquence to persuade me to live with him, but my resolution is & was unshaken — did beggary salute me — even compelled to live in one room with my children — I would bear all without one complaint but never, never will I live with a man devoid of honor & truth — he has threatened me with his actions — let him bring them, and prove <u>one</u> single thing against his wife, but having carried him thro' every difficulty — & last by having saved his life from the revenge of a poor, wounded wretch & from the laws of the country — let him & anybody go to Byron & let them blush that he must be called a man.

He proposed a private divorce in Scotld — I consented — anything — but him — peace, my children & health, all I wish. Would you, whose mind is unaccustomed to infamy, believe — I truly heard it 3 days ago — that when he came here last year, he forced his way into Lady Warrender's house, he does not know her, & remained for an hour, inventing every horror of me! He sent to see me Mr Smythe who he met at Lausanne and who came with a young heart believing all he had heard & talking of Mr. W.'s affection for me — I smiled — & forced upon me I showed him a letter written the very time he had these conferences with Mr. W. — he knew his writing — I said, 'I have done.' This person assured me that it was his constant wish to be reconciled to me, tho' he had not directly authorized him to make the proposal — the same to you — you speak his <u>wishes</u>, but not his words — I foretold it months ago — his object is reconciliation, but not in a noble, handsome manner — 'Fanny, I have injured you, I have destroyed yr happiness, tarnished yr fame — forget it & look to ye future' — No! He wishes to live with me, but it must be brought about by manoeuvring, that it may appear <u>my</u> wish & not his — Can he propose to be again ye husband of a woman who he has accused of profligacy, that the most abandoned would blush at — or he must be the greatest villain to have defamed his wife — or even greater to wish to live with a person who he has suspected guilty — I repeat, when Mr. W. confesses every word he has uttered to be false, then & then only with [sic — she was very tense at this point] I live with him — or let him bring his actions — I am ready to meet him in <u>any court</u>.

For months he does not communicate his address, for ye purpose of writing to his friends about my neglect in not letting him hear of his children — his whole life is devoted to petty intrigue. He now torments me about a Swiss journey. I really cannot degrade myself by replying to these repeated charges — if he has any cause, let him act as any other man wd — I ask no mercy.

Fortunately for me, I have been seen every day by those whose word will stand against his—'tis for this I live in a great city & in the house with friends— my husband would wish me to live in ye country, where, unprotected, unseen, all libels might be credited—At one time, disgusted with all—and in misery—I had thought of retirement—Sir James Cockburn forbid it—& my mother ordered me to remain in Paris. He [Webster] makes the late illness of my boy an excuse for annoying me—I, who have given up all for my children, who have devoted myself to & live but for them—who have begged a night's shelter from strangers, to save them from his grasp, he who never cared for them, & only now, in order to annoy me— Blighted in my first affection, I have fixed my true heart on them. I have fought for them, & he will find what a mother can do, if he <u>attempts</u> to steal them. Never has he given one shilling to their maintenance. I have devoted every farthing to their comfort & maintenance & sometimes have been without 5 francs and not one friend to whom I could turn— Who has the best right to these innocents?— With them I will brave every want or privation & the time will come when Mr. W. will lament, bitterly lament, the part he has acted towards one who feels nor malice nor ill will towards him, who left him to vindicate her character from his accusations & who lives from him to prove to ye world <u>what she really is</u>— My life is open to ye whole— See what I am— My heart is tranquil & will be so, when his will be tortured by Remorse—

 The greatest proof I can give in confidence in yr friendship is offering no excuse for this long, tedious letter— Yr kind assurances have given me a new life— Your heart will understand mine—and appreciate the motives that have dictated a conduct that leaves me alone in ye world—but I feel I have acted right—& my mind feels stern in armour— You may make ye use of this letter you will, the contents are well known to him and to hundreds in the world—for finding out his plan to villify [sic] every act pervert every word—I ceased to move but in public, or to speak but before witnesses— yes! he <u>does</u> want to live with me again—after having defamed me in the North, in England— he goes to Italy in hopes of arranging a reconciliation there, unknown to the world— to have to say, 'poor thing! what could I do, she wished it— my affection triumphed over self interest—I sacrificed myself—& I did'—I know him too well to be deceived— his full length character is before my eyes in cruel reality and I would risk my life on stating the exact conversations that have taken place between him & you— he has played ye same game with Numbers— you— who are deeply read in human nature, be not deceived by general conversation— ask him three simple questions— ask him, 'W. do you wish to live with your wife; No or yes?' 'Do you authorize me to propose to her a reconciliation?' 'Are you prepared to retract ye horrors you have uttered about her, to all her friends?'— His answers to these questions will open yr eyes, and if he gives a simple No or yes. if [sic] instead he does not launch out in a volume of unmeaning, fine words and sentiments, I have done—A simple answer to those questions will shew you his <u>real intentions</u>, without which you are working in the dark—<u>if</u> he wishes to live with his wife he can have no objection to <u>confide</u> it to his <u>friend</u>— but if he is not willing to <u>clear</u> her character, he cannot wish to live with one so defamed— Dear Lord Byron, for your own sake see clearly your way— for myself I am indifferent. I lament, bitterly lament, ye cruel circumstances that rendered separation an imperious Duty— but I have one consolation that never can forsake me— I have tried to forget the past & have not laboured in vain, & never to any body do I mention his name or conduct, but when forced upon me in self defence— he threatened to get himself naturalized to force me to live with him— but I send you my letter to him of Sept. 1821 in all its rough language—forgive it—You will see what my feelings were & a small portion of my injuries— to repeat to you all I have suffered w'd be to torture a sensible mind— I have been the victim of— a husband! How gladly do the many embrace the persecutions which such a sacred character sanctioned!— Forgive this tiresome volume— I feel you will— shall I hear from you again— I hope so—& if any thing requires explanation, ask it freely, my heart is open—I seek no disguise, I wish to hide no faults— whatever I am & only that, I wish to appear to the world, & to my friends.

 Adieu, my dear Lord Byron. Your patient perusal of these sheets, your candid opinion & judgement & bringing Mr. W. to a candid explanation, will prove I have, indeed, not been forgotten by one who I have never ceased to think of with sincere friendship.

 Ever your affectionate, F.W.

Then, in form of a post script, she adds, "I shall answer my husband's last letter tomorrow, but I shall not mention having heard from you; you are then at liberty to do as you please, indeed, I always confine my letters to answers to his several questions— I have to beg you will make him shew you my letter— Would that Genoa was near this!"

On February 10, 1823, Byron wrote to James a letter (now in the Stark Library, University of Texas, in manuscript form). It goes:

> My dear W—the Bankers have answered that as yr. own Banker has declined—and also another (Quantana—by name) it could hardly be expected that they should run the risk from a Stranger not recommended by their Correspondents.—I shall however send down again to them enclosing your book which proves the sums paid or received by you in 1822—through Hammersley—and so far indicates yr. correspondence with that House.—I have added whatever I could say on the occasion but I regret that I cannot myself either endorse bills nor cash them—nor advance the amount after the heavy expences [sic] of last year in England—and the many claims of different kinds which I have had to satisfy—and some (I am sorry to say) to refuse—I assure you that it [sic] at this very moment—I have five different letters before me—all requiring money—by the last two days posts—on one pretext or another—and they are but five of fifty of the same kind—my own interference therefore is out of the question.—I have no doubt that the bill is a good bill but I really have not the amount to spare—even for a week—and I have already become responsible for two hundred and fifty drawn on England by J H [John Hunt, publisher of Old Bond Street] besides having to fee lawyers for his Counsel in his Coming on Cause, in London.—Within the last January I have [had] to pay upwards of one thousand pounds in London—the greater part of a lawyer's bill.—You imagine then how far I am in a position to turn banker.—yrs. ever & truly NB.

In the previous October Hunt, who was poet Leigh Hunt's brother, had published Byron's *Vision of Judgement* in his periodical *The Liberal*. Eleven months later Hunt was put on trial for publishing this work, which was purported to slander the late George III.

Hammersley & Co., the banking house mentioned in this letter, was started in 1796 by Thomas Hammersley, who had been a partner in Ransom, Morland & Hammersley. This year, 1823, saw them move from 76 to 69 Pall Mall. The bank would finally be absorbed by Coutts in 1840. Ransom, Morland & Co. were Byron's bankers, and Scrope Davies.' Coutts was the bank of choice of Bold Webster's son Major George Webster-Wedderburn and his daughters, granddaughter and great-grandsons. It was a tightly knit world back then.

On February 12, 1823, Byron wrote to Douglas Kinnaird from Genoa,

> By the way could you not get sold (at any discount) Wedderburn Webster's bond with interest of ten years due upon it—it is in Hanson's hands—and has a judgement and is good against property or person—and it seems that he has the former still—I'll tell you who would buy it—his own Attorneys or mine?—The youth is here—has been Diddling his landlord &c.—and wanted me to endorse a bill for seventy pounds—I refused—but at last he bored me into the endorsement of a smaller one for thirty pounds of which I know not what will be realized—it is on Hammersley's house.—And all this time the fellow owns to the possession of twenty thousand pounds and the receipt of many thousands since I lent him the thousand in 1813—and now there is ten years interest due—try what it will fetch (his bond that is) I will take what it will bring in—.

Leigh Hunt referred to Sir James as "a fat dandy who came upon us at Genoa, and, pretended to be younger than he was, and to wear his own hair."

On February 16, 1823, Byron wrote: "Dear W—I cannot keep the book and take [J's ?] money too, for the bindings, and if I do not keep it, I have still less right to it. I therefore return it & request that you will not remand it on pain of proscription.—My 'chilblains' are I assure you no joke—and I can scarcely move for them.—To be sure the weather is not very inviting for this assistance. I beg your pardon for altering your nomenclature [Byron had failed to address James as Sir James on the envelope of his last letter], but old recollections are apt to float uppermost. Believe me yrs. ever & very truly NB."

The next day, February 17, 1823, the poet wrote to Lady Hardy from Genoa:

> Your Chevalier errant is here and more errant, though still stationary—than usual—and that is much.—He has embroiled himself with two absent friends—a Sir F.V. [Sir Francis Vincent]—

and some Caledonian Chiefs of the race of Diarmid, — Mr Campbell of Glensaddle [there apparently was such a man] — I believe — both of whom have cut him by letter — for reasons which — as I have nothing to do with — I cannot pretend to explain. There are also some high and doubtful questions with his landlord of the 'Croix de Malthe'— his tailor — his shoe-maker — and finally his Valet — also his banker — and two other Bankers— who have manifested an unaccountable aversion from his bills— unless guaranteed by an amicable endorsement —'a backing of one's friends' which Plyades himself would probably have avoided [reference to Plyades and Orestes, the two great friends of Greek mythology].— All these woes— to say nothing of others— he lays to your door — for having lured him with deceitful hopes to this mercenary country — where a Man must actually pay for his provisions— To console himself for your rigour, — on his return he paid his court to a very pretty Madame Quantana — the wife of a rich banker — but his bills seemed no less unacceptable to the Lady than her husband — for neither of them would cash his love or money at whatever discount — Messrs Gibbs were equally inexorable in the pecuniary part, but we will see what is to be done and get him back to Lausanne, and if possible to his wife — for he is moving Heaven and Earth — for a reconciliation. — She is at Paris. — I knew her soon after their marriage — and him some years before — when he was in the Hussars — and I was a Collegian. — She was very beautiful — and more romantic than wise — and that unlucky kind of woman — who can do nothing without an Éclat — so that the wonder is that they were not separated before.— He has bored me into being a Mediator in his behalf — attracted doubtless by my own signal success in amicably arranging my own matrimonial affairs — I have consequently addressed the Lady — in a respectful and conciliatory epistle — representing with all the elements of common place — that very trite truism — that all quarrels are bad — but those of holy Matrimony the very worst of all. — I do not know that it will do any good but at least it can only hurt myself — if they make it up — well and good, — if not — they will both fall upon the Pacificator according to the ancient custom.

Early in the morning of February 20, 1823, Webster left Byron and headed north for Turin, and thence Lausanne, in Switzerland. The weather was so bad that his progress was painfully slow. In the hour before he left Byron, he jotted down a brief a note which he had conveyed to his host:

My Dear Byron, I send you this note to beg you to <u>defer</u> writing to Paris untill I have <u>time to breathe</u> at <u>Turin</u> & you hear from me at that place — for my mind has been so harrassed [sic] by Duns— piastres & chattels— that I [last two words deleted] & you gave me so little time (with all possible deference for y'r vegetables) to masticate the letter — & to discuss ye subject with you, as ye interests of both require — In short my mind as to that subject is now like an ocean with no shore, or point on wh to fix — I trust tho' my vetturin [driver of a vettura, an Italian cab] may produce a better digestion before I reach Turin & I will then write you fully — in ye mean time — if you do not write as in Curtesy [sic] to answer the interminable MS [manuscript] before you, I wish you w'd call for a more explicit & less irritable expression of her own sentiments—for some thing in short that can justify the exaction of ye conditional queries or points put to you — good faith & its harbinger — Candour — is what I seek & expect —
    adieu. God Bless You — JWW.
    5 A.M. Thursday.

Lady Frances, however, still looked upon Byron as the chivalric hero she had always conceived him to be since he had "spared" her in 1813. As she wrote, her sentiments grew warmer toward Byron than toward her husband (not a difficult chore). Byron ignored her flattery and replied with seriousness and frankness. But, as he had anticipated, his efforts were unavailing. His letter from Genoa, of February 21, 1823, to Lady Frances, is now in the Nottingham Public Library. It reads:

My dear Friend — I saw your husband soon after receiving your letter and the enclosed statement which I need not say shocked me very much — neither did I conceal the impression it made upon me from himself.— As he expressed a strong wish to see your letter I availed myself of your permission to show it, more particularly, that he might not take any fancies into his head — which is a Windmill of suspicions of all kinds.— I then put your three queries to which he answered 'yes' — expressing at the same time great attachment to yourself. — He is gone to Lausanne. Since his departure I have received from him a note desiring me to delay writing — except 'in courtesy'—therefore this present epistle is not to be considered as committing him &c. &c.—I really do not know exactly what he would be at—nor do I think he knows himself.—He is to write to me from Turin—more explicitly he says—and requires on your part something 'still more explicit as an expression of your sentiments to justify his answer in the affirmative to your queries.' I certainly think that you should soften a little—I do not mean to say that you have not been injured—but when a reconciliation is proposed—resentments must of course be forgotten.—He wishes to know in case of a renewal—if you would live at Lausanne as he cannot stay at Paris—on account of his affairs.—I still do not despair of your reunion,—and, as to his Self-love—about who should yield first, &c. &c.—these are mere weaknesses—and may be indulged without any great harm.—But I do not wish you to act precipitately—or without consulting your friends—though I trust that you will reckon me among the number.—You can write to me what you wish to be done—or said—or unsaid—and I will scrupulously follow your directions as I have done.—I began this sheet intending to enclose his note—but perceive on looking at it—that I am not authorized to do so.—He certainly answered the three queries—contrary to your expectation but his note leaves them again in abeyance.—I will address you when I have anything to interest you.—Pray believe me in all events as one most truly and affectionately yrs. NB.

By February 22, 1823, on his way to Lausanne, Webster had been able to proceed only as far as Asti, not too far from Genoa, when he got hemmed in by the weather. He decided to write Byron from there, that day:

Asti, Saturday. My Dear Byron, The dreadful state of ye roads & ye depth of snow impeded my further progress & I rather avail myself of this day's post from here than defer ye subject on wh we last met, to an uncertain period—you have indeed cause to congratulate yourself on y'r Genovese climate with all its versatility, for this is Siberia exaggerated——

I never felt such intense cold at any period in our Island [i.e. in Britain] & ye whole face of ye country is buried in all parts two—and in many, four & six feet under snow.

Now in regard to ye correspondence & ye Object for who you are good enough to feel an interest—I leave ye reply entirely to your Judgment—you know my feelings on that subject & you know ye Interests inseparable from all connected with it—The impression however left on my mind by ye hasty perusal I had of ye Document in question is that it breathes throughout not only a feeling of animosity—but one of vindiction & if not it surely betrays none of a gentle or conciliatory nature wh certainly sh'd precede any communication of ye character expected—In reference again to ye Queries—They are not put with a desire to have my answer but merely necessary to convince you that you are mistaken in regard to y'r conception of my feelings—Therefore it appears to me that y'r reply sh'd be to call expressly for a declaration of those sentiments & intentions wh must necessarily guide & impel mine, for wh you may give an undertaking conditionally—& subject to such sentiments——

Another year gone by & it will no longer be in ye power of any one to befriend that individual by ye purpose you have in view—& ye very conduct pursued now will ensure a dreadful & long & raw hereafter—when children & all will be no longer objects of consolation—or care—finally whatever my sentiments may be (& what they are, or rather w'd be, you know)—you sh'd prop'ly require those of y'r correspondent instead of the transcription of calumnious absurdities & impossible relations—only to be equalled in length & rancour by our late Bill of Paris & Penalties at home—& which can avail nothing—

Write therefore soon with this view & then you will tread on sound ground & perhaps have ye satisfaction hereafter of saving much from (unhappily) a noble wreck—

My whole view & feeling is directed towards those unconscious little victims of ye present state of things & not evy [every] year (as you say properly observed) must render worse—you should have r'd [read] more Desolate [what he means is that "desolate" is a better word than "worse"]—You have ye feelings of a father—I know—& have seen—You know ye rest—& I need therefore add nothing of wh you will not lose sight—not to advance with preliminary declarations from ye one without having them first justified by ye unequivocal sentiments (under such hypothesis, as we understand) of ye other——

God bless you Dear Byron—send me a few lines by return of Post to Chambery & B'le me ever y'rs JWW.

The P.S. says, "Remember, I expect to have your advice written fully—& therefore shall be anxious to hear from you at Chambery, wh I shall wait for, en passant."

On February 24, 1823, Byron wrote to Mary Shelley, "Would you have the goodness to request Lh [Leigh] Hunt to return the two vols of Napoleon (if finished) as Sir J W promised to lend them to the Countess D'Isson of Cannes."

On February 27, 1823, Byron from Genoa replied to the letter of February 22 that James had written while snowed in at Asti. This reply was auctioned by the Swann Auction Galleries on May 17, 1951. Part of the reconstruction of this letter comes from a fragment quoted in the Swann catalog, and another part from a Manuscript fragment. It reads (as much as we have, anyway): "I do not quite understand your letter — if I have full power I can treat. The proposition must come directly from you. I cannot become involved in a long correspondence to determine who is to write first, etc. — the only thing to be said is will you make it up? and then she will give her answer. I wrote to her since your departure; if her answer is favourable, you shall hear.... I cannot go from the point to wander into sentimental discussions — that were childish."

On March 1, 1823, in a letter from Byron to Douglas Kinnaird, written from Genoa, the poet says, "I agree with you that we must have nothing to do with Lord Mountnorris [Lady Frances's brother], who is a litigant and bad debtor."

Lady Frances replied to Byron's letter to her of February 21. It was dated "Paris, 7th March," and addressed to "The Rt. Hon. the Lord Noel Byron, Genova, In Italia." The poet received this letter on March 19.

"My dear Byron," it begins:

> your 2d letter has given me unfeigned pleasure, and I would try & thank you for ye kind interest you take in my affairs, did I not feel quite equal to repressing the full force of my sentiments.
>
> That I prize your friendship and value it beyond all this world holds for me besides, is indeed true, & ye happiest, the proudest feeling to me is contained in those four words, 'Consider me your friend' — not in the world's definition of that sacred name, no! That lovely passion, which Byron alone can understand, Byron only can feel — Sir J.W.'s replies did not astonish me, when followed by his note from Turin — 'tis ye same — had he given <u>unconditional</u> answers, I should have been surprised — Byron, I consider you my friend from this — my living again [this last word added as a caret] with Mr. W is <u>impossible</u> — Honour, duty to myself, my children & the World. Pride, nay, even common <u>decency</u>, demand that I should not — Our separation arose not from common caprice. 'Twas an act of duty after deliberate consultation and calm reflection — 'twas a step forced upon me by a series of pre <u>meditated</u> infamy, by accusations, by plots, against whom? <u>His Wife!</u> — If you could have witnessed one moment of those months you would say never — hear him — married again. Where are his actions that he has trumpetted [sic] from one end of Gt. Britain to ye other? — and does he wish to live again with a woman who he has accused not of laxity, not of profligacy <u>only</u>, but of horrors I dare not, cannot repeat.
>
> Take not my word. Write to <u>any body</u> in England who may have ever conversed with him, and they will tell you, 'If what he says is true, 'tis a <u>monster</u> & not a woman! [she forgets to close the quote] — Am I not bound in honor to prove to ye world what I am — Now I stand alone & unprotected — I may now be judged, and those who know human actions may judge whether the <u>abandoned profligate</u> can, in almost youth, suddenly abandon her hideous life, be contented without a solitary acquaintance & find happiness in her children & escape from a moral assassin.
>
> 'Tis ere long I shall be judged, & I feel I shall not be disappointed amongst those worthy of thought — You say you know not what he w'd be at. I will tell you. There are many windings in his path — 'He wishes something still more explicit, &c' — My questions were merely put to open your eyes. I anticipated the storm of his eloquence, but his 'yes' proves that his plan is further advanced than I had anticipated. My sentiments have been clearly given to him in multiplied repetition, perhaps some will say in too strong language, but let it be remembered that I spoke & wrote under ye agony of exaggerated accusations & that ye moderation belonging to [a] woman sunk under ye load of calumny.
>
> I left him, to defy him. I called upon him loudly to prove one word he had uttered about me — I offered, promised, bound myself to appear in any court in Europe — What was his conduct? No open, generous proceedings, which all men may claim, were his line of conduct — No! <u>His honorable</u> plan was to force his way into every house in Engld & Scotld, and bow to those who turned

their backs upon him, in order to poison their minds against his wife, even to my dearest friends, has he not tried ye form of eloquence, artfully mingling his 'Pity' and 'affection' with a volley of defamation, & boasted of his '<u>success</u>'!! and you would say live with him! Byron! Byron! Thy noble, manly heart can never speak those words, illy do I know it, if it does not feel generous indignation & say, 'continue as you have begun'—I long ago, 6 months or more, when he was last here, foretold that he would, as his finances diminished, try to recommence a reconciliation—I was a faithful prophet, he has made several attempts, & as I before started to make it appear <u>my</u> wish, not his—witness his wish for me to write 1st, which you, whose heart is good, attribute to innocent self love, but <u>I</u> who know him, read inst. [i.e. instantly] his scheme—My living with him again is <u>quite impossible</u>—no friend can advise it—therefore it matters not, but ask yrself if a man wished to live with a woman, if he felt he had acted honorably, where ye necessity of so much manoeuvring? <u>He does</u> wish to live with me, but he has acted so venomous, so dishonorable a part that he cannot come forward in the face of man—is it to be credited, is it in human nature to suppose that he can publickly avow himself to be ye greatest villain in existence, which he must by denying ye horror he has circulated about me—would he not be obliged to cloak his conduct under his eternal themes, 'pity' and 'affection'—What trumpet would blow his confession, even did he make one, to ye ears of all those who have imbibed his poison & when he even contradicted his falsehoods, numbers, numbers w'd hesitate to receive conviction—Oh, Byron! Mine are deadly injuries—I may forgive, but never can forget—Ages could never restore what I have lost—Myriads of tongues w'd never unsay what that man has said—Look at my situation and not be ashamed to name it, alone, the finger of ye world pointed at me, and who has brought it on me?—I do not utter a complaint—I have learnt to detest ye world—& this proud spirit of mine supports me under all my trials & enables me still to find happiness in my home & children. But 'tis a cruel situation & not a common one—all, but what that man has done to me might be undone, but let any <u>man</u> look at my situation & say live with the author of it, your defamer, ye assassin of your peace—I w'd say—But no, it never could be Byron, Byron is my friend—Forgive this long story—I owed it to you, after ye trouble you have taken—You now have my whole heart before you, its <u>secret</u> feelings—talk to me no more of impossibilities & what your own noble heart in itself forbids—Tell him <u>simply</u> you cannot interfere anymore, for I am tired of the subject—Let me hear from you whenever you wish to please me & ever believe me, Your affect. F.W.

The post script read, "Do not from this shew him my letter. It will make him write & turn toad—Did he shew you my letter to himself—?—"

The unpredictable Webster was back in Genoa in March, but soon left again. A letter to him from Byron, written on March 9, 1823, was the last the poet wrote to his old friend Bold Webster: "Dear W—Part of your news is rather interesting—as I was present at the marriage of the earl [of Portsmouth] by request of the father in law & thought that all had been very regular—I suppose there is some statute against his marrying any but a woman past bearing which his last wife was & his brother intended his next to be—but he chose for himself very perversely.—Pray step over & tell me more of these fine things—which are vastly amusing.—ever yrs. B."

The bride Byron refers to was Mary Anne Hanson, daughter of Byron's lawyer, John Hanson. J.C. Wallop, the 3rd Earl of Portsmouth, was notoriously insane. His family had married him off to a much older woman (Lord Grantley's daughter), who, fortunately, had been able to keep his more bizarre eccentricities in check—or at least, somewhat hidden from public view. When this good lady died in 1813 interested parties moved with great speed to set the rampant earl up with a replacement bride. Hanson, who was also lawyer for the Wallops, went as far as to donate his own daughter to the cause, and persuaded Byron to give her away the following year. Despite the whip she kept under her pillow in order to beat down the more dangerous of Portsmouth's nocturnal naughtiness, Mary Anne did not have the firm grip of her predecessor; in truth, any firm grip she had was bestowed instead upon one William Rowland Alder, lawyer, whom she moved into Huntsbourne Park with her, and by whom she had three children, right under the nose of the demented earl. She would subsequently marry Alder. By 1823 Lord Portsmouth had been wreaking havoc among his domestic animals for the best part of a decade, and in February of that year, sine pecus intactus, it was determined legally that he had been insane since 1809. The case was a cause of considerable public interest in the early 1820s.

From "Lausanne — 19 m'ch 23 [March 19, 1823]" Webster wrote to "The Lord Noel Byron, a Gênes [i.e. Genoa], par Turin — £2.1 [i.e. 2 pounds and one shilling]." "My Dr. Byron," the letter opens:

> As I have neither heard from London or Genova since my return to this country [i.e. Switzerland] I am in a mood of both hope & fear as to Hammersley & ye Bills — But having left nothing undone that I thought w'd concentrate my scatter'd forces, I can only wait ye issue — Tho' neither are yet due by a considerable time —
> As you have no doubt heard from Paris since I heard from you at Chambery, I am very anxious to rec'e your report & beg you not to delay sending me a few lines on recpt of this —
> I found my canine friend still in statu quo — & amazingly increased in magnitude, tho' not in beauty, therefore you have no loss, as the man will not sell him now under 8 louis & rejects my old bargain of ye 5 — his maxim is 'Qui tenet teneat, possessio valet' [possession is nine points of the law] — & not a bad one —
> Made de B. [i.e. Madame de B.] (the mother wood of Helvetia) is in Paris — & her chateau to be had for abt 200.000 if well furnished — the place produces abt 150 louis per ann: independent of ye house, wh w'd always let for 200 a y'r & w'd be (I have no doubt) inestimable if dedicated to ye same pious purposes, as report affirms it to have been of latter years — if you have any idea of purchasing it for y'r residence (& it is out of ye question as a pecuniary speculation) I shall be happy to obey y'r commands — .

Clearly James was angling for an agent's commission here. In those days, as now, estates 'produced' so much per annum, which offset the outgoings. Madame de B. was a mysterious society figure of the day, wife of Dominique Bazaine, some said.

Webster goes on to ask,

> Have you seen ye report of Lord Portsmouth's cause in ye Journal des Débats? Poor Lady P is described as Miss Hanson, autrefois tres [sic] liée avec le celebre [sic] Lord Byron [formerly very tied up with the famous Lord Byron] — I fear she has nothing to lose — or to acquire — but to favor ye world ever with its fallen angels — Tho' Chancery Lane is certainly abt ye last place I sh'd have expected to find one — her Lords [sic] eccentricities appear on a new scale — his grt jest was slaying oxen — & ye Witness (a butcher) declared his Lordship so good a 'Headsman' [i.e., executioner] — that he never missed — this & ringing church Bells for ye departed, was his occupation whilst ye indefatigable Alder was labouring to perpetuate both his follies & his honors —
> How is [?] —? — Badinage apart — with Gibbs — & a few more such, anglo-Genoese, jesuitical looking fellows — you might soon get up a 'Cato St. scene' — apropos of Jesuits, Lethbridge tried to convince ye house ye other day, that a dangerous body of them existed in Ireland — & our friend Hobhouse replied — 'he had often heard of a Jesuit & travelled far — but had never seen one — & he sh'd like to see such a thing' —
> a [sic] War — (with ye neutrality of Russia & Austria) seems decided — & if so when I have disposed of my friends — I shall take a look at our enemies —
> Portarlington is gone in as a cornet again, therefore there is no lack of precedent, L'd Barnard Le ——— I hope you stick to ye Hock, wh Haller & Hoffman call'd 'Le Pégase des Poètes' — wh [i.e. which] tho' w'd be a reason I suppose for you to abandon it — .

John Dawson, 2nd Earl of Portarlington, had served gallantly against Napoleon throughout the Peninsular campaign, but something controversial happened at Waterloo. As colonel of the 23rd Light Dragoons he seems to have lost his way to the battlefield. Some say he was ordered to do so by the surgeon, others said the idea was his own. Regardless, he reported late and came under a cloud of cowardice that never went away. He resigned from the Army almost immediately, but his friend, the Prince Regent, feeling sorry for him, offered him a cornetcy in his old regiment, saying that he was still young enough to start again (he was 34). He accepted Prinnie's offer, and as a consequence was made one of the Prince's aides-de-camp and thus a colonel. He retired as a captain (real rank) in 1821 and died unmarried and somewhat unheralded in December 1845. Anyway, this news of the cornetcy was old hat when Webster retailed it to Byron, and one wonders why he bothered.

As for his more liquid reference, Webster's statement is undoubtedly true and correct, but it was Pontanus who described wine in general as 'the Pegasus of the Poets.'

He continues:

> Wine tho' is necessary decidedly to health & probably to happiness—at least wiser heads (Solon & Cato) so held it—if Seneca is ay [any] authority in y'r opinion—I got a terrible fright passing through Piemont, in my quality of heir, as I was credibly assured, women there are not out of gunshot, & bearing at <u>55</u>—God grant ye infection may not reach ye Grampians———
> Pray let me hear from you soon & B'le me ever y'rs with regard, JWW.
> P.S. If we <u>descend</u> in <u>worldly goods & chattels</u>, we don't in blood at all events—I have just heard of ye marriage of a near relation (Mr Wedderburn) with Lady Helen Ogilvie [sic]—she is both mad [these last two words careted, which, in a way, makes sense of the subsequent seeming solecism] beautiful & young!—.

Webster was a prophet, this time ahead of the news. Not until April 30 would his cousin John, son of John Wedderburn of Spring Garden, marry the daughter of the 3rd Earl of Airlie.

From rue d'Anjou, N. 8, Paris, on March 25, 1823, Lady Frances received a letter from her husband, then in Lausanne. After reading it she wrote to Byron a letter he received three days later:

> Am I importunate—or may I hope you will not consider my so soon writing to you an intrusion—judging from the kind expressions in your 1st letter, amiable professions, I will not offer any apology but trust to ye truth of those assurances to plead my cause for breaking in on yr valuable time—in truth, my dear Lord Byron, I know not why, but I had hoped to have had the pleasure of hearing from you before this, and again, I know not why, I am impressed with a suspicion of your not having rec'd my letter, which would give me real pain, not from its contents being of any importance, but that you should, for a moment, suppose me capable of leaving your kindness one hour unanswered & unthanked—
> Pray favor me with one word to this point, and then please yourself as to the continuation of a correspondence which will always afford me the most heart felt pleasure. The sight of your handwriting affords me a pleasure I wish not, nor will I pretend to conceal—it ranges a pure, delightful sensation, & revives the full recollection of hours never, never forgotten—I have this day a letter from Lausanne, <u>two sheets full</u>—after a long story about affection for his children, which he is very anxious to impress upon my mind & denial of having forced his way into Lady Warrender's house at Versailles, he comes to the expression of his anxiety to do anything that will contribute to my happiness, <u>consistent with his honor</u>. He assures me the interference of a 3rd person can tend to no good, as if I was the proposer, or had applied to you, and hopes that I have sufficient confidence in him to express my sentiments to himself—finding he could not influence you to take a dishonorable part in his negociations he now wishes to exclude you. My sentiments are too well-founded to change, as my last letter will have shown you. Therefore I shall not reply to that part of his letter. He accuses me of malice in my communications with you, not so, God knows, it was my duty to state to you the facts as they were—had he not urged you to write, I should not have named him. I never do but when the subject is forced upon me. I will not longer detain you, God bless you, my dear Friend. Believe me ever, sincerely yours, Frances W. Rue d'Anjou, No. 8, Paris, 25th March.

On March 28, 1823, Byron wrote to Lady Hardy from Genoa, "I had an epistle from your Chevalier this morning—he is at Lausanne—my negociation to reconcile him with his wife—had the luck of a Congress.—It produced a long (married) State-paper from the Lady—full of the most extraordinary charges against your admirer—and invoking discussions—in which I had no wish to enter.—I have therefore written to both parties to decline interfering further in so delicate a matter."

Byron continues, in the same letter:

> Your despairing 'W.W. who never more will trouble you trouble you' effected at length his retreat from Genoa—after some not very creditable skirmishes with the Bankers—tailors—hatters—

and innkeepers of this mercenary city—who manifested an unaccountable repugnance to his bills on England—To extricate him in a small way—I endorsed two of them for him—to no very great amount luckily—for I am given to understand that my virtue in this instance is likely to become it's [sic] own reward.—He departed in company with about fifty pounds sterling of mine—a circumstance which by no means diminished my regret for his return to a country where they have more Christian faith with an embarrassed traveller—what he will do next I do not know—but as he attributes his loss of time—heart—and monies—to your having led him by the most awful [sic] coquetry to Florence—I hope that he will discover some Armida more destined to repay his affections—or at least his expences. [The beautiful witch Armida, from Tasso's *Gerusalemme liberata*, was a favorite literary character of Byron's]—You see what mischief you have done—I had a great mind to send you his unpaid bills—enclosed in an ode of my own inditing—with an excellent moral to it.—But on second thoughts—considered the subject too serious for poesy.—Donat and Orsi had actually written from F[lorence] to have him stopped here for some banking business or other—but the law could not reach him in another state.

Austin K. Gray, the author of *Teresa* (a book primarily about the Countess Guiccioli), unbelievably fails to understand Byron's sarcasm in this letter to Lady Hardy. Gray says, "Byron scolded her for tormenting the poor man, and regaled her with his own domestic trials and a great deal more about Webster's in the past than he had a right to tell." Again, Gray has failed to understand the mores of the time concerning gossiping, dissembling, and railing. Ultimately Gray has failed to come to grips with his subject. However, Gray does understand J W when he says, "James Webster was fussy and talkative, suspicious out of season."

On April 19, 1823, Byron wrote to Kinnaird, "You have never answered about Webster's bond—(in Hanson's hands).—I see similar sales (Ld. Moira's bonds for instance) in the papers daily—and I would willingly sell it—for what it may fetch—Rowley and Capron in Savile Row would be likely to buy it?"

"Fr. Webster" wrote from Paris to "The Rt. Honble Lord Byron, Genova, In Italia," on April 22, 1823 (Paston and Quennell misread the date as April 23). The letter was franked in Chambéry, where Sir James was living at the time, and received by the poet in Italy on May 2. "My dear Friend," it begins, "I fear I must prepare you for a very dull & selfish letter, but knowing your generous, kind disposition I will not pretend to offer one apology which to ye common race of man would be indispensable—."

The letter continues:

And then, My Dear Byron, I had yesterday ye pleasure of receiving your letter of the 11th brought to me by a Mr. Malapeyre or Lake to whom I gave a receipt, as your friend or acquaintance Mr. Clarke requested in his letter to this said Editor of Sheridan's works & historian of a singular man who perhaps he never saw—but this is nothing in this age of wonders—yr letter gave me as usual perfect pleasure, tho' in fact it contained nothing but the reassurance of your friendly disposition towards me, which is truly grateful & of your ever having been my friend, which I never doubted from ye known nobleness of your nature—I <u>did</u> receive your letter of ye 16th March, but not till the 4th April, long after ye departure of mine, expressive of my anxiety at your silence, & so long did your letter tarry in this <u>fine hand</u> that I was forced to fear my volumes of self had fatigued even Byron—my not having since written to you—the following detail will explain, & all Paris is ranged with indignation at what I assume will not fail to enrage you.

21

The Kidnapping

Although all Paris was probably not raging (or even enraged — Paston & Quennell misread this obvious word as "enraged"), something quite newsworthy had, indeed, happened. Paston and Quennell say, "It appeared that Sir James had contrived to kidnap his little boy, who was in wretched health, had carried him across the border to Nantes and handed him over to mauvais sujets. He had abused Lady Frances to his valet, and had slandered her to her friends and relations, describing her as a woman of gross appetites, 'ready to rush into the arms of any man.' She had no funds wherewith to rescue her boy, or make her children wards in chancery."

That's a fairly good summary, but Lady Frances goes into detail in her letter to Byron:

> You remember my announcing Sir J.W.'s intention of residing at Lausanne — a few, I may say, hours after his letter arrived, Mr Fawkes, a mutual acquaintance, came to me to announce Sir J.'s being in Paris, & his request to see ye children, which I declined in consequence of a conspiracy last year to carry them off — Mr F. said he had pledged his word of Honour as a gentleman not to annoy me and that he w'd give his that his object was only to see ye children, but that he would return to Sir James, & if he did not feel quite certain of his honorable intention he w'd himself recommend me not to send them — all appeared satisfactorily pledged, oaths were even given, & ye children went, but only 2 returned, 1 he kept. I called on Mr. Fawkes, who went to Sir J., but all in vain — he had taken ye child off — an infant of 2½ who had been for 16 months in a dreadful state & who only left his room to see his father, which I risked to avoid misrepresentation.

I have been unable to identify this Mr. Fawkes. Evidently a friend of both Sir James and Lady Frances, he may well have belonged to the Yorkshire family who lived at Fenley Hall. She continues:

> Heaven only knows where he put ye child — I called upon ye police, ye whole engine was set in motion, he was followed from place to place, but never once did he go to see the poor baby — every house was searched — all was vain — every authority lent me the hearty assistance — I risked arresting him but upon his proving himself ye father he was, of course, liberated — ye next day I brought it before ye 1er [première] Chambre & after a very fine speech of feeling & in consequence of ye physician's statement of ye health of ye child the judgement was given for ye restitution of ye child to its mother's care — but before the judgement could be put into a form to act upon he had removed ye child from ye horrid place he had it in, & sent it with a common mauvais sujet to wait for him in ye road, & assisted by a Sir Frs. Vincent, without a passport he makes off, Sir Francis finds ye child, takes it to ye father, gives him his passport, & leaves Sir J. with ye woman & infant to proceed — So soon as we heard they were gone couriers were sent off — who brought these seats, he was travelling past, offering any money to get on — and travelling with a courier, having taken ye road to Lille tho' he pretended he was going to England — the next day the Minister de Police telegraphed them, but they had passed thro' Lille half a hour before, ye maid & child, he on foot — asking for ye nearest Frontier — I then set off for Lille — & I found them in ye little town of Menin, in Belgium — when I used every exertion, but he was out of france [sic] & nothing could be done — having forced him before ye Procureur du Roi [the King's Procurator] at Courtray [sic] and coming with one of ye judges, I met him at ye door of ye Hotel talking to my maid & begging to see me — I walked in & he followed me — he began by reproaches & continued by professions & imploring me to live with him — I repeated to him my

ideas & sentiments which I have already written to you — I only came to claim & save my child, if I failed, at least I had done my duty & trusted to God for ye rest — he said what c'd he do — his living with me again would contradict all reports of itself — upon my expressing my opinion of his object & ye manner in which he w'd be obliged to explain living with me, he offered to write a paper & sign it — I told him I never would do in secret what I would not openly voice — if he wished to live with me, he should make his proposal to me in writing & if I saw him sincere I would not refuse — oh, no! he wished it then or never, that if I w'd not he w'd go to Scotld — & get a Divorce — but that if I lived with him, I could do as I like, of course now there w'd be no such thing as Jealousy & we w'd live near Byron — such a mixture of dishonour & infamy is rare — finding me firm, he then proposed my <u>lending</u> myself to a Divorce in Scotld — to enable him to marry again, but not me — I assured him I had no ambition — my heart is as my children's, & I implored my boy — he assured me ye child tormented him but it w'd give me too much pleasure to have it — however, he had not ye means of keeping it [i.e. the child] & if I w'd remain 3 weeks at Ostend, 100 miles from where we were, he w'd give it up when he embarked — I assured him I would make any sacrifice to save my boy, but that was not in my power, as I had no funds — I had already anticipated my allowance to enable me to make ye journey, that living at an Hotel was impossible — that my embarrassment is increased & no fault of mine & I had no secret funds or ways of getting money like him — & in truth, my dearest Friend, how does he get on — he has had money at command, to purchase my misery — and I who lead a hermit's life — embark in no expense — labour to make so little do, am forced into expences [sic] & debt (this last affair I see 1100 fr. [francs] debt) — am obliged to suffer ye misery of embarrassment & every privation — I have not one <u>relation</u> to whom I could turn, happen what may & at a moment when I know not what to do — nor a friend — no, no! I will not say that — but I only know 2 people in ye world to whom my heart owns sufficient friendship — not to make ye load of obligation severe, to them I would not apply — where does he get his money?

She continues:

After several hours conversation, he promised to send ye child at ye end of 3 days if I remained near. I did, at Lille — but all in vain, & mind & body exhausted, disgusted at his villainy, & without funds, I returned home yesterday & 2 hours after my arrival, I received your letter — you will then continue to write to me, & I will, on my part, promise you to abridge my replies — do not let this letter alarm you — its length is fearful, but I promise amendment — there is no person here who can interrupt my letters — ye fault is at ye Post Office — where there is great neglect, but yr letters, tho' delayed, did not appear to have been opened — write to me, I pray you — & believe me ever Dear Byron, your sincere FW.

Byron may well have hoped that this was the end of the letter, but it wasn't. She carried on, in an unannounced and rather lengthy postscript:

Sir J, tho' avowing his only object was to live with me, & confessing to me 'twas for money, yet ye day he left, having called on Sir C. Stewart [sic — the ambassador] to complain of ye Police, ran on with such execrable abuse of me that Sir Charles said this is different to your sentiments to Lord Byron (for I had copied the parts of your letters relating to him, shewn them to Ldy Elizabeth [the ambassador's wife, daughter of the 3rd Earl of Hardwicke], upon which he said if Lord B. ever expressed other views, said I was anxious to live with her — 'tis false — I never did — the same to my lawyer here & to ye secretarys at ye Embassy. When I named this to him at Menin he denied ever having spoken of me but with affection — then, said I, perhaps you spoke of me this morng, to ye Maire [French for mayor] of Menin — 'I did' — I then repeated to him the infamy of a 2 hours conversation, being almost in ye same room — 'Oh, ye Rascal, I asked him if you were in ye same house, he said no!" — That Sir F. Vincent is a refined villain! — I saw him for ye 1st time the day he had himself carried off ye child — & he gave me his honor he knew nothing of it — & calmly heard ye cries of this unhappy infant who had never been an hour away from its mother, had been accustomed to her tenderest care and carried it away with a mauvais sujet, to gratify what feeling? I confess I know not human nature enough to decide — you asked my plans — to remain here in peace or war — here I am beyond ye reach of his vile intentions, & ye world shall now see what I really am — patience, & my enemies will fly — .

On May 22, 1823, "the Lord Noel Byron, Albaro, a Genova, in Italia" received, after a delay of almost three weeks, a package and letter from Bold Webster, in effect Sir James's version of

Lady Frances's story of a few weeks before. This delay between the writing and the receipt of the letter was due to the fact that Sir James wrote it in London, then brought it with him from London to Chambéry, and mailed it from there.

> London. 2 May. 1823. My Dear Byron, I am happy to find that my bill for 30£ (ye more onerous paid of y'r kindness) is <u>p'd</u>, & ye latter one of 20£ is not due yet for some time, you may be assured that my anxiety to meet all such obligations is unlimited, & that no effort wh[ich] my reduced fortunes will allow shall be left untried.
>
> My bill to Leonart. Orsi [Florentine banker] being also paid, leaves Italy at least, untainted by ye pestilential effects of dilapidated resources.
>
> I found Sir F.V. [Sir Francis Vincent] in Paris & nothing c'd be more kind, or friendly, than his conduct & ye epistolary ebullation [sic] at wh I was annoyed when at Genoa, was meant in any but an offensive spirit, as all his subsequent acts proved.
>
> I conclude you have a 'green Bag' full [the Green Bag scandal involved seditious papers during the Regency period], at least of my 'Plots & conspiracies' in Paris transmitted from ye rue D'Anjou—The <u>facts</u> however of such memories are far too serious & atrocious for ay [any] plaisanterie on my part.
>
> First in regard to y'r correspondence with Lady F., (wh as you know I never saw), I found that it had been made a part of British Diplomacy—at least that our ambassador [Sir Charles Stuart] had ye benefit of its perusal—for what purpose I can form no opinion. You, however, will form y'r own estimate of ye motives & feelings wh submitted the letter in question to such inspection.
>
> On passing through Paris, I was determined at least to have my little Boy, & I therefore kept him after Lady F. had sent all ye children to my hotel.
>
> In doing this I am free to avow, I was obliged to <u>manquer</u> towards an old friend (Mr. Fawkes) who had pledged himself to her that they w'd be restored—The <u>necessity</u> of such a step was as painful to me as I contend that ye principles upon wh it is perfectly defensible, are not to be called in question—for ye rights of parental authority are not to be compromised under such unparelled [sic] circumstances, or can they, by any Sophistry be held analogous to the common incidents & daily occurrences of Society—Such cases form their own rules & exceptions—They become indeed ye Preceptor of one's Duty—Fawkes being compromised by ye circumstances towards her. I offer'd him ye only reparation in my power, at least Vincent did for me, & each his friends has properly advised him was unnecessary, indeed, as 'tis, F. told him it w'd have been a gratuitous piece of knight-errantry by no means called for—failing by these means to regain ye child Lady F.—or rather those who advised her had recourse to measures wh it is difficult to imagine, ye Government of ay country in alliance with one of wh I ye victim am a subject c'd have lent itself.
>
> I must first tell you that ye moment I had kept my boy I wrote to assure Lady F. If she w'd send my girl over to Lady M'tnorris care by me, I w'd return him—or if she w'd join me in appointing 10,000 of my trust property to ye Boy at our Deaths—These offers—or assurances were treated with contempt & 2 days afterward my room was enter'd by Two Commissaires de Police & 2 Gens d'armes, with an order of ye Prêfet [sic] to arrest me, 'accusé d'avoir enlévé [sic] un enfant'—My arrest you see was obtained & granted by fraud—Vin. [Vincent] representing me as an indifferent person—a stranger to ye parties & such a suggestion was indeed worthy of ye French Police for it is impossible to suppose such an idea c'd have enter'd ye mind of Lady F.
>
> I was taken to, & kept almost au secret at ye Prefecture of Police from 10 in ye morning till 4 in ye afternoon—in vain I demanded to be examined by ye Prefet [sic]—or Sous Prefet—in vain I asked to send to <u>Sir C. Stewart</u> [sic] or for an avocat. In short had I been Louvel or Berton more rigour & insolence c'd not have been shewn—.

Louis Pierre Louvel was the assassin, in 1820, of the Duc de Berry. The execution of General Auguste Berton, Carbonari insurrectionist, as he sang out "Vive la France," was still fresh news when Bold Webster wrote this.

The epistle continues:

> The only reply I w'd give to a dirty little commissary who at length appear'd to insult, rather than to examine me, was my passeport & a refusal to give up my child—with this determination—He & Lady F. & her advisers (Dr. Hyde & Mr. Allen, an English attorney) went before le Procureur du roi who said the arrest was perfectly illegal, as I had proved my right to ye child, that Lady F.

might appeal to ye courts, but that I c'd <u>there</u> also stop all proceedings by pleading this incompetency I have wh there is not a clearer point in the whole code of Napoleon — notwithstanding this authority, those infamous wretches to whose counsel poor Lady F. had abandoned her cause, were resolved to try by fraud & imposition what they c'd not attain legally — two days therefore after the arrest a citation was left at my hotel at 6 in ye eve'ng, summoning me to appear & plead ye next morning by 9 — There I went to ye Tribunal de la Première Instance & there, I blush to say, appear'd Lady F. with her aunt [Deborah, wife of Sir Richard Musgrave, 1st Bart, was sister of Lady Mountnorris].

That is the end of Page 1. Page 2 (and headed as such) begins mid-sentence:

Lady Musgrave (whom I had never seen before) & Allen, ye attorney — my lawyer in vain asked a Day's delay to plead & equally so did he insist on the incompetency of the Court, tho' both ye President & ye Procureur du roi admitted it!

Lady F.'s counsel demanded a Jugement Provisoire on 3 grounds— to prevent my taking ye child out of ye country & an order to arrest me untill I restored him — 1st Allen produced a certificate that Lady F. had instituted Proceedings of Divorce ag'st me! in England & to wh fabrication & absurdity this person had ye audacity to get Sir C. Stuart's signature — 2nd they asserted ye child to be only 28 months old when he is 3 yrs ye 1st of May — & lastly a certificate of ye redoubtable Dr. Hyde that his [i.e. the child's] health was so delicate, 'I w'd most manqué à mourir plusieurs fois' [the French translates as "missed death several times"; Webster's meaning or what he is quoting is unclear] — on these 3 points, wh my avoué [attorney] in vain offer'd to <u>prove</u> diabolically false & in defiance of ye <u>admitted</u> point of incompetency, they gave a Judgment in favor of Lady F. & ordering my arrest — after <u>such</u> measures I was determined to shew them they had an Englishman to deal with & therefore not so ready a victim to their Inquisitorial Proceedings [an interesting self-description, in that Sir James was only a tad more genealogically English than, say, Napoleon] — Vincent got a carriage & with his passeport. So I passed into Belgium by ye next day — They actually telegraphed us at Lille 5 minutes after I passed the Gates— when at Menin, Pays Bas, Lady F. followed me with ye Judgment. She attached me with another Commissary of Police, instigated by ye French authorities untill ye procureur du roi at Courtrai said the Judgment was invalid in Belgium, & that no one c'd dispute my possession of ye child — As I was obliged to leave all my things in Paris, not daring to return to my hotel after ye Judgement you may imagine my situation as ye intrigues of ye Police have as yet not only prevented their being sent after me, but intercepted all my correspondence, so that I am literally almost without a change of clothes & what is worse, can't afford to buy what w'd be useless to me when I get my things again — To you who hold in abhorrence evy [every] species of tyranny, I need make no comment on ye infamy of those hirelings lending themselves to such measures — If my private interests did not, as you have often heard me say, demand privacy, I w'd positively have ye case b't [brought] before Parliament. If Stuart c'd, or w'd not remonstrate & it sh'd at least be known for the future to what extent a British subject in France might expect persecution or protection.

But I am fetter'd & bound by worldly policy & Temporal Difficulties, to say nothing of ye security wh my wife being ye Instigator, affords ye movers of the scene — in short they knew well & calculated on ye indemnity wh that fact assured them.

If you continue ay correspondence with her, Pray never name me — tho' I feel it an unnecessary caution, still [he deleted this last word] The curtain has fallen on ye last act of our Tragedy —

Pray let me hear from you — that you are well & happy will always be a source of Interest with me — Write to ye care of Messrs Hammersley & Co, Pall Mall, & B'le me ever affect'ly yrs, JWW.

Some weeks later, on May 17, 1823, Byron wrote from Genoa to Lady Hardy about Webster:

Your chevalier — whom you do not again allude to— has not closed his career yet.— He has been to Paris— ran away with one of his wife's children (by mistake it is supposed for one of his own) has been taken by the police — ran away again — been telegraphed to Lisle — but escaped — bearing away this paternal trophy of his prowess — after having broken his word to a Mr Fawkes — to whom he pledged himself that he only wanted to see the children — and would restore them immediately to Lady Frances — who had recourse to the Ambassador &c. &c.— But this is not all — he involved me — when he was at genoa [sic] — 1stly in a correspondence with Lady F. to reconcile them — well — he had the impudence to deny to Sir Charles Stuart — having ever authorized me to address her upon the subject!—

This comes of peace-making! 2ndly — I endorsed two bills for him here — to enable him to get away — my banker here says— that they were protested by his banker — and of course I have had to pay them.— All this has somewhat stirred my meekness.— I have written to England to have him arrested (if he appears there) on a bond for a thousand pounds which I lent him ten years ago— with ten years interest due upon it — I am tired of [keeping ?] measures with such a mauvais sujet — I remember lending him that sum on condition that he would not go to the Jews — he took it — went to the Jews notwithstanding — and never paid me a farthing from that hour to this— I hope I shan't be deemed a hard Creditor — in being at length provoked to teach him some articles of faith.

Also from about this time (although that's a guess) is an undated letter from James to the poet:

My Dear B — I enclose you a note of my Distemper — I sh'd if possible — that is if yr kindness wills it, be sorry to leave a part of so small a Bill here & my effects— wh w'd most likely never reach me & if they did, at a vast expense — if therefore you will desire them to make ye bill for 45 or 50 — it will completely clearly [sic] me now d'un embarras I shall not <u>easily</u> forget & you will serve yours ever, JWW.

But I leave it all to you & as to ye Pay't of ye Bill, I cannot add to ye assurances I have already given & wh I trust are satisfactory to you.

22

When We Two Parted

On June 10, 1823, Byron wrote to Lady Hardy:

As to yr. chevalier W Wne *** to be sure I learnt from himself all about his [?] surprise — but there is some little doubt of his accuracy. — At least it is very strange that he could never prove so public a voyage of discovery. — She — poor thing — has made a sad affair of it altogether. — I had the melancholy task of prophesying as much many years ago in some lines — of which the three or four first stanzas only were printed — and of course without names — or allusions — and with a false date — I send you on the concluding stanza — which never was printed with the others. —

> Then — fare thee well — Fanny —
> Now doubly undone —
> To prove false unto many —
> As faithless to One —
> Thou art past all recalling
> Even would I recall —
> For the woman once falling
> Forever must fall. —

There's morality and sintiment [sic] — for you in a [?] — but I was very tender hearted in those days. — If you want to know where the lines to which this stanza belongs — are — they are in I know not what volume — but somewhere (for I have no copy) but they begin with

When we two parted
In silence and tears
&c. &c. &c.

So here is a treasure for you in honour of our relationship — rhymes unpublished — and a secret into the bargain — which you wont keep —.

The poem in question was listed erroneously in the old Byron collections as being an 1808 piece, but that was long before the Byron letters were published, which gave the answer to the poem entitled, "When We Two Parted." The published four stanzas go like this:

> When we two parted
> In silence and tears,
> Half broken-hearted
> To sever for years,
> Pale grew thy cheek and cold,
> Colder thy kiss;
> Truly that hour foretold
> Sorrow to this.
> The dew of the morning
> Sunk chill on my brow —
> It felt like the warning
> Of what I feel now.
> Thy vows are all broken,
> And light is thy fame;
> I hear thy name spoken,
> And share in its shame.

> They name thee before me,
> A knell to mine ear;
> A shudder comes o'er me —
> Why wert thou so dear?
> They know not I knew thee,
> Who knew thee too well: —
> Long, long shall I rue thee,
> Too deeply to tell.
> In secret we met —
> In silence I grieve,
> That thy heart could forget,
> Thy spirit deceive.
> If I should meet thee
> After long years,
> How should I greet thee? —
> With silence and tears.

Although it seems indisputably clear that "When We Two Parted" was written with Lady Frances in mind, Tim Burnett in *The Rise and Fall of a Regency Dandy* questions this long-held belief. He says, "It has been stated that Byron wrote his poem 'When we two parted In silence and tears' in response to the news that on 16 February 1816 James Wedderburn Webster was awarded 2000 [pounds] damages against one Baldwin proprietor of the St James's Chronicle, who had alleged in his issue for 5 August 1815 that Lady Frances had been the mistress of the Duke of Wellington. The presence in the British Library, however, of a MS of the poem in the hand of Lady Byron with corrections by Byron (Add. MS. 31038) would appear to make this unlikely since the Byrons had parted, never to see each other again, on 15th of January."

Miss Frances Williams Wynn, in her *Diaries of a Lady of Quality* (1864), wrote:

> In England we are apt to exclaim with Byron, in his suppressed lines [she means the original poem, rather than the one that was printed]:
>
>> Then, fare thee well, Fanny, thus doubly undone,
>> Thou frail to the many, and false to the one.
>> Thou art past all recalling, e'en would I recall,
>> For the woman so fallen for ever must fall
>
> These lines about which frequent enquiry has been made, were given me by Scrope Davies. They originally formed the conclusion of a copy of verses addressed by Lord Byron to Lady Frances W W to whom he was devotedly attached until she threw him over for the Duke of Wellington, then in the full blaze of his Peninsular glory. 'Byron,' said Davies, 'Came one morning to my lodgings in St James's Street, in a towering passion, and standing by the fire, broke out, 'D--- all women, and d--- that woman in particular.' He tore from his watch-ribbon a seal she had given him, and dashed it into the grate. As soon as I left the room, I picked it up, and here it is.' He showed it to me, and allowed me to take an impression of it, which I have still. It was a large seal, representing a ship in full sail, a star in the distance, with the motto, "*Si je la perds, je suis perdu.*" Two or three days afterwards his Lordship presented himself again with a copy of verses addressed to his fickle fair one, from which Davies with some difficulty induced him to omit the four concluding lines.

23

The Death of Byron

In 1823 Sir James's application to become a consul overseas was turned down. That year Byron went to Greece. He died there on April 19 of the following year, at Missolonghi, of marsh fever.

Whatever Byron's loss meant to Sir James, it meant considerably more to his wife, who, just as Byron's Memoirs were about to be published after his death, wrote to John Cam Hobhouse, one of the executors of Byron's will (the other being John Hanson), from "Paris. May 31 [1824]":

> My dear Sir, In you, whom intimate acquaintance with Lord Byron enabled you most thoroughly to know & appreciate him, to you his loss must be most severe — all Europe must lament him, but you & all others who also enjoyed his friendship must deeply & for ever deplore him — amongst them you, I know, are aware that from circumstances unnecessary to repeat, his loss is severely felt by me — My knowledge of your honour, his opinion, my own, my confidence in you — all prevents me having a single fear about any thing relating to me that may have been confided to you, but I am naturally anxious to know whether Ld. B's memoirs are to be published or not — the papers have many versions of a story on their subject, perhaps you will oblige me by a statement, and, if not asking too great a favour, I should like to know what mention was or is made of me — but in ye event of publication I feel convinced I should be safe in yr hands—
>
> In a letter a long time since, Lord B. mentioned to me that my letters to him were in either Mrs Leigh's hands or yrs — I forget which — If in yours, may I hope that you will either destroy them or send them to me — they can afford no amusement, no interest to any body, and are best destroyed — and, my dear Sir, I am going to ask you a favor; which I must trust to your generous kindness to forgive — Have you a print of our dear departed friend that you could let me have, one that you think like him & if you could send me one, you would confer the greatest favour — I shall be for ever grateful — if you can — & enclose it for me under cover to Sir Charles Stuart, Ambassador here, & sent to Downing Street it will come safe. — I also venture to remind you of a promise you made me some years ago of a copy of those invaluable works — I claim it in order to have your selection of the copy but now only on condition of your librarian sending me a memorandum of ye value.
>
> Excuse me, my dear Sir & believe me in real grief for our dear friend, ever your obliged & faithful sevt. Frances Wedderburn. No. 8, rue d'Anjou St Honoré.

Hobhouse never complied. As Paston and Quennell say, "But Lady Frances's letters were never returned to her, and still remain among Byron's amatory archives."

The will (drawn up on July 29, 1815, with a codicil dated November 1818 and made when he was living in Venice) was proved before Byron's remains came back to London on July 1, 1824.

24

Baronet

From 1824 on Sir James seems, hardly surprisingly, to be have been in renewed financial trouble. In a letter of that year he speaks of a visit to Scotland as having to be "attended with the circumspection that my circumstances require." In January 1825 he wrote a *Farewell to thee, Scotland*, which he inaccurately calls "the land of my birth." In the John Wedderburn collection is a printed leaflet of this song by James Webster Wedderburn.

In 1825 Hatchard's of London published the political tract *Letter to Henry Broughton, Esq., M.P., on the subject of Catholic Emancipation, and the sentiments of H.R.H. the Duke of York on that subject considered*, by Sir James Wedderburn.

Washington Irving, the American writer, was living in Paris in 1824–25. His journal includes the following entries:

> Sunday, 19th [December 1824] — Called with Matthews on Lady Francis [sic] Webster — Talked about Lord B.'s memoirs. She seemed apprehensive that more disclosures would appear concerning his private writings, letters, etc.
>
> June 2d [1825] — Thursday — went to Ital[ian] opera — 'Italiana in Algiere' — sat in Matthews' box — Lady Frances Webster there — introduced me to Mr Gowen.
>
> Tuesday 7th [June, 1825] — supper at ten — return home at past twelve in carriage of Lady Francis Webster.
>
> Saturday, 11th [June, 1825] — Dine at Lady Francis Webster's — present Lord and Lady Bolingbroke — Mr Eugene Laglandiere, Mr---, Dr Hyde.

Irving was ten years older than Lady Frances. Who knows?

Sir James Webster Wedderburn was importuning Home Secretary Robert Peel about this time, again on the subject of Catholic emancipation. There is a letter from May 1825 and another from June 1826, both now in the British Library (Add: 40378, vol. 198, f. 253 and Add: 40378, vol. 207, f. 235).

On July 13, 1826, Lady Frances's sister, Lady Catherine Somerset, gave birth to her third daughter, Juliana Lucy Sarah.

Sir James settled for a while at Auchterhouse in 1827, near the home of his ancestors in Scotland. Here he began a revised edition of his book on his family. Another book was published that year, a novel called *The Guards*, in three volumes, scribblerus incognito, published by T. Clerc Smith and printed by Bentley. On page 188 the author is describing the occupants of boxes at the ballet. Golden Ball is mentioned, and then reads, "Lady F.W.W.———, the Right Honourable spouse of a very simple knight and an X MP [sic]. This lady should support the Opera, for she gained a fine fortune, per legacy, from being admired there by one who was contented to look and sigh — look and sigh, look and sigh, nay, and sigh again, and that was all."

Evidence of Bold Webster's reconciliation — no matter how impermanent — with his wife came with the birth of their final child, George Gordon Gerard Trophime de Lally-Tollendal Webster-Wedderburn, on December 12, 1827, at Paris. The infant was baptized in Brussels not

George Gordon Gerard Trophime de Lally-Tollendal Webster-Wedderburn, youngest son of Sir James and Lady Frances Webster-Wedderburn. By kind permission of Tatton Hewetson.

long afterwards, surprisingly surviving the immersion despite being so weighted by nomenclature. His godparents were the Duchess of Richmond (wife of the 5th Duke) and the Marquis de Lally-Tollendal (the Marquis had married, in 1779, Elizabeth Charlotte, only child of Sir John Wedderburn-Halket — and a distant relation of Sir James — by his wife, Elizabeth Fletcher. In the John Wedderburn collection is a letter from Sir James Webster-Wedderburn to John relating to the Marquis.)

Just at this time, the immortal Scrope Davies wrote, in 1828, to Francis Hodgson from his apartment in Ostend: "James Wedderburn, whom you must have met at Newstead, has passed a few days here on his road to Paris. Did you ever see Lady Frances? She is the only person I ever beheld on whom was everything the eye looks for in woman. She, and she alone, of all I have ever seen, the 'vultus nimium lubricus aspici' [he is quoting here from Horace's *Odes*], 'that beauty over which the eye glides with giddy delight, incapable of fixing on any particular claim.'" He continues, in the same letter, "Sir James has survived Waterloo, but he has not survived his love of writing. He makes 'born' rhyme to 'storm,' and 'suspect' rhyme to 'respect.' About the latter, in vain do I assert that in English Poetry a rhyme, to be just, should not be an 'idem,' but a 'simile.' He goes on rhyming and reasoning, and both with the same success."

James's (and Lady Frances's) money problems became acute after 1828. He and his wife made repeated entreaties from this time on to the Duke of Wellington for money, but these were politely and steadily turned down.

Tom Moore, in his journal entry for April 11, 1828, says, "The Executors are engaged in something of the same kind [as with Francis Hodgson, in the matter of Byron's estate] with Webster — the sum in question 1500 pounds [which was the £1000 plus interest]. Hobhouse confirmed to what I had heard already from S. Davies that Byron never actually [the manuscript is torn away here] possession of Lady Francis [sic] Byron himself said to Hobhouse that he feared he had once let [again, the manuscript is torn away here] think that such had been the case, but it was by no means so — he had never had her —."

Again then, here, a confirmation that Byron did, indeed, spare Lady Frances as he had claimed.

On November 11, 1828, Sir James Webster-Wedderburn wrote to John Wedderburn, his cousin, from Brigton this time, giving particulars of the arms and supporters of Sir Alexander Wedderburn, 2nd Baronet of Blackness, and his mottoes "Spernit pericula virtus," and "Consilio et cura," found by him in an old Latin history of Scotland in the library of Mr. Hunter of Blackness. This letter is in the John Wedderburn collection.

Sir J.W. Wedderburn was invited to, and duly attended, the King's first levee of the season, on April 29, 1829.

On February 15, 1829, old Charles Wedderburn of Pearsie died up in Scotland, and by the terms of his May 1829 London will left a small annuity of 50 pounds to his nephew, Sir James. James was much disappointed when he found himself cut out of the entail, and speaks of "the unparalleled injustice" of this having been done. His disappointment was deepened by the fact that he regarded himself not only as the heir to his uncle, but as entitled to assume the Blackness baronetcy. He seems to have thought that all the descendants of the executed Sir John Wedderburn of Blackness were to be regarded, by reason of Sir John's attainder for high treason in 1746, as dead in law though not so in fact, and that the honors of Sir John's father thus devolved on the senior male descendant of his second son, i.e. Robert Wedderburn of Pearsie, James's grandfather. There is a logic to that, but it wasn't shared by anyone else.

James wrote to his cousin, Henry Scrymgeour-Wedderburn, the de jure 7th Earl of Dundee, on December 16, 1829, from 115 Park St., Grosvenor Square. This letter, which is part of the Scrymgeour-Wedderburn papers, contains the following:

> As I fear that the unparallelled injustice of my late uncle's settlements does not afford me an early prospect of visiting my native country [sic] and having the pleasure of seeing you, I must be excused for troubling you on this occasion and begging you the favour of your friendly services, I am about to undergo in Edinburgh what I believe is termed general service as heir of line to my great grandfather Robert Wedderburn of Pearsie [he means grandfather, or, if he really does mean great-grandfather, then it should be Sir Alexander Wedderburn of Blackness]. As we merely want evidence or proof of the births, or register thereof, it would, as I am informed, very much facilitate matters: any parole testimony of repute, such as the representative of a family or other member of consequence.
>
> Now when my jury is convened, should you happen to be then in Edinburgh, perhaps you would not object to do me the kindness merely to appear and state what you know either from documents or general repute, viz:— that old Pearsie was a son of Sir Alexander, and that David Webster, my father, was Robert Wedderburn's son, &c.
>
> Will you at all events oblige me with a few lines in reply as soon as convenient? Lady Frances & my daughter, who are still in town, unite in my best regards to Mrs Wedderburn & my cousins.

This plan of getting himself served heir to the fourth baronet, however, which he seriously entertained, was never acted upon, and he was content with assuming the title and getting others to treat him as having the right to do so. So, at this stage, Sir James unlawfully assumed the title of 5th Baronet Wedderburn of Blackness. Many people would call him this for the rest of his life.

In 1829 Rivington's of St. Martin's Lane printed 250 copies of the political tract *A Reply to Mr Gally Knight's letter to the Earl of Aberdeen on the foreign policy of England, with remarks on the present state of the nation*, by Sir James Wedderburn, Bart. Henry Gally Knight was a gentleman-author and expert on architecture, who lived at Firbeck Hall, in Rotherham, very close to Sir James's old Aston Hall home. Naturally, James did not pay the printers; given his prominence, he was allowed over three years by his creditors, until, eventually, they brought the case before a jury (see below). Copies of correspondence between Rivington's and Sir James are in the British Museum (pressmarks T.1002,7, and T.1282,8).

It was also in 1829 that Sir James Webster Wedderburn and his wife were plaintiffs in a case against George Cavendish. This has to be Lord George Cavendish, uncle of the 6th Duke of Devonshire.

On June 15, 1829, Tom Moore went to see Lady Hardy, and the two of them sat for an hour and a half, discussing Byron and the letters he had sent to her. Moore wrote in his journal for that day, "... parts in them (particularly about Wedderburn Webster), which, though highly comical, cannot be published. The worst of Lady F. Webster's faiblesses was that they were all for money — no matter how old or ugly the man — even a new gown (said Lady H.) would do it."

Had it really come to that for Lady Frances, or was Lady Hardy merely retailing maliciousness she had got from Sir James? One is more inclined to believe the latter. We will probably never know. These people all knew each other's business, or at least thought they did, and they talked freely among themselves, but as for print, they would truly have been damned if they had.

Lady Frances's sister, Lady Catherine Somerset, had her fourth child and only son, Sir Alfred Plantagenet Frederick Charles Somerset, on September 5, 1829.

There is a Lady Frances Webster letter in Robert Peel's general correspondence, from December 1829 (Add: 40399, vol. 219), and two Sir James Webster Wedderburn letters from January 1830 (Add: 40400, vol. 220, ff. 112, 114).

The Marquis de Lally-Tollendal died on March 15, 1830. The next day Lady Frances's brother-in-law, Major-General Norman Macleod, died. His widow, Hester Annabella, Lady Frances Webster-Wedderburn's sister, would die on August 14, 1844.

On April 30, 1830, James wrote in a note in his manuscript for his book on the Wedderburns, "The Marquis of Lally Tollendal, recently created a Knight of the Holy Ghost by the King of France, has lately died at Paris as full of honours as of years, leaving many literary works to prove his talents, and a character which has gained him the appellation of the 'eloquent and noble' from one of his most distinguished contemporaries. He compiled some account of his family, which was ancient, and gave a printed copy of the memoir to Sir James Webster Wedderburn, whom he met in Paris [for this incident, see page 82 of James's manuscript]. He had also some correspondence with the late Charles Wedderburn of Pearsie, with the kind but fruitless intention of healing the breach between him and his nephew, Sir James. It was, however, too late to change opinions which, however founded, age had strengthened."

25

Wedderburn vs. Wedderburn

Sir J.W. Wedderburn was invited to, and duly attended, the King's levee of December 15, 1830. In 1831, his son, Charles, entered Charterhouse as a gown boy. On February 1, 1831, James was, as ever, short of money, and dreamed up a way to get some. He inveigled some of his relatives into what would become a cause célèbre. He initiated, along with his brother Charles, his sister Mrs. Hawkins and her husband, and Archibald Douglas (James's brother-in-law) as co-plaintiffs, the long Chancery suit of Wedderburn vs. Wedderburn, which was partially the basis for the fictional Jarndyce v. Jarndyce in Dickens's *Bleak House* (1853). The defendants were the partners in the company of Wedderburn. The plaintiffs claimed that in 1801 David Webster's estate had not been given enough money, and that this missing money had, after having worked for the company, produced profits. The plaintiffs wanted to re-open the company's books.

This suit would drag on for 26 years (until 1857, when all parties still alive settled for a miserable sum) as the longest ever Chancery suit, and would ruin everyone concerned, including the initiator, who had long since died. In connection with this suit, James's name, and the name of his brother, Charles, appears in the index to "heirs at Law, Next of Kin, etc," by E. Preston, 1 Great College St., Westminster, thus, "51576–77. Sir James Wedderburn-Webster, Charles Wedderburn-Webster." As Dickens says in his preface to his famous novel, "At the present moment there is a suit before the Court which was commenced nearly 20 years ago; in which from thirty to forty counsel have been known to appear at one time; in which costs have been incurred to the amount of seventy thousand pounds; which is a friendly suit; and which is (I am assured) no nearer to its termination now than when it was begun." Dickens assures us that there was an even older Chancery suit, still going on in 1852, that was begun in the 18th century, and had used up more than double that seventy thousand he talks of for Wedderburn v. Wedderburn.

In between all this the Queen held a drawing-room at the King's Palace, St. James's, on May 28, 1831, to celebrate the birthday of His Majesty. Lady Frances was presented by the Dowager Duchess of Richmond.

Tom Moore's *Life of Byron* came out in 17 volumes in 1832. It gives three references to Webster in the index. In volume 3, page 52, there is reference to a letter from Byron to W ... W ... Esq., dated February 28, 1814, in which the poet begs James to do nothing in his defense, adding that his enemies "are more chagrined by my silence than they could be by the best defence in the world." Volume 4, page 317, refers to a letter, June 1, 1820, from Byron to Moore, saying that W.W. had written Byron "a well-meaning letter stating his belief that a reunion might be effected between Lady B. and myself," but asking Moore to let W.W. know that "the thing is impossible." The third reference, to volume 4, page 31, seems to be an error. In his copy of Moore, John Cam Hobhouse wrote in the margin, "Though Webster is & was a very poor creature it is too bad to tell the story." In the second edition, Moore represented Webster's name by asterisks only.

Mary Shelley, the author of *Frankenstein*, wrote to John Murray on June 10, 1832, from Somerset Street, discussing Byron's works. She says, "... and in Canto XIVc. where the dangerous passion arising from a game of billiards alludes to Lady F.W.W. the heroine of the Bride — and the Ginevra of the Sonnets...."

What Mary Shelley means is verse 100 of Canto 14 of Byron's *Don Juan*, which was written in 1823, and reads:

> But great things spring from little: — Would you think,
> That in our youth, as dangerous a passion
> As e'er brought man and woman to the brink
> Of ruin, rose from such a slight occasion,
> As few would ever dream could form the link
> Of such a sentimental situation?
> You'll never guess, I'll bet you millions, milliards—
> It all sprung from a harmless game at billiards.

This also shows how people not only read every word that Byron wrote, but analyzed it as well. At least those in the know did. Such a seemingly obscure piece about the billiards game could be known only by the in-crowd, at least until the 1920s when Byron's correspondence revealed the truth about the game with Lady Frances. It is also interesting that in 1823, when the relevant canto came out, Sir James did not pick up on it, as Mary Shelley did. But then James could be obtuse at times.

In 1832 James published another political tract, *Essay on the Foreign Policy of Great Britain*, and in March of that year, motivated primarily by cowardice and sycophancy, he set in motion a train of events that would have violent consequences for his wife. Preparing to go to the Continent — ostensibly for his health, but really to escape his legion of pressing creditors, to get away from Lady Frances, and to try to see Sir Walter Scott in Naples — he assigned the lease of his house, Number 14 Chesterfield Street, Mayfair, to the Rev. James M'Donald, an old friend of Lady Frances and one of her trustees. The lease included the proviso that Lady Frances be allowed to let the house from M'Donald, furnished. It was no skin off M'Donald's nose, as he had a house on Brook Street (13 Upper Brook Street, which he had been leasing since just before Christmas 1831), so he readily agreed. Also, being pressed mightily by an ironmonger, to whom he owed a vast sum, James sold his furniture in April to M'Donald, for £600, or rather, gave it to him in partial exchange for the huge sums he owed the clergyman. However, the ironmonger had already put a lien on the furniture. This did not worry James. Nothing did now. Uppermost in his mind was to escape to warmer climes and to bask in the glow cast by one of the greatest writers of the century — and a real baronet at that. Abdicating every shred of responsibility, he departed Britain without even looking back. At which point the sheriffs of Middlesex seized the furniture, which caused consternation to M'Donald, he thinking the furniture was now his. The sheriffs did not see it his way, so M'Donald brought suit against them. On a technicality, M'Donald lost his case on February 10, 1833. This put him in foul humor for some time to come, and he determined upon vengeance.

In the meantime, on the Continent, James made his way to Naples in a desperate bid to see the great Scotch historical novelist, who incidentally did not have long to live. Somehow James managed to secure to himself the position of second to Scott's Neapolitan host, Sir William Gell, in a duel. At least that is how rumor has it, although it is exceedingly difficult to imagine the bent and gouty 55-year-old in a duel. In addition to this difficulty, even good biographies of Gell fail to mention this duel. However, it did take place, according to Alexander Ogilvy Wedderburn in *The Wedderburn Book*. This was much more exciting than being at home, where nasty things were about to happen.

Richards, representing Rivington's — the company owed £141 7s 6d by Sir James Webster

Wedderburn, Baronet, for printing 250 copies of his pamphlet *Upon the Policy of Britain* (as it was known in its necessarily abbreviated form)—brought his case, Richards vs. Wedderburn, before Justice J. Parker and a common jury in the Bail Court on January 18, 1833 (deferred from January 16). Of course, James was abroad, and there was no defense. The jury awarded in full for the plaintiff. The John Wedderburn collection contains a newspaper clipping of the action brought by Richards.

26

The Robbing of Lady Frances

In the *Times* of March 29, 1833:

> Marlborough Street [i.e. the Marlborough Street Magistrates Court]. Charles Fuller, Ann Fuller, and Penelope May, were brought before Mr. Dyer yesterday, the two former for stealing property to the amount of about 400 l [pounds] from the residence of Lady Wedderburn, and the latter [i.e. Penelope May] with receiving the same.
>
> It appeared from the evidence that Goddard [Henry Goddard, police officer] was sent for yesterday to the house of Lady Wedderburn to make some inquiry after some jewellery which was missing. On examining Ann Fuller he discovered several duplicates relative to very valuable property, and he immediately suspected that Her Ladyship had been robbed. He then charged the prisoner and her husband, when the latter admitted that he had stolen two hampers full of old china, glass, antique and bronze ornaments. Upon hearing this statement Lady Wedderburn gave them into custody, and Goddard proceeded to make further inquiries, and succeeded in finding between 300 l and 400 l worth of property, a great portion of which had been pledged at Mr Jones's, South Street, by the prisoner May, who represented it as belonging to a lady of the name of Forbes. He also found a great portion at the house of a gentleman in York-place. Fuller, it appeared, was acquainted with the butler, who permitted him to leave a hamper, filled with very rich property, on Monday; but he was ignorant of the contents.
>
> Lady F. Wedderburn identified nearly all the property, part of which belonged to her, and some to a gentleman the name of Macdonald [sic].
>
> Mrs May denied all knowledge of the robbery. Her son (Fuller) informed her that Lady Wedderburn had made a present of it to his wife.
>
> Ann Fuller said that there was an execution in her Ladyship's house in October last, when the broker said to the servants, — 'Now, girls, help yourselves,' on which she took some of the articles, but she knew nothing of their being pledged.
>
> The other prisoner declined saying anything, and they were all remanded until Wednesday next.

The case of theft, simple grand larceny, was heard in two parts at the Old Bailey on April 11, 1833. Mr. Phillips conducted the prosecution:

> In the first Charles Fuller and Hannah Fuller were indicted for stealing, on the 23rd of February, the following goods of Sir James Webster Wedderburn, Knt: ten china plates to the value of one pound; a writing-desk, same value; one etwicke case to the value of five shillings [etwicke case is what it says, even though that must be a mistake]; two china bottles with a grand value of five shillings; two flowerpots, grand value five shillings; one print valued at ten shillings; one sheet valued at seven shillings; three china jars with the grand value of a pound; and twelve books, valued at a total of two pounds. Also the following goods of James McDonald: one salad dish and stand, valued at ten shillings; one butter dish and cover, valued at a pound; and five books, with the grand value of a pound.

Lady Frances testified:

> I am the wife of Sir James Webster Wedderburn, Knt. We live in Chesterfield Street, Mayfair. Hannah Fuller was our servant — she had to take care of the house, which was let to me furnished. I missed a case of diamonds, and sent for Goddard, the officer, who searched her box, in

her presence, and found a pearl knife and some duplicates—I had missed a writing desk, two china bottles, two flowerpots, a print, three china jars, and some other articles. She said the duplicates were her husband's, and that he gave them into her charge to keep—he had come to the house on the Saturday before these duplicates were found. I had spoken to her about the books, and she said they were to be looked for. I had never permitted either of the prisoners to dispose of any of these things. I know this print to be mine. I had coloured it myself. I had not missed that. I thought it was locked up in my closet.

The Rev. James M'Donald then testified:

The house is mine. I let it furnished to this lady. The prisoner Hannah had been living in my service. This salad bowl and butter-boats, some of the books, and some knives and forks are mine. I never allowed either of the prisoners to take any of the property. The woman was there purposely to guard it.

Mr. Doane, cross-examining M'Donald, asked, "Was this part of the property which was assigned to you by Sir James Webster Wedderburn?" to which M'Donald replied:

No. I purchased some property of him; he assigned to me the lease of his house, but I purchased the furniture of him for 600 pounds. He has been in my debt upwards of fifteen years. There was no execution in the house at the time I purchased the furniture, which was, I think, in April last. Lady Wedderburn was residing in the house on the 23rd of February.

John Haigh was next to testify:

I am shopman to a pawnbroker in South Street, Manchester Square. These china plates, this salad bowl and stand, this glass butter-dish and writing-desk, were pawned at our shop by Penelope May.

Penelope May herself was next up:

I am the mother of Charles Fuller. He gave me all these articles to pawn. I think he gave them to me about November. He said his wife's lady had made her a present of them. He told me to pawn them in my own name, which I did, for Mrs Forbes. I had been in the habit of going to that pawnbroker's. I never saw Hannah Fuller about these things, but she told me repeatedly that her mistress had made her a present of these articles.

James Moody then testified:

I am shopman to Mr Ross, a pawnbroker in East Street, Manchester Square. This print was pawned by the male prisoner on the 13th of December, in the name of Charles May.

Then Henry Goddard, the constable, testified:

I am an officer. I was sent for by her ladyship, and found the duplicates in the trunk, which referred to this property. I went to the pawnbrokers and they were readily given up to me. The female prisoner said her husband gave her the duplicates to take care of; he was in the house at the time. I went to him, and asked him if he had any duplicates. He said No. I then showed him these, and asked if they were his. He said they were. I asked if he was quite certain of that, as Her Ladyship had missed articles of various descriptions; he said they were his. I said he had better go with me to the pawnbroker's, and in going along I again asked him if they were his; he said Yes, but when he got to the shop he said some of the property belonged to Her Ladyship. I then took him. The nine plates were pawned on the 13th of December.

Lady Frances then took the stand:

The man came on the 23rd of February. He had no opportunity of coming to the house in November. I had seen him there in July, and desired him not to come. I believe the prisoners are married. I saw the certificate of their marriage.

Then came Charles Fuller's defense:

I was sent for by Her Ladyship's servant to assist in getting some of the things away at the time the execution was in the house. I was in want of money, and pawned these articles.

This crime, if proved, carried a mandatory sentence of transportation. Charles Fuller, aged 28, was found guilty, and transported for seven years. Hannah Fuller was found not guilty.

It wasn't over for Hannah Fuller. In the next case on the docket Hannah Fuller was again indicted for stealing, on the 23rd of February, one mother of pearl knife, valued at five shillings; and one waist-buckle, of the same value; the goods of Sir James Webster Wedderburn, Knt. After a short trial she was found not guilty through lack of evidence.

27

The Molesting of Lady Frances

The year 1833 was not a good one at all for Lady Frances, and the strange and complex relationship between her, Sir James and the Rev. M'Donald was far from over. The *Times* of August 7, 1833 reported:

> Bow Street [i.e. the Bow Street Magistrates Court]. Yesterday John Richards, George Dodds, and Richard Moffatt, were charged under the following circumstances:—
>
> It appeared that Lady Frances Wedderburn occupies the house No. 14 Chesterfield-street, Mayfair, to which a gentleman named M'Donald lays claim. On Thursday last Lady Wedderburn received a message from Mr M'Donald, requesting to know when it would be convenient for the family of Sir James Wedderburn to leave the house. To this message Lady Wedderburn returned no answer, and on the Saturday following, in the afternoon, the defendant Richards was observed pacing backwards and forwards in front of the house, looking up at the windows in a threatening manner. He then went round to the stable, and inquired of the coachman when Lady Wedderburn would require her carriage. The coachman could not give him an answer and he went away. In the course of the evening the defendant Dodds, who was also observed walking in front of the house for some time previous, knocked at the door and inquired if Lady Wedderburn was at home, at the same time attempting to push into the hall. The servant, however, would give him no answer, and succeeded in shutting the door in his face. He [Dodds] was then heard to say that he was determined to get into the house before night, but after some time both he and Richards went away. On Monday morning the defendant Richards was seen by Lady Wedderburn and her servants to resume his former position in front of the house, in company with the defendant Dodds, and, soon after, Richards attempted to force open the area of the gate, but did not succeed. They then went away for about an hour, and returned in company with another man, supposed to be Moffatt. During their absence, Mr Flower, the partner of Alderman Harmer [Harmer & Flower, of Hatton Garden] arrived at Lady Wedderburn's house to act as her solicitor; and Her Ladyship, having ordered her carriage, was about to enter it when another attempt was made by the three defendants to force an entrance into the house through the street door, but they were successfully resisted in the attempt by Her Ladyship's servants. A warrant was obtained in the course of the day against the defendant Richards, and, on the return of Lady Wedderburn in her carriage, at 3 o'clock, he was taken into custody by Stevens, the officer. Her Ladyship was then conducted by her solicitor, Mr Flower, to the door of her house, and, immediately upon her entering, the defendants Dodds and Moffatt attempted, in a violent manner, to obtain an entrance to the house. In the scuffle that ensued Mr Flower was struck on the breast by the defendant Dodds. Admiral Maitland [Anthony Maitland, then admiral of the blue, and later the 10th Earl of Lauderdale, was nephew of Tom Maitland, the late governor of the Ionian Islands], a friend of Lady Wedderburn, who happened to be passing at the time, now interfered, and succeeded in pulling Dodds from the door. The assistance of the police was then obtained, and the two defendants were secured, and conveyed to the station-house of the C Division. During the whole of the transaction the defendants, although several times questioned, refused to tell their object in attempting to force their way into the house of Lady Wedderburn.
>
> The defendants, in answer to the charge, stated that they had acted under the written directions of Mr M'Donald, a copy of which they produced. It was to the following effect: 'I hereby authorize you, and each of you, to enter and take possession of my house, No. 14 Chesterfield-street. May-fair, and also to take possession of the furniture and fixtures therein, and proceed to

take an inventory thereof.' This document was addressed to John Richards and George Dodds, and was signed James M'Donald and witnessed by Richard Moffatt.

Mr M'Donald was then called forward on behalf of the defendants, and, according to his statement, it appeared that Lady Wedderburn was inhabiting the house in question merely on sufferance. About six weeks ago he discovered that the conduct of Her Ladyship towards him was such that he could not consent to her remaining any longer in his house. He accordingly, by advice of his solicitor, authorized the defendants to obtain possession of it by stratagem or otherwise.

Mr Halls said that, however Lady Wedderburn might have acted, Mr M'Donald should have sought his remedy against Sir James Wedderburn, and not against his wife. The proceedings of the defendants were illegal throughout; for the lady being in possession of the house, whether lawful or not he would not pretend to say, ought not to be disturbed by threats or violence. He should, therefore, call upon the defendants to find bail, themselves in 40 l [pounds] each, and two sureties each in the sum of 20 l, to keep the peace towards Lady Wedderburn, and to answer any charge that might be preferred against them at the sessions.

Mr M'Donald was also held to bail, himself in 100 l, and two sureties in 50 l each, to keep the peace towards Lady Wedderburn, who declared that she apprehended personal violence from him.

She was right to be afraid of McDonald. On August 23 he broke his warrant and sank to a new level of egregiousness.

The *Times* of September 4, 1833 reported the trial at the Bow Street sessions:

Yesterday, the Rev. James M'Donnell [sic], of No. 13 Upper Brook-street, appeared before Sir F. Roe, Mr Minshull and Mr Halls, to answer to a charge of assault preferred against him by Lady Frances Wedderburn, the wife of Sir James Wedderburn, who is at present abroad. Her Ladyship came in her carriage, accompanied by Admiral Maitland and two ladies; and Mr Charles Phillips and Mr Flower, the solicitor of Hatton-garden attended professionally on her behalf.

Mr Alley and two solicitors appeared for the rev. defendant [sic], and a great number of witnesses were in attendance on both sides.

It may be remembered that about six weeks ago the rev. defendant was held to bail at this office to keep the peace towards Lady Wedderburn, and also for assaulting Mr Flower, her solicitor, and the transaction at present in question took place while the rev. gentleman was under recognizances which he entered into at that time.

Mr C. Phillips, after a few introductory observations, said he should at once proceed to call Lady Wedderburn forward to state the nature of the assault of which she complained.

Lady Wedderburn, who appeared to labour under the effects of illness, was then sworn, and stated that on Friday week, the 23rd ult., she was residing at No. 14 Chesterfield-street, when, between 3 and 4 o'clock in the day the defendant rushed into the house with so much violence that the servant who had opened the door fell against the wall. Witness was in the hall at the time, and the defendant, advancing towards her with something in his hand, struck her a blow on the head, which, however, fell upon her comb, and therefore did not hurt her. The defendant exclaimed, 'Now I'll be revenged upon you.' He then caught hold of her arm, and struck her other blows on the head, which she partly warded off by raising her hand, and her arms and hands were black and blue from the effect of the blows which she received. She struggled to get away from the defendant, who fell upon her like a tiger, and one of her maid servants, who entered the door at the same time with the defendant, took up an umbrella to defend her. If it had not been for that circumstance, she believed she should have been killed, for she felt convinced that the object of the defendant was to murder her. Another of her maid servants also endeavoured to defend her, when the defendant took up one of the hall chairs and flung it at her. She called murder as loud as she could, and her servant boy, who had run for assistance, returned with a policeman, when 12 or 15 ruffians, who had been hired by the defendant, rushed into the hall. Her Ladyship, in reply to questions by Mr Phillips, said that she showed the bruises she received to two doctors, one of whom was now present. She was allowed by the defendant but half an hour to pack up her goods and quit the house.

Mr Alley said he did not wish to be ungallant to a lady of rank and fashion, and therefore he should not cross-examine her, but merely ask he if she had been sworn?

Lady Wedderburn replied in the affirmative.

Mr Alley: Then I am instructed to say that in the statement you have made you have not spoken one word of truth.

Mr C. Phillips: That assertion is not very gallant on the part of my friend, Mr Alley.

Mr David Gregory, a medical gentleman, proved that on the morning after the fracas he saw Lady Wedderburn's arms and fingers, which exhibited marks of violence.

William Purdy, a lad in the service of Lady Wedderburn, proved that when he opened the hall-door the defendant rushed in and pushed Her Ladyship against the wall. Witness immediately ran into the street for a policeman, and when he returned there were several men in the hall.

Mr Alley: Was there not a poker behind the hall-door?

Witness: There was.

Mr Alley: By whose orders was it placed there?

Witness: I heard my lady order it to be brought there.

Mr Alley: Did you not see your lady strike the defendant two or three good thumps with the poker?

Witness: No, I did not.

Ann Terry, a well-looking and smartly-dressed young woman, deposed that she lived in the service of Lady Wedderburn, and at the time in question she was coming into the house, when the defendant struck her on the mouth, without any provocation whatever on her part. He then rushed into the hall, and pushed Lady Wedderburn with great violence against the wall. He then pushed a chair against Her Ladyship's legs. The sister of witness, who was also a servant in the house, called 'Murder,' and witness, seizing an umbrella struck the defendant with it in the head, but not until after he had struck her mistress and herself. Finding the top of the umbrella loose, witness seized the poker, and aimed a blow at the defendant, but did not strike him, as someone seized her arm. Some men then came to the door, and the defendant said, 'All who belong to me come in.' Five or six men then rushed in, some of whom appeared to be watermen, and took possession of the house. The defendant allowed Her Ladyship but half an hour for the removal of herself and servants from the house, but the time was subsequently extended to three or four hours.

Mr Alley: The fact is, the house belongs to my client, and he considered he had a right to regain possession of it.

Mr Phillips: Not by illegal means, Mr Alley.

Mr Alley then proceeded to cross-examine the witness, with a view to show that she struck the defendant on the head with the poker more than once. She denied, however, that the poker struck him, but said she conceived she should have been justified in defending her mistress and herself from the violence of the defendant as far as she was able.

Mr Alley: If what you have stated be true, no one could blame you, but I am instructed to say that you have fibbed from beginning to end.

Mr C. Phillips said that he had omitted to ask the witness whether anything passed between her and the defendant after the affray in the hall took place.

Witness: Yes, the defendant acted very rudely towards me about four hours after.

Mr C. Phillips: Explain in what way he used you.

Witness: He met me on the stairs, and followed me into a room, and while I was there, and no one present, he clasped me round the waist in a most insolent and indecent manner, and crushed my bonnet.

Mr C. Phillips: Pretty conduct for a clergyman.

The sister of the witness (also a very well-looking young woman) was then called forward, and proved that she saw the defendant strike her sister on the mouth at the street-door, and afterwards saw him strike her mistress in the hall, and kick the chair against her legs. She saw Her Ladyship's arms the next morning; they were quite black and bruised.

Mr C. Phillips: Did the defendant take liberties with you as well as your sister?

Witness: He did. About four hours after he got into the house he met me upstairs, caught hold of me round the waist, and attempted to salute me.

Mr C. Phillips: Indeed! Why, he is a perfect Don Giovanni.

Mr Alley: There was no harm in a little innocent embrace; and, as to a kiss, I don't wonder at it, when the temptation is considered.

Mr C. Phillips: Has your mistress, up to the present moment, obtained possession of her wearing-apparel, which she was forced to leave behind her?

Witness: She has not.

Mr Penny proved that he was tutor to Lady Wedderburn's children and resided in the house. On the day in question he was unwell in his room upstairs, and heard the witness Ann Terry cry out as if she was insulted by someone in a gross manner.

Mr Alley: It was nothing more than a struggle for a kiss.
(A laugh).
Mr C. Phillips: Oh! nothing more; a clergyman is accustomed to such things, and knows the most approved method, no doubt. It is rather a curious way, however, to make love, first to strike a lady in the mouth, and then kiss the spot to make it well again. I am sure that is not the way my friend Alley manages these matters.
(Renewed laughter).
Mr Alley: Perhaps not; but my friend must allow that it is no easy matter to kiss a lady now-a-day without spoiling the shape of her bonnet.
Mr C. Phillips: That is my case.
Mr Alley: I am instructed to deny, on behalf of my client, that he used any unnecessary violence whatever. He found the door open, and entered the house in a peaceable manner, when he was assaulted with a poker. The learned gentleman then called forward Charles Hall, who stated that he was a clerk in the employment of Mr Stevens, a broker, and on the day in question he went to make a distress at the house in which Lady Wedderburn resided. Witness and the defendant entered the street-door nearly at the same moment, and he saw the defendant receive a blow from the witness Ann Terry.
Mr C. Phillips: On your oath did he not strike her first?
Witness: Decidedly not. He did not use any violence whatever, but in less than a second after we got in he was attacked by Lady Wedderburn and her two servants, one of who, the witness Ann Terry, struck him over the head with a poker, and was about to repeat the blow when the weapon was wrested from her. Lady Wedderburn was very active with the umbrella, and called upon her servants to murder the ruffians. The defendant had no weapon in his hand, and merely raised his arms to defend himself from the blows that were aimed at him.
Mr C. Phillips: Do you mean deliberately to swear that all he did was to put his arms up to defend himself? Don't bow to me, Sir, but answer the question. We can't allege perjury on a mere bow.
Witness: He did nothing more than defend himself from the blows by raising up his arms.
Mr C. Phillips: Now, on your oath, did you see Lady Wedderburn strike a blow?
Witness: I can't say that I did; but she made use of abusive epitaphs.
Mr C. Phillips: And what were those abusive epitaphs, as you call them?
Witness: She urged on her two maids to the murderous attack on the defendant.
Mr C. Phillips: Did you hear her cry murder?
Witness: I did.
Mr C. Phillips: Was that while she was beating the defendant with the poker?
Witness: I can't say; she was fighting away as hard as she could.
Mr C. Phillips: And not a soul touching her?
The witness made no answer.
Mr C. Phillips: I am afraid, my friend, when it comes to your own epitaph, that you will be in a bad way.
Mr Langley Maddox, a broker residing at Maida-hill, proved that on the day in question he was employed by the defendant to take an inventory of the goods in the house inhabited by Lady Wedderburn. He saw the defendant receive a very rough compliment, to wit, a smack on the face, from the witness Ann Terry, and saw a poker raised to strike the defendant. Did not see Lady Wedderburn take any active part in the scuffle, except that she used language calculated to urge her servants to acts of violence. He did not see any personal violence offered to Lady Wedderburn or her servants.
Thomas Jane proved that he was in the service of the defendant, at No. 13, Upper Brook-street. He saw the witness Ann Terry strike his master, without any provocation, and he afterwards saw her with a poker in her hand attempting to strike the defendant.
The witness, in his cross-examination by Mr Phillips, said he was page to the defendant, but he did not wish to say what his duties in that capacity were. He subsequently admitted that he had lived with the defendant but a fortnight and that he was employed for the purpose of entering the house in which the complainant resided. He heard Lady Wedderburn cry murder when no one attempted to touch her.
James Wilson, who described himself as a general servant in the defendant's employment, corroborated the statement of the other witnesses for the defence with respect to the scuffle.
On being cross-examined he admitted that he had been but three weeks or a month in the defendant's service, that he was by trade a master dyer, and that the defendant used to employ him to scour and renovate his clothes.

Thomas Waters, a butcher out of business, saw the defendant shrink by the young woman, but did not see Lady Wedderburn attempt to strike anyone. Heard her Ladyship cry 'Murder' and 'Police.'

Thomas Smith, a waterman, residing at Deptford, came forward and produced the poker spoken to by the witnesses. Saw it in the hand of the young woman now present, and wrenched it from her as she was about to strike a blow that would have laid open the defendant's head. He was employed to assist the page, or anything else. He was not regularly engaged by the defendant, but only on liking as yet. His business was to wait upon the servants at the kitchen-table.

Mr Alley: That is my case, and as there is a cross-warrant obtained by my client against the witness Ann Terry, I submit that Mr M'Donnell ought to be heard.

Sir F. Roe said that it was rather unusual to hear two warrants arising out of the same transaction. After what had passed he conceived that the best course would be to refer the matter to the sessions, where both parties would have the benefit of a jury.

Mr Alley having conceded to this course on behalf of his client, Sir F. Roe said that as he was not called upon to decide the warrant in a summary manner, he should refrain from making any observations on the case, but simply call upon the defendant to put in bail on two charges of assault.

Mr C. Phillips: I hope you will remember, in fixing the amount of bail, that the defendant has already forfeited his recognizances, and also that he is under bail on a charge of conspiracy arising out of these transactions.

Sir F. Roe: I think, under such circumstances, that the bail I now require from the defendant should be hardly less than himself in 300 l [pounds] and two sureties in 150 l [pounds] each.

Mr C. Phillips, at the request of Lady Wedderburn, hoped that the magistrate would call upon the defendant to promise that he would not insult or annoy her Ladyship any more.

The defendant assured the magistrate that he had no such intention, and the required sureties having been put in, the parties retired.

Sir James, overseas, heard of the case and spluttered outrage in a letter written September 12, 1833, and published in the *Times* of September 18:

Sir, though I have neither the folly nor the vanity to suppose that what affects me can interest the public, the impertinent and vulgar letters signed 'James Macdonald' which appeared in the Sunday Times of last week, compel me, partly, at least, to break the silence which I had imposed upon myself in reference to his late conduct towards Lady Frances Wedderburne. When extreme ill-health and the (I trust but temporary) entanglement of my affairs induced me to go the Continent a year and a half ago I certainly assigned the lease of the house to Mr Macdonald, whom I then considered the oldest and most *unalienable* [italics in original] friend of Lady Frances and my family, under circumstances which will shortly be made public, and upon the most sacred assurances and confidence in my right, that Lady Frances could not be disturbed in the occupation of the house. How little, then, could I have foreseen or expected the brutal and un–English attack which by the magisterial examination of Mr Macdonald last week I see he perpetrated upon Lady Frances to gain the illegal possession of that house? Mr Macdonald knows I am incapable of vindictiveness towards any man, but the grossness of his conduct to Lady Frances Wedderburne compels me to adopt but one, and that a determined line of conduct in this business. Mr Macdonald is to be tried by indictment this session for the first part of these proceedings, and I have desired my solicitor immediately to proceed against him for the second and last assault. The assignment of the house shall be submitted to the Court of Chancery. Mr Macdonald will *then* [italics in original] see whether my determination and the laws of the country are not equal to the defence of Lady Frances. I am, Sir, your obedient servant, James W. Wedderburne. September 12.

The day after this letter was published, Magistrate Rotch, at the Middlesex Sessions, fulminated against persons of education sending him letters trying to influence a case. He was referring specifically to one sent very recently, by a man, and that involving the Lady Wedderburn case, although the judge did not actually name the case. Either Sir James wrote the letter, or the Rev. James M'Donald did. Either way, the case had already been settled out of court.

28

The Death of Lady Frances

On October 10, 1833, Lady Frances's sister, Lady Farnham, died. Lord Farnham would die in Paris on September 20, 1838.

Sir James, by now back in England, wrote to Henry Scrymgeour-Wedderburn on March 22, 1834, from 5 Baker St., Portman Square (this letter is in the Scrymgeour-Wedderburn papers), asking him for information to aid him in his suit v. Wedderburn, Colvile & Co., with draft answer in full (dated 29 March 1834) in which Scrymgeour-Wedderburn says that he is unable to give the requested information.

On August 23, 1834, at Norwood, near London, Bold Webster's daughter, Lucy, married the Rev. Alfred Caesar Bishop, an Oxford graduate who in 1851 would become rector of Martyr Worthy, Hants.

Another cause for familial joy was that James's brother Charles produced another child, a daughter this time, Rebecca Georgina, on September 22, 1834. Rebecca would live most of her life in France, marrying first a Monsieur Dufour, and later Léon-Jean Consigne. She died in 1890, in Paris.

Sir James wrote again to Henry Scrymgeour-Wedderburn, on November 13, 1834, from 15 Hertford Street, Mayfair (the final home together of Sir James and Lady Frances):

> Having been in Germany all summer and only lately sufficiently recovered from ye dreadful illness with which it pleased God to afflict me last year, I am only now enabled to reply to your extraordinary letter of the 29th March. As to its being 'out of your power' to give me the information I require as to the sale of an estate by which you recd 5000 pounds or more, I think I have some right to request an explanation of that. If you refuse me this, I shall give my Counsel your letter, & have it read in court when the Wedderburn suit is heard which will be very shortly, & the world will recognize in it a part of the friendly and honourable conduct which my father's family have met with from his relatives and friends in business.
>
> I don't know that any information you can give me will be of any great import to the suit. But I feel I have a right to the information which I again request you to send me, or a good reason for yr refusal to do so.
>
> Tho' it is a matter of perfect indifference to me how you address me, I think it proper to inform you that I have assumed the Baronetcy of Nova Scotia, since the death of Mr Charles Weddn of Pearsie, as the heir of my great grandfather Sir Alexander, that our King always receives me as such, ministers, &c, and that in consequence (now I think I am able to make it out) I shall have printed a case of all the law opinions which for years past I have taken upon my claim, proving it to be as good as that of any man to his lands which he now occupies. My duty to my son has imposed this upon me, tho' no one can suppose me weak enough in such times to care about the rank, &c. &c.

This last phrase of James's has a glare and a magnificence about it that must rank it with either the great self-mockeries of letters or the most startling self-delusions in history.

Number 15 Hertford Street was a suitable address. It had five bedrooms, a dressing room, two very nice drawing rooms communicating by folding doors, an eating room, a breakfast parlor, a spacious hall, water closets, a detached kitchen, housekeeper's and men-servants' rooms, pantry, larder, domestic offices, arched wine-cellar, and so forth.

Lady Frances's sister-in-law, Anne, wife of the 2nd Earl of Mountnorris, died on January 6, 1835. She had been Anne Courtenay, eighth daughter of Viscount Courtenay. On March 18 that year, Arthur Macleod, Lady Frances's nephew (son of her sister Hester), married Mary Bradley.

Lady Frances had sufficient income at this time to be a subscriber to the Rev. F.H. Hutton's volume of sermons. As did Master Wedderburn (i.e., her son Augustus). But then, heaven was a buyer's market.

On August 8, 1835, James's mother was widowed again. She and her son William Douglas continued on at Brigton, and in June 1846 she bought a winter residence, Carbat House, in the seaside town of Broughton Ferry, on the Firth of Tay, about a dozen miles from Brigton. Her Douglas son would spend some of his time at Brigton, managing the farm, but most of his life was idled away yachting.

James Webster-Wedderburn's first grandson, James Francis Joseph Wedderburn Bishop, was born at Thornton Beacon, Yorkshire, and baptized in nearby Thornton by Pocklington on November 8, 1835. This lad would grow up to be rather spectacular.

On March 2, 1836, Tom Moore wrote in his journal, "In talking of Lady Frances Webster and her having had the glory of captivating two such men as Lord Byron and the D. of Wellington, Sir Pulteney [Admiral of the White Sir Pulteney Malcolm, not long for this world] said that the Duke found time every day (I suppose while at Paris) to write some pages to Lady Frances. Told of himself (Sir P.) having sat next Webster at the Duke's table, without knowing who he was, and talked pretty freely to him [i.e., to Webster] about the liaison between his wife and the Duke, she sitting opposite to them. His [Sir Pulteney's] horror, afterwards, in finding out who it was he had been speaking to."

Five years elapsed between the filing of the Chancery suit and the first hearing on May 31, 1836. In November a judgment was made against the defendants. Yet still the case was contested, to higher courts.

On January 18, 1837, Sir James and Lady Frances's second grandson, Howard Arthur Wedderburn Bishop, was born, and a mere four days later, on January 22, Lady Frances herself died at her (and James's) home in Hertford Street, Mayfair, London. She was buried at South Audley Street Chapel Burying Ground. At the time she and James had been living apart for some time by mutual consent, he most of the time in Paris.

Quoting Paston and Quennell, "Zuleika, Genevra, the White Rose — already withered and drooping — lived on till 1837, thus surviving her lover [Byron] just thirteen years."

The *Times* of January 23, 1837, said, "On Sunday morning, at [her] residence in Hartford-street [sic], to the inexpressible grief of her family and friends, and after a long and melancholy illness, which she bore with Christian fortitude and resignation, the Right. Hon. Lady Frances, wife of Sir James Webster Wedderburn, Bart., in the 42nd year of her age. Her Ladyship was sister to the Earl of Mountnorris, and sister-in-law to Lord Farnham, Lord John Somerset, &c."

The burying ground in South Audley Street has now been laid out as a garden, and there is no record of her gravestone.

Lady Frances's nephew, Viscount Valentia, elder and now only son and heir of George, 2nd Earl of Mountnorris, married Frances Cockburn on October 21, 1837. Young Valentia died just over three years later, with no issue, thus terminating the line. On October 26, 1837, at St Mary's, Bryanston Square, the late Lady Frances's youngest sister (the younger of the two Juliana Lucys) married Robert Bayly of Ballyduff, nephew of William Bayly of Moreland's House, Kilkenny. Lady Juliana would still be alive in the 1850s.

In 1837 James and his gang brought suit in the Scottish courts to prevent the defendants in the Chancery suit disposing of any of their North Britain properties until the case was solved.

28. The Death of Lady Francis

Another sad coda, this time William Fletcher, Byron's old valet. The poet, it seems, in his death throes, had attempted to create a legal document whereby a certain annuity was to be settled on the faithful Fletcher, but marsh fever moved too fast. However, all was not lost. Augusta, Byron's half sister, made sure the valet got £70 a year, but by 1837 that had dried up and Fletcher, now in his mid–50s, was in deep financial trouble and working as a pickle warehouseman in London. John Murray, the publishers, and Ransom, the lawyers, and some other well-meaning souls had a whip-round for the poor fellow, but his fate is uncertain. One suspects that Byron's daughter, Ada, aided him.

On April 26, 1838, Sir James Wedderburn, Baronet (sic), was sued by Thomas of Bond Street, and tried in absentia. On May 2, 1838, James wrote to the *Courier* to explain that he knew nothing of it till judgment had passed, and that it was untrue that he was now within the rules of the Queen's Bench. (This letter is in the John Wedderburn collection.)

On April 29, 1839, James's second and third grandsons, Howard and Henry were baptized at Tichborne, Hants. Less than a month later, on June 20, 1839, Lady Frances's goods were administered in Westminster, and granted to her husband, Sir James Webster Wedderburn, Baronet (sic).

29

James's Death at Cooney's Tavern

On August 13 (although the *Annual Register* erroneously says August 6), 1840, a mere four months after his old crony Beau Brummell expired a raving syphilitic in Caen, Sir James died suddenly of a paralytic stroke brought on by apoplexy at *Cooney's Tavern* in Dublin (although the *Wedderburn Book* wrongly tells us it was on the streets of Dublin), aged 52 (the *Annual Register* refers to him as aged about 50, and calls him Sir Jas. Webster Wedderburne, knt).

The *Times* of August 17, 1840 reported:

> Ireland. Dublin. Aug. 14. Awfully sudden death of Sir J.W. Wedderburne, Bart. It is our painful duty to have to record the demise of the above-named baronet, which took place a few minutes to 11 o'clock last night, under the following most distressing circumstances. It appears that the deceased had been stopping for some time in this city, at Elvidge's Hotel, Kildare–street. He had dined and spent the evening of yesterday at the house of a friend in Harcourt-street. Between 9 and 10 o'clock he left, took a car, and called at one or two shops in Sackville-street, at which having transacted some business, he desired the driver of the vehicle to wait for him at the corner of the same street, turning into Upper Abbey-street. Some time afterwards, within 10 or 12 minutes to 11 o'clock, he went into the public house, 77 Abbey-street. He was accompanied by two females, and was shown up to the front drawing-room. There he seated himself on a box in a recess of one of the windows, and ordered the waiter to bring up two glasses of punch for his companions. One of the latter, however, declined drinking punch, and in its stead a glass of lemonade was ordered. The waiter was in the act of having the beverage prepared at the bar below, when a fall, as if of some heavy substance [a nice way to describe Sir James], was heard on the floor of the drawing-room immediately over head. He stopped till the drink was got ready, and he proceeded with it up stairs. There, on entering the apartment, he beheld the deceased extended on the boards, all but a lifeless corpse, breathing convulsively, but without the slightest motion of body or limbs, the females still seated, and looking upon the awful scene before them apparently with about as much emotion as they would the shivering of a drinking-glass, for the payment of which they might be held responsible. The waiter hurried off immediately for medical assistance. Dr Heron, of Sackville-street, was most prompt in attendance, a vein was opened in one of the temples, but all was over — the vital spark had fled for ever. Notice of the melancholy event was, without loss of time, communicated to the police by the inmates of the house. Mr Inspector Dunden went to the place. The two women in question were interrogated, and their account was, that the deceased had met and invited them to take a glass of punch; they, of course, consented; after they had ordered the drink, and the waiter had left the room, they observed him to suddenly laugh loudly, and then a change seemed at once to come over him. He begged of them not to feel alarmed, that he was subject to fits of weakness, and that this was one of these, but he would recover in a few minutes. In a moment, and almost as he spoke, he fell from the box on which he had been sitting, they occupying accompanying chairs on either side of him. He did not utter a word afterwards. He had not the slightest appearance of drink whatever on him when he entered the house, nor had he then ordered any for himself. The officer having given the women in custody to some of his men, proceeded to examine the deceased's pockets. A gold watch, some money, amounting to between 5 pounds and 6 pounds, a ticket from one of the steam packet offices, by which it appeared that he had paid his package to England for the following (this) day, his card, and some other matters, were found on him. A policeman was left in charge of the mortal remains of the ill-fated gentleman until a coroner's inquest shall be held on

them this day. Deceased appeared to be upwards of 50 years of age, of handsome countenance, but rather corpulent in person. In his walk he halted considerably, as if suffering from a paralytic affection.

The Times of August 18, 1840 (page 7, column e):

Inquests— Sir J.W. Wedderburn, died from apoplexy. From the *Dublin Freeman's Journal* of Saturday. "An inquest was held yesterday on the body of this lamented gentleman, the Lord Mayor presiding as Coroner, with a very respectable jury. Anne Cooney was the first witness examined. She stated that the deceased came into her house on Thursday night, accompanied by two females. There was no light, but he went upstairs, and immediately after called for two tumblers of punch for his companions, one of whom refused to take it, and he then ordered lemonade for her; she was in the act of giving what was ordered when she heard a noise above stairs, and when the boy went up he was lying on the floor. By one of the jurors:— he was not in the house more than five minutes when she heard the noise, and, on learning what had happened, she sent immediately for Mr Heron, of Sackville-street. Mr Alexander Disney was next examined. He said that the deceased, having dined with him on Thursday, left his house about 10 o'clock, apparently in good health. He had been complaining a little the day before, and after dining with him complained of feeling plethoric. He had one or two apoplectic fits some years since, but he (the witness) could not tell how long it was. He took very little at or after dinner, and when going away was perfectly cool and collected. He (Mr Disney) walked with him to the door, at which a car was awaiting to take him to Elvidge's Hotel, at which he was stopping, and having put his cloak upon it, drove off. By a juror:— He was brother-in-law of Lord Mountnorris. He had acted as aide-de-camp to the Duke of Wellington at Waterloo, where he was wounded, the effect of which was a slight lameness, and some years ago fought a duel with the present Earl of Harrington, then Lord Petersham, in which he was slightly wounded; neither that or the wound he received at Waterloo had, however, injured his health in the slightest degree. Maria Walsh, one of the young women, next deposed that she was coming up Sackville-street, near the print-shop at the corner of Abbey-street, when she perceived the deceased standing at the corner, and joking with some girls who were selling pocket-handkerchiefs. A female who was bare-legged was also talking to him, and he was in the act of following her into a lane facing Abbey-street, when upon turning round he saw the witness and her companion, and immediately walked toward them, saying, he had appointed to meet a poor woman with a child, to whom he had given some money before, and promised to give her more that evening, but she did not make her appearance. He then inquired if there was any place in the neighborhood where they could get a glass of punch, but the witness's companion refused to take any, and he then ordered her a glass of lemonade. She then asked him was he not going to take anything himself, when he replied, no, and added that the room was extremely warm. He then threw off his cloak, and told them not to be alarmed, as he had a fit often before, immediately after which he laughed very loud, and fell on the floor. She thought at first it was joking the deceased was; and the waiter having come into the room, he ran and took off his stock. The face of the deceased was, at that time, very flushed. The witness, in reply to questions put to her by the jurors, stated that she did not see him get off a car, and that it was about half past 10 o'clock when she first saw him smoking a cigar at the corner of the fruit-shop. A juror asked Mr Disney if he had any knowledge of what brought him to Sackville-street after he had left his house. Mr Disney:— He told me, when leaving my house, that he intended going to Mitchell's to buy some cigars; and fearing that his being found in that house, which he understood to be a very respectable one, might give the manner of his death a colorable complexion, he wished to state that he was an exceedingly charitable man, and possessed an enormous fortune. Thomas Neill, the waiter, deposed that having got directions from the gentleman to get a glass of punch and a glass of lemonade, he went downstairs for that purpose, and while there heard a noise above as if something had fallen. He returned very shortly after, when he discovered him lying on the floor, and upon asking the two females what the matter was, they desired him not to be alarmed, that the gentleman would recover in a few minutes. Not seeing him recover, he then ran across to Mr Heron's, in Sackville-street. Mr Heron was next examined.— He stated that he was called on about half past 10, or very near 11 o'clock on Thursday night; and when he saw the deceased he considered him quite dead; but not wishing to act by himself he sent for a surgeon to assist him. It was all, however, useless; and though he poured some spirits of anomine on his eye it had no effect whatsoever. By a Juror.— He unquestionably considered the cause of death was apoplexy. John Mullan, M.D., examined.— He deposed that

Surgeon Hatchell opened the body in his presence, and upon examining the head found sufficient cause for his death. The vessels on the surface of the brain were filled with blood, which left no doubt whatever that he died of apoplexy. By a Juror.— The fall he received could not have affected his head. George Hatchell sworn.— He was a member of the Dublin College of Surgeons, and, on examining the body of the deceased, found the cause of his death to be, that on the base of the brain there was a coagulum of blood, and in both temples; he was a person exactly fitted for an attack of apoplexy, having a short neck, and his person altogether such as would be easily attacked with such a fit. Mr Inspector Dunden here produced six powders in a paper, which the deceased appeared to have purchased shortly before his death. Mr Heron, on examining them, stated that in his opinion, they were Seidlitz powders, and, of course, perfectly harmless. Mr Dunden also produced a box of cigars, five sovereigns, and 10s. [10 shillings], in a purse, with a splendid gold watch, which he found on the person of the deceased. The Lord Mayor directed that all his property should be given to Mr Hamilton, the solicitor, who was then in attendance. The Jury then, without a moment's hesitation, found a verdict.— The deceased came by his death in consequence of a fit of apoplexy. Mr Disney said that the deceased was plaintiff in the great case of Wedderburne, by the decisions in which, given by the Lord Chancellor of England, he had received 400,000 pounds; he was also worth 20,000 pounds a year, and had considerable property in Ireland. The Lord Mayor inquired if any arrangements had been made with regard to the receiving of the body. Mr Disney replied that Mr Hamilton had made the necessary arrangements for having the body removed. It would be placed, in the first instance, in a shell, until they heard from the trustees of the deceased, after which it would be removed to Scotland, to be interred in the family burial place. He wished to ask his Lordship whether he would give directions to have the property found at Elvidge's Hotel to be given up to Mr Hamilton. The Lord Mayor said he had no power to give such an order, but was certain that all his property would be given up. Mr Hamilton observed, that he was then in possession of all the property which the deceased had at his hotel. The inquest then terminated.

An anonymous writer (but it had to a member of the family, one supposes, perhaps Lucy Bishop) had read these articles, and responded in the *Times* of August 20, 1840:

The late Sir James Wedderburn was knighted by George IV. His grandfather had been a baronet [this, of course, is an error committed by the corrector — it should have said great-grandfather], but through an attainder in 1745 that distinction was not descendible to heirs. He was not entitled under the Lord Chancellor's decree to any such sum as 400,000 l. [pounds], but only to a fourth share of about a fourth part of that amount, his proportion being greatly encumbered by charges and liabilities. Indeed, it is not supposed that any division of the sums involved in the Wedderburn suit can take place for many years to come, the accounts to be gone into being of the most complicated nature. Instead of 20,000 l. a year, Sir James having expended his original property, has been known for years as unable to fulfill his wish to settle the claims which his want of income created, and he has undergone privations of the most painful kind. Sir James quitted the Army in 1811, when he married Lady Frances Annesley, daughter of the late Lord Mountmorres [sic and wrong]. He was at Brussels in 1815, but positively did not act as aide-de-camp to the Duke of Wellington on that or any other occasion, neither was he present at the engagement. His lameness was from paralysis (treated by Mr Guthrie), and not by any wound. Lord Petersham, post Earl of Harrington, did not wound Sir J. Wedderburne in the duel which unfortunately took place between them. Sir J. Wedderburne never had any property in Ireland — Evening paper.

He was buried in Dublin. On November 6, 1840, administration of the estate (granted in Middlesex, by the Prerogative Court of Canterbury) of Sir James Webster Wedderburn, knight, late of Hertford St., Mayfair, was placed in the hands of his daughter, Lucy Sarah Anne Bishop, one of the natural and lawful children of the deceased.

30

Post Mortem

Only five days prior to the administration of Sir James's goods, his daughter Lucy had given birth to Herbert Alfred Bishop, at Tichborne, Hants. The Bishops would have twelve children in all, only three of whom would carry on the line, mostly in the Antipodes. Two of the daughters—Matilda and Frances—became college principals; one of the sons died in a ballooning accident; but only the eldest, James, would become a star.

Bold Webster's mother, Elizabeth Read-Wedderburn-Webster-Douglas, died at Carbat House, on September 9, 1857, aged 86. William, her son by her second marriage (to Douglas), had discovered a girl in Bond Street, in Westminster, and, as secretly as he knew how, was wooing her. His mother's death freed young Douglas to commit all manner of unpardonable sins. Within days he had sold the Broughty Ferry house and moved to Bond Street. The next few years saw a few illegitimate Douglas children produced by Miss Ellen Rigge and finally a marriage between the parents. Young Douglas died, amid lawsuits, on February 16, 1869, a credit to his deceased half-brother.

Then came James Bishop. After Marlborough, his health being fragile from infancy, he left England for Italy in the 1850s and became involved with the recently deposed king of the Two Sicilies, and was converted to the Catholic faith in 1860, at the time the Risorgimento was nearing its climax. He broke into the headlines in April 1862, when he was arrested for spying for the old Bourbon king and for engaging in treasonous activities to bring about a restoration of said ex-monarch. He was imprisoned for ten years. It caused quite a stir and became known as the "Bishop Case." The family intervened, and the case was debated mightily in the House of Commons, and eventually James was freed in November 1863 under a King's armistice.

Driven to it partly by having borne a dozen children, and partly by the strain placed upon her by the misadventures of her eldest son, Lucy died suddenly at Martyr Worthy on April 24, 1864. Mr. Bishop moved to Bramdean House, where he married again, on April 4, 1866, to Louisa Frances Katherine Legge, granddaughter of the 2nd Earl of Dartmouth.

Young James Bishop wasn't finished yet. He hit the headlines again, this time in Germany. He bribed a German sergeant to steal the mobilization orders of the Prussian Field Artillery. The sergeant informed his superior, and James was arrested for spying in December 1877. On June 25, 1878, he was tried by the Berlin Criminal Court and sentenced to 30 months imprisonment. It took his family again, notably his sister Matilda, to get him out, and he was pardoned on January 21, 1880. Then he came back to Bramdean and lived with his father. After that he disappears.

Bold Webster's son Charles Francis was an Army man in India. By his second of three wives, Ann Helyar, of Coker Court, Somerset, he had several children. He died in 1886. (Another Webster relation in the Army was James's nephew, Charles Adrian, son of James's brother Charles by his wife, Rebecca Chatterton. Charles Adrian was an Army captain. He died on January 16, 1885.)

Charles's second son, Arthur Augustus, became Inspector of Constabulary and Deputy Inspector-General of Police in Kingston, Jamaica. By his first wife, Katharine Elspeth Maude Hamilton, he had a daughter, Dorothy Hamilton Webster-Wedderburn. Arthur Augustus was injured in the Kingston riots of January 1891, and his wife died on June 5, 1907, as the result of having had both legs broken in the Jamaica earthquake of January 14 of that year. Arthur Augustus died in 1919. His daughter, Dorothy, is the mother of Tatton Hewetson. Gertrude Violet Webster-Wedderburn, Captain Charles's daughter and Bold Webster's granddaughter, was, by her first marriage, the ancestor of Simon Heneage. By her second marriage, she became Lady Savile. She died in 1912. Captain Charles Wedderburn's youngest child, Albert Annesley Webster-Wedderburn, went to Australia. His line continues in that country.

Augustus, Bold Webster's fourth child, died in 1845, in Jamaica, unmarried, and was buried there. The fifth and last child, George, also an Army man, married Caroline Dixon, whose aunt was Jane Austen's second cousin (the former Anne Austen, one of the world's first two women photographers), and whose uncle Dr. Fred Dixon, of Worthing, was one of the first dinosaur hunters and a geologist and paleontologist of the first water. Major George Webster-Wedderburn died in 1875. Two of his daughters became nurses (Frances was trained by Florence Nightingale), while the youngest of his seven girls, and by far the most interesting — Maude — decided to follow in the footsteps of her grandparents.

She married Henry Alexander Hadden, solicitor, son of F.J. Hadden, one of the great lace manufacturers of Nottingham and twice Lord Byron's third cousin. F.J.'s great-grandfather, John Innes, 7th of Edingight, was the brother of Byron's great-grandfather, Alexander Innes of Rosieburn. Another great-grandmother, Jean Duff, was the sister of Byron's great-grandmother, Margaret Duff.

The newly married Haddens produced only one child (this author's grandmother) before Maude ran off to Paris with Willie Rider, the publisher. The Hadden divorce provided scandal for the papers in 1902. Incidentally, Rider's daughter by his first marriage was the mother of Robert Newton, the actor.

Rider introduced Maude into the world of the occult, the Golden Dawn, Swinburne, MacGregor Mather, drugs and orgies. It was during this period that she became Maude Annesley, novelist. More than anything it was being one of "Aleister Crowley's girls" that spelled her doom. Her third husband, Major Harry Blaikie Brownlow, was forced to put her into Camberwell House, an asylum in Peckham, where she died in 1930, her mind shot to pieces.

Maude wrote a piece called "Byron and the Wedderburns," which was published in the *Illustrated London News* of April 19, 1924 (this author is in possession of the original typed manuscript). This was hot on the heels of the spring 1922 publication, by John Murray, of *Lord Byron's Correspondence*. Maude says, "During the time Byron was staying at Aston Hall, James Wedderburn's place, in 1813, his letters to Lady Melbourne have a considerable portion of them devoted to his great love for his hostess, Lady Frances Wedderburn. Later on he began his famous journal — undoubtedly, from what he says, to distract his thoughts. At the very beginning of the journal in November 1813 he says 'if this had been begun ten years ago and faithfully kept!!! — heigh ho — there are too many things I wish never to have remembered, as it is.'"

Sir James is mentioned in many contemporary and later references, albeit some in a cursory manner, or in passing. For example, Peter Quennell, who edited the 1950 standard, *Byron: A Self-Portrait*, calls James "an irrepressibly foolish personage, whose wife, Lady Frances, was destined to play a part in Byron's later career." John Gore, in his book about the Hardys, accurately says, "Webster was a bad man, a weak man, a bore and a buffoon." Tim Burnett, in his Scrope Davies biography, refers to Sir James as "James Wedderburn Webster, a somewhat asinine friend of Scrope and Byron."

André Maurois describes Webster as a commonplace, tow-headed young man, whom Byron

Maude Annesley, granddaughter of Sir James and Lady Frances Webster-Wedderburn. From the author's collection.

had known at Cambridge and later at Athens. He was "a chatterbox, indiscreet, awkward, always putting his foot in it — in a word, insufferable; but Byron was always indulgent to creatures of this species because of his sense of the comic." While Maurois's historicity is, at times, questionable, his assessment basically rings true, except that James Webster was far from commonplace. However, Maurois' explanation as to why Byron put up with James all those years is not only facile but wrong. Maurois simply never thought it out.

George Paston and Peter Quennell write, in *To Lord Byron*: "Some men achieve absurdity through force of circumstances; there are others whose destiny it is to be born absurd. To the latter class must be assigned Byron's much abused and considerably misused friend, James Wedderburn Webster, author of *Waterloo and Other Poems*. Whatever Webster did tended somehow to ridicule." These two writers conclude that "Bold Webster's fatuity was overwhelming." And they are right, except that James was certainly not born to absurdity. He truly worked at it.

James's "friendship" with Byron has long been open to question. That he knew Byron well is beyond doubt, but as to how friendly they were is a matter for calculation. Another question scholars have always asked is "why?" Why would Byron pick such a specimen as a friend?

All manner of explanations have been offered up to explain this, yet the answer is simple. Byron and Webster fell in together in 1806, when they were both a year or two short of 20. In those early days Byron more than tolerated James, even liked him. James was one of his set. There seems little doubt, given all the evidence and the prevailing opinion in those early days, that James was a buffoon even then, but he was still Bold Webster, daring, handsome, rich, well-connected, athletic, resourceful, and fun, and as such definitely a young man acceptable in any set (of that class). But Webster's decline into adulthood, his repeated demands for money (which he never paid back), finally wore Byron down to a point where he came to dislike the fellow, even by 1813.

That explains Byron's attachment to the young Webster, but how does one rationalize the continuing relationship between the two, which extended over the next decade or so?

Maurois offered the suggestion that the poet picked Webster as a friend for his amusement value. Many later scholars took up the Frenchman's cudgel, assuming he had inside knowledge, but all the time Maurois was just guessing. Others have put forth the idea that Byron kept Webster on mainly with Fanny in the back of his mind, and this is true, to some extent, especially over the 1813–1814 period. Yet others have hinted that it might have been a homosexual relationship, which is a totally uninformed stab in the dark. However, all scholars have agreed that there must have been more to James Wedderburn; it is just that nobody seems to have been able to find it.

Bernard Grebanier, for example, sums up the scholars' attitude to this question in his book *The Uninhibited Byron*: "There must have been some significant compensations in the friendship of Webster, but what they could have been escapes one. Did Byron enjoy him as the unwitting clown among his acquaintance? It is hard to believe that, for he was not usually one to suffer foolish men patiently for any length of time. Yet this friendship was of some date. It took years for Byron to weary of him, as he at long last did. But even then, it was unquestionably Webster's wife who supplied the complicating factor that soured the relationship."

Yet, having digested all this, the answer was there all the time. As Byron reminds us in his 1822 letters, on more than one occasion, it had been nine years since he had seen Webster. Byron and Webster had known each other since 1806. Those nine years, 1813–22, represent well over half of the entire span of their relationship. When Byron finally met up with James again in Italy he was, frankly, disgusted. What had enabled the relationship to exist over all those missing years was because they were ... missing. It was all done by correspondence. If at any time during that nine-year period Byron had run into Sir James, he would have ended the relationship then and there.

An interesting movie note: *The Iron Duke* (1935), starring George Arliss as Wellington, featured Walter Sondes as Wedderburn Webster and Lesley Wareing as Lady Frances Webster.

Bibliography

Annesley, Maude. *Byron and the Wedderburns.* Unpublished manuscript in possession of the author, 1924.
Bingham, Caroline. *The History of Royal Holloway College, 1886–1986.* London: Constable, 1987.
Burton, Anthony, and John Murdoch. *Byron: An Exhibition to Commemorate the 150th Anniversary of His Death in the Greek War of Liberation, 19 April 1824. 30 May–25 August 1974.* London: Victoria and Albert Museum, 1974.
Byron, George Gordon. *The Poetical Works of Lord Byron.* Boston: Lee & Shepherd, 1869.
Byron, a Self Portrait: Letters and Diaries 1798–1824. New York: Scribner's, 1950.
Clark, Roy Benjamin. *William Gifford: Tory Satirist, Critic and Editor.* New York: Russell & Russell, 1930.
The Creevey Papers. Northumberland Record Office (Ref: NRO 324/L.18/23 — refers to Lady Frances's correspondence). Diaries and correspondence of Thomas Creevey, MP, (1768–1838), natural son of Lord Sefton.
Davies, Scrope Berdmore. Contents of his trunk.
Despatches (1839) and *Supplementary Despatches* (1858) of the Duke of Wellington.
Edgecumbe, Richard (ed.). *The Diary of Frances Lady Shelley.* London: 1912.
Ehrsam, Theodore G. *Major Byron: The Incredible Career of a Literary Forger.* New York: Charles S. Boesen; London: John Murray, 1951.
Eisler, Benita. *Byron.* New York: Alfred A. Knopf, 1999.
Elwin, Malcolm. *Lord Byron's Wife.* New York: Harcourt, Brace & World, 1962.
Extracts from the Notebook of the Comtesse d'Assche, née d'Ives.
Fox, Sir John C. *The Byron Mystery.* London: Grant Richards, 1924.
Gore, John. *Nelson's Hardy and His Wife.* London: John Murray, 1935.
Gray, Austin K. *Teresa.* New York: Scribner's, 1945.
Grebanier, Bernard. *The Uninhibited Byron.* New York: Crown, 1970.
Gross, Jonathan David (ed.). *Byron's "Corbeau Blanc": The Life and Letters of Lady Melbourne.* College Station: Texas A & M University Press, 1997.
Gunn, Peter. *My Dearest Augusta.* New York: Atheneum, 1968.
Hardcastle, The Hon. Mrs. (ed.). *The Life of John, Lord Campbell, Lord High Chancellor of Great Britain, Consisting of a Selection from His Autobiography, Diary and Letters.* American edition. 2 vols. New Jersey: Frederick D. Linn, 1881.
Henning, Fred. *Fights for the Championship: The Men and Their Times.* 2 vols. London: Licensed Victualler's Gazette, 1900.
Jackson, Lt.-Col. Basil. *Notes and Reminiscences of a Staff Officer.* Ed. R.C. Seaton. London, 1903.
Knight, G. Wilson. *Lord Byron's Marriage.* New York: Macmillan, 1957.
Laforce, Patrick. *Wellington the Beau: The Life and Loves of the Duke of Wellington.* Gloucestershire, England: Windrush, 1990.
Lennox, Lord William. *Three Years with the Duke of Wellington in Private Life.* London: 1853.
Longford, Elizabeth. *Wellington: The Years of the Sword.* New York: Harper & Row, 1969.
_____. *Wellington: Volume II.* London: Weidenfeld & Nicholson, 1972.
MacCarthy, Fiona. *Byron: Life and Legend.* New York: Farrar, Straus & Giroux, 2002.
Marchand, Leslie A. *Byron: a Biography.* New York: Alfred A. Knopf, 1957.
Maurois, André. *Byron.* Trans. from the French by Hamish Miles. New York: D. Appleton, 1930.
Moore, Thomas. *Memoirs, Journals, and Correspondence of Thomas Moore.* Ed. Lord John Russell. London: Longman, Brown, Green & Longman, 1853–56.
Ogilvy Wedderburn, Alexander Dundas. *The Wedderburn Book,* 1898.

Paston, George, and Peter Quennell. *To Lord Byron: Feminine Profiles Based Upon Unpublished Letters 1807–1824*. London: John Murray, 1939. [Unfortunately, this book cannot be trusted. Its quotes from letters are so inaccurate as to render them seemingly different letters from the originals.]

Quennell, Peter. *Byron: The Years of Fame*. New York: Viking, 1935.

_____. *Byron in Italy*. New York: Viking, 1941.

Radford, Peter. *The Celebrated Captain Barclay: Sport, Money and Fame in Regency Britain*. London: Headline, 2001.

Schultess-Young, Henry (ed.). *The Unpublished Letters of Lord Byron*. London: R. Bentley, 1872.

Sitwell, Osbert, and Margaret Barton. *Brighton*. London: Faber & Faber, 1935.

Wedderburn Webster, James. *A Genealogical Account of the Wedderburn Family*. Privately printed, 1819.

Williams, R. *Royal Holloway College: A Pictorial History*, 1993.

Index

Numbers in ***bold italics*** indicate pages with photographs. Entries in **bold** refer to principals.

Abbey St., Dublin 195
Abbotsford (Walter Scott's home) 115
Academy of Sciences, Moscow 34
Addison (writer) 131–132
Adriatic Sea 120, 122, 135
Aeneid (poem by Vergil) 63
Agar, Felix (a blood) 24
Agar, George Charles 45, 62, 133
Aiken, Capt. (pedestrian) 15
Ainsworth, Sarah 121
Airlie, 3rd Earl (Ogilvy) 166
Alava *see* De Alava
Albany, London 88, 91
Albaro, Italy 153, 169
Albemarle, Lord 41
Albemarle St., Clapham 20
Albemarle St., London 84, 106
Alcon Malanzore: A Moorish Tale (by Stuart) 105
Aldeburgh, Suffolk 11, 92
Alder, William Rowland 164
Alexander, Czar of Russia 99
Alfieri (writer) 45
Allen, Mr. (lawyer) 170
Alley, Mr. (lawyer) 187–190
Almack's (London club) 141, 142
Alpine Journal (by Lord Byron) 115
Alumni Cantabrigienses (book) 12
Alvanley, Lord (dandy) 24
The Amicable Society 16
Angus *see* Forfarshire
Annesley, Arthur *see* Mountnorris, 1st Earl
Annesley, Catherine *see* Somerset, Lady Catherine
Annesley, Frances Caroline *see* Webster-Wedderburn, Lady Frances
Annesley, George *see* Mountnorris, 2nd Earl
Annesley, Henry Arthur (called Arthur; Lady Frances's brother) 18, *19*, 121, 149
Annesley, Hester *see* Macleod, Hester
Annesley, Juliana *see* Bayly, Juliana
Annesley, Juliana Lucy *see* Farnham, Lady
Annesley, Maude *see* Webster-Wedderburn, Maude Gertrude Annesley

Annesley Hall, Notts 35
Annual Register (publication) 18, 100, 194
Antwerp 94
Apsley House & Walmer Castle (book by Ford) 96
Arbuthnot, Harriet 99, 114
Argument (by Lord Byron) 115
Argyll, 6th Duke (dandy) 24
Ariosto (writer) 84
Arkwright, Sir Richard 108
Arliss, George (actor) 200
Ashbrook, Lady 125
Assche, Comtesse 94, 98
Asti, Italy 157, 162–163
Aston Hall 2, 31, 32, 33–85, 87, 90, 92, 111, 178, 198
Athens, Greece 16, 122, 199
Athol, Mr. (pedestrian) 15
Auchterhouse 176
Austen, Anne (photographer) 198
Austen, Jane (writer) 35, 198
Australia 198
Austria 165
Autissier, Louis-Marie (painter) 17
Avignon, France 89
Aylesford, 5th Earl (Heneage Finch) 38

Baartman, Saartjie (the Hottentot Venus) 43
Bacon, Sir Francis 36, 40
Bacon, Thomas 57, 78, 91
Bagshot, Hants 78, 91
Baker St., London 191
Baldwin, Charles (newspaper proprietor) 113, 174
Balindean 9
Ballantyne & Co. (printers) 138
Ballyduff, Ireland 192
Balmuir 8
Bankes, George 137
Bankes, Sir Henry 137
Bankes, William John 28, 29, 137
Barber of Seville (opera) 136
Barclay, Capt. Robert (pedestrian) 15
Barclays Bank 123
Barnes, Gen. 95
Barnet, Herts 10
Barry-Maxwell, John *see* Farnham, Lord

Barrymore, 8th Earl (dandy) 24
Barton, Margaret (author) 13
Bath, Somerset 126, 150
Baviad (poem by Gifford) 29, 107
Bayle, Pierre (philosopher) 40
Bayly, Juliana (born Annesley; Lady Frances's sister) 18, *19*, 81, 83, 94, 192, 92
Bayly, Robert 192
Bayly, William 192
Bazaine, Dominique 165
Beaufort, 5th Duke (Henry Somerset) 92, 97
Belcher, Jem (pugilist) 14
Bengal 33
Bennet St., London 34, 36, 37, 39, 66, 84
Bentley (printer) 176
Berdmore, Margaretta *see* Davies, Margaretta
Berkeley, Col. 95
Berlin, Germany 197
Berry, Duc de *see* De Berry
Berton, Gen. Auguste 170
Berwickshire (Scotch county) 106
Bessborough, Countess (born Lady Henrietta Spencer) 97
Bessborough, 3rd Earl (Frederick Ponsonby) 97
Best, Serjeant (lawyer) 113
Beverly, Yorks 62
Billiards 46, 181
Birkhill 132
Birmingham, Warws 33
Bishop, Rev. Alfred Caesar (Sir James Webster-Wedderburn's son-in-law) 191
Bishop, Frances (Sir James Webster-Wedderburn's granddaughter) 197
Bishop, Henry (Sir James Webster-Wedderburn's grandson) 193
Bishop, Herbert (Sir James Webster-Wedderburn's grandson) 197
Bishop, Howard (Sir James Webster-Wedderburn's grandson) 192
Bishop, James (Sir James Webster-Wedderburn's grandson) 192, 197
Bishop, Lucy Sarah Anne (Sir

James Webster-Wedderburn's daughter) 7, 32, 64, 100, 102, 150, 156, 170, 196, 197
Bishop, Matilda (Sir James Webster-Wedderburn's granddaughter) 197
Bitton, Isaac (pugilist) 13
Blachisserie, rue de la (Paris street) 94
Blackness, Forfarshire 5, 87
Blackwood, William (publisher) 99
Blade's Hotel, London 16
Bleak House (novel by Dickens) 180
Blessington, Earl and Lady 72
Blucher, General 88, 95
Bold Webster *see* Webster-Wedderburn, James
Bolingbroke, Lord and Lady 176
Bonaparte *see* Napoleon
Bond St., London 92, 138, 197
Bonnie Prince Charlie *see* Stewart, Charles Edward
Bordeaux, France 105
Borrow, George (author) 35
Boston, Mass 132
Boulogne, France 145–147, 150
Bourbon dynasty 88, 104, 197
Bow St., London 186
Bowdery & Kerby (printers) 138
Bowles, William Lisle (writer) 111
Boxing 12, 13, 14
Boyne (ship) 39
Bradley, Mary 192
Bradshaw, Mr. (dandy) 95
Bradshaw, Mr. (Lady Frances's uncle) 146
Brahe, Tycho (astronomer) 40
Bramdean House 197
Bride of Abydos (book by Lord Byron) 65, 70, 74, 75, 77, 86, 124, 153, 181
Brighthelmstone *see* Brighton
Brighton (book by Sitwell and Barton) 12
Brighton, Sussex 13, 14, 16, 26, 101, 136, 138, 143
Brigton, Forfarshire 9, 11, 32, 115, 150, 177, 192
Bristol, Glos. 16
British Library 123, 174
British Museum 139, 178
British Museum Catalog of Political & Personal Satires 139
British Press (publication) 139
Broadway, London 141, 143
Brook St., London 181
Brooks's Club 144, 145
Broughton, Baron *see* Hobhouse, John Cam
Broughty Ferry 192, 197
Browne, Sir Thomas (writer) 84
Brownlow, Major Harry Blaikie 198
Bruce, Michael 121
Brummell, George "Beau" (dandy) 23, 24, 29, 194
Brussels 32, 92, 94, 95, 97, 100, 102, 105, 113–114, 149, 151, 176, 196

Bruton St., London 10
Bryanston Sq., London 192
Buccleuch, Duke of 115
Buckingham, Duke of 41
Buckinghamshire (English county) 24
Buenos Aires 135
Bullen, Mr. 147
Buonaparte *see* Napoleon
Burdett, Sir Francis 121
Burghersh, Lord (i.e., Napoleon) 89
Burnett, T.A.J. (author) 3, 97, 123–124, 138, 174, 198
Bury, Lord 41, 45
Busby, Thomas 70, 105
Bute, Earl of 94
Butler, Dr. (headmaster of Harrow) 11
Butler, James *see* Ormonde, 1st Duke
Buzzard (Sir James Webster-Wedderburn's horse) 12, 13
Byng, Poodle 24
Byron (book by Eisler) 14, 26
Byron (book by Maurois) 41, 50
Byron, Ada (Lord Byron's daughter) 134, 193
Byron, Allegra 124, 132, 134, 137
Byron, Annabella (born Milbanke; Lord Byron's wife) 20, 37, 38, 84, 87, 92, 101, 102, 112, 114, 122, 134, 135, 138, 174, 180
Byron, Augusta *see* Leigh, Augusta
Byron, Caroline (Lord Byron's mother) 11
Byron, George Anson (Lord Byron's uncle) 120
Byron, Major George Gordon de Luna (forger) 37, 92, 102, 116, 134
Byron, Mad Jack (Lord Byron's father) 11, 34
Byron, Lord 1, 2, **8**, 89, 97, 100, 106, 111, 112, 114, 119, 121, 123, 124, 125, 128, 131, 132, 137, 145, 149, 153, 166, 176, 178, 192, 193, 198–200; affair with Lady Frances 33–85; aging 133; Aston Hall 32, 33–85, 87; bankruptcy threat 17; birth 11; boxer 14; Brighton 14; Cambridge 12, 16; contracts malaria 26; death 175; education 10, 11, 12, 13, 16; estate 177; Europe 15, 16, 17, 26, 37; forged letters to Sir James Webster-Wedderburn 37–38, 89, 102, 116–117, 134–135; forms university clubs 16; Genevra 76–77; Harrow 10, 16; homosexuality 30, 31; journal Nov. 17, 1813 70; journal Nov. 25, 1813 74; journal Jan. 16, 1814 80; *Alpine Journal* Sept. 22, 1816 115; Lady Sitwell's party 91; leaves England for good 114; letter to Augusta Leigh, Sept. 21, 1818 122; letter to Hanson Oct. 13, 1813 51; letter to Hobhouse, June 19, 1811 26; letter to Hobhouse, Nov. 2, 1811 30; letter to Hobhouse, Nov. 3, 1811 31; letter to Hobhouse, Nov. 8, 1811 31; letter to Hobhouse, Nov. 17, 1811 31; letter to Hobhouse, Dec. 15, 1811 32; letter to Hobhouse, Jan. 26, 1815 92; letter to Hobhouse, March 17, 1817 117; letter to Hobhouse, April 6, 1820 136; letter to Hobhouse, May 11, 1820 136; letter to Hobhouse, Dec. 14, 1822 155; letter to John Jackson Oct. 4, 1808 14; letter to John Murray, Feb. 5, 1817 116; letter to John Murray, March 9, 1817 117; letter to John Murray, April 9, 1817 117; letter to John Murray, Aug. 15, 1820 138; letter to John Murray, Nov. 9, 1820 138; letter to John Murray, Sept. 20, 1821 145; letter to John Murray, Sept. 28, 1821 145; letter to Kinnaird, Feb. 24, 1817 116; letter to Kinnaird, July 5, 1819 133; letter to Kinnaird, Dec. 1, 1822 154; letter to Kinnaird, Feb. 12, 1823 160; letter to Kinnaird, March 1, 1823 163; letter to Kinnaird, April 19, 1823 167; letter to Lady Frances, Feb. 21, 1823 161–162; letter to Lady Hardy, Dec. 1, 1822 154; letter to Lady Hardy, Feb. 17, 1823 12, 160–161; letter to Lady Hardy, March 28, 1823 166–167; letter to Lady Hardy, May 17, 1823 171–172; letter to Lady Hardy, June 10, 1823 173; letter to Lady Melbourne, Sept. 21, 1813 41, 42; letter to Lady Melbourne, Sept. 28, 1813 43; letter to Lady Melbourne, Oct. 1, 1813 20, 44–45; letter to Lady Melbourne, Oct. 5, 1813 45; letter to Lady Melbourne, Oct. 8, 1813 45–47; letter to Lady Melbourne, Oct. 10, 1813 47; letter to Lady Melbourne, Oct. 11, 1813 50; letter to Lady Melbourne, Oct. 1813 50–51; letter to Lady Melbourne, Oct. 13, 1813 51; letter to Lady Melbourne, Oct. 14, 1813 51–52; letter to Lady Melbourne, Oct. 17, 1813 52–53; letter to Lady Melbourne, Oct. 19, 1813 55–56; letter to Lady Melbourne, Oct. 21, 1813 58–59; letter to Lady Melbourne, Oct. 25, 1813 61; letter to Lady Melbourne, Nov. 22, 1813 72–73; letter to Lady Melbourne, Jan. 8, 1814 78–79; letter to Lady Melbourne, Jan. 11, 1814 79; letter to Lady Melbourne, Jan. 13, 1814 79; letter to Lady Melbourne, Jan. 15, 1814 79–80; letter to Lady Melbourne, Jan. 21, 1814 81, 91; letter to Mary Shelley, Feb. 24, 1823 163; letter

to Moore, Sept. 27, 1813 42; letter to Moore, Oct. 2, 1813 45; letter to Moore, Dec. 8, 1813 75–76; letter to Moore, Jan. 6, 1814 78; letter to Moore, Feb. 28, 1817 116–117; letter to Moore June 1, 1820 137–138; letter to Scrope Davies, March 7, 1817 117; letter to Scrope Davies, April 10, 1817 117; letter to Sir James Webster-Wedderburn, April 12, 1809 16; letter to Sir James Webster-Wedderburn, July 29, 1811 26, 27; letter to Sir James Webster-Wedderburn, July 31, 1811 27; letter to Sir James Webster-Wedderburn, Aug. 24, 1811 27, 28; letter to Sir James Webster-Wedderburn, Aug. 31, 1811 29; letter to Sir James Webster-Wedderburn, Oct. 10, 1811 29, 30; letter to Sir James Webster-Wedderburn, Dec. 7, 1811 32; letter to Sir James Webster-Wedderburn, July 25, 1813 34; letter to Sir James Webster-Wedderburn, Aug. 12, 1813 35, 36; letter to Sir James Webster-Wedderburn, Sept. 2, 1813 12, 39, 119; letter to Sir James Webster-Wedderburn, Sept. 6, 1813 40; letter to Sir James Webster-Wedderburn, Sept. 15, 1813 40; letter to Sir James Webster-Wedderburn, Sept. 25, 1813 42; letter to Sir James Webster-Wedderburn, Sept. 30, 1813 43–44, 105; letter to Sir James Webster-Wedderburn, Nov. 22, 1813 73, 145; letter to Sir James Webster-Wedderburn, Jan. 18, 1814 81; letter to Sir James Webster-Wedderburn, Feb. 20, 1814 83; letter to Sir James Webster-Wedderburn, Feb. 28, 1814 84; letter to Sir James Webster-Wedderburn, March 21, 1814 85; letter to Sir James Webster-Wedderburn, March 30, 1814 (or April 6) 85; letter to Sir James Webster-Wedderburn, June 11, 1814 90; letter to Sir James Webster-Wedderburn, Sept. 4, 1815 101–102; letter to Sir James Webster-Wedderburn, Sept. 18, 1815 103–104; letter to Sir James Webster-Wedderburn, April 16, 1816 114; letter to Sir James Webster-Wedderburn, May 31, 1818 120; letter to Sir James Webster-Wedderburn, July 25, 1818 122; letter to Sir James Webster-Wedderburn, July 2, 1819 132–133; letter to Sir James Webster-Wedderburn, Oct. 5, 1819 133–134; letter to Sir James Webster-Wedderburn, Oct. 26, 1822 153–154; letter to Sir James Webster-Wedderburn, Jan. 12, 1823 155; letter to Sir James Webster-Wedderburn, Feb. 2, 1823; letter to Sir James Webster-Wedderburn, Feb. 10, 1823 160; letter to Sir James Webster-Wedderburn, Feb. 16, 1823 160; letter to Sir James Webster-Wedderburn, Feb. 27, 1823; letter to Sir James Webster-Wedderburn, March 9, 1823 164; letters to Lady Frances 33; loan to the Websters 52, 55, 59, 73, 92, 114, 115, 133, 135–136, 145, 154, 155, 160, 167; Manton's 14; marriage 37, 114; meets Sir James Webster-Wedderburn for first time 10, 11; Newstead party 15; singing religious songs 76; will & testament 175

Byron: A Biography (book by Marchand) 26
Byron: A Self Portrait (book by Quennell) 198
Byron and the Wedderburns (by Maude Annesley) 198
Byron Correspondences 87
Byron in Italy (book by Quennell) 76
Byron: Life and Legend (book by MacCarthy) 18, 30, 41
Byron Mystery (book by Fox) 86–87
Byron: The Years of Fame (book by Quennell) 20, 42
Byron's Letters and Journals (by Marchand) 33
Byron's Poems (ed. by Coleridge) 86

Cadiz, Spain 37
Caen, France 194
Caen Cathedral 119, 151
Café de la Paix, Paris 136
Cairnie (Cairney) Lodge, Fife 113–115
Calais 146–148
Cam, Charlotte see Hobhouse, Charlotte
Cam River, Cambridge 16, 27
Camberwell House, Peckham 198
Cambridge (university) 12, 16, 27, 28, 30, 31, 41, 199
Cameron, Caroline (Lord Byron's prostitute friend) 14
Campbell, John 9, 10, 13, 50, 113–114
Campbell of Glensaddle 161
Cannes 163
Canning, Col. 95
Cape Town, South Africa 43
Capel, Lady Caroline 94, 96
Carbat House 192, 197
The Carbonari 170
Carew, Pike 146–147
Carib Chief (play by Twiss) 131
Caricatures 139–143
Carmarthen, Lady 34, 42
Carmarthen St., London 57, 63, 71, 74

Carr, John (architect) 33
The Castle (Bob Gregson's pub) 20
Castle Inn, Salt Hill, Bucks 24, 25
Castle Mahon, County Cork 155
Castlereagh, Lord 88
Cat Law, Forfarshire 5
Catholic emancipation 14, 30, 131
Cato 166
Cavendish, Deborah see Musgrave, Lady
Cavendish, George 178
Cavendish, Sir Henry, Bart (Lady Frances's grandfather) 18
Cavendish, Sarah see Mountnorris, Countess
Chalk Farm (dueling ground) 141
Chambery, France 156, 162, 165, 167, 170
Champs de Mars, Paris 89
Champs Elysees 89
Charterhouse (school) 180
Chatterton, Sir James, Bart. 155
Chatterton, Rebecca 155, 197
Chatterton, Thomas (writer) 84
Chaworth, Lord 35
Chaworth, Mary see Musters, Mary
Chaworth family 35
Cheese 42
Chesterfield St., London 29, 181, 183, 186, 187
Childe Harold's Pilgrimage (book by Lord Byron) 16, 26, 32, 35, 112, 120, 123, 125, 132
Ching's Lozenges 98–99
Christabel (poem by Coleridge) 111
Christie, James (London auctioneer) 10, 11
Christina, Queen of Sweden 135
Churchill, Charles (poet) 37
Clairmont, Claire 134
Clapham, Surrey 7, 8, 9, 10, 20, 21, 150
Clare, 3rd Earl (Richard Fitzgibbon) 155
Claridge, John J. 16, 30
Clark, Roy Benjamin (author) 107
Clarke, Mr. 167
Claughton, Thomas 51, 90, 121, 131, 137, 154
Clichy, Plain de 99
Clova, Forfarshire 5
Clubs 24
Cockburn, Frances see Valentia, Lady
Cockburn, Sir James (pronounced Coburn) 148–149, 159
Coker Court, Somerset 197
Coleridge, E.H. 86
Coleridge, Samuel Taylor (poet) 111
Coliseum (in Rome) 118
Colman, George (playwright) 32
Colville-Wedderburn 8
Comus (poem by Milton) 56
Conan Doyle, Sir Arthur (author) 8
Concealed Griefs (poem by Lady Frances) 74–75

Concorde, Place de la (in Paris) 89
Conduit St., London 10
Consigne, Léon-Jean 191
Constable & Co. (publishers) 115
Constantinople 134
Conversations with Lord Byron (by Lady Blessington) 72
Cooke, Gen. 95
Cooke, George Frederick (actor) 83
Coombe Wood, Kingston (duel site) 139–145
Cooney, Anne (publican) 195
Cooney's Tavern, Dublin 194–196
Corfe Castle 28, 137
Corfu 25, 26
Cork, Ireland 155
The Corsair (poem by Lord Byron) 67, 81, 86, 105
Cossacks 88, 89
Cottles House, Wilts (the Hobhouse home) 16
The Courier (publication) 193
Courtenay, Ann *see* Valentia, Lady
Courtenay, Viscount 192
Courtney, Lord 30
Courtney, Mr. 147
Courtrai, Belgium 171
Coutts Bank 160
Creevey, Thomas 101
Cribb, Tom (pugilist) 14, 74
Crimean War 94
Criminal Conversation 98, 142
Croce di Malta Hotel, Genoa 153, 161
Croix de Malthe *see* Croce di Malta
Croker, John Wilson (critic) 111, 116, 119
Crowley, Aleister 198
Crown and Anchor Tavern, London 121
Cruickshank, I.R. (engraver) 139, 141–143
Culloden (battle) 5
Cumberland, Duke of 5
Cumberland, Richard (playwright) 46
Cupar, Fife 9, 113–115
Currie & Co. 147
Curzon, Nathaniel *see* Scarsdale, 2nd Baron

D'Aix, Ile 97
Dallas, Robert Charles 84, 120
Dalrymple, Capt. (bigamist) 30
Dandies 23, 24, 29, 123, 139
Dandy of the Desert *see* Wilson, Sir Robert
D'Anjou, rue (Paris street) 166, 175
Dante (writer) 45, 84
Dartmouth, 2nd Earl (Legge) 197
Darwin, Charles (scientist) 35
Davies, Margaretta (born Berdmore; Scrope's mother) 16
Davies, Martin 20, 124
Davies, Rev. Richard (Scrope's father) 16

Davies, Scrope 2, 3, 14, 15, 16, 24, 29, 38, 43, 47, 92, 97, 107, 117, 123–30, 132, 137–138, 160, 174, 177, 198
Davies St., London 14
Dawson, Capron & Rowley (solicitors) 136, 167
Dawson, John *see* Portarlington, 2nd Earl
De Alava, Gen. Don Miguel 94, 100
Dean's Court, Wimborne, Dorset 26, 28, 30, 31, 32
De B, Madame 165
De Bathe, James Wynne 136
Debden Hall, Essex 152
De Berry, Duc 170
De La Warr, 4th Earl (George West) 39
De Lally-Tollendal, Elizabeth Charlotte 177
De Lally-Tollendal, Marquis 177, 179
De Lancey, Col. 95
De Luna, Countess 37
De Maryn, Capt. 152
Denon, Vivant (director of the Louvre) 105
d'Epernon, Duc 40
Deptford, London 190
Derby races 38
Derbyshire (English county) 18
De Ros, Lady 94
Despatches (by Wellington) 96
De Staël, Mme 114
Devizes, Wilts 124
Devon (English county) 69
Devonshire, Duchess of 28
Devonshire, Duke of 38, 52, 178
Diaries of a Lady of Quality (by Williams Wynn) 130, 174
Diary of Frances Lady Shelley 100
Dickens, Charles (writer) 180
Didot, Firmin (Parisian publisher) 106–111, 132
Disney, Alexander 195–196
Disobedience (poem by Milne) 132
D'Isson, Countess 163
Dixon, Annie *see* Wakefield, Annie
Dixon, Caroline *see* Webster-Wedderburn, Caroline
Dixon, Cecilia Pierina (born Gironci) 26
Dixon, Dr. Fred 198
Dixon, Capt. William 26
Doane, Mr. (lawyer) 184
Dodds, George 186–187
Dolphin Hotel, Southampton 126–127
Don Juan (by Lord Byron) 124, 134–135, 181
Donat 167
Doncaster Races 42
Doncaster, Yorks 42, 43
D'Orsay, Count (dandy) 24
Dorset (English county) 26, 28, 30, 31, 32
Dorset, Earl of 39

Douglas, 1st Bart. (born Kenneth Mackenzie) 151
Douglas, 6th Bart. 151
Douglas, Sir Alexander, 7th Bart. 151
Douglas, Anne (Sir James Webster-Wedderburn's sister) 7, 92
Douglas, Archibald Murray (Sir James Webster-Wedderburn's brother-in-law) 7, 92, 151, 180
Douglas, Elizabeth (Sir James Webster-Wedderburn's nephew) 7, 92
Douglas, Mary (Sir James Webster-Wedderburn's niece) 7, 92
Douglas, Robert (Sir James Webster-Wedderburn's stepfather) 9, 10, 11, 32, 92, 151, 197
Douglas, Sylvester 151
Douglas, Col. Sir William 151
Douglas, William (Sir James Webster-Wedderburn's half brother) 11, 192, 197
Douglas, William (Sir James Webster-Wedderburn's nephew) 7, 92
Douglas, William, of Brigton 9, 32, 92
Dover St., London 84
Doveridge Hall, Derbys 18
Downes, Mr. (pedestrian) 15
Downing St., London 175
Dragoons 12, 17, 94, 95, 165
Drury, Rev. Joseph (headmaster of Harrow) 11
Drury Lane, London 83, 131
Dublin 131, 194, 196
Dublin College of Surgeons 196
Dublin Freeman's Journal (publication) 195
Duels 152, 181
Duff, Jean 198
Duff, Margaret 198
Dufour, M. 191
Dunciad (poem by Pope) 37
Dundee, 7th Earl *see* Scrymgeour-Wedderburn, Henry
Dundee, Forfarshire 5, 6, 7, 8
Dunden, Inspector 194, 196
Durham (English county) 92
Dyer, Mr. (judge) 183

East & West India House 5, 6
Edgecumbe, Richard 100
Edinburgh 22, 74, 77, 99, 115, 134, 138, 178
Edleston, John (friend of Lord Byron's) 30
Edward, Isobel *see* Wedderburn, Isobel
Edward St., London 123
Egypt 107
Ehrsam, Theodore G. (writer) 37, 92, 102, 116
82nd Regiment 151
Eisler, Benita (author) 14, 26, 31, 56
Elba 88, 107
Elegant Extracts 12
11th Dragoons 12

Index

11th Light Dragoons 150
Elizabeth I, Queen 135
Elvidge's hotel, Dublin 194–196
Elwin, Malcolm (author) 13
Endymion (poem by Keats)
Enniscorthy, Ireland 30
Epistle to Robert Lloyd (poem by Churchill) 37
Epistles (by Horace) 32
Epsom Downs 14
Erskine, Charles 115
Erskine, Esme Stuart (born Eliza B. Norton) (writer) 105
Essex (English county) 152
Eton (school) 16, 29, 114
Euganean Hills 120–121
Every Man in His Humour (play by Jonson) 52
Examiner (publication) 141

Fairburn, John (publisher) 141, 143
Farewell to Thee, Scotland (by Sir James Webster-Wedderburn) 176
Farnham, Lady (born Juliana Annesley; Lady Frances's sister) 18, 191
Farnham, Lord (John Barry-Maxwell; Lady Frances's brother-in-law) 18, 191, 192
Farquhar, George (playwright) 55
Farrington Diary 13
Fawkes, Mr. 168, 170–171
Felix, J.H.
Fermor, Thomas William *see* Pomfret, 4th Earl
Ferney, France 152
Field of Waterloo, and Other Poems (by Scott) 106
Fielding, Henry (writer) 73
Fife (Scottish county) 9, 113–115
52nd Foot 7, 92, 151
Fights for the Championship (book by Henning) 12, 14
Finch, Heneage *see* Aylesford, 5th Earl
Fingal, Lord 31
Firbeck Hall 178
Fitzgibbon, Richard *see* Clare, 3rd Earl
Fives Court, London (boxing venue) 13
Fletcher, Ann *see* Read, Ann
Fletcher, Elizabeth *see* Wedderburn-Halket, Elizabeth
Fletcher, Col. Sir Robert 150
Fletcher, William (B's valet) 16, 82–83, 91, 193
Fletchers of Ballinshoe 150
Florence, Italy 120, 122, 154, 167
Flower, Mr. 186–187
Foley, Thomas, 3rd Baron (dandy) 24, 139, 141–145
Fops 23
Forbes, Mrs. 183
Forbes, S.W. (publisher) 143
Ford, Richard (author) 96
Forfarshire (Angus) (Scotch county) 5, 7, 9, 21, 150, 151

Forged Lord Byron letters 37–38, 92, 102, 116, 117, 134–135
'45 Rebellion (1745) 5
Foscolo, Ugo (writer) 121
Foster, Lady Elizabeth 52
Fouche (French minister) 104
Four Horse Club 24
Four-in-Hand Club 24
Fox, Sir John C. (author) 86–87, 125
France 32, 88, 94–104, 107, 113, 120–121, 131, 133, 136, 150, 152, 179
Frankenstein (book by Mary Shelley) 181
Fredolfo (play by Maturin) 131
Fryston Hall, Yorks 97
Fuller, Ann (Hannah) 183–185
Fuller, Charles 183–185
Furey, Edward B. 114

Galignani, Giovanni Antonio (publisher) 132, 134, 156
Galli-Curci, Amelita (opera singer) 37
Gamba, Count 153
Gambier, Samuel 10
Gay, John (playwright)
Gell, Sir William 181
Genealogical Account of the Wedderburn Family 132
Geneva 116, 152
Genevra sonnets 76–77, 81–82, 153, 181
Genoa 12, 72, 153, 155, 157, 159–161, 163–167, 170
Genoa Gazette 155
Gentleman's Magazine 18
George II 5
George III 8, 23, 136, 160
George IV 1, 13, 14, 22, 23, 26, 105, 136, 152, 165, 191, 196
George, Dorothy 139
Germany 191, 197
Gerusalemme liberata (by Tasso) 167
Giaour (book by Lord Byron) 35–37, 60, 69, 74–75, 106
Gibbs, Messrs 161, 165
Gibbs, Vicary 113
Gifford, John (judge) 121
Gifford, William 29, 107, 111, 116, 119, 121
Gight, Scotland 11
Gironci, Cecilia Pierina *see* Dixon
Glamorganshire (Welsh county) 29
Glen Prosen Company 5
Glenarvon (novel by Lady Caroline Lamb) 111
Glenbervie 151
Gloucestershire (English county) 16, 127
Goddard, Henry (policeman) 183–184
Godsall, Philip (carriage maker) 26, 28
Godwin family 124
Golden Dawn 198

Golden Square, London 10
Gordon, Caroline *see* Byron, Caroline
Gore, John (author) 198
Gottingen University 27
Gowen, Mr. 176
Grady, Mr. 147
Graham, Elizabeth (born Elizabeth Wedderburn; Sir James Webster-Wedderburn's aunt) 8
Graham, James, of Balmuir (Sir James Webster-Wedderburn's uncle) 8
Grampians 77, 166
Grand Canal (in Venice) 120, 122
Grantley, Lord 40, 164
Gray, Austin K. (author) 20, 154, 157, 167
Great College St., London 180
Great North Road 10
Grebanier, Bernard (author) 31–32, 111–112, 200
Greece 16, 26
Green Park, London 28
Gregory, David (doctor) 188
Gregson, Bob (pugilist) 13, 20
Grenadier Guards 29
Greville, Charles Cavendish Fulke 139, 143
Greville, Lady Charlotte 99, 114
Greville family 94
Grey, Countess (born Mary Elizabeth Ponsonby) 62
Grey, 2nd Earl 62, 97
Grey de Ruthyn, Lord 14
Gronow, Capt. Rees Howell 14, 29
Grosvenor Sq., London 178
Grosvenor St., London 10
The Guards (anonymous novel) 176
Guiccioli, Count 133, 136
Guiccioli, Teresa 132, 135–136, 153, 156, 167
Gully, John (pugilist) 13
Gunn, Peter (author) 41
Gurwood, Col. 96
Guthrie, Mr. (doctor) 196

Hadden, Betty Valentia *see* Stewart, Betty Valentia
Hadden, Frederick John 198
Hadden, Henry Alexander 198
Haigh, John (shopman) 184
Hall, Charles (clerk) 189
Halls, Mr. (magistrate) 187
Hamilton, Anthony (writer) 52
Hamilton, Katharine 98
Hamilton, Mr. (lawyer) 196
Hamilton Place, London 143, 144
Hammersley, Thomas (banker) 160
Hammersley & Co. (bankers) 160, 165, 171
Hammersmith, London 25
Hampshire (English county) 45, 57, 70, 78, 126–127, 191, 193, 197
Hanger, Col. (dandy) 24
Hans Carnal/Carvel 92–93
Hanson, John (Lord Byron's

lawyer) 17, 51–52, 93, 136, 154, 164, 167
Hanson, Mary Anne *see* Portsmouth, Lady
Harcourt St., Dublin 194
Hardwicke, 3rd Earl 169
Hardy, Admiral 153
Hardy, Lady Anne 12, 153, 155–156, 178
Hare, Naylor 28, 29
Harmer, Alderman 186
Harmer & Flower 186
Harnish House, Wilts 151
Harrington, 3rd Earl 38, 139, 141
Harrow (school) 10, 11, 12, 16, 39, 136
Hastings House 92
Hatchard's (London publishers) 176
Hatchell, George (surgeon) 196
Hatfield 40
Hatton Garden, London 186
Havre (Le Havre), France 120–121
Hawke, Lord 24
Hawkins, Sir Caesar, 1st Bart. 151
Hawkins, George (Sir James Webster-Wedderburn's brother-in-law) 7, 43, 133, 151, 180
Hawkins, John 151
Hawkins, Mary (Sir James Webster-Wedderburn's sister) 7, 150, 180
Haydon, B.R. (painter) 89
Heath, W. (engraver) 143
Heaven and Earth (by Lord Byron) 149
Helen of Troy 52
Hellespont 16
Helyar, Ann 197
Helyar, Gertrude Violet *see* Savile, Lady
Heneage, Simon 94, 139, 140, 152, 198
Henning, Fred (boxing author) 12, 13, 14, 20
Heron, Dr. 194–196
Hertford, Lord (dandy) 24
Hertford St., London 191, 192, 196
Hertfordshire (English county) 10, 13, 21, 150
Heutsch (Swiss banker) 116
Hewetson, Capt. (pedestrian) 15
Hewetson, Tatton 8, 150, 198
Historical Memoirs of Napoleon 155
History of Duelling (book by Millingen) 145
Hitler, Adolf 105
Hobhouse, Ben (John Cam's father) 16, 83
Hobhouse, Charlotte (born Cam; John Cam's mother) 16
Hobhouse, John Cam 14, 16–17, 20, 30–32, 39, 62, 70, 83, 95, 112, 116, 121, 123, 128, 134, 136, 138, 165, 177, 180
Hodgson, Francis 28, 29, 30, 92, 93, 177
Hodgson, James T. 93
Holborn, London 20

Holford, Miss (poet) 111
Holland family 97
Holland House, London 37, 44
Holmes, James (painter) 73, 75
Holte family 33
Home, James, of Linhouse (Lyon depute, Scotland) 21, 22
Home Office 9, 11
Homosexuality 28, 30, 31, 44
Horace (writer) 32, 43, 132, 177
Hornby, Capt. 26
Hornby, Rev. George 26
Horne, Mr. (lawyer) 150
Horse racing 38, 40, 42
Horsley, Glos. 16
Horton, Anne *see* Wilmot, Mrs
Hottentot Venus *see* Baartman, Saartjie
Howard, Charles *see* Norfolk, Duke of
Howe, Mr. (pedestrian) 15
Hughes, Golden Ball (dandy) 24, 176
Hume, Dr. John 94
Humphrey, G. (printer) 139, 142
Hunt, John (publisher; brother of Leigh Hunt) 160
Hunt, Leigh 160, 163
Hunter, Mr., of Blackness 177
Huntingdonshire (English county) 42
Huntsbourne Park 164
Hurt, Sitwell *see* Sitwell, Sir Sitwell, Bart.
Hussars 1, 12, 16, 17, 94–95, 121, 139, 142, 161
Hutchinson, Col. 107
Hutchinson, Mrs. 158
Hutton, Rev. F.H. 192
Hyde, Dr. 170, 176

India House 9
Innes, Alexander, of Rosieburn 198
Innes, John, 7th of Edingight 198
Inveresk 8
Ionian Islands 186
Ipswich, Suffolk 12, 13
Ireland 14, 18, 31, 131, 155, 165, 192, 194, 196
Iron Duke (movie) 200
Iron Duke *see* Wellington
Irving, Washington (writer) 176
Islington, London 16
Italiana in Algeri (opera) 176

Jackson, Basil 78, 98
Jackson, Gentleman John (pugilist) 12, 14, 28, 40, 43, 136–138
Jacobites 5
Jamaica 5, 121, 198
Jane, Thomas (servant) 189
Jeffreys, Mr. 148
Jersey, 5th Earl (George Villiers) 46, 78
Jocelyn, Robert *see* Roden, 3rd Earl
Johnson, Samuel (writer) 116
Jones, Mr. (pawnbroker) 183

Jonson, Ben (playwright) 52
Journal des Débats 165
Journal of H.E. Fox 142–143
Joy, William (painter) 150
Junot, Marshal 99

Kean, Edmund (actor) 83
Keats, John (poet) 111
Kedleston Hall, Derbys 37
Kelston House, Somerset 151
Kemble, John Philip (actor) 83
Kennedy, Lord 106
Kent (English county) 133
Kerby, Edward (printer) 138
Kerr, John (herald, Scotland) 22
Kerr, Mr. (friend of Petersham's) 145
Kildare St., Dublin 194
Kilkenny 192
King's Case Stated (by Sir James Webster-Wedderburn) 152
King's Palace, London 180
Kingston, Jamaica 198
Kingston, Surrey 139
Kinnaird, 7th Baron 114
Kinnaird, Douglas 114, 116, 121; *see also* letters by Lord Byron
Kinnoull, Earl of 21
Knight, Col. 147
Knight, G. Wilson (author) 76
Knight, Henry Gally (writer) 111, 178
Knighthood 21, 22

Lade, Sir John 24
Lady Jane Grey (poem by Hodgson) 28, 29
Laforce, Patrick (author) 89, 99
Laglandiere, Eugene 176
Lake (Sir James Webster-Wedderburn's servant) 147, 167
Lally-Tollendal *see* De Lally-Tollendal
Lamb, Lady Caroline (wife of 2nd Lord Melbourne) 20, 44, 49, 60–62, 73, 81, 95, 97, 99–101, 103–105, 111, 114, 121, 123
Lamb, Peniston *see* Melbourne, 1st Viscount
Lamb, William *see* Melbourne, 2nd Viscount
La Mira (near Venice) 117
Lancashire (English county) 30
Langham, Suffolk 11
Langham House, Suffolk 11
Lara (by Byron) 86
Latin 10
Lauderdale, 10th Earl (Anthony Maitland) 186–187
Lausanne 83, 161–162, 165–166, 168
Lavalette, Count Marie (deluded Napoleoniste) 107, 121
Lawrence, Sir Thomas (painter) 105
Leadenhall Street, London 6, 8
Legge, Louisa (2nd wife of Rev. Mr. Bishop) 197
Leghorn, Italy 155
Le Haye 95

Index

Leicester Sq., London 13
Leicestershire (English county) 136
Leigh, Augusta (Lord Byron's half sister) 34, 36, 41, 43–44, 47, 78, 84, 87, 92–93, 112, 120, 125, 127–128, 131, 135, 145, 175, 193
Leigh, Elizabeth Medora 36, 81–82, 120–121
Leigh, Col. George 36, 38, 92–93
Leigh, Georgiana 120
Lennox, William 100
Lens, Serjeant (lawyer) 113
Lerici, Italy 154
Lethbridge, Mr. 165
Letter to a Friend (by Browne) 84
Letters and Journals of Lord Byron (by Marchand) 86
Letters of Jacopo Ortis (by Foscolo) 121
Letters to Metternich (by Lieven) 139
Lewes, Sussex 16
The Liberal (publication) 160
Lido, Venice 135
Lieven, Dorothea, Princess 95, 139
Life and Letters of Lady Melbourne 20
Life of Byron (book by Moore) 180
Life of John, Lord Campbell 9
Light Dragoons 12, 94
Lille 89, 168, 169, 171
Lincoln's Inn 10, 13
Lion (man o' war) 13
Lisbon, Treaty of 88
Livingstone, David (explorer) 35
Logie, Forfarshire 7
Loire, River 96, 132
London 6, 7, 10, 11, 12, 13, 14, 16, 18, 23, 26, 27, 30, 32, 36–37, 39, 55–56, 63, 74, 81–84, 89–90, 97, 104, 114, 120–121, 131, 135–136, 138–139, 141, 143, 165, 170, 178, 181, 183, 186, 189–193, 196
London Spy (publication) 139
Long Acre, London 26
Longford, Elizabeth (author) 12, 94–95, 98, 114
Longman, Hunt, Rees, Orme & Brown (publishers) 115
Long's Hotel, London 92
Lord Byron's Correspondence 198
Lord Byron's Marriage (book by Knight) 76
Lord Byron's Wife (Elwin) 13
Lord Lyon King of Arms 21, 22
Louis XVIII 88, 108
Louvel, Louis Pierre (assassin) 170
Louvre (Paris art gallery) 88, 105
Lovelace, Earl of 134
Lucien (poet) 101
Lucretius (translated by Busby) 70, 105
Ludgate Hill, London 141, 143
Lumley, John *see* Scarborough, 8th Earl
Luxembourg, Paris 89
Lyttelton, Lord 28
Lyttelton, Lucy 18

Macaronis 23
MacCarthy, Fiona (author) 14, 18, 30, 41
Mackenzie, Kenneth *see* Douglas, 1st Bart. of Glenbervie
Mackintosh, Sir James 44
Macleod, Arthur (Lady Frances's nephew) 192
Macleod, Hester Annabella (born Annesley; Lady Frances's sister) 18, 179, 192
Macleod, Maj. Gen. Norman (Lady Frances's brother-in-law) 179
Maddox, Langley (broker) 189
Madeleine, rue de la (Paris street) 106–107
Madras 150
Mahon, Castle *see* Castle Mahon
Maida Hill, London 189
Maitland, Anthony *see* Lauderdale, 10th Earl
Maitland, Tom 186
Major Byron (book by Ehrsam) 37
Malapeyre, Mr. 167
Malcolm, Sir Pulteney 192
Malta 16
Malthen, Gen. 88
Manchester Sq., London 184
Mansfield, Notts 35
Manton, Joe (gunsmith) 14
Manton's shooting gallery, London 14, 141
Marchand, Leslie (author) 26, 33, 86
Margaret of Anjou (poem by Miss Holford) 111
Marks, J.L. (engraver) 141
Marlborough (school) 197
Marlborough St., London 183
Martyr Worthy, Hants 191, 197
Maryn *see* De Maryn
Mather, MacGregor 198
Mathias, T.J. (poet) 29
Matthews, Charles Skinner 13, 15, 16, 27, 28, 29
Matthews, Mr. 176
Maturin, Charles Robert (playwright) 131
Maurois, Andre (author) 20, 41–42, 48–50, 198
Maxwell, Murray 121
May, Penelope 183–185
Mayfair, London 29, 181, 183, 191–192
M'Donald, Rev. James 181, 183–184, 186–190
Mediterranean 39
Melbourne, Lady (born Elizabeth Milbanke) 20, 33–85, 95, 198
Melbourne, 1st Viscount (born Peniston Lamb) 20
Melbourne, 2nd Viscount (William Lamb; the PM) 20, 103–104
Mellish, Capt. Henry Francis "Harry" (a blood) 13
Melrose, Scotland 115
Memoir of the Rev. Francis Hodgson 93

Memoirs of Count de Grammont (by Hamilton) 52
Mendoza, Daniel (pugilist) 14
Menin, Belgium 168, 171
Meredith 132
Messenger (publication) 132
Metamorphoses (Ovid) 10
Metternich (French minister) 95
Middlesex (English county) 181, 196
Middleton Park, Oxon 46, 69, 71
Milan, Italy 116
Milbanke, Annabella *see* Byron, Annabella
Milbanke, Elizabeth *see* Melbourne, Lady
Milbanke, Lady (born Judith Noel) 37, 122
Milbanke, Sir Ralph, 5th Bart. 20
Milbanke, Sir Ralph, 6th Bart. 20, 37
Milbanke family 134
Mildmay, Sir Henry (dandy)
Milky Dandy 101
Millingen, John Gideon (author) 145
Milne, A.A. 132
Milnes, Robert Pemberton 97
Milton, John 56
Minshull, Mr. (magistrate) 187
Mira, La *see* La Mira
Miscellanous (poems by Sir James Webster-Wedderburn) 105
Missionary of the Andes (by Bowles) 111
Missolonghi 175
Mitchell's Cigar Store, Dublin 195
Mocenigo (palazzo) 120, 122
Moffatt, Richard 186–187
Moira, 2nd Earl (Francis Rawdon) 14, 104–105, 167
Month at Goodspeed's Bookshop 132
Moody, James (shopman) 184
Moore, Peter (politician) 131
Moore, Thomas 14, 16, 34, 45, 56, 76, 84, 86, 124–125, 136–137, 145, 177–178, 180, 192
Moreland's House, Kilkenny 192
Morgan, Capt. (Major) 13, 24
Morning Chronicle see St. James's Morning Chronicle
Morning Post (newspaper) 31, 139
Morritt, John Bacon Sawrey (traveler, scholar) 115
Moscow, Russia 34
Mountnorris, Countess (born Sarah Cavendish; Lady Frances's mother) **18–19**, 78, 94–95, 98, 102, 112, 121, 148, 150, 170
Mountnorris, 1st Earl (Arthur Annesley; Lady Frances's father) 1, 10, 18, 20, 21, 39, 81, 83, 95, 113, 115, 150, 192, 196
Mountnorris, 2nd Earl (George Annesley; Lady Frances's brother) 18, 20, 26, 30, 121, 148–149, 163, 195
Mullan, John (doctor) 195

Index

Murphy, Arthur (playwright) 47
Murray, Joe (Lord Byron's butler) 34, 36, 38, 39, 102, 138
Murray, John (Lord Byron's publisher) 2, 15, 35, 106–107, 114, 116–117, 128, 134, 181, 193, 198
Murray Archives 2
Musgrave, Lady (Lady Frances's aunt; born Deborah Cavendish) 171
Musgrave, Sir Richard, 1st Bart. 171
Musters, Jack 35
Musters, Mary (born Chaworth) 35, 79
My Dearest Augusta (book by Gunn) 41

Nairn (Scotch county) 44
Nantes 123, 131–132, 149–151, 168
Naples 120, 122, 181
Napoleon 24, 70, 83, 88–89, 96–97, 103–105, 109, 112, 116, 163, 165, 171
National Library of Scotland 2
Neill, Thomas (waiter) 195
Nelson, Lord 153
Netherlands, King of the 95, 96
Nettle (Lord Byron's dog, a gift from W) 42, 43
New Monthly Magazine 131
Newby Wiske, Yorks 32
Newmarket 13
Newstead Abbey, Notts (Lord Byron's home) 13, 15, 16–17, 26–30, 33–34, 36, 40–41, 43, 47, 50–52, 55–56, 60, 64, 73, 80, 82, 90, 92, 102, 121, 131, 133, 136–137, 177
Newton, Marjorie Balfour Rider 198
Newton, Robert (actor) 198
Ney, Marshal 103, 107
Nightingale, Florence 198
91st Regiment 151
9th Dragoons 95
Noel, Edward *see* Wentworth, 1st Viscount
Noel, Judith *see* Milbanke, Lady
Noel, Sophia *see* Scarsdale, Lady
Noel family 134
Norfolk, Duke of (Charles Howard; a dandy) 24
Normandy, France 120
Normanton, Lord 45
Northamptonshire (English county) 55
Norton, Eliza B. *see* Erskine, Esme Stuart
Norwood, Surrey 191
Notes and Reminiscences of a Staff Officer (by Jackson) 98
Nottingham, Notts 198
Nottinghamshire (English county) 14, 32–33, 35, 70, 83, 92, 121, 154, 198

Odes (by Horace) 177
Ogilvy, Lady Helen 166

Ogilvy, Lord 5
Ogilvy, Thomas Wedderburn 70
Old Bailey 183
Old Bond St., London 160
Old Pretender *see* Stewart, James
O'Meara, B.E. (translator) 155
102nd Regiment 45
Opposition (term coined by Hobhouse) 62
Orange, Prince of 96
Ord, The Misses 94
Ord, William 94
Ormonde, 1st Duke (James Butler) 62
Orsi, Leonart (banker) 167, 170
Ossian (poet) 109
Ossulstone, Lord 73
Ostend 92, 169, 177
Ovid (poet) 10, 83
Oxford, Lady 44, 51, 145
Oxford, Oxon 45, 191
Oxford St., London 138
Oxfordshire (English county) 46

Pack Horse (inn) 24
Paine, Tom 116
Pakenham, Capt., R.A. 94
Palafox, Gen. 109
Pall Mall, London 9, 10, 123, 160, 171
Palmer, Col. Charles 139, 142–143
Paris 32, 85, 88, 89, 92, 96–100, 104–107, 111–112, 114–115, 121, 136–138, 145–146, 149–150, 152, 156–159, 161–162, 167–168, 170–171, 176–177, 179, 191–192
Paris After Waterloo (by Simpson) 99
Park St., London 178
Parker, J. (judge) 182
Partridge (astrologer) 117
Partridge, Henrietta (landlady) 24, 25
Paston, George (author) 2, 40, 48, 49, 56, 82, 97, 152, 155, 167–168, 175, 192, 199
Paternoster Row, London 115
Pearsie, Forfarshire 5, 6, 8, 150, 178
Peckham, London 198
Peel, Robert 176
Penny, Mr. (tutor to Lady Frances's children) 188
Perregeaux, Messrs (bankers) 89
Perry, James (newspaper proprietor) 116, 117
Personal Recollections of the Great Duke of Wellington 94
Petersham, Viscount (Charles Stanhope) 24, 38, 41–45, 105, 139–145, 154, 195–196
Phillips, Charles 187
Phillips, Mr. (lawyer) 183–184
Phocion (ed. by Porson) 30
Piccadilly, London 32, 39, 70, 115, 133, 135–138, 141, 143
Piccadilly Terrace, London 101–103
Picton, Gen. 95
Piedmont (in Italy) 166

Pierrepoint, Henry (dandy) 24
Pius VII (Pope) 105
Platov, Matvei Ivanovich 88
Poems by a Gentleman and His Lady 101
Poetical Works of Lord Byron (1848) 86
Pole, Mrs 94
Polidori, John William (writer) 131–132
Pomfret, 4th Earl (Thomas William Fermor) 70
Ponsonby, Frederick *see* Bessborough, 3rd Earl
Ponsonby, George 97
Ponsonby, Mary Elizabeth *see* Grey, Countess
Pont Neuf (Parisian bridge) 105
Pontanus 166
Pope, Alexander (poet) 37, 101
Portarlington, 2nd Earl (John Dawson) 165–166
Portman Sq., London 191
Portsmouth, Lady (born Mary Anne Hanson) 164–165
Portsmouth, 3rd Earl (J.C. Wallop) 164–165
Post Office (in Paris) 107
Powerscourt, 5th Viscount (Richard Wingfield) 39
Prerogative Court of Canterbury 8
Prince of Wales *see* George IV
Prince of Wales's Own (regiment) 12, 16, 17
Prince Regent *see* George IV
Princes St., Edinburgh 134
Prisoner of Chillon 123
Prussia, King of 30
Prussian Field Artillery 197
Purdy, William (Lady Frances's servant) 188
Pursuits of Literature (by Mathias) 29

Quantana (banker) 160
Quantana, Mme 161
Quarterly Review (publication) 106, 107–112, 116–117
Quennell, Peter (author) 2, 20, 40, 42, 48, 49, 56, 76, 82, 97, 152, 155, 167–168, 175, 192, 198–199
Quentin, Col. 142

Raglan, Lord (Fitzroy Somerset) 94–95, 97
Ransom, Morland & Co (bankers) 114, 123, 160, 193
Ransom, Morland and Hammersley (bankers) 160
Ravenna, Italy 132, 133, 136, 138, 145
Rawdon, Francis *see* Moira, 2nd Earl
Rawlence, Miss 57–58, 62, 64–65, 69, 71, 74, 78, 91
Read, Alexander, of Logie (Sir James Webster-Wedderburn's grandfather) 7, 150
Read, Ann *see* Wedderburn, Ann

Read, Ann (born Ann Fletcher) (Sir James Webster-Wedderburn's grandmother) 7
Read, Elizabeth *see* Wedderburn, Elizabeth
Read, Fletcher (Sir James Webster-Wedderburn's uncle) 8, 12, 13
Recollections of Shelley and Byron (by Trelawny) 153
Reddish's Hotel, London 26
Redlands, near Bristol 16
Regency period 1, 23, 38, 136
Reid *see* Read
Reminiscences (by Gronow) 14
The Review (The Wags of Windsor) (play by Colman) 32
Rialto, Venice 122
Richards, John 186–187
Richards, Mr. (of Rivington's, the printers) 181
Richardson, Samuel (novelist) 39
Richelieu, Duc de (French minister) 104
Richmond, Duchess of 94, 98, 113, 128, 177, 180
Richmond, 5th Duke 88, 94, 113, 177
Rider, William (publisher) 198
Rigge, Ellen 197
Rise and Fall of a Regency Dandy (book by Burnett) 3, 97, 123, 138, 174
The Risorgimento 197
Rivington (printer) 138, 178, 181
Rochdale, Lancs 11, 30, 34, 122
Roden, 2nd Earl of 39
Roden, 3rd Earl (Robert Jocelyn) 39
Rodney Stone (novel by Conan Doyle) 8
Roe, Sir F. (magistrate) 187, 190
Rogers, Sir John 24
Rogers, Samuel 44
Rome, Italy 43, 104, 118, 120, 122
Romford, Essex 16
Ros *see* De Ros
Ross, Mr. (pawnbroker) 184
Rotch, Mr. (magistrate) 190
Rotherham, Yorks 33–34, 37, 178
Roxburghshire (Scotch county) 115
Royal Artillery 94
Royal College of Surgeons 42, 117
Royal Hotel, Edinburgh 77
Rushton, Robert (Lord Byron's servant) 16, 34–40, 66, 91–92, 103
Russia 165
Rutland, Duke of (dandy) 24

Sackville St., Dublin 194–195
St. Albans, Herts 10
St. Andrews Undershaft (London parish) 8
St. James's, London 34, 36–37, 39, 66, 142, 180
St. James's Morning Chronicle 31, 98, 99, 100, 107, 113–116, 154, 174
St. James's Palace 32
St. James's St., London 23, 26, 30, 139, 141–142, 144, 174
St. John, Mr. 148
St-Lazare, rue (street in Paris) 104
St. Martins St., London 13
St. Marylebone, London 18
Ste-Addresse, Normandy 120
Salt Hill, Bucks 24
Satires (by Horace) 132
Savile, Lady (born Gertrude Helyar; Sir James Webster-Wedderburn's granddaughter) 34, 198
Savile, 1st Baron (John Lumley-Savile) 34
Savile, 2nd Baron 34
Savile Place, London 136
Savile Row, London 136, 167
Savile-Lumley, John *see* Savile, Baron
Scaliger, Julius Caesar (scholar) 84
Scarborough, 7th Earl 33
Scarborough, 8th Earl (John Lumley) 33, 34
Scarborough, Yorks 115
Scarlet Pimpernel 23
Scarsdale, Lady (born Sophia Noel) 37
Scarsdale, 2nd Baron (Nathaniel Curzon) 37–38
Schwartzenburg, Prince 88
Scotland 5, 7, 9, 21, 62, 64, 66, 69–70, 75, 77–78, 83, 113–115, 117, 131, 134, 137, 158, 163, 169, 176–178, 192
Scot's Magazine 100
Scott, Walter (Scotch poet) 35, 70, 99, 101, 105–106, 115, 181
Scrymgeour-Wedderburn, Henry (7th Earl of Dundee) 178, 191
Seaham, Durham 92
Seneca 166
Seymour Rd., London 91
Shakespear, Arthur 94
Shakespeare, William (writer) 83, 110
Sheffield, Yorks 33, 47
Shelley, Lady Frances 99, 100, 114
Shelley, Mary 134, 181
Shelley, Percy B. (poet) 111, 123–124, 134
Shenley Hill, Herts 10, 11, 13, 21, 150
Shepperton, London 13
Sheridan, Richard B. (playwright) 44, 131, 167
Sibbald, William 114–115, 137
Sicily 35, 36
Simpson, James (lawyer) 99
Sitwell, Lady (born Sarah Caroline Stovin) 50, 90–91
Sitwell, Osbert (author) 13
Sitwell, Sir Sitwell, 1st Bart (born Hurt) 50
6th Dragoon Guards 150
Skeffington, Sir Skiffy (dandy) 24
Sligo, Lord 71
Slough, Bucks 25
Smith, T. Clerc (publisher) 176
Smith, Thomas (waterman) 190
Smythe, Mr. 158
Solon 166
Somerset (English county) 126, 151, 197
Somerset, Sir Alfred (Lady Frances's nephew) 179
Somerset, Lady Catherine (born Annesley; Lady Frances's sister) 18, *19*, 39–41, 43–45, 46, 50, 53, 57, 59, 62, 64, 68, 77, 80–81, 92, 94, 97, 116, 176, 179
Somerset, Fitzroy *see* Raglan, Lord
Somerset, Frances (Lady Frances's niece) 116
Somerset, Henry *see* Beaufort, 5th Duke
Somerset, Lord John (Lady Frances's brother-in-law) 18, 92, 94, 97, 158, 192
Somerset, Juliana (Lady Frances's niece) 176
Somerset St., London 181
Sondes, Walter (actor) 200
Song of the 4th of May (by Byron) 86–87, 125
Sotheby's (auction house) 95, 115
South America 134, 138, 153
South Audley St., London 192
South St., London 183
Southampton, Hants 126–127
Southey, Robert (poet) 44
Southwark, London 138
Spain 16, 37
Spectator (magazine) 132
Spencer, Lady Henrietta *see* Bessborough, Countess
Spring Garden, Jamaica 7, 8
Stable Yard, London 141
Staël, Mme de *see* De Staël
Stafford St., London 115, 138
Stanhope, Charles *see* Petersham, Viscount
Stanhope, Francis (Petersham's brother) 38, 41
Stanhope family 45
Stanzas for Music (by Byron) 86
Stevens, Mr. (broker) 189
Stewart *see* Stuart
Stewart, Betty Valentia (Sir James Webster-Wedderburn's great granddaughter) 17, 198
Stewart, Catherine (born Catherine Wedderburn; Sir James Webster-Wedderburn's aunt) 8
Stewart, Charles Edward (Bonnie Prince Charlie) 5
Stewart, James (the Old Pretender) 5
Stewart, Robert, of Dundee (Sir James Webster-Wedderburn's uncle) 8
Stewart, William (Sir James Webster-Wedderburn's great great grandson) 17
Stilton, Hunts 42
Stilton cheese 42
Stormonth, Isabella (born Isabella Wedderburn; Sir James Webster-Wedderburn's aunt) 8

Stormonth, Rev. James, of Airly (Sir James Webster-Wedderburn's uncle) 8
Story, Jack (squire) 136
Stovin, Sarah Caroline *see* Sitwell, Lady
Straube, Frances (born Webster-Wedderburn; Sir James Webster-Wedderburn's granddaughter) 198
Stuart *see* Stewart
Stuart, Lady Elizabeth (wife of Sir Charles) 169
Stuart, Sir Charles (ambassador) 94, 169, 170–171, 175
Suffolk (English county) 11, 32
Supplementary Despatches (by Wellington) 96
Surrey (English county; formerly Surry) 7, 8, 10, 21
Surry *see* Surrey
Sussex (English county) 16, 198
Swann Auction Galleries 163
Swift, Jonathan (writer) 107
Swinburne, Algernon (poet) 23, 198
Switzerland 115–116, 152, 158, 161, 165
Sydney (Sir James Webster-Wedderburn's dog) 14

Talleyrand (French minister) 88, 89, 104
Talma, Francois-Joseph (actor) 103
Tarleton, Banastre (dandy) 24
Tasso (poet) 30, 122, 167
Tay, Firth of 192
Tegart's (Paris restaurant) 145
10th Dragoons 36
10th Hussars 12, 16, 94, 139, 142
10th Light Dragoons 150
10th Royal Hussars 12, 16
Teresa (book by Gray) 20, 154, 157, 167
Terry, Ann (Lady Frances's servant) 188–189
Thanet, Lord 107
Then Fare Thee Well, Fanny (poem by Lord Byron) 114, 173
31st Foot 150
Thomas of Bond Street 193
Thompson & Wrightson, Messrs. 32
Thornton Beacon, Yorks 192
Thornton by Pocklington, Yorks 192
Thorwaldsen, Berthel (Danish sculptor) 118
Three Years with the Duke of Wellington (by Lennox) 100
Tichborne, Hants 193, 197
The Times (newspaper) 12, 15, 119, 143, 145, 152, 183–190, 192, 194–196
To Lord Byron (book by Paston) 2, 56, 80, 199
Tokay wine 134
Tottenham Court Road, London 57, 74
Tours, France 107
Towcester, Notts 70
Trelawny, Ernest 153
Trelawny, Jamaica 8
Trevanion, Henry 120
Trevanion, Marie 121
Trinity College, Cambridge 16, 27, 114, 137
Tristram Shandy (novel by Sterne) 46
Trois Frères Provençaux 136
Tuileries, Paris 89, 101
Tunbridge, Kent 133
Turin, Italy 157, 161–163, 165
Turnham Green, near London 24
Tweeddale, 8th Marquess (a blood) 20
12th Light Dragoons 150
23rd Light Dragoons 165
Twiss, Horace (playwright) 131
Two Sicilies, King of the 197
The Uninhibited Byron (book by Grebanier) 31–32, 111–112, 200

Upper Abbey St., Dublin 194
Upper Arley, Worcs 18
Upper Brook St., London 181, 187, 189
Upper Grosvenor St., London 10
Uxbridge, Lord 95, 121

Valentia (courtesy title) *see* Mountnorris
Valentia, Lady (Anne Courtenay) 192
Valentia, Lord (Lady's Frances's nephew) 192
Vampire (short story by Polidori) 132
Vansittart, Sir Nicholas 62
Vaughan, Serjeant (lawyer) 113
Vendôme, Place (in Paris) 88, 100, 101, 103
Venezuela 134
Venice 116–117, 120–122, 124, 131–136, 175
Verelst, Sir Harry 33
Vergil (writer) 63
Verona, Italy 116
Versailles, France 166
Verulam, Lord 94
Victoria, Queen 136
Villiers, George *see* Jersey, 5th Earl
Vincent, Sir Francis, 10th Bart. 152, 156–157, 160–161, 168–170
Vis à vis (carriage) 26, 27, 28, 56
Vision of Judgement (by Lord Byron) 155, 160
Volage (frigate) 26

Wags of Windsor (play by Colman) 32
Wakefield, Annie (born Dixon; Sir James Webster-Wedderburn's granddaughter) 17
Wall Street Journal 114
Wallop, J.C. *see* Portsmouth, 3rd Earl
Walsh, Maria (wench) 195
Wareing, Lesley (actor) 200
Warrender, Lady 158
Warwick St., London 10
Warwickshire (English county) 33
Waterford, Lady 73
Waterloo 17, 29, 94–95, 97, 103, 107, 108–112, 113, 114, 121, 143, 165, 195
Waterloo, and Other Poems (by Webster-Wedderburn) 105, 107–112, 115–117, 199
Waterpark, Baroness (Lady Frances's grandmother) 18
Waterpark, Lord 43
Waters, Thomas (butcher) 190
Way to Keep Him (play by Murphy) 47
Webster, Catherine (wife of old James Webster) 8
Webster, David (brother of old James Webster) 5, 8
Webster, David (Sir James Webster-Wedderburn's brother) 7, 115, 150
Webster, George (brother of old James Webster) 8
Webster, James (Sir James Webster-Wedderburn's great uncle) 5, 7, 8, 14, 21, 150
Webster, John (brother of old James Webster) 8
Webster, Lt. Henry 96
Webster, Sir James Wedderburn *see* Webster-Wedderburn
Webster, Messrs, druggists 5
Webster, Thomas (brother of old James Webster) 8
Webster & Co., of Clapham 5, 6
Webster family of Dundee 5
Webster-Wedderburn, Albert Annesley (Sir James Webster-Wedderburn's grandson) 198
Webster-Wedderburn, Arthur Augustus (Sir James Webster-Wedderburn's grandson) 198
Webster-Wedderburn, Augustus George Henry Desire (Sir James Webster-Wedderburn's son) **150**, 198
Webster-Wedderburn, Caroline (born Dixon; Sir James Webster-Wedderburn's daughter-in-law) 17, 25, 26, 198
Webster-Wedderburn, Charles (Sir James Webster-Wedderburn's brother) 7, 150, 155, 180, 191, 197
Webster-Wedderburn, Charles (Sir James Webster-Wedderburn's grandson) 132
Webster-Wedderburn, Charles Adrian (Sir James Webster-Wedderburn's nephew) 197
Webster-Wedderburn, Charles Byron (Sir James Webster-Wedderburn's son) 7, 100, 102, 119, 150
Webster-Wedderburn, Charles

Francis (Sir James Webster-Wedderburn's son) 136, **138**, 151, 168–172, 180, 197

Webster-Wedderburn, Dorothy Hamilton (Tatton Hewetson's mother) 198

Webster-Wedderburn, Frances *see* Straube, Mrs.

Webster-Wedderburn, Lady Frances (born Annesley) 1, 7, 10, 12, 18, *19–20*, 21, 31, **48**, 89, 120–122, 131, 132, 133, 136, 138, 139–144, 150, 155–156, 161, 170–171, 174, 176–179, 181, 183–190, 196, 198–200; affair with Byron 2, 33–85, 86–87; affair with Scrope Davies 123–130, 132, 137; affair with Wellington 2, 78, 94–118; at Aston Hall 32–85, 92; birth 20; death 191–193; divorce threat 148, 158, 169; estate 193; in Europe 85, 92, 145; family 20; fragility 20, 41–42, 47, 53; given lock of hair by Byron 48–50; given ring by Byron 47–48; leaves James 115, 123, 145–149, 152; letter to Hobhouse, May 31, 1824 175; letter to Lord Byron, Oct. 18, 1813 54–58; letter to Lord Byron, Oct. 22, 1813 59–61; letter to Lord Byron, Oct. 28, 1813 61–63; letter to Lord Byron, Oct. 29, 1813 65–66; letter to Lord Byron, Nov. 1813 67–69; letter to Lord Byron, Nov. 1, 1813 66; letter to Lord Byron, Nov. 14, 1813 69–70, 72; letter to Lord Byron, Nov. 19, 1813 71; letter to Lord Byron, Nov. 22, 1813 71–72; letter to Lord Byron, Nov. 25, 1813 74, 75; letter to Lord Byron, late Dec. 1813 78; letter to Lord Byron, Dec. 28, 1813 77–78; letter to Lord Byron, Feb. 1, 1814 82; letter to Lord Byron, June 17, 1814 91; letter to Lord Byron, Sept. 5, 1815 102; letter to Lord Byron, Oct. 3, 1816 85; letter to Lord Byron, Jan. 18, 1818 119; letter to Lord Byron, Feb. 7, 1823 157–159; letter to Lord Byron, March 7, 1823 163–164; letter to Lord Byron, March 25, 1823 166; letter to Lord Byron, April 22, 1823 167–169; letter to Robert Peel, Dec. 1829 179; letter to Sir James Webster-Wedderburn, Sept. 30, 1821 145–149; letters 2, 3, 33–85; loan from Byron 52, 55, 59, 73, 92, 114–115, 133, 135–136, 145, 155, 160, 167; marriage 12, 18, 20, 26, 123; pregnant 94, 96, 137, 145; at queen's reception 32, 180; in Scotland 62, 64, 66, 69, 70, 74, 75, 77, 83, 115

Webster-Wedderburn, George (Sir James Webster-Wedderburn's son) 17, 25, 26, 160, 176, *177*, 198

Webster-Wedderburn, James 1, 6, *8*, 25, 29, **89**, 91, 95, 102, 113, 114, 117, 119, 123–140, 149, 150, 152–154, 156, 159, 161, 163, 164, 166, 167, 173, 174, 176–177, 179–180, 183, 185, 187, 190, 192–193, 198–200; arms 21, 22, 23; Army 12, 16, 20; Aston Hall 32, 33–85, 90, 92; athlete 12, 13; birth 7; Blackness baronetcy 178; boxer 14; Brighton 14; buried 196; consulship 175; dandy 24; death 194–196; divorce threat 148, 158, 169; Dorset 26; duelist 139–145; education 9, 10, 11, 12, 13; estate 197; Europe 16, 85, 88, 92; family 5; France 145; gambler 14, 15, 20; gets name Bold Webster 13; homosexuality 30, 31; inheritance 8, 14, 178; kidnaps son 168–172; king's levee 26, 177, 180; knighthood 21, 22, 152–154; Lady Sitwell's party 91; letter to John Wedderburn, 1821 150; letter to John Wedderburn, Dec. 28, 1821 150; letter to John Wedderburn, Nov. 11, 1828 177; letter to Lady Frances, March 1823 166; letter to Lord Byron, 1809 15, 16; letter to Lord Byron, Aug. 25, 1811 28; letter to Lord Byron, July 31, 1813 34, 35, 36; letter to Lord Byron, Aug. 2, 1813 36; letter to Lord Byron, Aug. 12, 1813 37; letter to Lord Byron, Aug. 27, 1813 38; letter to Lord Byron, Aug. 29, 1813 38, 39; letter to Lord Byron, Sept. 4, 1813 39, 40; letter to Lord Byron, Sept. 13, 1813 40; letter to Lord Byron, Sept. 27, 1813 42, 43; letter to Lord Byron, Oct. 28, 1813 62; letter to Lord Byron, Oct. 29, 1813 66; letter to Lord Byron, Nov. 18, 1813 70; letter to Lord Byron, Feb. 17, 1814 82; letter to Lord Byron, Feb. 25, 1814 83–84; letter to Lord Byron, May 5, 1814 88; letter to Lord Byron, June 8, 1814 90; letter to Lord Byron, July 31, 1814 92; letter to Lord Byron, July 18, 1815 96–97; letter to Lord Byron, Aug. 31, 1815 100–101; letter to Lord Byron, Sept. 10, 1815 102–103; letter to Lord Byron, Sept. 28, 1815 104–105; letter to Lord Byron, Oct. 2, 1815 105–106; letter to Lord Byron, Jan. 15, 1816 106–107; letter to Lord Byron, Sept. 20, 1816 115; letter to Lord Byron, July 25, 1818 120–121; letter to Lord Byron, May 20, 1819 131–132; letter to Lord Byron, Sept. 23, 1819 133; letter to Lord Byron, Nov. 11, 1819 135; letter to Lord Byron, May 16, 1820 136–137; letter to Lord Byron, 1823 172; letter to Lord Byron, Feb. 4, 1823 156–157; letter to Lord Byron, Feb. 20, 1823 161; letter to Lord Byron, Feb. 22, 1823 162; letter to Lord Byron, March 19, 1823 165–166; letter to Lord Byron, May 2, 1823 170–171; letter to Robert Peel, May 1825 176; letter to Robert Peel, June 1826 176; letter to Robert Peel, Jan. 1830 179; letter to Scrymgeour-Wedderburn, Dec. 28, 1829 178; letter to Scrymgeour-Wedderburn, March 22, 1834 191; letter to Scrymgeour-Wedderburn, Nov. 13, 1834 191; loan from Byron 52, 55, 59, 73, 92, 114–115, 133, 135–136, 145, 154, 155, 160, 167; Manton's 14; marriage 12, 18, 20, 26, 123; meets Byron 12; miniature 17; name changes 8, 132; Nantes 131–138; Navy 12; Newstead party 15; pamphlets 138, 176, 178, 182; poems 106, 112, 116; politics 27; printing press 132; Scotland 62, 64, 66, 69, 70, 74, 75, 77, 83, 115; separates from Lady Frances 123

Webster-Wedderburn, Lucy *see* Bishop, Lucy

Webster-Wedderburn, Maude Gertrude Annesley 154, 198, *199*

Webster-Wedderburn, Rebecca Georgina (Sir James Webster-Wedderburn's niece) 191

Websters of Scotland 21

Wedderburn, Alexander Ogilvy (author) 181

Wedderburn, Sir Alexander, 2nd Bart. of Blackness 177

Wedderburn, Sir Alexander, 4th Bart. of Blackness 5, 21, 178, 191

Wedderburn, Ann (born Ann Read; Sir James Webster-Wedderburn's aunt by marriage) 8

Wedderburn, Anne *see* Douglas Anne

Wedderburn, Catherine *see* Stewart, Catherine

Wedderburn, Charles, of Pearsie (Sir James Webster-Wedderburn's uncle) 5, 8, 178–179, 191

Wedderburn, David (Sir James Webster-Wedderburn's father) 6, 7, 8, 9, 10, 11, 12, 21, 22, 150, 178, 180

Wedderburn, David, of Balindean 9, 62, 132

Wedderburn, Elizabeth (Sir James Webster-Wedderburn's mother) 7, 9, 10, 11, 18, 32, 92, 150, 192, 197

Wedderburn, Isabella *see* Stormonth, Isabella

Wedderburn, Isobel (Sir James Webster-Wedderburn's grandmother) 6

Wedderburn, James (Sir James

Webster-Wedderburn's cousin; solicitor-general) 131
Wedderburn, James, of Inveresk 8
Wedderburn, James, of Trelawny (Sir James Webster-Wedderburn's father's cousin) 7, 8
Wedderburn, John (Sir James Webster-Wedderburn's cousin; son of John of Spring Garden) 150, 166, 176, 177, 182, 193
Wedderburn, John, of Clapham *see* Wedderburn, John, of Spring Garden
Wedderburn, John, of Spring Garden 7, 8, 9, 166
Wedderburn, Sir John 5th Bart. 5, 8, 9, 178
Wedderburn, Sir John, of Balindean, 6th Bart. 8, 9, 11
Wedderburn, Louisa Dorothea 8
Wedderburn, Margaret (wife of David, of Balindean) 62
Wedderburn, Mary *see* Hawkins, Mary
Wedderburn, Messrs & Co. 5
Wedderburn, Robert (the Black Preacher) 43
Wedderburn, Robert, of Pearsie (Sir James Webster-Wedderburn's grandfather) 5, 6, 21, 150, 178
Wedderburn, Thomas, of Cantra 7
Wedderburn, Webster & Co 8–9, 150
Wedderburn Book 18, 181, 194
Wedderburn versus Wedderburn 180–182, 191–192

Wedderburn-Halket, Elizabeth 177
Wedderburn-Halket, Elizabeth Charlotte *see* de Lally
Wedderburn-Halket, Sir John 177
Wedderburn-Webster *see* Webster-Wedderburn
Weekly Messenger (newspaper) 13
Wellesley, Arthur *see* Wellington, 1st Duke
Wellington, Duchess of 125
Wellington, 1st Duke (Arthur Wellesley) 1, 2, 78, 88, 94–96, 98–100, 102, 105, 112–115, 154, 157, 174, 177, 192, 195–196, 200
Wellington, 2nd Duke 96
Wellington the Beau (book by Laforce) 89, 99
Wellington: The Years of the Sword see Years of the Sword
Wellington, Vol. II (book by Longford) 114
Wentworth, 1st Viscount (Edward Noel) 37
Werner (by Lord Byron) 156
West, George *see* De La Warr, 4th Earl
Westcombe, Nicholas 45
Westcombe, William 45
Westminster 18, 193, 197
Westminster Bridge, London 13
Wexford (Irish county) 30, 121
When We Two Parted (by Lord Byron) 173–174
Whig Club 16, 24
Whitbread, Samuel (brewer) 97
White Doe of Rylstone (poem by Wordsworth) 111

Whitechapel, London 12, 13
Wilde, Oscar (poet) 23
Wildman, Col. Thomas 51, 121
William IV 136
William Gifford: Tory Satirist (book by Clark) 107
Williams Wynn, Frances 130, 174
Wilmot, Mrs. (born Anne Horton) 91
Wilmot, Robert John 91
Wilson, James (servant) 189
Wilson, Sir Robert 107, 138
Wiltshire (English county) 16, 124, 151
Wimborne, Dorset 26, 28, 30, 31
Winchester, Hants 45
Wingfield, Richard *see* Powerscourt, 5th Viscount
Woodhaven, NY 114
Worcester, Lord (dandy) 24
Worcestershire (English county) 18
Wordsworth, William (poet) 111
Worksop, Notts 33, 83, 90, 92
Worthing, Sussex 198

Yale University 116
Yarmouth, Lord (dandy) 24
Years of the Sword (book by Longford) 12, 95, 98, 114
York, Duke of 176
York Place, London 183
Yorkshire (English county) 32, 33, 37, 97, 115, 192
Young Pretender *see* Stewart, Charles Edward

www.ingramcontent.com/pod-product-compliance
Ingram Content Group UK Ltd.
Pitfield, Milton Keynes, MK11 3LW, UK
UKHW050529150426
5217IPUK00026B/1854